Cambridge Imperial and Post-Colonial Studies Series

General Editors: **Megan Vaughan**, King's College, Cambridge and **Richard Drayton**, Corpus Christi College, Cambridge

This informative series covers the broad span of modern imperial history while also exploring the recent developments in former colonial states where residues of empire can still be found. The books provide in-depth examinations of empires as competing and complementary power structures encouraging the readers to reconsider their understanding of international and world history during recent centuries.

Javed Majeed
AUTOBIOGRAPHY, TRAVEL AND POST-NATIONAL IDENTITY

Francine McKenzie
REDEFINING THE BONDS OF COMMONWEALTH 1939–1948
The Politics of Preference

Gabriel B. Paquette
ENLIGHTENMENT, GOVERNANCE, AND REFORM IN SPAIN AND ITS EMPIRE, 1759–1808

John Singleton and Paul Robertson
ECONOMIC RELATIONS BETWEEN BRITAIN AND AUSTRALASIA 1945–1970

Kim A. Wagner *(editor)*
THUGGEE
Banditry and the British in Early Nineteenth-Century India

Cambridge Imperial and Post-Colonial Studies Series
Series Standing Order ISBN 0-333-91908-4 (Hardback) 0-333-91909-2
(Paperback)

(outside North America only)

You can receive future titles in this series as they are published by placing a standing order. Please contact your bookseller or, in case of difficulty, write to us at the address below with your name and address, the title of the series and the ISBN quoted above.

Customer Services Department, Macmillan Distribution Ltd, Houndmills, Basingstoke, Hampshire RG21 6XS, England

Enlightenment, Governance, and Reform in Spain and its Empire, 1759–1808

Gabriel B. Paquette
Junior Research Fellow,
Trinity College, University of Cambridge

First published 2008 by
PALGRAVE MACMILLAN
Houndmills, Basingstoke, Hampshire RG21 6XS and
175 Fifth Avenue, New York, N.Y. 10010
Companies and representatives throughout the world

PALGRAVE MACMILLAN is the global academic imprint of the Palgrave Macmillan division of St. Martin's Press, LLC and of Palgrave Macmillan Ltd. Macmillan® is a registered trademark in the United States, United Kingdom and other countries. Palgrave is a registered trademark in the European Union and other countries.

ISBN-13: 978-1-4039-8594-1   hardback
ISBN-10: 1-4039-8594-4   hardback

This book is printed on paper suitable for recycling and made from fully managed and sustained forest sources. Logging, pulping and manufacturing processes are expected to conform to the environmental regulations of the country of origin.

A catalogue record for this book is available from the British Library.

A catalog record for this book is available from the Library of Congress.

10   9   8   7   6   5   4   3   2   1
17   16   15   14   13   12   11   10   09   08

Trnasferred to Digital Printing in 2009

To my parents, Kathy and Gregory Paquette, and my brother, Jonah Paquette

Contents

Illustrations

Acknowledgements

It is a pleasure to acknowledge, with tremendous gratitude, the substantial intellectual, personal, and material debts that I have accumulated in the process of writing this book. Above all, I offer thanks to Richard Drayton, my mentor and editor, who taught me the techniques required to navigate the turbulent waves of Atlantic History. Though my research drew its original inspiration from his *Nature's Government*, it has been Richard's sage advice and astonishing erudition which have guided my *galeón* safely away from numerous shoals and into open water.

This project is the product of fruitful and enjoyable years of study at the University of Cambridge. I extend my sincere gratitude to T.C.W. Blanning (Cambridge) and Anthony McFarlane (Warwick), who examined the PhD dissertation from which this book emerged. Both offered many astute criticisms and stimulating suggestions. I thank Emma Rothschild (Cambridge and Harvard) who directed my initial exploration of Anglo-Iberian intellectual history and has encouraged my research ever since. Illuminating conversations with David Brading (Cambridge) enabled me to understand the complexity and importance of the Bourbon reforms.

During the course of my research for this book, five distinguished scholars beyond the Fens generously offered encouragement, insight, advice, and constructive criticism for which I shall remain forever grateful. I wish to thank John Elliott (Oxford), Kenneth Maxwell (Harvard), Jeremy Adelman (Princeton), Richard Herr (Berkeley), and John Robertson (Oxford) for confirming that Clio's province is the fairest in the Republic of Letters. I also profited from the good advice, useful criticism, and enjoyable conversation of William Callahan (Toronto) and Charles Noel (London), two eminent scholars of Bourbon Spain.

At every stage of my research in Cambridge, the Master, Fellows, and Staff of Trinity College have been extraordinarily helpful, caring, and generous. It is both an honour and a privilege to live and work in such a stimulating and staggeringly beautiful environment. I especially thank John Lonsdale, Boyd Hilton, and Jean Khalfa for the interest they have taken in my intellectual development. Without the material assistance provided by Trinity College, the archival research which underpins this book—undertaken in Spain, Cuba, Chile, and Argentina—would have been inconceivable.

I have accrued debts on my native shore of the Atlantic as well, especially at Wesleyan University in Connecticut. Philip Pomper, Richard Elphick, Vijay Pinch, and Cecilia Miller have nurtured my curiosity as teachers and inspired me by their example as scholars. Without their guidance and unflinching support, I would not have pursued History as a vocation. I am grateful to these four historians and to the entire Department of History for having invited me back to Wesleyan to serve as Visiting Instructor in 2005–06.

Various parts of this book benefited from the scrutiny and constructive criticism of academic audiences in Oxford, Montreal, Lexington, Florence, and Belfast. I thank those audiences for helping to improve the ideas contained in this book. I also wish to record my gratitude to the following organizations for generous material support towards archival research excursions: the Cambridge Faculty of History; the Cambridge Overseas Trust; the Universities UK Overseas Research Scheme; the Centre for History and Economics (King's College Cambridge); Harvard University's Atlantic History Seminar Short-Term Research Grant Program; the Program for Cultural Cooperation between Spain's Ministry of Culture and United States Universities; the Cambridge Historical Society; the Sir John Plumb Charitable Trust; the Electors of the Worts Travelling Fund (Cambridge); the Cambridge European Trust; the Electors of the Cambridge Centre for Latin American Studies Chile Fund; the Electors of the J.B. Trend Fund (Cambridge); the Ibero-American Society for Eighteenth-Century Studies; and the American Society for Eighteenth-Century Studies. I also am grateful for the one-year research fellowship in Lisbon from the Portuguese Fulbright Commission which both allowed me the opportunity for occasional trips across the border to check my sources, and to see the outlines of a future project on Pombaline imperial reform.

I appreciate and admire the patience and grace of staffs at the libraries and archives in Great Britain, the Unites States, Spain, Chile, Cuba, and Argentina in which I researched. I also thank the Board of Trustees of the National Gallery of Art in Washington, D.C., for kind permission to reproduce various details from Tiepolo's 'Wealth and Benefits of the Spanish Monarchy Under Charles III'. I acknowledge AKG-Images/Erich Lessing for permission to reproduce Mengs's 'Count Pedro Rodríguez de Campomanes' and Goya's 'Charles III as a Hunter'. I further appreciate the permission granted by the Special Collections and Archives Division of the Wesleyan University Library to reproduce the image 'Glory of the Prince' from Cesare Ripa's *Iconologia*. I thank Allynn Wilkinson of Wesleyan University's Information Technology Office for help in preparing these images for publication.

I offer my sincere thanks to Richard Drayton and Megan Vaughan, editors of the *Cambridge Imperial and Post-Colonial Studies* Series, for selecting my book for publication and for their encouragement and criticism throughout this process. I thank Michael Strang, Ruth Ireland, and their colleagues at Palgrave Macmillan for their patience, advice, and assistance during the revision, production, and publication of this book.

Research can be a lonely process. It has been much less so because of the wonderful friendships which were born and nurtured both in and beyond Cambridge. I wish to acknowledge my friend and fellow historian David Todd whose fraternal kindness, humour, and generosity of spirit were indispensable to the completion of this project. In Britain, I also wish to thank (in no particular order) Christian Wuthrich, Chloë Cyrus Kent, Matt and Cody Tunney, Andy Crawford and Monica Stassen, Alexander Kirshner, Lucie Campos, Radek Spicar, Michael Edwards, Cristina Miguel, Edith Bukovics, Jon Todd, Josh Byrne, Ravin and Roshni Ponniah, Florian Schui, Chris Warnes, Sunil Amrith, Tom and Georgia Flight, Bob McPhee, Inga Huld Markan, and Prav and Anatole Menon-Johansson for their friendship, loyalty, and laughter. In the United States, I wish to thank (in no particular order): Debbie B. Rosenberg, Nina B. de Fels, Lindsay Shortliffe Paquette, Robyn Creswell, Matt Goldstein, Ben Block, Danny Forster, Don Andy Toebben, Avi Spivack and Natasha Kogan, Jason Nebenzahl, Raina Blyer, Nina Kontos, Jessica Zweiman, Andy and Allison Davenport, Duk Blakaj, Lexy Bloom, John McGill, Max Rubenstein, Alex Himmelbaum, and Eloise Paul. They were, as always, unstintingly caring and generous with their kindness. My entire extended family—both Paquettes and Baumans—were wonderfully supportive during this entire process.

In spite of their great support and numerous helpful suggestions, the individuals mentioned are not to be held responsible for any errors of fact or interpretation that remain in my book.

I dedicate this book to my parents, Gregory and Kathy Paquette, and to my brother, Jonah, who created a loving environment in which learning, in all of its wonderful forms, was cherished for its own sake.

Brooklyn, NY, USA, and Cambridge, UK
1 May 2007

Introduction

'The majority of the maxims which guide the commerce of other nations, which enabled them to prosper, are unadaptable to our nation. Their circumstances are distinct from our own and following their path will upset the natural order of things'.[1] Royal ministers, who governed the Spanish empire in the reign of Charles III, were accustomed to this type of complaint from disgruntled subjects. Some of this dissatisfaction stemmed from the Crown's rigorous application of the 'axioms and calculations of economists and public writers of commerce' to all aspects of public affairs. It is possible to imagine these ministers climbing the stairs of Madrid's *Palacio Real* in 1788, making their way to the Throne Room. Waiting beneath Tiepolo's monumental fresco,[2] a superannuated king received their reports concerning his peninsular and ultramarine realms, neither aware of his impending death nor cognizant of the coming cataclysms which would undermine the empire which he had sought to revive from its torpor. Before examining these ministers and this monarch further, however, their affairs should be situated against a broader historical panorama.

This book analyses the political ideas animating the government reformers of Spain and its Atlantic empire in the second half of the eighteenth century. It focuses on the intellectual foundations of attempts at administrative, commercial, and fiscal restructuring which gathered momentum after the replacement of the Habsburg with the Bourbon dynasty, sanctioned under the terms of the Treaty of Utrecht. Efforts to reform government between 1700 and 1808 under the successive reigns of Philip V (1700–46), Ferdinand VI (1746–59), Charles III (1759–88), and Charles IV (1788–1808) are known to contemporary historians as the Bourbon reforms.[3] This monograph neither offers a comprehensive account of the dynamics of Bourbon government policy nor an analysis of the Spanish Enlightenment. Because many valuable and detailed studies already exist,[4] it strives to complement this formidable body of scholarship with an intellectual history of the central ideas employed by policymakers and political writers to revamp Spain's peninsular and ultramarine realms in the 50 years following Charles III's accession to the throne.[5] His reign, and that of his son and successor, Charles IV, traditionally is referred to as the 'Caroline' era and, in this study, will be used interchangeably with the overarching term 'Bourbon'. The evolution of the key ideas of this historical episode, the application of these ideas to policy, and the intellectual repercussions of this implementation are the historical changes traced in this book.

The Bourbon reformers sought to renovate a diffuse, haphazard, and unwieldy state apparatus, bolstering it with a centralized bureaucracy, emanating from Madrid, equipped with the revenue-generating mechanisms necessary to restore the prestige and influence of the monarchy. Repudiating the notion of Spain as an eclipsed, second-rate power through bold actions in Europe, Madrid also endeavoured to assert its rejuvenated sovereignty over its far-flung empire against the encroachments of foreign contrabandists and competitor imperial states. These threats, particularly the omnipresent spectre of war, propelled the Crown's predilection for the concentration of power. Bourbon reformers turned away from the stable and resilient, if inefficient, decentralized 'composite' monarchy structure bequeathed by their Habsburg predecessors.[6] The old order, with its robust corporate entities, superabundance of privileges, and regional semi-autonomy was to be suppressed. In its place, reformers sought to erect a unified nation state, subservient to the monarchy, and fashion it into the generator of a new patriotic spirit.[7]

In their quest to transform the federated kingdoms (*reinos*) of the New World into subordinate colonies (*colonias*),[8] Madrid's reformers necessarily revised and replenished their older political ideas through engagement with newer intellectual currents. Regalist jurisprudence was the solid ideological foundation of the Bourbon reforms. Centripetal absolutism, suffused by a nostalgia for an idealized past and an overly ebullient estimation of future glory, suggested the target of its ambitions, its force of character, its relentlessness. Political economy, smuggled over the Pyrenees and across the Cantabrian Sea, provided its intellectual basis and galvanized a generation of reformers. Much as the early nineteenth-century English Utilitarians would find a scope for agency in government in India, which they could not achieve at home, so the Caroline reformers of the late eighteenth century found their political laboratory in the colonies of the imperial periphery. Thwarted on the peninsula by recalcitrant mercantile and agrarian elites and entrenched ecclesiastical authorities, the rapidly modernizing Atlantic periphery provided an element of scale and expansiveness to this cohort of reformers, so essential for the deployment of its political ideals.[9] Regalism, political economy, and considerations stemming from international rivalry comprised the three chief components of the Caroline ideology of governance. Their origins, interactive blending, and implications for policy are traced in the four major chapters of this book.

In their haste to reach their sovereign, the ministers probably neglected to admire the fresco-adorned ceilings of the staterooms through which they passed, masterpieces by Anton Raphael Mengs and Corrado Giaquinto. They may not, upon reaching their destination, have shifted their gaze upward towards the *Glory of the Spanish Monarchy*, painted by Giambattista Tiepolo (1696–1770). This would have been unfortunate, as these frescos spurred an English traveller to exclaim that he had encountered 'no palace in Europe fitted up with so much true royal magnificence'.[10] In order to comprehend the Caroline epoch—particularly its political languages of governance and reform—it is useful to begin with its aesthetic ideals because they embody the aspirations of royal reformers, the pan-European character of their project, and the political vocabularies through which they formulated their intended overhaul of the Atlantic empire.[11] The fresco both conjures and reinforces the image of Charles III as a beneficent and omnipotent ruler under whom, consonant with Bossuet's description of the merits of the wise prince, 'wars succeed, peace is established, justice reigns, the laws govern, religion flourishes, commerce and navigation enrich the country and the earth itself seems to produce fruits more willingly'.[12] The fresco, as shall be shown, is a tribute to the beneficence of state power, an assertion of the Crown's capacity to promote public welfare and prosperity, and an argument for its expansion into all facets of political and economic life.

When Tiepolo accepted Charles III's invitation to paint the ceiling of the Throne Room in 1761, his talents had been long patronized by other European monarchs.[13] The iconography of his fresco has produced spirited debate since at least 1829, when Ferdinand VII commissioned Francisco José Fabre to elucidate its enigmatic symbolism. Fabre was confounded and, apologetically, resorted to the standard handbooks of Baroque iconography in order to decipher the frescos' enigmatic meaning.[14] Fabre's confusion suggests that these frescos require further meditation. What message did Charles III and his ministerial elite seek to convey through such imagery?

Tiepolo's symbolism suggests that monarchical government brings about, and remains responsible for, economic prosperity and maritime supremacy. In order to convey this intended meaning, Tiepolo selected an imperial figure enthroned between two monumental statues as his principal motif. In his preliminary sketch, reproduced in this book, Hercules and Apollo flank the throne. In the Madrid fresco, however, Tiepolo substituted Minerva for Hercules, perhaps intending to replace Strength with Wisdom.[15] Monarchy also is flanked by a bevy of figures associated with good government: Clemency, Moderation, Good Counsel, Princely Glory, Magnanimity, Affability, and Intelligence. These elements, however, are subordinated to the reciprocal gaze of the Monarchy and Abundance. In Tiepolo's preliminary sketch, Abundance does not occupy a pivotal position; in the fresco, by contrast, Abundance, whose hair now is sprinkled with sprigs of grain, offers wheat to the figure of Monarchy. Neptune, the fresco's second dominant figure, and the Lion of Spain, surrounded by two overflowing cornucopias of gold and fruit, comprise the only distractions from Abundance's courtship of Monarchy.[16]

Employing these devices, Tiepolo's fresco celebrates not only oceanic colonial commerce, but also peninsular Spain's potential agricultural prosperity. This dual emphasis is underscored by the artist's employment of an innovative local symbolism, depicting agrarian fertility with regionally specific indigenous produce: Andalusia, for example, is represented by a prosperous farmer with overflowing barrels of fruit. There are no prototypes for these figures in Spanish iconography and they are, instead, purely symbolic emblems, rooted in medieval heraldry.[17] They convey a fascination with agricultural prosperity and a nostalgic yearning for the vanished glories of an idealized past whose amalgam is emblematic of the reform ideology. The symbolism of Tiepolo's fresco suggests that ultramarine, peninsular, and European politics were interwoven in the minds of contemporary officials to a greater extent than acknowledged by recent historians. For this reason, this monograph aims to contribute to a 'Cis-Atlantic' history of Spain; that is, a national history situated in the context of overseas empire.[18]

While the symbolism of Tiepolo's fresco alludes to the Bourbon reformers' infatuation with the efficacy of state power on mercantile and agricultural prosperity on both shores of the Atlantic, Charles III's other artistic preferences suggest how such achievements might be brought about. The entire aesthetic of his first years in Madrid suggests a pan-European dimension, epitomized by Mengs's elevation to the position of *Primer Pintor de Camara*. Mengs (1728–79) stressed the value, even necessity, of emulation in the creation of art, just as the Bourbon reformers believed that emulation of foreign political practices was required to revive Spain's moribund empire. While Charles ruled in Naples (as Charles VII between 1734 and 1759), he commissioned Mengs to decorate the Chapel of Caserta and, subsequently, recruited him to Madrid in 1761. Having been appointed to the pre-eminent artistic post, Mengs exerted tremendous influence both on court taste and on Spanish academic artistic style.[19] 'Almost every court in Europe has wished to possess some paintings from his hand', claimed José Nicolás Azara in his 1780 eulogy. 'Poland raised and supported him as long as she was able to support herself; Rome acknowledges him as her greatest ornament; Russia, Naples and Florence courted him; and Spain looks on the ever-living monuments of his departed genius with all the ardor of religious adoration'.[20] Azara's grandiloquent description of his deceased friend should not distract attention from his crucial insight into the patterns of emulation of foreign models central to Bourbon political thought.

Mengs's theory of emulation suggests the degree to which the tastes, ideas, and policies developed in other European states were received, analysed, and integrated into Spanish cultural life. For Mengs, painting cannot be reduced to a 'mechanical trade'. Instead, he considered it a 'liberal art'.[21] Painting required the imitation of exalted predecessors because, as Mengs put it, he who 'effectively studies and observes the productions of great men with the desire of imitating them, makes himself capable of producing works which resemble them'. Such a painter, therefore, could 'adapt them to all things where they are suitable; and thus it makes him an imitator without being a plagiarist'.[22] His conception of emulation's creative dimension resonated in Bourbon reform circles.

Mengs's theory found a sympathetic and powerful audience in Count Pedro Rodríguez de Campomanes, a leading reformer, whose political writings figure prominently in this book. Campomanes lauded Mengs, who painted his portrait, claiming that his 'pictures compete with the most highly esteemed of Raphael's', and recognized the potential applicability of his theory of emulation to policymaking.[23] Campomanes linked the diffusion of new painting techniques with national advancement. He asserted the 'utility and necessity of drawing' and contended that 'all of the arts and professions [in Spain] had made progress' due to its instruction.[24] It was government's responsibility to 'remove barbarism and introduce good taste'.[25] This enterprise also required the participation of 'writers with the good intention of instructing the public' whose example 'should stimulate the activity' of their compatriots to 'embark on the Enlightenment of their country (*patria*)'.[26]

This link between emulation, patriotic cultural production, and national advancement provides a basis for the analysis of the Caroline government reform programme. Bourbon ministers siphoned foreign ideas—from Britain, Naples, Portugal, Denmark, Prussia, Holland, and France—and blended them with Spanish ones to produce a syncretic ideology of governance. The process was not copying pure and simple. Critical reflection on, and a correction of, a model distinguishes emulation from mere imitation. Emulation implied admiration combined with a desire to surpass an original model.[27] Foreign ideas often were refracted and adapted according to the dictates of local circumstances, and processes of re-ordering, aggregation, abridgement, and amplification proved inevitable.[28] As foreign models and ideas penetrated Spain, they mingled with deeply rooted Iberian traditions, producing an amalgamated ideology, which was, in turn, harnessed to satisfy the demands of the reform programme.

The use of foreign ideas was not mere fashion, but was crucial to state survival in the tumultuous decades of the late eighteenth century. The Bourbon state was embroiled almost continuously in global and local wars between 1759 and 1808.[29] These included: the misguided and belated intervention in the Seven Years' War; the botched invasion of Portugal (1762); the *Monitorio* conflict with the Papacy and the protracted expulsion of the Jesuits (1766–73) from Spanish dominions; the disastrously amateurish invasion of Algiers (1776); incessant conflict with Britain which led to intervention in the American Revolution (1779–83), wrangling over the Mosquito Coast (until 1786), and contention over the Nootka Sound (1790–1); a profligate war against revolutionary France (1793–6); economically crippling wars with regicide France against Britain (1796–1802 and 1804–8); and the eventual occupation of Spain by Napoleonic forces (1808–14).[30]

International conflict, paradoxically, gave impetus to the emulation of one state's institutions and policies by another. Faced with excruciating defensive and fiscal pressures, Spain's reformers necessarily coveted, and sought to reproduce, successfully implemented policy innovations. Policymakers thus mingled cosmopolitan sensibilities with patriotic allegiance and were committed to employing the common European stock of ideas for the improvement of Spain.[31] Bourbon reformers emulated rival European powers in areas of administrative, fiscal, or military policy in which the Spanish counterpart was deemed deficient by comparison. Emulation promised rapid improvement in Spain and reduced the risk of failure associated with experimentation.[32] Such emulation was highly pragmatic, a scramble for viable models with which to rouse a stagnant, if stable, system and compete with those same states whose policies were emulated. As foreign models were encountered, modified, and incorporated, Bourbon Spain's policy goals, content, and instruments increasingly came to resemble those of its rivals.[33] Incessant war, mercantile rivalry, and the drive for geopolitical power resulted in policy convergence and a move towards institutional isomorphism across Europe's Atlantic empires.

The intersection of ideas and governance in the eighteenth century traditionally has been studied through the lens of 'enlightened absolutism'. This term refers to the purported collusion of newfangled philosophical currents with the centralizing aspirations of monarchical regimes. Enlightened absolutism—with its emphasis on rational governance, reliance on philosophical ideas, and cosmopolitan tendencies—may seem, at first glance, capable of accommodating national idiosyncrasies in its framework. This framework tends to obscure, however, the juridical and historical underpinnings of Bourbon political thought. For this reason, 'regalist governance' is proposed as a fuller, more encompassing alternative which better fits the specific features of Bourbon Spain.

Complementing increased awareness of intellectual currents beyond the Pyrenees was a rejuvenated, deeply entrenched Iberian regalism. Regalism's core principle was the state's pre-eminence and supremacy in relation to the Church, accompanied by its protection and support of the Church and its attendant institutions.[34] The primary thrust of regalism was the aggrandizement of the state at the Church's expense. According to its proponents, the monarch possessed an unlimited jurisdiction to promote 'public happiness', a vague doctrine which proved pliable and conveniently applicable to disputes with corporate bodies besides the Church, including guilds, the nobility, mercantile elites, and local bureaucrats. Regalism's emphasis on the subordination of all institutions to the Crown dovetailed with the Bourbon policy elite's geopolitical and fiscal-military ambitions. It thus provided the overarching framework within which reform was contemplated. It structured debates on political affairs far beyond Church–State relations, catalysing the inaugural phases of government reform and decisively determining its subsequent trajectory, preoccupations, and rhetorical structures.

The rhetoric of peninsular and imperial revitalization, like regalism, originated, of course, in the two centuries preceding the one studied here. The Bourbon reformers enthusiastically acknowledged their debt to the previous century's royal reformers, including the Count-Duke of Olivares, and their reliance on an earlier generation of policy theorists, particularly the *Arbitristas*.[35] Caroline reform was distinguished, however, by its fervent regalism. Regalism's scope—normally confined to a description of the Spanish Crown's disputes with the Roman *Curia*—was enlarged in the late eighteenth century to encompass an expansive view of the state's function in society and the monarchy's role in the international order. These aspects often have been obscured by a tendency to concentrate exclusively on Church–State relations. The Church–State dispute incubated a broader, less coherent, yet more potent brand of regalism.

Regalism evolved, therefore, from a narrow concern with the perceived excesses of the Church's secular authority into a multi-faceted, flexible ideology of governance which justified the extirpation of all obstacles, ecclesiastical and otherwise, which impeded the expansion of monarchical power and infringed on its unencumbered exercise.[36] This amplification coincided with, and was galvanized by, the emulation of foreign institutions and ideas which entered through the permeable membrane of civil society institutions and philosophically inclined officials. European ideas and regalist precepts constituted, respectively, the bricks and mortar of Caroline enlightened governance.

The dynamics of the process by which regalism fused with European intellectual currents in Spain are analogous to the genesis of Josephism. In Austria, reformers employed the lingering cultural authority of the Baroque, but 'turned it on its head':

> By the 1740s, old institutions and their ideologies showed themselves unable to compete with other modern, centralised and proto-national states ... yet Maria Theresa and Joseph did not dismantle the existing edifice: they possessed no other. Rather they sought to redirect it, maintaining their alliance with church, nobles and intelligentsia ... Joseph II did not so much break from the past as turn the past on its head ... [Josephism] perpetuated much of the Baroque's own intellectual equipment: its categories, if not its content.[37]

A comparable process occurred in Charles III's Spain.[38] Regalism, a cavernous, antique vessel of medieval and Baroque origins, was re-outfitted with the new artillery of political economy. Its structures, rhetoric, and terms of discourse, all markers of the Old Regime's stability, however, underwent only minor alteration. The absolutist state was superimposed on a 'complex of inherited circumstances', whose continued existence depended on the preservation of traditional political forms.[39] Novelty, encouraged when it did not corrode the edifice bequeathed by the Baroque, flourished where it buttressed state aims.

The pressures spawned by international competition and rivalry, however, compelled Spain to galvanize its long-established, decentralized institutions. The reformers aimed to revivify the monarchy and to forge a modern instrument of geopolitical authority. This quest entailed both the elimination of entrenched corporate bodies and the installation of groups more amenable to Crown control. It involved nothing short of an overhaul of the political culture of the Spanish Atlantic World. This political culture, both in the peninsula and America, was characterized by negotiation, accommodation, and compromise. The Crown and local elites thus reached mutually satisfactory arrangements within an accepted, long-standing legal and constitutional framework.[40] The reformers' efforts, which undermined this well-established contractualism, triggered widespread resistance, including the Quito insurrection (1765), peninsular *Motín de Esquilache* (1766), the New Granada *Comunero* uprising (1781), and the Túpac Amaru rebellion in Peru (1780–1).[41]

The Crown's legitimacy in the Old and New Worlds nevertheless remained unchallenged, even if the scope of its authority remained severely cramped and its specific policies, especially its strident fiscal demands, faced a rising tide of popular dissent. For this reason, reformers did not renounce regalism, but rather sought to make it more palatable, to achieve their aims without inciting resistance. In the New World, the Crown settled for mutually advantageous arrangements, which bolstered Spain's geopolitical authority without eroding the privileges of local elites and corporations. This led both the Crown and local elites to embrace political economy, with its promise of public happiness and material betterment, as a common language of reform. This symbiosis led to the creation of numerous quasi-state and state-sponsored entities which aimed to promote economic prosperity through new trading regimes and extensive public works projects. The best of these innovations, the *Consulados* and Economic Societies, facilitated the entry of innovative and regenerative ideas into policy circles and also involved the devolution of small quantities of political authority to local elites.

Quixotic or not, attempts to reform government, increase revenue, and compete with rival imperial states brought an influx of new political ideas and institutions to Spain and its Atlantic empire and reinvigorated long-established Spanish conceptions of royal authority. Even if Madrid failed to realize its loftiest ambitions, the reform ethos helped to accelerate the assimilation of the periphery—Chile, the Río de la Plata, Cuba, Venezuela, and New Granada—into the international system. From the desiccated hills of the Andalusia's Sierra Morena to the verdant cane fields west of Havana,

Bourbon reformers emphasized the lofty aims of public happiness, prosperity, and population growth. Their instruments—military might and arbitrary government—were crude, but the political thought underlying these policies was sophisticated.

This study strives to contribute to the existing scholarship of the eighteenth-century Spanish world in three connected ways. First, the book contributes to the intellectual history of Spanish governmental reform, with an emphasis on jurisprudence, political economy, and historical thought.[42] It explores how, in the latter decades of the eighteenth century, Caroline policymakers came, under the influence of both peninsular and imported political-economic doctrines, to aspire towards a more interventionist state.[43] Second, the book reintegrates Iberian history into the framework of Atlantic and European History, thus further repudiating claims of Spanish 'exceptionalism'. Narratives of Spanish, Colonial Latin American, and non-Iberian European history are merged to reflect their mutual influence. Furthermore, they are placed in the broader context not only of other nation states, but of rival imperial systems as well.[44] Third, the book enhances the understanding of how actors in the colonies reshaped metropolitan policies. It examines both colonial administrators who proposed, modified, and implemented reform measures and colonial subjects who manipulated the reform programme's political ideas to serve their own purposes without openly resisting royal authority.

These aims are pursued in the following four chapters:

Chapter 1 contends that geopolitical rivalry catalysed important intellectual debates in Bourbon Spain. The attempt to replicate the prosperity achieved by competitor imperial states prodded Spanish political writers and policymakers to emulate foreign practices. Britain, in particular, held a central position in the Spanish political imagination, especially with regard to colonial commerce, naval affairs, and domestic agriculture. Yet if Spanish modernizers were enamoured of foreign ideas and practices, they also detested the disdain for Spain, emanating from the Black Legend, purveyed in contemporary European historical narratives. An analysis of the reception of Abbé Raynal's *Histoire des Deux Indes* (1770), it is argued, demonstrates the political function of History in Bourbon Spain. Envisaged as a refutation of foreign critiques, the Duke of Almodóvar's *Historia Política de los Establecimientos Ultramarinos de las Naciones Europeas* (1784–90) suggests how royal historians produced narratives which responded to, and helped to foster, international rivalry. Geopolitical struggle was waged not only from gunships and fortresses in the Caribbean, but from within the walls of the Royal Academy of History in Madrid as well.

Chapter 2 postulates that regalist-infused ideas converged with an enlarged conception of the state's function to promote general welfare in late eighteenth-century Spain. A syncretic ideology of governance galvanized and lent coherence to previously fitful reform efforts. This chapter first examines the ubiquitous and multivalent concept of *felicidad pública*, public happiness, and analyses how proponents of an interventionist monarchy employed it to justify a broader sphere of state control over society and the economy. After tracing the intellectual origins of regalism, it is shown that the Caroline variant was guided both by an ambition to expand state power and a predilection for the removal of obstacles to agricultural prosperity, commercial growth, and international competitiveness. Its aims, therefore, merged with 'enlightened' notions of public happiness to form a new and flexible ideology of governance, which moved far beyond regalism's initial link to Church–State jurisdictional disputes. In fact, it gave rise to a new conception of the role of the state which would reverberate across the Atlantic Ocean.

Chapter 3 traces Bourbon ideas and policies in Spanish America. It analyses the impact of concepts of population, commerce, slavery, and administration on the shaping of policy. Policy was not a process of metropolitan directives being implemented mindlessly by local administrators, the 'men-on-the-spot'. For this reason, the often-divergent discourses which emanated from metropolitan ministers and colonial governors receive significant attention. In order to illustrate how lofty principles and pan-imperial policies manifested themselves in practice, the chapter concludes with a case study of governance in the interlinked colonies of Cuba, Louisiana, and Florida.

Chapter 4 describes how colonial elites participated in the reform process. Focusing on the new quasi-state institutions of the colonial *Consulados* and Economic Societies, the chapter contends that members of these institutions actively sought to modify existing commercial, agricultural, and population policy, thus further dispelling the images of inert, complacent colonists and uncompromising proto-revolutionaries. Colonial elites pursued licensed privilege and moderate, incremental reform in the context of a revivified, socio-economically stable Old Regime.[45] Operating within a neo-patrimonial political culture, American merchants and planters used the Bourbon reform ideology to their advantage, embracing it until such a stance impinged deleteriously on their interests.[46] The relation between the nascent civil society and the state in Spanish America, at least until 1808, was 'amicable and mutually supportive'.[47] Chapter 4 traces the coalescence of a Creole intelligentsia that helped to renovate Spanish imperial governance while solidifying its socio-economic pre-eminence, and, ultimately, incubated a robust public sphere in the nascent republics after the collapse of Spanish royal authority.[48]

Before reviewing the existing historiography, the preference for certain terms, which may provoke the consternation of the reader, deserves pre-emptive explanation. The use of terms such as 'policymaking', 'governance', and 'reform' may at first appear anachronistic. Spanish ministers themselves wrote almost exclusively of *proyectos*, or plans. Yet 'policymaking', as employed here, refers to a process which may be discerned in Spanish ministerial and administrative circles, a 'flow of deliberation and argument, of calculation and mediation between differing impulses'. Drawing on methodological insights from both British Imperial and Colonial Latin American historiography, this book aims to 'disentangle the continuities of purpose from the play of circumstances and personalities' and to trace the 'broad notions, the illusions and apprehensions, the tone and the spirit' of Spanish governance between 1759 and 1808.[49] The dispatches of administrators, 'the most salient and enduring feature of any colonial regime', offer key insights in this regard. They provide a 'highly visible structure of command and a framework which encloses more formless processes of social, economic and cultural change'.[50]

The prominence of non-state and quasi-state actors, moreover, explains the preference for the term 'governance', and not 'government'. Governance refers to the processes and institutions, both formal and informal, which need not be conducted exclusively by the state, and which guide and restrain the collective activity of groups and individuals. Government refers to a smaller subset of actions in which authority creates formal, legal obligations.[51]

The term 'reform' also requires definition for the purposes of this book. The following processes, through which state and non-state actors in the Spanish Atlantic World endeavoured to modify the *status quo*, should be classified as reform initiatives: agrarian renewal; population promotion schemes; the foment of 'industry' through the dignification of manual labour; inducements offered to stimulate manufacturing; the internal free trade of grain on the peninsula and the partial deregulation of colonial commerce; limitations on ecclesiastical mortmain and jurisdiction; judicial reform and legal codification initiatives; the curtailment of the nobility's privileges; and the reconfiguration of imperial fiscal and bureaucratic structures. With these definitions in mind, the scholarly debates surrounding the Bourbon reforms may be appreciated more easily.

The historiography of the Bourbon reforms

The argument knitting this book together cannot be appreciated fully without reference to the long-standing scholarly debates with which this monograph engages. The remaining part of this introductory chapter, therefore, distils and analyses the existing historiography of four major themes: foreign influences and their relative impact in Spain and Spanish America; the concept of 'enlightened absolutism'; the concept of regalism; and the debate over the 'success' of the Bourbon reforms in both Spain and America. It shall be demonstrated that the Spanish eighteenth century is a vibrant province of History, much 'more than a desert, where a few modest plants flowered, all of little beauty and without much scent'.[52]

The extent, impact, and source of foreign ideas on Spanish intellectual life have been an abiding quarrel among historians since the early nineteenth century. On the one hand, conservatives portrayed the Bourbon period as an 'epoch of slavish imitation of foreign practices and despicable adulteration' of values believed to be archetypically 'Spanish'.[53] The alleged Bourbon fetish for French ideas wrought a 'great array of pernicious errors', a 'contagion of the ideas of new thinkers' and laid the groundwork for Napoleon's occupation of the peninsula between 1808 and 1814.[54] For conservatives, then, the Bourbon period was an age adrift from all patriotic tradition, without moorings in Spain's past, a period of utter rupture. On the other hand, liberals disputed this characterization. For them, Charles III's reign embodied the 'reforming spirit which corrects, creates and perfects', which 'had triumphantly pushed Spain along the path of civilisation and progress'. The liberals contrasted this beneficent orientation with the 'revolutionary spirit which shatters, destroys and extinguishes'.[55] The influx of foreign ideas was one aspect of the Crown-directed modernization of Spain rather than a harbinger of foreign occupation.

Towards the turn of the twentieth century, the historiographical, as well as popularly accepted, division of the 'Two Spains' emerged. One was rooted in a pristine, pious peninsular tradition whereas the other, its nefarious counterpart, was inspired by sinister foreign influences.[56] The 'ruinous consequences' wrought by the 'Encyclopedism' of heterodox French *philosophes*, it was claimed, 'infected kings, princes and ministers'. Political economy, embraced by the Bourbon reformers, was decried as the 'legitimate offspring of materialist philosophy' which corroded Spain's national genius, extirpating its Catholic roots.[57] The Bourbon embrace of foreign ideas, then, was deemed the prelude to national catastrophe.

In the 1950s, it was proposed that foreign ideas produced a salubrious, not deleterious, impact on Spanish intellectual life. Echoing the early nineteenth-century liberal position, Charles III came to be depicted as the 'leader of a national revival that carried the country to heights of prestige and prosperity unknown for centuries'. His reign marked the 'end of Spain's isolation from major European intellectual and economic currents'.[58] After crossing the Pyrenees, cosmopolitan Spaniards 'brought to their country useful knowledge and modern doctrines, skilful techniques and a more open spirit' which were subsequently used in the 'crusade to liberate Spain and served as an example to their more backward compatriots who still clung to ancient traditions'. Foreign, mainly French, inspiration permitted Spain to 'depart from its morose solitude and begin to follow the rhythm of the world'.[59] Whereas nineteenth-century historians bewailed the disastrous impact of such ideas in policy decisions, historians of the mid-twentieth century arrived at the opposite conclusion: the movement of ideas across the Pyrenees was the catalyst of Spain's modernization. Isolation was deemed the 'cause of decadence' whereas Europeanization was a 'symptom of new vitality, curiosity, and spirited recuperation'.[60] Notwithstanding their divergent judgments, however, most historians agreed on two points: first, foreign influences were predominant in the Caroline reforms; and, second, among foreign influences, French currents were pre-eminent.

Since the 1950s, scholars have been more attuned to additional sources of foreign ideas in Bourbon Spain. Charles III's installation of ministers carried over from his reign in Naples (1734–59), at the apogee of Spanish bureaucracy, suggests a pronounced Italian accent in the articulation of the reform ideology.[61] It is now recognized that 'Italy maintained a remarkable function of social stimulus for Spain' and that 'in a remarkably systematic way, Italians were incorporated into the work of bringing Enlightenment to Spain'.[62] Neapolitan political economists, in particular, found a receptive audience among Spanish policymakers because their 'decay-reversing' and 'growth-oriented approach to society and policy did not necessarily upset canonical views about the state as an ethical and teleological entity'.[63] Recognition of Neapolitan currents stimulated historians to rethink the relative sway of French ideas and, more generally, the dynamics of assimilation of foreign political and economic thought in Spain.

From the 1960s, the pendulum swung in the opposite direction, and scholars stressed the Iberian, not pan-European, roots of reform policies. 'Inordinate stress on this dependence on foreign ideas', they argued, 'oversimplifies the complexities of intellectual life and distorts its character'. They claimed that Bourbon 'ambivalence reinforced their desire to identify with earlier Spanish reformers'.[64] The formative influence of the doctrines of seventeenth-century *Arbitristas* in eighteenth-century political discourse was highlighted, thus drawing attention to the 'national foundation' of Bourbon policy, which was only 'enriched by foreign imports'.[65] Recent authors have refuted the notion that the Spanish Enlightenment may be reduced to a 'mere process of imitation or translation of foreign works and authors', claiming rather that it was distinguished by 'innovative [native] thinkers who articulated ideas responsive to Europe'.[66]

If foreign ideas entered Spain, to what extent did they penetrate Spanish America? The diffusion and impact of European political ideas in Spanish America is a contentious subject. An early twentieth-century Chilean historian disparagingly observed that colonial intellectual life was 'unmoving, rigid and inert like a corpse'.[67] While differing on the degree of impact, subsequent scholars have departed from this bleak portrait and argued that the Spanish American public sphere was influenced profoundly by eighteenth-century European thought. The debate concerns which ideas had the greatest impact and from which country they derived. One scholar has claimed that the European enlightenment had little impact in Spanish America. Bourbon governance, he argued, was guided primarily by precepts of late Scholastic political thought, especially Suárez.[68] The majority of historians, however, concur that eighteenth-century ideas were abundant in Spanish America. Some note the 'overwhelming impact' of peninsular ideas which left a 'deep imprint' on the colonial public sphere.[69] The argument for predominant peninsular influence is congruous with Creole reformers' 'presentation of their designs as measures to rescue the monarch and his realm from the spectre of collapse'.[70] Substantial evidence also exists for the role of non-Spanish European ideas in colonial intellectual life, notwithstanding religious and state censorship, a capacious category which encompasses both the subversive ideas of French *philosophes* and the regime-bolstering concepts of Neapolitan political economy. Like their peninsular counterparts, historians of colonial Latin America are moving away from the notion, now denounced as a '*post hoc* fallacy', that the penetration of enlightened ideas precipitated Spanish American independence. Neither inert receptors of European thought nor radical revolutionaries, colonial elites operated in a more varied, textured intellectual milieu.[71]

The notion of Spanish Americans as passive recipients of European thought, or inert altogether, then, has been dismissed by scholars in recent decades. Spanish Americans modified the ideas which they obtained from Europe, contributed original concepts, and creatively adapted ideas to the peculiar circumstances of the New World. Exogenous ideas, whether from Spain or Europe at large, are now reduced to 'co-factors which complemented unique qualities of Spanish Americans'.[72] The transmission of European ideas 'gave educated creoles tools for criticizing the colonial regime and developing a new assertiveness'.[73] Spanish Americans depended on Europe, but 'succeeded in creating an intellectual tradition that was original, idiosyncratic, complex and quite distinct from any European model'.[74] Instead of imitating a single model, colonial intellectuals drew on an 'eclectic range of sources to create a "mobile rhetoric" of reform' in order to 'articulate a new balance between colony and empire'.[75] The trend in current research, then, is to avoid the often-confounding question of origins and instead to study how the Creole elite, 'with the aid of existing doctrines', approached public affairs.[76]

With regard to the contentious question of the impact and function of foreign ideas in Bourbon Spain and Spanish America, this book proposes a compromise solution. Claims for the predominance of French, Neapolitan, and Spanish influence are each, taken alone, unsatisfying. A turbulent coexistence of foreign and peninsular ideas best characterizes the intellectual atmosphere in which the Bourbon reformers and colonial organic intellectuals operated. Emulation of foreign models was tempered by patriotic priorities and the dictates of local circumstances, resulting in intellectual hybridity. The main areas discussed here—political economy, regalism, reform, imperial administration, absolutism, historiography—are distinguished by, and incomprehensible without, the interpenetration of foreign and peninsular, the interplay of older and newly fashioned ideas of different national origins.

A second major historiographical debate concerns whether 'enlightened absolutism' is the proper optic through which to view the Bourbon reform period. To what extent were newfangled political and economic ideas incorporated into the policymaking process in the Old World and the New? Although it was not used in Spain itself, the term *'despotisme éclairé'* or *'despotisme legal'* surfaced in the writings of Grimm, Gorani, Diderot, and Raynal in the second half of the eighteenth century.[77] The contemporary debate concerning the concept of enlightened despotism, however, was inaugurated in the late 1920s.[78] It was considered to refer to the following transnational characteristics: religious tolerance, educational reform, centralization, and concern for public welfare.[79] In the 1960s, however, scholars began to view the analytical category of enlightened absolutism—the latter word began to replace 'despotism', at least in European scholarship—with a heightened degree of scepticism. While acknowledging the existence of a 'community of interest between "enlightenment" and "despotism"', some scholars contended that, beyond a superficial allegiance to new ideas, 'cold political and economic requirements of their states and their thrones had the ultimate voice in determining both the specific character of the reforms undertaken and the limits of their own reform goals'.[80] The concept was derogated as 'irritating in its fluidity' because the 'exact nature of the different elements in the compound and the proportions in which they were combined are less easy to identify'.[81] Enlightened absolutism was dismissed as 'little more than a set of theories and aspirations' which lent an 'intellectual veneer' to policies which were 'seldom genuinely new and frequently selfish'.[82]

This judgment was queried in recent decades as historians detected the 'direct influence' of the enlightenment in the legislation of numerous eighteenth-century European rulers.[83] Two fundamental misconceptions, these scholars contended, have prejudiced historians against the proper appreciation of enlightened absolutism. First, it had been 'assumed too readily' that there existed a 'natural antagonism' between the enlightenment and the exigencies of the state. Enlightenment was not necessarily a subversive movement, but rather 'developed within and in support of the established order, not outside and against it'. Second, a tendency to conflate the French with other national enlightenments generated further confusion, resulting in a failure to recognize that the reforms undertaken in many countries had but a 'tenuous connection with the ideas of the French enlightenment, but were firmly rooted' in other intellectual traditions.[84] The enlightenment now is conceived as the intellectual context within which political reforms were fashioned, but was not the direct inspiration of specific legislative acts. Enlightened absolutism, then, is understood as a matter of 'mental attitudes, not of trying to plant physiocratic doctrines in foreign soils'.[85]

These insights, drawn primarily from non-Iberian history, have not been incorporated yet into the debate on the applicability of the concept 'enlightened absolutism' to Spain. This constitutes one of the scholarly lacunae which this book intends to fill. Assessing the applicability of the appellation 'enlightened absolutism' to Spain and its overseas empire presents tremendous difficulties. Emphasis on Charles III's position at the apex of the political system, for example, leads inevitably to the conundrum that the monarch was not 'enlightened in the eighteenth-century sense'. His upbringing had been conventional and he was 'pious and traditional in his religious practice. He read little and had few cultural interests'.[86] Spanish enlightened absolutism thus has referred to the cadre of ministers who formulated and implemented Crown policy.

Yet even these ministers' commitment to the application of ideas to policy is not uncontroversial. Contemporary foreign observers of the Bourbon reforms arrived at opposing conclusions: in 1780, Joseph Townsend deemed the reforms undertaken as not only defective, but also outmoded: Spain's 'best political writers resemble lag hounds hunting the stale scent while the fleetest are already in possession of the game'.[87] In contrast to this view, Scottish historian William Robertson in 1777 wrote admiringly of reforms inspired by 'sentiments more liberal and enlarged'.[88] He praised Charles III for his repudiation of 'narrow prejudices'; embrace of limited, free, and 'reciprocal intercourse'; and his 'arduous' effort to 'revive the spirit of industry where it has declined'.[89] In Spain, the reforming minister Gaspar Melchor Jovellanos shared Robertson's glowing assessment. Under the late king, he claimed, 'both population and industry prospered, and new sources of public wealth were opened up. The laws not merely kept order, but, what is more enlightened, promoted the greatness' of Spain.[90]

Though eighteenth-century commentators were intrigued by the connection between ideas and policy, this topic was neglected in the nineteenth. The tendency to view eighteenth-century Spain through the optic of enlightened absolutism coincided with the rise of its contemporary usage in the 1930s. Scholars associated it with the influx of 'French and Italian ministers who influenced Spanish governance and customs' and distinguished it by its 'protection, friendship and enthusiasm for renovative ideas', the pervasive influence of Versailles in politics and administration, and the infiltration of Spanish culture by the 'salons and encyclopedic ideas of Paris'. Yet, simultaneously, it was maintained, a 'profound sense of Spanish tradition' was retained.[91]

By the 1950s, enlightened absolutism fell out of favour among Spanish historians. Crown officials, it was argued, had manipulated the enlightenment in order to enhance their own personal power. Enlightened ideas 'coincided perfectly with the effort to invigorate royal power as the "principal nerve" of reform'.[92] In anglophone scholarship, however, enlightened absolutism was embraced as a viable concept. It was defined as an 'alliance of absolute monarchs, progressive thinkers, and those who profited from industry and commerce, bound together by feelings of mutual advantage'.[93] The concept of the 'enlightened, dynamic, authoritarian state' thus became a keystone of Spanish historiography.[94]

In 1970, the 'ideology of enlightened despotism' was defined as Spain's quest for modernization. 'Liberated from the institutional residues of the feudal past', the Bourbon reformers sought to 'realize, without perturbation, the will of the sovereign in accordance with the demands of public utility'.[95] Crown officials, it was claimed, aimed to shepherd Spanish society towards juridical, administrative, economic, and fiscal homogeneity. In order to achieve this goal, the Crown employed an 'active interventionism' to 'suppress' the power of the Church; to 'eliminate the feudal vestiges which weighed down agrarian society'; to 'diffuse an educational system which established social integration'; and to construct an instrument capable of 'destroying traditional barriers of resistance to the state's authority'.[96]

After an abeyance of 30 years, this argument was pushed one step further when one historian recently contended that Charles III was not the patron, but rather the nemesis, of enlightenment. The 'first' enlightenment, which flourished prior to 1759, was driven into 'crisis precisely' at his accession. His regime was 'in no way the apotheosis of principles born in the previous period'.[97] A chasm separated the conservative ideas animating Crown policy from the progressive political thought articulated by intellectuals in civil society. No longer the benign overseer of a cultural renaissance and the apostle of the public good, recent scholars have reduced Charles III to an ordinary despot who eschewed philosophy in favour of canon jurisprudence and older justifications of monarchical power.

Underpinning Caroline absolutism, it has been argued recently, was a combination of 'conservatism and arbitrariness', nourished by an 'anti-philosophy' which was labelled 'regalism'. This 'anti-philosophy' relied on older theses concerning the divine basis of royal authority. Allusions to foreign ideas by reformers merely served as a 'cloud of smoke' which obscured the 'obstinate traditionalism' of their aspirations.[98] The 'supposedly' enlightened regime 'became reduced to its essence; that is, mere absolutism, without need of enlightenment' by the turn of the nineteenth century.[99] This reinvigorated absolutism aspired to 'control, direct and manage' all aspects of social, cultural, political, and economic life.[100] Enlightened governance, according to this most recent historiography, would consist of an autonomous civil society, an ample sphere of cultural enterprise free from Crown interference, and liberal government institutions. Regalism encroached on this terrain and thus precluded the formation of an autonomous civil society.

To what extent have such revisionist conclusions penetrated analyses of enlightened absolutism as conceived by historians of colonial Latin America? The evidence is mixed. Older assumptions, which maintained that the 'speculative ideas of the enlightenment ... penetrated as well into official circles in Spain and resulted in important innovations in political administration and in trade', continue to persist.[101] Enlightened absolutism in Spanish America recently has been defined as the 'intent to apply the rational principles of the age to the resolution of problems in the imperial sphere'.[102] 'Enlightened officials', it is argued, 'constructed a narrow goal-oriented ideology designed to achieve material prosperity' and made the state 'responsible for definite economic performance'.[103] Colonial reforms thus are described as 'profoundly inspired by the Enlightenment'.[104]

Many historians of colonial Latin America, however, anticipated these revisionist assessments of Bourbon enlightened absolutism. They argued against a strong link between ideas and policy. They encountered little evidence of enlightened ideas in archival documents[105] and, based on this supposed scarcity, some have concluded that political and economic doctrines had 'none or very little' effect on the formation of policy.[106] Bourbon reformers did nothing but 'adapt traditional mercantilism to new exigencies'.[107] Spanish policymakers were 'simply pragmatic nationalists administering a fragile state and porous empire'. They 'merely proliferated traditional structures' in order to shore up the 'gothic edifice' of the imperial system.[108] While such 'pragmatism often combined with principle', it has been argued recently, 'principle gave way to pragmatism' for it was 'power, more than the power of ideas, that determined' Spanish policy.[109] The 'partisans of tradition' prevailed in what was a 'limited and largely superficial renovation of empire'.[110]

This latter set of analyses would appear to cast doubt on the argument that ideas animated Bourbon policy on both sides of the Atlantic. This book, however, seeks to demonstrate that advanced political and economic ideas circulated at the highest echelons of government and decisively impacted policy, notwithstanding the competing pressures—fiscal, geopolitical, military, religious—which hampered their application. This impact has been overlooked for several reasons: the first reason is that not all of the ideas informing policy were 'enlightened' in the traditional sense. Though it serves to sharpen the link between ideas and policy, 'enlightened absolutism' obscures more antiquated theoretical justifications for absolutism which prevailed in Bourbon Spain; the second reason is that advanced ideas often were used to bolster radically conservative and anti-reformist policy. Iberian politics, as one eminent scholar observed, is a 'complex interaction between the two major strands of the Enlightenment: its absolutist form, which involved a reformulation of imperialism along neo-mercantilist lines' and its 'more liberal form, which served as a guide to experimentation with new forms of governance and constitution-making'.[111] Developing this keen insight and applying it to Spain, this monograph suggests how older, though rejuvenated, political and legal ideas about kingship, particularly regalism, came both to justify and to inform the expansion of state power into previously unperturbed spheres of political and social life.

The third major historiographical debate with which this book engages, therefore, concerns regalism. What, precisely, have historians understood by the term 'regalism' and how has their understanding evolved since the nineteenth century? Debates about regalism typically have centred on disputes between Church and State concerning property and other forms of temporal authority. A leading Bourbon political writer contended that the 'immense riches of the clergy ... hindered national industry' and represented 'one of the gravest illnesses that threatened Spain'.[112] Crown officials endeavoured to correct this perceived calamitous imbalance.

Some nineteenth-century historians sympathized with the aims of the eighteenth-century regalists, asserting that

> the regalists did not debate theological issues of any sort; they did not aspire to enslave the Church to the state. The only thing that they sought was to free the state from its condition as a vassal of the Roman Curia.[113]

Opponents of regalism, however, attacked it an 'abuse which converted privilege into a law, artfully exploiting the Church's wealth'.[114] They asserted that it was an imported, un-Spanish, phenomenon. Its deleterious impact, therefore, could be attributed to the perversion, by interlopers, of Spanish piety, particularly infected by the 'regalist teachings of the clerophobe' Bernard Tanucci, Charles's chief minister when he reigned in Naples. Tanucci's purported 'hatred of the Church, his opposition to amortization, and his skeptical, heterodox and revolutionary tendencies', particularly his role in the expulsion of the Jesuits from Naples, were specifically derided.[115] Much of the nineteenth- and twentieth-century debate over regalism, then, would concern whether it was a foreign or peninsular phenomenon, the contours of a livelier debate limited by this binary straitjacket.

Until the mid-twentieth century, regalism was represented in Spanish historiography as a 'pathological situation', an 'illness' which produced a 'century of tyranny over the Church', even denigrated as the 'great sin of modern Spanish history'.[116] Anglophone historians inherited this tendency to interpret regalism as both hostile to the Church and distinct from the enlightenment. It was claimed that the regalists 'destroyed the independence and authority' of the Church and in so doing 'breached the thickest wall that stood between Spain and the Enlightenment'.[117] By the late 1970s, however, scholars of all nationalities had repudiated 'the myth of a heterodox, encyclopedist and imported regalism'. Instead, regalism was depicted as a phenomenon consonant with Iberian precedent.[118] Regalism was rooted in the *real patronato* privileges enjoyed by the Crown in the New World.[119] It was, therefore, neither a 'rupture' with the Spanish past nor a 'change of direction', but rather an 'evolution'.[120] Regalism 'symbolized a process of readjustment, the transfer of mechanisms of social control' to the state, which previously had not 'been sufficiently institutionally developed to use them'.[121] Bourbon regalism, then, was recognized as derived from Iberian jurisprudential traditions revivified by foreign intellectual currents.

Few contemporary scholars, however, acknowledge regalism's formative impact on policymaking or find it an intellectually compelling concept.

It has been derided as an intellectual 'cul-de-sac', boasting less of a 'creative and innovative capacity' than 'pure despotism', and a major force in the 'petrification and collapse' of the Old Regime.[122] This judgment, which conflates enlightenment with proto-liberalism, ignores the crucial, if neglected, role played by regalist ideas as catalysts in the crucial, inaugural stages of governmental reform. The regalist conception of the state's function in political and economic affairs was, this book contends, among the most decisive influences in the making of the Caroline ideology of governance. State reform necessitated the creation of a new language of politics which simultaneously was embedded in peninsular tradition, but also borrowed concepts from rival European nations which had pulled ahead, both militarily and economically, of Spain. Regalism provided the necessary grammar and new European ideas fused with older peninsular ones to make up the vocabulary of this new political language. Its concoction of cosmopolitanism, patriotism, and traditionalism adds a more nuanced conception of Spanish Crown reform than that afforded by enlightened absolutism.

To the debates over the role of foreign ideas, the applicability of enlightened absolutism, and regalism, a fourth contentious topic must be added: did the Bourbon reforms—whether enlightened, absolutist or regalist—of the Spanish Atlantic Empire succeed? Notwithstanding the difficulties inherent in developing an adequate criterion to assess 'success', historians have reached three, competing conclusions: first, the reforms devised were implemented comprehensively and produced the intended, beneficent result; second, the reforms pursued by the Spanish Crown were not formidable and of limited efficacy; and third, Spain and Spanish America underwent a significant transformation, particularly robust economic growth between 1760 and 1810, but that other factors, not Crown policy, were responsible for this change.

The first group of historians have hailed the extensive accomplishments of the Bourbon reforms. They point to the 'creation of a bureaucratic absolutist state, dedicated to the principle of territorial aggrandisement', predicated on a 'salaried bureaucracy, supported by an extensive army of guards, [which] enabled the Spanish monarchy to reap an extraordinary fiscal harvest from the expansion of economic activity effected by its reforms in commerce and its encouragement of colonial exports'.[123] While acknowledging that reforms represented an 'Indian summer, a fragile equipoise, easily broken asunder by changes in the political balance in Europe', the accomplishments of the Caroline ministers were vast.[124] In the short run, at least, royal officials were 'remarkably successful' in raising revenue through new tax levies, establishing more efficient collection procedures, and imposing royal monopolies.[125] Authority was centralized and contraband declined in some regions.[126] Throughout Spanish America, it is claimed, the 'overhaul of imperial government' centralized the 'mechanisms of control' and 'modernised the bureaucracy' through the creation of new viceroyalties, the appointment of intendants, the 'prime agents of absolutism', among other innovations.[127] In spite of lingering minor disagreements about their scope, scale, and legacy, this first cohort of historians maintains that the Bourbon reforms served to rationalize administration, produce higher revenues, and centralize political and economic control.

A second group of historians repudiated this glowing portrait of the Bourbon reformers and their policies. These historians derided the 'pervasive myth' of the Caroline era as one of 'unhindered progress, when the implementation of a rational imperial reform program awakened Spain and its imperial possessions from their Habsburg slumber'.[128] The Bourbon reformers, it is argued, were 'constantly beset by difficulties', 'proceeded fitfully', 'inefficiently applied' their loftier principles, and experienced 'reversals of policy and long periods of inaction'.[129] Crown policy was not animated by a 'vision of a new trading regime, composed of new markets or new products'. Charles III's reforms, then, were not a 'decisive rupture with past practices— hence the preference to describe this effort as a reconstitution of empire rather than a full-blooded revolution'.[130] According to this second, more sanguine historiographical perspective, the monarchy did not direct the reform process, but rather desperately attempted to keep pace with developments which sprang from the private initiatives of colonial elites or arose from the pressures of international rivalry.

Government reforms, in this second view, amounted to little more than a response to the exigencies of 'defensive modernisation' galvanized by the 'external stimulus' of geopolitical threats to the Spanish American empire. Bourbon reformers 'responded only where and when circumstance made change unavoidable'. Even this action did not prove the 'hoped-for panacea for the structural problems of delayed industrialization and colonial undersupply'.[131] Caroline reform amounted to 'calibrated adjustment, methodical incrementalism, never radical change or restructuring'.[132] Methods of revenue collection may have changed but the fiscal system had not undergone any fundamental reform.[133] Such incrementalism and half measures were necessary due to the Spanish imperial state which remained 'weak by European standards. It delegated functions, tolerated high levels of illicit violence, failed to consolidate territory'.[134] The incapacity of the Crown, especially at the municipal level, to implement the comprehensive reform it devised revealed that, 'for all the centuries of expanding royal authority, Spain remained in many ways a federation of self-governing municipalities'.[135] The Bourbon reforms, according to this second view, failed to create the necessary conditions to reverse the decline of Spain's Atlantic Empire.

Those historians who have espoused a third perspective on the relative success of the Bourbon reforms acknowledge the tremendous growth of the colonial economy in the final 20 years of the eighteenth century. They have denied, however, that government-led reforms were instrumental to this burgeoning prosperity. It is contended that the tendency to interpret this shift as the result of 'institutional intentionality' was attributable to the Bourbon 'strategem of propaganda', claiming responsibility for fortuitous results to which their actions had not contributed directly.[136] The success of the reforms may be 'exaggerated because of an assumption that fiscal reforms were responsible' for rising production and commercial activity.[137] Crown reformers 'simply took credit for other men's toil and ingenuity'; the true protagonist was the 'entrepreneurial elite composed of merchants, planters and miners'.[138] This third cohort of historians reject analyses which appraise Charles III's reign according to the myriad projects which his ministers devised because they 'sustain a view of his rule as an epoch of reforms' whereas 'more than reforms, what proliferated were *proyectos*, the majority of which never came to fruition'.[139] This latter group of historians, then, is sceptical of the reformers' efficacy and the extent to which they realized their grandiose objectives, regardless of whether prosperity coincided with their tenure in power.

Many eminent historians, then, have issued widely divergent verdicts concerning the ultimate efficacy of the Bourbon reforms. Indeed, the conclusion reached by each historian often hinges on the particular ultramarine colony or peninsular kingdom under consideration and the exact chronological period in which it is studied. Far from seeking to resolve the debate, this book shifts the focus towards the political ideas and sentiments which guided the reformers, regardless of their success or failure in particular instances. It examines the political vocabulary employed in the articulation of policy across the empire rather than the failures or successes associated with implementation.

The most salient conclusions to be retained from this brief survey of the four major historiographical debates are: first, the pan-European and syncretic character of the Caroline ideology of governance has long been obscured by a historiographical tradition suspicious of cosmopolitanism and inclined to celebrate Spanish exceptionalism; second, the term 'enlightened absolutism' has been applied imperfectly to the Bourbon reform period and served to shroud its most original characteristics; and third, regalism, formally a phenomenon studied exclusively by ecclesiastical historians, may facilitate a more textured understanding of the political anxieties and ambitions which animated the Caroline epoch, traditionally studied under the rubric of enlightened absolutism.

Plate 1: Giambattista Tiepolo, 'Wealth and Benefits of the Spanish Monarchy under Charles III' (1762). Reproduced with the kind permission of the Board of Trustees of the National Gallery of Art, Washington, DC, USA.

Plate 2:   Francisco de Goya, 'Charles III as a Hunter' (c. 1786–8). Museo del Prado, Madrid, Spain. Reproduced with the kind permission of AKG-Images/Erich Lessing.

GLORIA DE' PRENCIPI.
Nella Medaglia d' Adriano.

Plate 3: 'Glory of the Prince'. Published in Cesare Ripa, *Iconologia* (Venice, 1603). Reproduced with the kind permission of the Special Collections and Archives Division of the Wesleyan University Library, Middletown, Connecticut, USA.

Plate 4: Detail, Giambattista Tiepolo, 'Wealth and Benefits of the Spanish Monarchy under Charles III' (1762). Reproduced with the kind permission of the Board of Trustees of the National Gallery of Art, Washington, DC, USA.

Plate 5: Detail, Giambattista Tiepolo, 'Wealth and Benefits of the Spanish Monarchy under Charles III' (1762). Reproduced with the kind permission of the Board of Trustees of the National Gallery of Art, Washington, DC, USA.

Plate 6: Anton Raphael Mengs, 'Count Pedro Rodríguez de Campomanes' (n.d.). Real Academia de la Historia, Madrid, Spain. Reproduced with the kind permission of AKG-Images/Erich Lessing.

1
The Intellectual Impact of International Rivalry

Since at least the sixteenth century, Spanish governance enkindled the scorn of many foreign commentators. In the middle decades of the eighteenth, Montesquieu faulted Spain's 'internal vice of bad government'. John Campbell concurred, contending that its plight was attributable to 'nothing but errors in government'.[1] Extending this indictment to culture, Nicolas Masson de Morvillier's infamous entry in the *Encyclopédie Méthodique* answered, in unflattering terms, the question 'Que doit-on à l'Espagne? Et depuis deux siècles, depuis quatre, depuis six, qu'a't'elle fait pour l'Europe?' These negative assessments help to explain the Inquisition's censure of *The Spirit of the Laws* in 1756 and the *Encyclopédie* in 1759. In spite of the prohibition, Masson's unfavourable characterization was read by and incited furious respondents, the most notable of whom was Juan Pablo Forner. In his *Oración Apologética*, Forner conceded that Spain had 'produced neither a Descartes nor a Newton'. But, he added, it had nurtured 'wise legislators and excellent practical philosophers, who had preferred the ineffable pleasure of working for the benefit of humanity to the lazy task of constructing imaginary worlds in the solitude and silence of a study'.[2] No less effective was José de Cadalso's ridicule of the 'rapid style of certain French pens, agitated by superficial, flippant, and hardly impartial fantasies. How few Spanish books Montesquieu has read! What limited knowledge he has of our literature!'[3]

Yet Forner's and Cadalso's impassioned defence was not shared universally by their compatriots. Lamenting the backwardness of the university curriculum, Pablo de Olavide noted that, 'to our detriment, not even a ray of light has entered ... whereas the cultured nations occupy themselves with the practical sciences, determining the shape of the earth or discovering new luminous objects in the sky to improve navigation, our time is wasted ... in answering frivolous scholastic questions'.[4] Subsequent commentators would extend Olavide's pessimism to encompass additional facets of culture, 'the great backwardness in which all of Spain's arts and sciences, which flourish in other nations, are found'.[5] Knowledge of the world beyond the Pyrenees was considered indispensable to the advancement of commerce. Travel, which facilitated 'knowing men in their own countries, their customs and their whims', was required. 'Without visiting many countries, seeing their cities and meeting their inhabitants', one observer remarked, it would be impossible to 'distinguish between a polished and an uncivilized nation' and thus enrich Spain with '*las luces*' acquired abroad.[6] Industry also would benefit from such foreign contact, Madrid's Economic Society argued, as learning from foreign models would permit Spain to train the 'necessary artisans so that we will not require recourse to foreign goods'.[7]

Critical admiration for foreign ideas and practices is a phenomenon, which sheds intense light on the intellectual milieu from which the Bourbon reform ideology emerged. Geopolitical rivalry had cultural and intellectual repercussions. Reformers depended on ideas, as well as fleets, militias, and tax receipts, to pursue their ends while political writers contributed to heightening inter-state rivalry through intellectual production. The chapter first analyses the reception of foreign ideas in Spain, particularly the phenomenon of emulation. It examines the process by which foreign ideas were fashioned into models, deployed in political debate, and manipulated in practice. Using the image of Britain as a case study, this chapter offers a panorama of Spanish engagement with foreign ideas, the process of selecting the useful and discarding the inapplicable. The chapter then explores Spanish reactions to the histories of Spanish America written by foreign writers. The primary focus of the second part of the chapter is the Duke of Almodóvar's translation of the Abbé Raynal's *Histoire Philosophique et Politique des Établissements et du Commerce des Européens dans les Deux Indes* (1770), which bore only slight resemblance to the original in ideology, content, and structure. His five-volume work, which appeared as the *Historia Política de los Establecimientos Ultramarinos de las Naciones Europeas* [Political History of European Overseas Settlements], was published in Madrid between 1784 and 1790. It is the most distinguished Iberian contribution to the genre of the enlightened narrative.[8] It provides an appropriate lens through which to observe the critical reception and use of foreign ideas in Bourbon Spain. The chapter demonstrates that the enlightenment in Spain drew inspiration from foreign ideas and practices in an active and critical, not passive and derivative, way. These ideas were viewed as instruments in the revitalization of Spain and its Atlantic colonies, an aspiration which inevitably led to clashes with competitor imperial states.

The dynamics of emulation in eighteenth-century Europe

Imperial rivalry had major cultural repercussions, including emulation by one state of another's successful practices. The late eighteenth century witnessed a spike in intellectual exchanges and transnational borrowing of practices, a phenomenon due as much to the exigencies of international competition as to cosmopolitanism. Everything, from literary devices to the mechanics of sugar mills, was eligible to be siphoned, borrowed, or adapted. A 'spirit of ambitious emulation' was rampant across eighteenth-century Europe.[9] Far from an anachronistic framework imposed by modern scholars, contemporaries were keenly aware of emulation's role in the diffusion of foreign ideas, practices, and institutions as well as its link to inter-state rivalry. Portugal's future enlightened despotic minister, the Marquis of Pombal, observed that 'all European nations have improved themselves through reciprocal imitation', adding that 'each one carefully keeps watch over the actions taken by the others [and] they take advantage of the utility of foreign inventions'.[10] Emulation was a strategy by which a state could modernize its administrative, fiscal, and military structures in order to compete with its rivals.

It was a paradox of inter-state conflict that each nation sought to emulate the most successful practices of its rivals and to adapt them to local conditions. By critically copying its rivals, each state sought to surpass the competition and to dominate international affairs. Although the emulation of successful practices of other states was urged, failed or misguided policies also served as an albatross, symbols of potential actions whose replication would prove deleterious to the pursuit of geopolitical greatness. Political writers, therefore, dissected, analysed, and either lauded or repudiated, the ideas, institutions, reforms, and character of rival empires.[11]

Emulation was contrasted with, and seen as the positive counterpart of, jealousy or envy throughout Europe in the eighteenth century. It was considered to be the competitive pursuit of national excellence. Both emulation and envy were instances of rivalry, but were of 'divergent moral quality: one fair and constructive, the other unfair and malevolent'.[12] Emulation, in contrast to jealousy and envy, was considered a 'generous, ennobling passion, productive of integrity and virtuous ambition'.[13]

Emulation and envy often were used as synonyms. Edward Gibbon deployed the composite term 'jealous emulation' to encompass its multiple meanings whereas Adam Ferguson depicted emulation as an 'unhappy disposition rarely unmixed with jealousy and envy'.[14] It was Adam Smith, however, who defined emulation's relation to statecraft. In *The Theory of Moral Sentiments*, published in 1759, the same year as Charles III's accession to the Spanish throne, Smith contrasted emulation's constructive character with the pernicious effects of jealousy or envy: 'the love of our own nation often disposes us to view, with the most malignant jealousy and envy, the prosperity and aggrandisement of any neighboring nation'. Smith argued that a nation should endeavour to 'promote, instead of obstruct, the excellence of its neighbours. These are all proper objects of national emulation, not of national prejudice or envy'.[15] As one recent scholar has demonstrated powerfully, emulation could be a 'vehicle for *grandeza*, a quest for national pre-eminence'. It became a 'patriotic duty, motivated by the love of country and serving national honour'.[16]

Emulation was not, of course, an exclusively anglophone concept. In France, the Parisian *Société Libre d'Émulation*, founded in 1776, promoted inventions applicable to agriculture, commerce, and manufactures, justifying its *concours* on the grounds that emulation was a worthy objective. The word 'emulation' appears frequently, with positive connotations, for example, in the writings of Helvétius and Mirabeau.[17]

In Spain, some political writers disagreed that emulation was a path to national regeneration. 'Every nation', Juan Sempere y Guarinos contended, 'esteems itself above the others, and believes that its land, practices and customs are better than those of the rest of the universe'.[18] He maintained that Spanish writers furnished adequate resources, making recourse to foreign writers superfluous. Sempere y Guarinos argued that 'it is not necessary to turn to Montesquieu, Hume, Melon or any other foreign writer, whose ideas are suspicious for not having been careful always to unite the demands of religion with those of politics'.[19]

Although they were influential, critics of emulation's benefits, like Sempere, remained in the minority. Most embraced it as salutary or, at least, inevitable. Forner described fierce competition as a 'kind of furore, each nation wanting to raise and enlarge its literary merit over and above the other contestants'.[20] A high-ranking official reached a similar conclusion concerning the political utility of emulation, arguing that nations whose commerce flourished 'emulate that which is most advantageous'.[21] An influential political economist urged the creation of learned academies modelled on English and French precedents. These institutions would, he asserted, 'enable [Spain] better to imitate the curious inventions of others, and also to make useful discoveries ourselves, of such things that are serviceable to a foreign and home trade'.[22] Campomanes concurred, pleading that 'by means of their academies, the empire of the arts has been appropriated, and the rest of the Europe merely copies their inventions'. With the establishment of academies, this minister declared, Spain could 'reach the same level and, within a few years, overcome its backwardness and regain the time that it has lost'.[23]

Crown ministers and colonial officials remained keenly aware of the mutual influence exerted by states upon one another. The most chauvinistic claimed that the 'discovery and progress achieved by our nation in the New World awakened the emulation and covetous ambition of the other European powers' and provoked continuous wars.[24] 'Emulation, or better put, jealousy', Almodóvar wrote, 'has produced malignant detractors against the name of Spain'.[25]

Yet if national envy produced belligerence, it also could factor in the establishment and maintenance of peace. 'Our great distrust of war' and 'great hopes for peace' hinged, the normally bellicose general Alejandro O'Reilly told his friend Antonio Bucareli, the viceroy of New Spain, on 'our preparations. The great effect that they already have had in Paris and London is widely observed and everywhere it is said that never has such vigour been witnessed'.[26] The prevalence of foreign observation triggered a fear that policy missteps would be spotted and exploited by rival, and perpetually vigilant, nations. In the wake of the Túpac Amaru and *Comunero* uprisings, disillusioned commentators in the Americas fretted that the 'French watching this lamentable drama from their more comfortable position, will win the benefits of commerce, the most useful dominion, to which, it is observed, the Dutch and Danes also aspire, being themselves only poorly established in those places'.[27] This amalgam of chauvinism and cosmopolitanism, of national self-interest, and keen awareness of the practices of competitors, infused the Caroline reform ideology.

The failures and successes of rival nations were employed as evidence in Spanish political debates, often to urge a departure from current policy. This tendency may be detected in two of the period's most prominent political analysts: Bernardo Ward argued that 'by following the plans [of foreign nations] and imitating their models, I am certain that Spain will become the most powerful monarchy in Europe'. Jovellanos similarly conceded that 'our industry is not particularly inventive, and in its present state, the best we can achieve will be done by imitating and approximating foreign practice'.[28]

Explicit borrowing, nevertheless, remained rare even in the heyday of ideological imports and the integration of non-Spanish ideas usually acknowledged, perhaps hid behind, peninsular precedents. The acceptance of an idea of foreign origin often hinged on its congruence with one promulgated by a Spanish political writer. In his effort to introduce his readers to seventeenth-century English political economy, for example, Campomanes reassured his audience of its applicability by praising Uztáriz as 'the first Spaniard to use political calculus', derived from William Petty, in order to 'show others how to recognize the loss or gain of our balance of trade and the means by which they can be made to incline to Spain's favour'.[29]

It must be emphasized, however, that Spanish writers did not merely copy and servilely imitate, but rather engaged actively in criticizing, adapting, as well as rejecting, foreign ideas.[30] Following Mengs's theory of emulation, Campomanes contended that imitation and adaptation were potentially creative acts. He insisted that certain 'arts and professions originated in a new combination of [existing] objects, and this is what is called invention'.[31] These 'new combinations' and 'inventions', based on the successful practices of other European states, would prove vital to Spain's capacity to compete with its geopolitical rivals. In this sense, the union of cosmopolitanism and patriotism defines emulation in late eighteenth-century Spain.[32] Campomanes encapsulated the prevailing attitude when he stated that 'only ignorance of the progress and transmigration of the arts' can cause or produce 'ideas so contrary to the public good and the true interests of the native land [*patria*]'.[33] Ideas and concepts developed abroad, he and others argued, must be allowed to flood Spain and then be employed, where appropriate, in the service of national enlightenment.

The most direct source of foreign ideas in Spain was published books. While the latest currents of European ideas circulated among the intellectual elite, the fetish for foreign books always was dwarfed by the magnificent quantity of Spanish ones. The rampant republication of older Spanish works in the eighteenth century recounts only part of the story: the majority (51 per cent) of these re-issued books contained religious themes whereas non-religious works of history, political economy, and geography composed a paltry 21 per cent of the total, lagging behind the 36 per cent dealing with religious themes.[34] Where translations from modern European languages existed, a whopping 65 per cent came from French, 23 per cent from Italian, roughly 7 per cent from English, almost 4 per cent from Portuguese, and 1 per cent from German.[35] Among these translations, works of political economy and technical manuals were prominent, though the persistent paucity of books 'which teach the mechanic arts' was bemoaned as 'one of the principal causes of the backwardness of our factories'.[36] Whereas in the decade of the 1750s there were a mere nine translations of works of political economy from all languages, the 1770s witnessed 35, and the 1780s 49.[37] This upward shift was catalysed in part by the activities of the Economic Societies, which compiled and sought to disseminate works of political economy, and by the rise and growing sophistication of periodicals, which carried abundant news of foreign technological innovations.[38]

Percentages did not always reflect proportional influence: the impact of German ideas, in spite of the numerical paucity of translations, was considerable. The *Nuevas Poblaciones*, for example, the internal colonization scheme for the barren Sierra Morena region, discussed in Chapter 2, not only was modelled on Prussian and Russian precedents, but a Bavarian colonel recruited the 6,000 German and Flemish settlers. Moreover, Frederick the Great's economic initiatives often were cited in support of analogous Spanish *proyectos*, such as the formation of a monopoly company for the Philippines. The Prussian king, one advocate argued, 'knowing that by commerce alone he can make himself as powerful as he desires, ignored the great difficulties and inconveniences which oppose his object and formed a company for the East Indies'.[39]

Influential ideas and practices were transmitted not only through print, but also flowed from the observation of the experiences of other European states. Most were recorded by travellers, merchants, ambassadors, and administrators on the borderlands of empire, as well as ministers in Madrid. Often no correlation existed between the pervasiveness of a foreign culture in published literature and its impact in the domain of policy. For instance, Campomanes admired the Danish West Indies whose privileged company had been disbanded by royal decree due to its dismal economic performance. 'Commerce is their principal object', he gushed, 'and since [the end of monopoly] their Danish traffic in America has flourished'. 'This example',

Campomanes continued, 'so near to our own colonies is new proof of the necessity of stopping the spirit of pernicious regulation which has been ruinous to the nation'.[40]

Not all foreign practices, however, were deemed appropriate models for emulation. Some were models to be avoided. Campomanes's admiration for Danish practice, for example, contrasted with his disparagement of the 'causes of decadence' afflicting the Portuguese empire. He noted that Portugal had raised taxes by 4 per cent after the 1755 Lisbon earthquake in order to finance that city's reconstruction and that public credit subsequently 'deteriorated terribly there'. The broader cause of Portugal's predicament, however, he asserted, was its 'oppression of the liberty of commerce' through the formation of trading companies for the north of Brazil, predicting that 'spirit of privileged trade and the restrictions placed on commerce will hasten the downfall of that nation'. Portugal's experience, Campomanes admonished, 'should alert Spain to avoid such ideas concerning this mode of commerce'.[41] Trade, he contended, 'must neither be conducted by companies, nor at ports which enjoy exclusive privilege'.[42] Through critical assessment of the policies of rival nations, Spain could learn from precedent, avoid their competitors' calamities, and surpass them by virtue of superior practices.

The rapid economic progress of nations considered inferior to Spain also was cited to demonstrate the assured success of a new, foreign-inspired course of action. The Russians, 'a stupid and brute people', in one commentator's opinion, recently had 'distinguished themselves' in the sciences, arms, as well as the mechanical and liberal arts. This was a 'sudden and prodigious' shift which was attributable solely to the 'wise government' of Peter the Great.[43] Campillo stressed that other European colonies benefited from 'good government, to which is owed the great industry shown by their inhabitants ... and rather than using some of their methods, which are neither adaptable nor applicable to our circumstances, we can nevertheless borrow the principal spirit of their system'.[44] Foreign examples also were invoked to convey frustration and confusion when reforms yielded few of their intended benefits. 'We observe some nations without essential materials are nonetheless masters of manufactures', one high-ranking official remarked, 'while others, possessing everything, lack manufactures ... without ports and great stretches of coast, some have the most flourishing merchant marine; whereas others, who possess the most secure ports and are ideally situated, lack skilled sailors'.[45]

This heightened awareness of foreign practices was not exclusive to the metropolitan ministerial elite. It was a widespread phenomenon, pervasive even among the royal governors and Creole intellectuals of the imperial periphery. In attempting to extricate the empire from political–fiscal peril, colonial officials and civic-minded Creoles frequently drew inspiration from the practices of foreign states. In his 1804 inaugural oration at the newly founded university in Santiago, the Chilean jurist Juan Egaña heaped praise on the 'brilliant models which wise and generous Europe furnishes' and lambasted the Creole literary establishment which remained 'plunged in mediocrity while that of Russia today compete with those of Paris and London'.[46] Trinidad's governor, following Campomanes, employed the example of the Danish colonies to contend that Spanish trade policy required radical reform: 'without men [i.e. population], without money, without credit, without manufacturing, without commerce', Denmark's colonies flourished due to the existence of free ports 'for the entry of provisions and useful necessities', and to the freedom of commerce which they enjoyed.[47] Caracas's captain-general invoked foreign practices to urge the expansion of its agricultural sector, which, he claimed, constituted the foundation of prosperity. 'Foreign nations', he claimed, 'contend for wealth by means of emulation [*emulación*] or lose it through envy'. For this reason, he reported:

> the Swedes, who live in a sterile country, have developed many happy remedies to correct the defects of the northern climate; and Denmark has followed their example; for the same reason, Germany teaches rural and political economy at its universities, to the great advantage of its youth; similarly, the King of Sardinia sends the children of the most distinguished families to learn this noble art in the interior of Germany; likewise, Naples encourages its labourers to take care of, and to examine, the natural resources of its dominions; Florence established an Academy of Agriculture composed of first-rank Tuscan nobility; England, too, commenced the epoch of its greatness when it founded its commerce on the solid basis of agriculture; France has replicated this experience to which it must be added that even China's prosperity is built on its natural resources.[48]

This inventory of successful foreign practices draws attention not only to the cosmopolitan proclivities of certain administrators, but also highlights the manner in which foreign examples were utilized to urge concrete policy shifts in the national interest. Beyond a merely superficial vogue of enlightened ideas, a pan-European outlook informed policymaking in the pursuit of security and state prosperity.

'Una Verdadera Universidad de Política': the function of Great Britain in Bourbon political thought

Diplomatic alliances, geographic proximity, and cultural exchange ensured robust French influence in Spain. The successive 'Family Compacts' between the two nations indubitably facilitated the sanctioned entry across the Pyrenees of French ideas and fashions. As Almodóvar noted in 1785, 'the same family sits on both thrones in perpetual alliance, sharing an extensive border, the same religion and almost identical interests'.[49] Yet the preoccupation of Crown officials and political writers with colonial economy and agricultural improvement produced a deep, if often overlooked, fascination with Britain. Spain's recovery lay in following the recommendations of 'a variety of authors, both our own and foreigners, and even of our enemies'.[50] In late eighteenth century, there was no greater threat to Spain's Atlantic empire than England, which aspired, many Spaniards believed, to be 'master of universal commerce in both hemispheres'.[51]

The impact of this particular geopolitical rivalry in the political thought of the Bourbon reform period deserves closer examination. Efforts to draw connections between English and Spanish ideas are stymied by the pervasive assumption that foreign influence was confined to French and Neapolitan incursions. Misconceptions abound due to a tendency to conflate the ubiquity of French ideas and robust diplomatic alliance with influence on the ideas that undergirded policy.[52] Most accounts of Spanish reform thus minimize English influence in Spanish intellectual life and policy.[53]

War with England, whether hot or cold, was the most constant factor in Spanish foreign affairs between 1713 and 1808.[54] During the War of Spanish Succession, England captured Gibraltar (1704) and came away with the *Asiento*, the exclusive right to import slaves into Spanish dominions, in the negotiations which culminated in the Peace of Utrecht. War broke out again in the 1740s and Anglo-Spanish rivalry reached a fevered pitch during the Seven Years' War when the British captured both Havana and Manila in 1762. An uneasy détente and intermittent bellicosity between the two Atlantic Powers dominated the subsequent three decades. The key moments were the conflict which led to Madrid's cession of the Falklands to Britain, Spanish interference in favour of England's recalcitrant North American colonists from 1779–83, the diplomatic crisis over the Nootka Sound in the Pacific Northwest in 1790, and the broken truce of 1796 which engendered more than a decade of unremitting war with devastating consequences for Spain's ultramarine empire. Interspersed between these watershed events were lower intensity conflicts over Gibraltar, British settlements on the Mosquito Coast as well as at Darien in Central America, and ubiquitous contraband activity, usually launched from British Caribbean islands or the estuaries of the Río de la Plata.[55] Since the demands of geopolitical competition spurred Bourbon reform, it is logical that Britain, Spain's chief adversary, would impact profoundly ideas about political and economic reform.

The phenomenon of eighteenth-century Anglomania in other national contexts is well established. In France, England functioned as a 'catalyst in the formation' of nationalism. Anglophilia often served as a guise for an 'appraisal, unstated and thus uncensurable' of French society whereas Anglophobia was part of an effort to 'reawaken a sense of patriotism and pride'. The transmission of eighteenth-century British economic and historical writing in Germany displays how foreign ideas complemented, and were assimilated into, national debates.[56] An examination of British ideas in Bourbon Spain similarly sheds light on the proclivities and prejudices of its political writers and helps to identify the exogenous inspiration which infused the reform programme.

The recognition of this Anglo-Spanish cultural link has broader implications: first, it dispels the entrenched but erroneous notion that Spanish political thinkers were impervious to foreign penetration; second, it establishes the centrality of foreign sources and images in reform ideology, suggesting that England's potential utility as a national development model worthy of emulation captured the imagination of the policymaking elite;[57] and third, it contributes to the debate over to which geographical unit 'Enlightenment' belongs.[58] Assessing the Bourbon reformers from the perspective of rivals, admirers, emulators, and critics of Britain hints at a new interpretation of Iberian reform ideology, one obsessed with restoring the crumbling edifice of state power through a comprehensive transformation of society inspired by foreign models. While Britain may have been an inveterate geopolitical foe, Spanish political writers found many of its political writers' policies worthy of engagement.

Many references to England were frivolous or outright absurd: the *Consulado* of Santander, for example, boasted that its factory 'made excellent beer, as good as the best of England'.[59] In a moment of frustration with the Curia's tactics, Spain's ambassador in Rome asserted that 'the Pope had an English heart'.[60] The references to England treated in this section, however, had serious policy consequences and influenced six fundamental themes: industrial growth, colonial commerce, ultramarine governance, naval capacity, agricultural development, and the perceived link between patriotism and economic development.

As early as 1722, Philip V's minister, Melchor de Macanaz, had argued that the best way to promote industry was to arrange for English artisans to come to Spain, 'since they are the best in Europe. Entrusting factories to their care, within a brief amount of time we will not envy the English in this skill'.[61] With regard to colonial commerce, Campillo implored Spain to emulate England's method of 'giving to its vassals all manner of assistance to enrich themselves, the most secure path and measure to enrich the Treasury and the State'. Campillo considered liberty to be the 'soul of commerce, without which [nothing] can flourish or survive', that which 'enlivened agriculture, the arts, manufacture and industry'.[62] Campillo's verdict would be reiterated later in the century. The 'conditions of total liberty', one observer noted, permitted England's colonies to make 'great and rapid progress'.[63] Colonial governance received comparable approbation for British America was 'watched by all of Europe, a true theatre, in which outstanding achievements are performed'.[64] Pablo de Olavide's agrarian reform proposals explicitly endorsed Spain's imitation of the historical trajectory of English agriculture as a guarantor of prosperity:

England, that powerful and populated kingdom, was before in the same situation in which Spain finds itself today. It was devoted to the same erroneous principles and was poor, depopulated and miserable. Then a ray of light penetrated its government and transformed its legislation. Since then, it has protected agriculture and encouraged the utilisation of fallow lands. And, by changing this aspect of its legislation, it became populated and wealthy. This system is followed today by all nations that pursue the well-being of their people ... If we desire to increase our population and wealth, we should do what they have done and follow in England's footsteps by protecting and encouraging agriculture.[65]

In naval affairs, Antonio de Ulloa praised England's diligent, aggressive nurturing of its marine: '[England] always attends to its navy, dedicating to it a firm determination, [an attitude] which has long been sustained ... far from having waited for other nations to invent useful things for its use, it has hurried to make the most ingenious discoveries, to its great benefit'.[66] Ulloa also praised the conversion of Britain's non-strategic colonies from military to civil administration. 'If we should imitate this style of government', he argued, the cost of colonial administration could be 'reduced to a less burdensome figure'.[67]

Even the English form of government was invoked favourably by reformers. Whereas Spain and France were 'compound' monarchies and 'disconnected pieces linked to one another without mutual adhesion', Almodóvar argued, in England 'nothing is divided and, therefore, one senses the immense power of royal authority' which 'helped to form a close union between the nobility and the people'.[68] Beyond specific institutions, Britain's public-spiritedness, which assisted in the 'triumph of its government', mesmerized Spaniards while simultaneously provoking self-pity because 'patriotism sparks in the hearts of our rivals a vigorous activity which is [still] unknown to us'.[69]

These depictions and attitudes toward Britain reveal a fascination with its enviable prosperity, stable institutions, and national character. Yet Bourbon political writers moved beyond vague stereotypes. They delved deeper, fully engaging with texts of British political economy. Some scholars have questioned the extent of this interest. One scholar has argued that before 1760, with the notable exception of the 1753 Spanish translation of Joshua Gee's *The Trade and Navigation of Great Britain Considered* (1729), 'references to British authors were practically non-existent and of little significance'.[70] Translations from French to Spanish of the works of Herbert (1755), Mirabeau (1764), and Forbonnais (1765), among others, preceded those of Grenville (1770), Davenant (1779), Hume (1789), and Smith (1794).[71]

The absence of direct translations and relative paucity of English books, however, did not preclude the formative influence of English ideas.[72] News concerning, and précis of English books was widespread in the 1760s, finding expression in publications like the *Diario Estrangero* (1763) and the *Estafeta de Londres* (1762).[73] English texts often were transmitted through a third language, most commonly French. Some routes of transmission proved more circuitous. The Neapolitan political economist Antonio Genovesi, for instance, exerted a tremendous influence on Spanish political economy: his *Lezioni di Comercio* was translated in 1784, becoming a leading textbook in the Spanish world over the next 30 years, first in Zaragoza in 1785 and in Chile by 1813. Genovesi drew inspiration from an earlier generation of English commercial writers, most notably Joshua Gee and John Cary, and arranged for an Italian translation of the latter's *Essay on the State of England* (1695), to which he added an extensive preface.[74] In this manner, Spain's exposure to English commercial writers occurred, rather circuitously, via the Spanish translation of a text of an Italian political economist.[75]

The Bourbon reformers also engaged with, and disseminated widely, works of British political economy. Representative of the policy intelligentsia, Campomanes's primary goals included public happiness, national regeneration, and the enlargement of the state.[76] In order to realize these goals, Campomanes stressed the urgency of diffusing useful innovations, regardless of national origin. He contended that 'government is obligated to supply the public with advancements achieved in other places, so long as [Spanish] law can accommodate them, without distinction between indigenous and foreign. The accident of being born outside of Spain does not deprive them of the privileges which they deserve'.[77] Foreign political and economic ideas, Campomanes argued, had been neglected egregiously and he sought to attract the public's attention to meritorious institutions and practices of other nations.

Among these innovations, support for the advancement of economic knowledge was pre-eminent. 'Academic chairs for the teaching of the true rules of commerce have been established in Naples and Milan ... the reading of economic works is absolutely necessary in order to learn certain cardinal rules'.[78] He informed his readers of several of the 'excellent works published abroad, which recently have been translated', but reassured them that 'notes and reflections to accommodate them to our soil' would be appended.[79] He referred his audience to 'J. Child on the progress of the Spanish colonies in the Americas'.[80] Furthermore, among Campomanes's unpublished works was a translation of Davenant's 'On the Use of Political Arithmetic'.[81] English political economy was, therefore, a key source for Campomanes's proposals concerning Spain's potential regeneration.

Campomanes often extolled the utility of seventeenth-century English political economy. As early as 1761, he lauded 'this most useful calculus to compare the strength of nations with respect to one another, drawing on the principles of Petty and Davenant in England, which also were praised by our Uztáriz'.[82] In his *Industria Popular* (1774), he argued that the English 'have been those who most accurately used this type of calculation, whose books should be consulted' and, subsequently, observed that 'the study of the English language is of great importance to understand the excellent writings and insights relative to the improvement of industry'.[83] Indeed, a perusal of the catalogue of Campomanes's library (as of 1778) reveals multiple works by English writers in French translation, including John Cary, Josiah Child, David Hume, Joshua Gee, Bernard Mandeville, Charles King, and Arthur Young.[84]

Other Spanish observers in Bourbon Spain besides Campomanes hailed England as the first nation to 'think, meditate and calculate its interests upon solid and constant principles, the first to consider commerce as a science'.[85] Francisco Peñaranda y Casteñeda noted that 'this knowledge of economic science' permitted the enactment of 'wise economic measures' which under-pinned British prosperity and were 'worthy of the attention and imitation' of Spain.[86] This attitude was articulated most fully in Nicolás Arriquibar's writings. He translated an excerpt of Davenant's *Discourse on the Publick Revenues* (1698), publishing it as the first part of his own *Recreación Política* (1779). In his introduction to the translation, Arriquibar noted that 'this Englishman teaches us the secret with which the British government has reached its high level of perfection, the origin of its power, and the methods which any country can follow in order to enjoy the same happiness [*felicidad*], which is the art of calculating'. Utilizing this method, Arriquibar asserted, England had become 'a true university of politics', for these techniques were pur-portedly employed by all inhabitants in the conduct of daily affairs. He added that 'every Englishman considers himself to be the Prime Minister insofar as he tries to further the interests of his nation'.[87] Arriquibar was not alone in his assessment: Britain realized, according to one advocate of commercial education, 'how much [knowledge of] commerce contributes to the training of great men of state [*grandes hombres de estado*] which are found in abundance in England'.[88] The writings of Arriquibar and Campomanes, therefore, indicate the ubiquity of British models, however vaguely referred to or imprecisely analysed, in Madrid's political circles.

Establishing the importance of these commercial writers to eighteenth-century Spanish debates, begs a further question: what, precisely, was useful about seventeenth-century 'political arithmetic'? What lessons did it offer eighteenth-century Iberian admirers? English commercial writers addressed three themes which reverberated in Arriquibar's and Campomanes's political writings: the causal relation linking population, industry, and national advancement; a conception of good governance which endowed statesmen with a robust responsibility in economic affairs; and divergent stances con-cerning the utility of overseas colonies with detailed prescriptions for reme-dying the pernicious consequences of certain modes of ultramarine dominion.

Seventeenth-century English political writers' views on links between population growth, commercial expansion, and state action proved useful to the Bourbon reformers. Thomas Mun equated good governance with the promotion of mercantile activities:

so many well-governed states highly countenance the [mercantile] profession and carefully cherish the action, not only with policy to increase it, but also with power to protect it from all forraign [sic] injuries: because they know it is a principal of Reason of State to maintain and defend that which both supports them and their estates.[89]

Mun's justification of the state's central role in regulating and encouraging commerce while simultaneously protecting against 'foreign injury' coincided with the Madrid policy elite's attempts to revitalize peninsular and transoceanic trade.

Following Mun, subsequent English writers linked an industrious population with national upliftment. This conviction underpinned an interventionist effort to move all segments of the population into forms of employment which would contribute to overall national prosperity. John Cary, known in Spain through Genovesi's translation, contended that 'people are or may be the wealth of the nation, yet you must find employment for them, or else they are a burden to it, as the idle drone is maintained by the industry of the labourious bee'.[90]

In Spain, the nobility's antiquated codes of conduct proved incompatible with the newfangled rhetoric of industry. As a consequence of a ubiquitous aristocratic ideal, which held manual labour in low esteem, commercial and moneymaking pursuits were disdained. 'Our political system', one commentator observed, 'scorns commerce as a vile profession ... the nobility deprecates the word "business."'[91] From 1759, the Crown campaigned to dignify commerce and manual labour by ennobling merchants and discouraging idleness. Further legislation illegalized begging and vagabondage.[92] In its promotion of trade and industriousness, the impact of Mun and Cary on eighteenth-century Spanish reformers cannot be underestimated.

Another important link between English commercial writers and Spanish reformers involved the state's promotion of economic activity. An emphasis on the efficacious actions of individual ministers and policies saturates these writings, coalescing around a conviction that, in Petty's phrase, a 'small country and few people, may be equivalent in wealth and strength to a far greater people and territory'.[93] Davenant asserted that 'great statesmen have always taken care, not only to know the exact posture of their country, but likewise to understand perfectly the power or weakness of other people with whom they have wars or alliances; and the judgement formed from thence is political arithmetick'.[94] He praised the 'deep judgements of the ministers of state, Richelieu and Colbert, and not [that of] the merchants, that France owes the prosperity their trade was lately in, and 'twas their wisdom, more than the industry of their merchants, that laid the foundations of it'.[95] The state's primary responsibility, in his view, was the pursuit of national, political, and economic prestige. It cannot remain 'unarmed, sit still and suffer another country to enlarge its dominions' for this would demonstrate a 'mean courage; than which nothing is more odious to the multitude, who love valour in a prince, tho' it be unsuccessful'. The sovereign who 'would shine, and attract the love of their subjects' must be strenuously active when 'the rest of the world is in motion', eschewing the condition of a 'passive looker on'. Such a prince 'must make a figure, and have a share in all affairs abroad, or [he] can hardly give content at home'.[96] The refashioned Caroline monarchy drew on these and similar ideas as it reinserted itself into geopolitical conflicts after 1759.

The relation between colony and metropole was theorized by British commercial writers and picked up by Bourbon reformers. Josiah Child argued that if colonies were not 'kept to the rules of navigation' then the 'benefit of them would be wholly lost to the nation ... leaving us only the trouble of breeding men, and sending them abroad to cultivate the ground'.[97] Spanish political writers, preoccupied with the deleterious impact of smuggling, were guided by a similar principle. Davenant argued that colonies constituted a 'strength' so long as they remain 'under good discipline' and 'are strictly made to observe the fundamental laws' of the mother country. Under any other circumstances, however, colonies degenerated into 'members lopped off from the body politick, being indeed offensive arms, wrested from a nation, to be turned against it'.[98] British trade practices with its colonies were lauded by Spanish commentators. Campomanes credited the Navigation Acts for the discrepancy between the Spanish and British Empires: 'by means of [the Navigation Acts] the English violate commercial treaties ... by ill fortune Spain was oppressed by wars in all parts of the world while England prepared the foundation for its mercantile revolution; it is possible to infer that [from this point] Spain's backward slide began, ignorant as it was of the true principles of commerce'.[99] Spain, Campomanes implied, might match Britain's ascendance if its policies were underpinned by such 'true principles'.

Caroline political writers neither disparaged older Spanish economic doctrines nor viewed foreign and Spanish ideas as mutually exclusive. Instead they sought to republish and disseminate the most pertinent of their neglected peninsular predecessors. The widely circulated appendices to Campomanes's *Educación Popular* brought the commentaries of the *arbitristas*, including Martínez de Mata, Álvarez Osorio y Redin, and Navarrete to the attention of a broad range of audiences. Furthermore, Campomanes specifically recommended early eighteenth-century writer Gerónimo Uztáriz to his readers, whose work 'demanded to be re-read always for its excellent principles' of commerce.[100]

As 'excellent' as these works may have been, however, the exigencies of state required new strategies. In the preface to his 1794 translation of Adam Smith's *Wealth of Nations*, José Alonso Ortíz praised the preceding generation of Spanish political economists, but added that it had never 'attempted to reduce the subject to a science, a general system' or to express its ideas 'in an abstract way'.[101] Fourteen years earlier, Campomanes had reached a similar conclusion. The 'common defect' of those 'patriotic and well-intentioned writers', he noted in an unpublished essay, was the 'inexact' nature of their 'facts and figures' which, in turn, led them to faulty 'deductions and proposals'.[102]

The admiration of Britain by Spanish political writers should not obscure the critical dimension of their treatment. Contrary to the commercial maxims which it espoused, one observer would mock the British government for not having 'calculated according to its science of political arithmetic' in its 'inhumanly bloody' and 'profligate' war against its North American colonists.[103] Hostile assessments of Britain's quintessential values percolated as well. Some commentators castigated the 'dominant character of the English, the love of liberty, its most violent passion'.[104] The future minister of the Indies, José de Gálvez, distanced himself from this 'violent passion': 'We do not aspire', he wrote, 'to entirely adapt the liberty and other maxims of the English, because we recognize of course the great differences between the two states'.[105] Such recognition of the contradictions and potential fallibility ensured that admiration for English models never became sycophantic.

Most political writers, in fact, did not estimate Britain to be superior to Spain. It is implicit, perhaps, in all Spanish analyses, that the gap between the prosperity and power of the two nations was not insuperable. In the wake of the British capture of Havana in 1762, one influential optimist compared the two empires, noting that Spain's superiority in geographical size, the fertility of its land, and the produce of its colonies should have precluded such a debacle had resources been exploited properly and allocated efficiently. Everything, he argued, suggested that Spain should be a 'great, happy and powerful' country. Britain's greater revenues, then, were attributable to 'the better disposition' of its 'arts, fishing industry, agriculture, navigation and commerce' whereas Spain, if it possessed any of such things, remained 'quite languid'. He rejected attributing the divergence of fortunes, as many of his contemporaries did, to a 'different genius, or character' dismissing the notion of the 'laborious and diligent' Englishman and the 'lazy and distracted' Spaniard. The difference lay in government policy. 'If Spain were governed in the same way that England is', he predicted, 'within a few years it would be the superior in power and wealth'.[106]

This goal could be accomplished in myriad ways. One possibility was to deprive England of its illegal commerce with Spain's colonies. Grimaldi justified his rejection of an application from Asturian merchants for a privileged trading company with the Yucatán due to the prospective advantages which Spain would accrue in its rivalry with Britain if that trade were kept open to all Spaniards: 'We know', Grimaldi wrote, that 'the English currently conduct this commerce almost exclusively ... it would be a great advantage to strip them of it, substituting our own in its place ... no opportunity to improve our shipping and diminish that of England's should be lost'.[107] Britain's threat to Spain and its empire, then, gave impetus to many Bourbon initiatives. The threat, however, was not solely military or commercial; rather, it also was intellectual and moral. Britain, along with other European competitor states, was considered hostile to Spain's national character and intent on the besmirchment of its national past.

Imperial rivalry and History in Bourbon Spain

The twin forces of international rivalry and emulation impacted Bourbon Spain's revaluation of its own past. History furnished policymakers with prescriptive formulae as well as cautionary tales.[108] Policy and history were considered intimately linked in the minds of the Bourbon reformers. In the 1780s, a newly elected member of the Academy of History, founded in 1737, declared that since 'legislation is the soul which invigorates, makes robust and enlivens all types of government, national history should be formed from the law. When there are no laws, or those that existed have fallen into disuse, History will lack the most dignified object of its narrative'.[109] The study of History, therefore, was considered essential for governance. As a leading member of the Council of the Indies noted, 'the study and meditation of universal history not only satisfies our curiosity and entertains us, but rather is a factor in the formation of prudent judgment in the concerns of government'.[110] Campomanes echoed this sentiment in a letter to Jovellanos, grumbling that his fellow ministers 'do not know our History and they do not understand ecclesiastical affairs. How, then, are they ever going to counsel our sovereign about legislation?'[111] These sentiments determined that debates concerning the historiography of empire attracted the attention of figures at the highest echelons of Spanish government.

Piqued by unfavourable depictions by foreigners, Spanish reformers gazed at the past as often as they peered across borders as they sought to revitalize their Atlantic empire. The reception, translation, and dissemination of works of History, including Almodóvar's *Historia*, in Bourbon Spain were not passive processes. International rivalry provoked patriotic indignation, which, in turn, engendered a genre of counter-historical narrative which endeavoured to reprove and contest the unflattering images of Spain promulgated by foreign writers. In addition, Spanish historians gleaned practices of rival states which could be used either to vindicate existing policy or to provide support for a policy shift. Almodóvar's *Historia* sought to defend Spanish policy from foreign indictment neither by direct confrontation of the charges levied against it by purveyors of the Black Legend nor through effusive praise for Spain's conduct in its Atlantic dominions.[112] Instead, he negatively depicted

Spain's rival empires in the New World, especially that of Britain. Almodóvar's purpose, however, was not solely to deflect attention away from the ubiquitous Black Legend, but rather to prod Spain to renovate its empire through the critical emulation of its rivals.

Many historical epochs captured the political imagination of the reforming elite. Neoclassicism flourished, as it did elsewhere in Europe. The Iberian-born Roman Emperor Trajan, in particular, enjoyed renewed popularity. According to a leading periodical, Trajan was the 'most perfect prince ever recorded in history; no kingdom was ever so happy, nor as glorious ... he was a great man of state and a great captain, the man most fit to uplift human nature, pushing it toward the divine'.[113] Charles III remained obsessed not only with the antiquities unearthed at Herculaneum during his Neapolitan reign, but with the figure of Trajan himself. In the *Salon de Columnas* at the Royal Palace in Madrid, he had himself represented by a full-length statue garbed as a Roman General. The pose and costume of the figure repeat the design of Felipe de Castro's statue of Trajan on the palace façade.[114] Several years later, the monarch commissioned Mengs to paint the fresco 'Apotheosis of Trajan', which graced the ceiling of his private dining room. The composition of this work focuses on the figure of Glory, represented by a nymph clothed in white, surrounded by iconographical representations of the virtues of a Prince: liberality, firmness, fortune, economy, the military arts, and abundance. The figures of Public Happiness, Charity, and Love of Glory predictably occupy key positions.[115] Yet the Caroline era's historically conscious statesmen were not content with classical allusions. They were more interested in the less distant Iberian past.

Numerous historical episodes resonated in the contemporary politics.[116] The Visigothic period, as shall be discussed fully in Chapter 2, was highly esteemed by the regalists because of the existence of a national Church independent of Rome. The *Reconquista* often was extolled before the ill-fated siege of Algiers in 1776.[117] The epoch of Isabel and Ferdinand, *Los Reyes Católicos*, was praised by commentators lamenting Spain's departed prosperity and industriousness. 'There were many rich and populous cities where the arts and commerce flourished', Danvila y Villarrasa marvelled, 'laziness was loathed and work highly-esteemed as the companion of virtue; industriousness was common to the entire people'.[118] The unified Iberian Peninsula under Philip II was eulogized before the 1762 invasion of Portugal.[119] While the potential list of these uses of the past were myriad and the political impact of each was formidable, all of them looked toward an imagined time past when the machinery of state and society presumably had functioned more effectively.[120]

The period which captured the imagination of the Bourbon reformers, however, was the Spanish conquest of the New World and the subsequent establishment of its American empire. For Spaniards, as one eminent historian has noted, the 'discovery and possession of the Indies was further, and conclusive, evidence that they were the chosen race'.[121] But Spain's colonization had been pilloried by rival claimants to the imperial mantle. The Dutch depiction of Spanish brutality during their revolt against the Habsburg yoke in the late sixteenth century was taken up by the English and French in the subsequent two centuries, giving rise to the ubiquitous Black Legend. Spain was regarded suspiciously by European observers as an aspirant to universal monarchy, a barbarous destroyer of America's indigenous peoples, and, to borrow Gibbon's characterization, a nation marked by 'gloomy pride, rapacious avarice and unrelenting cruelty'.[122] European depictions of Spain invariably made use of such deeply entrenched attitudes concerning its rapacious conduct in the New World.

By the mid-eighteenth century, the seismic shifts in international relations and the ubiquity of the Black Legend had done little to perturb Spain's triumphal judgment of the conquest and colonization of America. Foreigners, a leading minister for ultramarine affairs complained, 'possessed by emulation and jealousy of our achievements and great aptitude, have endeavoured to tarnish the glories and triumphs of Spain, and, toward this depraved end, have concocted histories based in inaccurate perceptions, in no way justified, and for the most part false'.[123] Spanish officials at all echelons of government went on the offensive: one administrator stationed in New Granada asserted that English atrocities were responsible for a 'greater number of European victims of their caprice and passions, we would certainly find, than the number of native people' who suffered as a result of Spanish imperialism.[124] In fact, one prominent apologist asserted, of all of the European powers, only Spain had adopted a 'voluminous code of laws whose every sentence and every word breathe an admirable humanity and grants Indians full protection'.[125]

Responding to foreign vituperation was a major activity undertaken by Bourbon historians. William Robertson's *History of America* (1777) and Raynal's *Histoire* attracted the lion's share of the attention. Almodóvar's work, which will be examined at length, formed part of a broader, coordinated effort which sought to vindicate Spain's colonial past and to contest foreign polemics, thus 'confounding a certain class of [foreign] writers who have dedicated themselves to defaming an illustrious and honourable nation'.[126] The protracted debate over the introduction into Spain of Robertson's *History* and Raynal's *Histoire* signals History's elevated place in the genesis of Bourbon reform ideology. Foreign intellectual currents neither were received passively nor dismissed as impertinent to statecraft, but rather provoked spirited reactions and critiques which, in turn, produced syncretic ideas with which policymakers sought to galvanize the reform of the state.

The Spanish translation of Robertson's *History* ultimately was rejected in the late 1770s after a protracted debate.[127] Before Almodóvar undertook his translation of Raynal, another Spanish historian received a royal commission to write a history of the New World, which would respond, in a comprehensive and newfangled way, to foreign derision of Spanish colonialism. Juan Bautista Muñoz (1745–99), Royal Cosmographer of the Indies, lobbied Charles III to write such a history, claiming that its absence had been 'greatly prejudicial to the honor and to the interests of the nation'. Foreign writers, he fulminated, with Robertson's and Raynal's accounts foremost in his mind, 'unjustly indict the conduct of Spain, deprecate the merit of our discoveries, and obscure the glory of our heroes'. Such a history, which Muñoz volunteered to pen, would correct the record, demonstrating 'the righteous conduct and good intentions' of the Spanish Crown. He would thus 'dissipate the clouds which shroud the truth with ignorance and accusation' and vindicate 'the benevolence of [Spanish] government' in the Americas.[128]

The royal permission solicited by Muñoz was granted in 1779 and his *Historia del Nuevo Mundo* was published 11 years later. In the introduction to the first and only completed volume, Muñoz argued that Spain had encountered in the New World a 'field of glory worthy of its elevated thoughts' and, in spite of obstacles, the 'genius along with the ardour of religious belief ensured the happy attainment of its most arduous enterprises'. Spain, far from destroying the New World's wealth, persevered heroically in the worst of conditions, until America's 'steadily increasing wealth sparked the emulation, competition, industry, commerce, and interest of all of Europe'. Muñoz's bleak account of the pre-*Conquista* New World served to accentuate his claim for Spain's status as the indispensable conduit of European culture, without which the Americas would have remained mired in barbarism.[129]

The first volume of Muñoz's *Historia* was presented and approved by the Royal Academy of History for publication in 1791. In the final general session to approve it, however, normally a formality, his work was attacked bitterly. His detractors argued that Muñoz's *Historia* was not merely a 'modest individual effort', but rather represented a 'special responsibility' given by the late Charles III, who had died in 1788. 'Announced to both the nation and the rest of Europe' for many years, it must, therefore, be treated as 'work of the nation' and judged by a higher standard. The most damaging criticism was that Muñoz's work added 'nothing substantial to what has been written by previous historians of the Indies', both foreign and Spanish. Muñoz's history had 'omitted to include many reflections', thus lacking the 'philosophy proper to the century' and 'required of a History so long anticipated'.[130]

Almodóvar headed the Academy's commission which approved Muñoz's work and, subsequently, defended him against rearguard attack: '[our committee] has gained much [from reading his work] and we expect the same of the good judgment of the Academy'.[131] Almodóvar's opinion was not to be taken lightly: not only was he in line to assume the top post at the Royal Academy, but his five-volume translation of Raynal's history had appeared several years before the appearance of Muñoz's *Historia*. An unfavourable judgment of Spain's colonization of the New World also lay near the heart of Raynal's narrative, the harshness of which Almodóvar contested.

Yet Almodóvar's project differed from previous efforts, including that of Muñoz, which pursued strategies of either debunking the Black Legend or defending Spanish conduct and motives in the New World. Almodóvar shifted the focus away from Spain. He instead analysed the imperial trajectories of England, France, Portugal, and Holland, focusing on both efficacious practices as well as failed policies. Combining a cosmopolitan outlook with a ferocious patriotism, Almodóvar's *Historia*, which he published under the pseudonym (and anagram) Eduardo Malo de Luque, strongly insinuated along what lines the Spanish empire should reform in order to compete with rival imperial states.

Pedro Francisco Jiménez de Góngora y Luján (1727–96), later elevated to title of the Duke of Almodóvar, was director of the Royal Academy of History from 1791 until his death in 1796. Almodóvar was long accustomed to such public power, which followed naturally from his career service as an ambassador to the courts of various European states. Almodóvar's diplomatic career began in 1759 as an envoy to Russia, with a special commission to discover the full extent of Russian designs on the Pacific Coast of North America.[132] He remained in St. Petersburg until 1765 when he was named ambassador to Portugal during the age of Pombal. His tenure in Lisbon culminated with the Treaty of San Ildefonso (1778), which ended the numerous squabbles and skirmishes which had plagued Luso-Spanish relations since the Seven Years' War.[133] In 1778, he became ambassador to Britain, though Anglo-Spanish belligerence circumscribed his diplomatic efficacy. These biographical details are important because Almódovar's 35-year diplomatic career is highly relevant to the interpretation of his *Historia* offered in this book. Containing imperial rivalry and negotiating overseas disputes were key duties in Russia, Portugal, and England. From his diplomatic posts, he corresponded extensively with, and knew intimately, the Madrid-based architects of Bourbon imperial reform.

The imprint of these professional experiences and relationships are discernible in, and pertinent to, the arguments of his *Historia*.[134] In a 1767 letter to Spain's foreign minister, Almodóvar's preoccupation with British expansion is starkly revealed. He warned of the 'grave damage which would result from further English establishments' in the Americas. He proposed an alliance of mutual protection with Portugal on the condition that it closed its European and Brazilian ports to British shipping.[135] Almodóvar's suspicion of, and hostility towards, British ultramarine designs, which he claimed, in a 1779 epistle, emerged from a combination of 'dark and hidden maxims', 'ambition', and 'excessive pride', would become a significant subterranean anxiety of his *Historia* when it was published twenty years later.[136]

Throughout his diplomatic career, Almodóvar balanced intellectual pursuits and public duty in three ways: first, his observations abroad inspired policy proposals for peninsular Spain. He took special interest, for example, in the improvement of land-based communication and drafted a 'Proyecto de

Establecimiento de Postas de Ruedas en España' which drew upon his stints in Russia and Poland[137]; second, writing under a pseudonym, he introduced the public to French intellectual currents in his *Década Epistolar Sobre El Estado de Las Letras en Francia* (1781); third, he synthesized observations from his diplomatic career in his *Historia*.

Although the exact reasons for Almodóvar's decision to undertake a translation of Raynal (1713–96), whose work was banned in Spain, remain obscure, his remarks in the *Historia* provide certain clues: in the second volume, Almodóvar lamented that 'foreign writers have endeavoured to discredit Spain without having read or examined its long-verified and true histories'.[138] Almodóvar presented his project as part of the broader refutation of the Black Legend and the restoration of Spain's international reputation. 'Emulation, or better put, jealousy', he wrote, 'has produced malignant detractors against the name of Spain'.[139] But Almodóvar's project went beyond mere apology, the rejection of Raynal's indictment, and instead sought to show how a revivified empire could enable Spain to further reverse its decline and, ultimately, outstrip its rivals.

Raynal unequivocally condemned the Spanish Monarchy for its complicity in the devastation of the New World. He pursued his indictment through three channels. First, Raynal denied that the unsavoury character of the original Spanish inhabitants mitigated the Crown's responsibility because proper regulation would have produced a benign outcome. 'Rigid laws and equitable administration, an easy subsistence, and useful labour soon infuse morals', Raynal argued, into the former 'scum of the nation'. Although he acknowledged the possibility of rehabilitation, Raynal lamented the 'bandits' whose 'alloy debased the first colonies'.[140] Second, Raynal maligned the 'regular and constant system of oppression [that] succeeded the tumults and storms of conquest', an epoch of unbridled rapacity unleashed by the conquest and unabated to this day. Third, he blamed Spanish national character, imbued with 'prejudice' and 'pride', for hastening the 'perversion of human reason'. He claimed that Creoles had inherited the 'barbarous luxury, shameful pleasures, romantic intrigues', and 'superstition' of peninsular Spaniards.

Raynal linked Spain's 'blind fanaticism' and 'absolute contempt for improvements and customs' with its 'visible decay' into 'inaction and barbarism'; this language partially accounts for the vigorous censorship which Raynal's *Histoire* suffered in the Spanish World. But Spain's actions in the New World, repeated to varying degrees of rapacity by subsequent European competitors, were detrimental not only to non-European peoples, according to Raynal (and his collaborator Diderot), but to Europeans as well, whose prospects for stability and freedom were diminished by the persistence of imperial rivalry.[141] Raynal therefore implored all European governments to relinquish colonial monopoly and remove 'every obstacle ... that intercepts a direct communication' between the Americas and all European states.

For Raynal, the world historical purpose of commerce was to corrode relentlessly the fences of colonial fiefdoms.[142]

In his response to Raynal's grand narrative, banned in Spain after 1779, Almodóvar did not disguise his partiality. 'I am both Catholic and Spanish', he declared, explaining his intention to purge the Abbé's work of its impieties and chauvinism. He insisted that he was not 'obliged to translate the original which guides us, but rather its general method, select its seed, and add pertinent information to update the work'.[143] In claiming that it was not a strict translation, Almodóvar accurately assessed his own work for Raynal's *Histoire* served merely as a point of departure for the Duke's vision of the Atlantic World. While the first two volumes of Almodóvar's *Historia* mirror Raynal's design, the Spaniard added a voluminous appendix, entitled 'The English Constitution and the Affairs of the English East India Company', a feature not found in Raynal's original work. Moreover, in Almodóvar's third volume, he appended a 68-page essay entitled 'The Political and Economic State of France'. Whereas both Almodóvar's fourth and Raynal's third volumes, respectively, examine Scandinavian, Prussian, and Russian colonial ventures, Almodóvar supplemented the Frenchman's account with 'Analytical Memoirs Relative to the History and Present State of Russia', drawn primarily from materials and recollections of his diplomatic stint in St. Petersburg.

In addition to the three crucial appendices, Almodóvar's *Historia* differs most starkly from Raynal's in its failure to discuss America. Whereas Raynal's final seven volumes exhaustively treat Spanish, Portuguese, French, Dutch, and English colonial activity in the New World, Almodóvar remains conspicuously silent, concluding his work with a comparatively technical overview of Spanish settlements in Asia, including an extensive treatment of commercial prospects in the Philippines.[144] Almodóvar's strategy avoids directly disputing the judgment of Spanish colonialism purveyed by Raynal. Instead, he utilized contemporary reports of English atrocities in India to undermine the cultural chauvinism that he perceived permeated European accounts of the Spanish Conquest. While conceding the existence of 'some avaricious, cruel and misfortunate individuals' among the *Conquistadores*, he insisted that 'the times, the circumstances, the distances, and the scope [of the colonizing project]' served as mitigating factors, whereas the English commenced 'with the charitable motive of commerce, with the pretext of friendship, with the guise of a lamb', but subsequently 'transformed into a carnivorous wolf'.[145] Almodóvar, then, devotes scant attention to Spanish colonial practices and aimed to analyse, and extract useful lessons from, the conduct of rival European imperial powers. In this way, he declined to refute the specific charges of the Black Legend and, instead, analysed foreign practices in order either to vindicate certain Spanish practices or to urge policy shifts.

Almodóvar's narrative vindicated three Spanish imperial practices. First, he attacked the notion that a monarchical form of government caused Spain's seventeenth-century decline or impeded its economic recovery. As a corollary, he sought to dispel the notion that Spanish decline was linked to something intrinsic about its national character. Second, he highlighted the idiosyncrasies, if not depravities, of English and French colonial establishments. Third, he offered an account of colonial commerce which, though drawing selectively on Raynal, favoured the expansion of privileged monopoly companies which the Abbé had eschewed.

Almódovar instructed his readers to inspect the historical trajectories of Holland and Portugal, formerly 'tiny crumbs of the great Spanish monarchy'. He argued that forms of government and the fortunes of empire had no causal relation: the Portuguese empire 'flourished and degenerated under monarchical government' whereas the Dutch Republic had undergone a similar transformation while its form of government remained constant. The underlying cause in both cases, Almodóvar contended, was the relative abundance, or absence, of 'great men or great virtue'.[146] Employing Portugal repeatedly as a test case, Almodóvar repudiated the notion that Spain's national character precluded the profitable colonization of distant territories. The primary problem encountered by Portugal in its eastward expansion lay, in Almodóvar's view, in its 'desire to be a conquering power, to govern extensive territory which no nation would have been capable of conserving without debilitating itself'.[147] These two examples indicate Almodóvar's preference for monarchical institutions and his inclination to attribute geopolitical decline to the inexorable tendencies of imperial overstretch, rather than to the peculiarities of national character or intrinsically defective modes of government.

Almodóvar's circuitous apology for Spain's imperial legacy commenced with a superficially innocuous appraisal of its rivals, particularly Britain. As either an 'enemy or ally', he insisted, 'Great Britain is the power with which our interests are most linked, by very close-knit political and mercantile relations'. Almodóvar postulated, however, that Britain never would 'rule Europe or the rest of the world', a judgment which probably reflected Britain's humbled international stature after its 1783 capitulation in American Revolution. In an appendix to Volume II, Almodóvar lavished considerable attention on the English East India Company, which previously 'had conducted itself well relative to other companies, better conserving the customs, discipline and vigor than those of other nations'. In Bengal, however, this laudable conduct degenerated and had 'altered and corrupted all the sources of confidence and public happiness'. He did not refute the Black Legend, but rather tarnished England's reputation for being 'so reflexive, philosophical, generous, and such a good friend of liberty'. England, according to Almodóvar's account, had 'stained its glories' by its recent reprehensible conduct in India and revealed its policy to be 'cruel, haughty, avaricious, and unjust'.[148]

Britain's conduct in India, moreover, Almodóvar claimed, was unmitigated by the factors which produced Spain's excesses in its sixteenth-century conquest of the Americas. 'After the lessons and experiences of three centuries, the advances in the sciences, the arts and politics', he chided, not to mention the 'bitter criticisms and absurd calumny levied against Spain', Britain still engaged in 'barbarism'. In this way, Almodóvar appropriated the language of the Black Legend, formerly exclusively used to denigrate Spanish colonialism, and imposed it on the British.[149] Unlike Raynal, who believed that parliamentary action could ameliorate the East India Company's conduct, Almodóvar refrained from speculation on this question, preferring to draw attention to Britain's egregious crimes in South Asia. In this way, a type of counter-emulation was urged, in which Britain's imperial excesses were impugned as conduct to be both derided and avoided.

Yet Almodóvar nourished a patriotic aim in his lengthy treatment of Britain's empire which went beyond disputing the Black Legend and casting aspersions. For him, as for Adam Smith, emulation was a path to national greatness. He identified mutuality and rivalry as key factors in the imperial policy of Britain and France who 'fear, contemplate, insult, bore and highly estimate one another'.[150] Referring to these Powers as 'masters of the century in which the spirit of moderation reigns, [along with] the good correspondence of humanity and philosophy', he called on other 'great nations', transparently Spain, to 'open their eyes' and 'follow the right methods'. In such a way, Almodóvar claimed, the Crown could sustain its 'legitimate and lofty independence and perhaps achieve parity' with its rivals.[151] Through critical emulation, Spain could further bolster its geopolitical standing.

Almodóvar's *Historia* attracted the attention of the Spanish Enlightenment's leading figures. His approach to the translation and interpretation of Raynal's work earned both their approbation and dismay. Juan de Sempere y Guarinos summarized the positive evaluation: 'he endeavoured its correction, purging it of many defects, adding some useful parts, which both manifest the good judgment of the author and his skill in affairs of state'.[152] Jovellanos, by contrast, censured the first volume of Almodóvar work in late 1783, just prior to its publication, noting that it was 'unblemished by errors and impieties', but the scrupulousness needed to achieve this result also led Almodóvar to excise many 'beautiful discourses' of Raynal's original and the 'integrity of the work was lost, something essential to "philosophical" history'.[153] Fidelity to Raynal's text, however, never appears to have been Almodóvar's aspiration. Almodóvar's cosmopolitan outlook was primarily instrumental, an enlightened narrative to vindicate certain Spanish colonial policies and to promote the reform of other practices.

Almodóvar's conception of international and colonial commerce did not strictly mimic Raynal's views. Certain passages of the *Historia* undoubtedly echo the *Histoire*: 'war and navigation have mixed the destinies of societies and peoples', Almodóvar declared, and 'commerce invites all nations to consider the others as part of a single society, whose members can participate in the goods of all the rest'.[154] Other pronouncements, however, suggest economic priorities in the colonial sphere distinct from Raynal's.

Though he overcame some of the most rigid tenets of mercantilism, Almodóvar maintained greater affinities with it than with Raynal's nascent liberalism.[155] For example, Almodóvar praised the 'fortunate tyrant' Cromwell for his 'famous Acts of Navigation [1651] by which the commerce and marine of England flourishes even today'. Privileged companies also were meritorious in Almodóvar's view, especially when their 'ancient relations and established credit made them indispensable'. He implored the reader, 'the man of healthy judgment', not to be seduced by the cries of '"commercial liberty" and 'civil liberty'". He warned that economic writers purveying such schemes promised advantages which often proved to be nothing but a 'chimera'.[156] Almodóvar instead advocated the expansion of privileged trade, specifically the creation of a monopoly company for the Philippines as the most effective mode of extracting resources and generating revenue.

Exploiting a political climate favourable to privileged trading companies, Almodóvar proposed the establishment of one for the Philippines which he described as the ideal mechanism to exploit the natural abundance of that archipelago.[157] He insisted that such a company be founded on 'true principles', subject to revaluation every 25 years to determine whether monopoly privilege should be extended, or should be superseded by a policy predicated on different principles.[158] In a probable allusion to the physiocratic ideas professed by Raynal, he contended that the 'most powerful' method to develop the Philippines would be the 'cultivation of its extensive lands', a goal best achieved, he maintained, through the formation of a privileged trading company.[159]

Almodóvar's advocacy of a privileged company was not uncontroversial as a strategy for colonial development in general, as shall be developed in Chapter 3, and for the Philippines in particular. Some officials proposed abandoning distant outposts of empire altogether. Even the governor of the Philippines wrote to Charles IV urging that Spain attempt to exchange that far-flung archipelago with Britain for Gibraltar or Jamaica. The Philippines, in his view, were neither 'comparable in importance nor in usefulness to augment its power and commerce'. Considered together with Bengal, the governor predicted, Britain could create an Asian empire 'capable of recovering the decline which it feels in Europe', thus providing Spain with a freer hand in the Americas.[160]

In spite of such weighty reservations, the Royal Philippine Company, which was empowered to conduct trade between Manila and the rest of Spain's empire, as well as exclusive right to import slaves into Venezuela, received a royal charter in March 1785. Like the scheme Almodóvar had envisaged, the company received a 25-year charter and a capitalization of eight million pesos, of which the Crown purchased one million, thus demonstrating its backing of, and confidence in, the venture.[161]

The trading company's history indicates the role played by Almodóvar in the critical emulation of rival imperial states. It also suggests the impact of geopolitics on the writing of History. Far from a banal process of passive reception, dull translation, and desultory dissemination, an analysis of

Almodóvar's five-volume version of Raynal's *Histoire* urges at least two conclusions. First, historical translation was a politically charged process of omission and replacement, a process in which emulation was a crucial force. Second, Almodóvar's *Historia* demonstrates the Spanish Enlightenment's critical engagement with, and intellectual appetite for, the political practices of other European states, especially the administration of their overseas possessions. This engagement both served to refute the Black Legend and to compare Spain's conduct favourably with the imperial experiences of rival imperial states. Almodóvar's *Historia* highlights the mechanisms through which European ideas, particularly historical tracts, were incorporated into Bourbon political discourse and applied to contemporary policy decisions confronting the Spanish Empire.[162] The traces of critical emulation found in Almodóvar's work provide further evidence that the Spanish Enlightenment was not a derivative affair, a pale shadow of developments in France and Britain, but rather was characterized by intellectual cross-pollination, a cosmopolitanism tempered by patriotic duty and religious piety, and a conviction that History might furnish contemporaries with the insights required to propel Spain to recover its diminished geopolitical *grandeza*. Almodóvar's *Historia* suggests how innovative policy suggestions emanate from a historical text, which professes to operate faithfully within the confines of national and religious tradition. Grappling with these facets of this text, and the robust spirit of critical emulation with which it is imbued, may help to clarify the mechanisms by which ideas were transmitted between cultures, among rival states, and across intellectual boundaries in the long eighteenth century.

The preceding chapter thus sought to describe and analyse the various mechanisms by which Bourbon reformers encountered and processed non-Spanish ideas. It emphasized emulation's role in this process. The transmission and assimilation of foreign ideas occurred as much through traditional conduits, including published translations, as via first-hand observation of practices, institutions, and legislation. By the late eighteenth century, then, Spanish ideas neither were insulated from wider European trends nor isolated from intellectual currents from beyond the Pyrenees. Far from either static or passive, Spanish policy makers critically engaged with, and contributed forcefully to, broader European debates about state power, the value of empire, and its proper administration, political economy, and national character.

The chapter also attempted to clarify the relationship between geopolitical rivalry and historiography in Caroline Spain, arguing that mutual influence existed and was a fundamental component of the Bourbon ideology of governance. If imperial considerations permeated historiography and the latter, in turn, was employed as a tool in state affairs, it would be unsurprising if other intellectual fields were to infiltrate policymaking circles or, by the same token, were politics to stimulate intellectual activity. The next chapter therefore traces the interplay between legal thought, political economy, and policy in Bourbon Spain.

2
Felicidad Pública, Regalism, and the Bourbon Ideology of Governance

How will posterity pardon the eighteenth century for permitting such infamy to continue ... [that kings], in their own territory, cannot impose tribute without first seeking permission from the Bishop of Rome?[1]

'There are some critics', jurist Manuel de Abad y la Sierra tremulously declared in 1781, who 'will censure me and believe themselves to insult me by calling me a *regalist*, an expression which, in their minds, signifies a man of profane and pernicious studies [*hombre de estudios profanos y perniciosos*]'.[2] What did regalism signify to the eighteenth-century Iberian mind? Regalists disputed the scope of the Pope's authority over the Church in Spain and its overseas territories. While this conflict long preceded the Bourbon replacement of the Habsburg dynasty, the Caroline regalists were distinguished by a hybrid ideology, which combined new, broadly European currents of legal–political thought and older Iberian juridical principles. They employed this cross-pollinated political language of royal responsibility for public welfare in order to expand the scope of centralized state authority and undermine the matrix of local and regional juridical privileges, unmolested since the Middle Ages, which circumscribed the Crown's sovereignty.

   This chapter first describes the political language of *felicidad pública*, public happiness, which served to redefine and enlarge the state's overall function in society. After discussing its fundamental features and impact, the historical contours of Church–State disputes in Spain up until Charles III's accession are reconstructed. The analysis then turns to the regalism which animated the Crown reformers of the 1760s, looking at both the pan-European and peninsular origins of their ideas. The process by which the political vocabularies of public happiness and political economy were harnessed to bolster regalist political objectives receives extended treatment. The chapter concludes with the analysis of two ultimately failed projects, the *Nuevas Poblaciones* and the *Novíssima Recopilación de las Leyes de Indias*.

These projects embodied not only the interpenetration of regalist and enlightened political thought, but also suggest that Caroline regalism metamorphosed from its original parochial concern with Church–State relations into a flexible, sweeping ideology of governance which transcended the disputes from which it initially arose and was utilized as Spain reformed its American empire.

The new role of the state: public happiness, population growth, and commerce

According to Havana's newspaper, the quality of governance in a given state could be ascertained from whether, under its auspices, the 'sciences enlighten, the arts progress, commerce advances, and taxes decrease; from which one may infer that the treasury will swell, subject will dwell in greater opulence, and the country [*patria*] will have more sources on which to rely for its greatness, adornment and lustre'.[3] Most political observers in the eighteenth-century Spanish Atlantic World, notwithstanding its grandiloquence, would have found the Cuban gazette's criteria of good governance convincing. Public happiness and patriotism were connected intimately in the Spanish Enlightenment.

Public happiness merits special consideration not only because of its ubiquity in late eighteenth-century political discourse, but also because it was a malleable concept to which government reform initiatives appealed. The notion of public happiness drew heavily on Ludovico Antonio Muratori's ideas. Translated from Italian into Spanish and printed by royal decree in 1790, his *La Pública Felicidad: Un Objeto de los Buenos Príncipes* [Public Happiness: An Object of Good Princes] circulated widely in Spain following its original publication in Venice in 1749. Muratori defined public happiness in a polity as the condition 'in which everyone could be or could call themselves happy ... no greater nor more secure glory exists than governing well, with both the knowledge and desire to make the people happy'. Muratori maintained that the interests of the prince were synonymous with those of the state and necessarily consonant with those of his vassals: 'the public good is the good of the prince; the sovereign who thinks only of his own personal interest, forgetting that of his vassals, renounces his obligation and his glory. These two interests always should be united'. Nothing in Muratori's doctrine contradicted regalism's basic tenets. There should exist, he contended, a 'perfect and constant harmony between the *Sacerdocio* and *Imperio* ... both strive together to deliver to the people spiritual and temporal happiness'.[4] In the hands of Caroline ministers, public happiness became 'that which we are obligated to sustain and propagate, by means of the exact and zealous observance of the *regalía*'.[5] The increase of public happiness in Spain became, like 'improvement' in contemporary Georgian Britain, a 'new criterion for responsible authority and a mission towards which government might legitimately expand its powers'.[6]

Francisco Carrasco, a senior *fiscal*, attorney, of the *Real Hacienda* in the early 1760s, argued that public happiness consisted in the 'abundance of products; that which augments populations, fills the kingdom with riches, facilitates industry and the arts'.[7] For Carrasco, who feared deviation from political equilibrium, public happiness involved not merely net increase in itself, but equal, proportionate growth of the various sectors of the society:

> Health [*sanidad*] is nothing but the internal economy of [the body's] organs, humours, and parts in a true equilibrium ... in the same way, a state is healthy when its humours and parts are in equilibrium ... legislation is required to ensure that no single part grows disproportionately so that it becomes detrimental to the whole.[8]

Like French physiocrat François Quesnay, who applied medical metaphors to politico-economic affairs, Carrasco adopted a similar vocabulary in order to equate political legitimacy with the salubrious functioning of the physical body. This ardent defender of the monarchy emphasized harmonious balance while disparaging disruptive, radical change in his order-seeking political framework. As shall be analysed in this section, material plenty was considered a requisite attribute of public happiness, measurable chiefly by population increase.

Government policies and institutions were deemed defective if they failed to produce the increase of both subjects and goods. Campomanes argued that 'the greatest happiness of a republic consists in being very populated, and an abundant population is the greatest treasure that a prince could ever desire'.[9] Like population and wealth, public happiness, too, was calculable and its increase determined the relative glory of the legislator. 'The arithmetic expression of the glory of the legislator', one Chilean governor postulated in a similar spirit, 'may be measured by the number of persons that he has made happy multiplied by the number of obstacles that he had to overcome [in order to] achieve the epoch of happiness and strength [*firmeza*] of his government'.[10] Happy vassals, New Granada's viceroy contended, were synonymous with patriotic ones, who would in turn advance the aims of the state: 'the greatest power of a monarch certainly does not consist in the domination of vast kingdoms, but in being inhabited and cultivated by useful vassals, who are happy, and whose happiness's greatest ambition always will be the glory, splendor, enlargement and predominance of their nation over all others'.[11] This conception of princely power stressed the symbiotic relation between the state and its subjects. Natural resources and sheer size of possessions were deemed inadequate barometers of power. More secure was a state founded upon the mutual reliance of, and synergistic relations between, the prince and his subjects.

Such allusions to the intimate connection linking national strength, public happiness, and the greatness of legislator have been interpreted by some scholars as a convenient and transparent justification for absolutism. An analysis of the texts, however, reveals that the responsibilities, as well as the limits, of royal authority featured prominently in Bourbon political thought. The notion of mutual interest between prince and subject is both pronounced and pervasive: reformers sought not only to gild despotism, but to strike upon a new formula to uplift Spain and propel the monarchy's interests both within and beyond Europe. Francisco Cabarrús summarized the advantages which government could accrue, for example, by spreading educational opportunities widely. 'Governments have the greatest interest in the progress of *las luces*', he argued, and 'our people, brutalized and infected by oppression and error, are not susceptible to any pacific reform while they remain untreated'.[12] The embrace of state power, therefore, should not be construed as an endorsement of arbitrary government. Nor should public happiness be interpreted as a merely instrumental tactic to raise royal revenues.

Spanish political writers contended that an enormous gulf separated princely government, when it functioned properly, and was subject to fixed and established laws, from petty tyranny. While few institutional restraints on the exercise of monarchical power existed, this absence was counterbalanced by a political culture marked by lobbying, petitioning, and compromise.[13] The Crown's legitimate claim to promote public happiness depended on the preservation of this political culture. The *Diario Curioso* observed that it is 'commonly thought that tyrants are usurpers of that power which the laws of the nation prohibit them from appropriating and who regularly commit crimes to acquire this power or retain it'.[14] The Duke of Almodóvar, for whom monarchy represented the unchallengeable pillar of the social order, the 'genius, complexion and character of the nation', maintained that all forms of authority operated within limits. Overstepping such boundaries, which were 'sufficiently recognized', inevitably produced 'terrible effects'. According to this rationale, Almódovar distinguished between 'despotism' and a 'prince by justice'. For the latter, authority had 'fundamental laws for its principle, means and rule'.[15]

The *Diario Curioso* and Almodóvar were not isolated voices. A one-time professor at Huesca and later controversial judge [*oidor*] at the *Audiencia* of Charcas, Victorián de Villava, rejected despotism outright, defining it as a government without laws in which political decision-making was arbitrary. Free government, Villava asserted, existed 'when the laws identify limits to power, firmly determining its use and eliminating all arbitrary authority ... despotism's chief characteristic is its failure to recognize fundamental laws and fixed rules, transforming the despot's will into the only thing which is acknowledged and venerated'.[16] 'Even if despotism brought together all the attributes of sovereignty in a single subject', political economist Antonio Muñoz echoed, 'it lacks the reciprocal interest which constitutes the essence of sovereignty'.[17] State interest, commercial prosperity, and individual happiness were not only reconcilable, but convergent as well: 'the [common] interest of the property owner, the colony and the state is that the land produces as much as is possible'.[18] There existed, therefore, a vaguely defined, yet certain, limit beyond which royal power could not trespass without deteriorating into tyranny. Failure to strictly adhere to the rule of law threatened to undermine the reciprocal interest of Crown and subject.

The acknowledgement of a boundary which the monarch should not transgress, however, did not imply that the subjects maintained an extensive sphere of autonomy or that existing laws were pliable. Prominent writers agreed that sovereignty was restricted, but they did not champion an ample sphere for the individual's autonomous conduct. 'Liberty in politics', a Chilean governor argued, does not 'consist in the license for every person to do whatever attracts him, but rather only to do what is not against the public good [*bien general*]'.[19] This valuation of public good over individual liberty entailed that subjects's behaviour had to conform to certain norms. The political economist Lorenzo Normante y Carcavilla asserted, in the 1780s, that the 'object of political or civil education is that all citizens fulfil their social obligations'.[20] Some political writers entertained an even more austere conception of the public responsibility of individual subjects:

> all men are debtors to the *patria* and to the State. To it, they owe their industry, strength and talents ... he who does not contribute to the public good and does not work to the benefit of society may earn the reputation for being a corrupted member of the community, deserving of amputation and extermination.[21]

The strident tone of this passage suggests the weighty obligations of subjects in a state which strove to extend the public happiness of its members.

Expressions of dissatisfaction were, nevertheless, admissible within narrow limits, so long as such modest dissent was offered to further the public good. Dissent was permitted so long as the fundamental basis of the political system remained unchallenged. Misgovernance never undermined the legitimacy of the monarchy *qua* institution, but rather represented a perversion of the will of the sovereign, always attributable to administrative incompetence. Faulty administration could be criticized by subjects and merited the sovereign's sympathetic attention and corrective action. The policies enacted by Charles III's ministers in the early 1760s inspired a poem dedicated to the 'Bad Government of Esquilache', named for the minister of Treasury and War, the Sicilian-born

Marqués de Squillace, against whose policies the famous 'motines', or uprisings, of 1766 were directed:

> The revenues have decreased,
> But it is supposed that they have increased.
> Throughout the kingdom there are laments,
> But none is heeded.
> The factories are destroyed,
> Industry is damaged,
> Agriculture forgotten,
> The Church is seen oppressed,
> And the nation is dejected.[22]

The acceptability of the criticism articulated in such verses lies in the Crown's preservation of the contract by which, according to one contemporary, 'the People transfer to the King, through laws which limit the natural right of man, that which assures the solemnity of contracts, that which ensures the public calmness, and the happiness of the state ... from which is born the supreme power of kings to take the possessions of their subjects'.[23] Adherence to this contract, and the monarchy's pursuit of public happiness, was less of a choice than a necessity. As Cabarrús expressed the matter: 'the only method of perpetuating and preserving monarchies is to reconcile them with the general interest and will, or with the object of the social compact'.[24] Legislation, therefore, neither could be arbitrary nor disregard the public good. Sempere y Guarinos remarked that attempts to 'increase the tax receipts of the state by multiplying the tax burden of individuals is absurd and ruinous'. The 'improvement of agriculture, the arts and commerce' was exigent.[25] Even among the monarchy's staunchest defenders, then, there existed a consensus that rapacious absolutism was both undesirable and impractical.

How, then, did political commentators conceive that the Spanish monarchy could best preserve itself, secure public happiness, and simultaneously increase its prestige and power vis-à-vis rival states? This result, they argued, was possible only through the expansion of the state's revenues and administrative apparatus, the diminished autonomy of privileged corporations, and increased royal intervention in all spheres of society. Government action could mould the character and shape the aspirations of the Crown's subjects. 'No nation possesses a genius or character determined by Nature', one key commentator noted, 'on the contrary, it is formed and determined by government. A government cannot change the character of a single rude, pusillanimous, weak or listless subject, but it can shift the genius of the nation taken as a whole'.[26] Scientific administration in the pursuit of public happiness justified state intervention in the economy and most other spheres of public life. 'The science of government', one observer argued, 'maintains great empires and raises small ones [to greatness]; yet though customs and chance contribute in the short term to the prosperity or decadence of a state, the science of government teaches how to correct and prevent such occurrences'.[27] Governance guided by sound and verifiable principles, then, legitimated the expansion of state power.

Policymaking gravitated away from, not towards, utopianism and abstraction in the Caroline period and justified its proposals on the strength of their purported scientific basis. 'There are many policies [*proyectos*] which are beautiful on paper and pathetic in execution', Gandara declared, 'policymaking [*proyectar*] is already considered an art of many, but to very few has it become a science'.[28] Efficiency and productivity emerged as necessary criteria for policy. In his argument for the amortization of the Church property, for example, Sempere y Guarinos appealed to neither state nor individual advantage, but instead bemoaned the efficiency forfeited from fallow fields. Were it possible for these neglected lands to become well cultivated, it would, 'far from being prejudicial', be fully justified for the Church to retain control over their use. For the regalists, however, the state was the unique repository of this formula.[29] Such a proto-technocratic orientation was the means by which the monarchy's *grandeza* could be expanded.

Far from superseding divine justifications for princely authority, responsibility for public happiness endowed statecraft with new prestige and a renewed sense of purpose. The king, regalists argued, was obliged to foster manufacturing because, 'as a trustee of the happiness of the entire state, he must promote, ensure and increase it for everyone by every means available'.[30] In a similar spirit, increased taxes provided the revenue to 'maintain the dignity of the sovereign and equip him with methods conducive to the promotion of the happiness of his vassals and to make his state appear formidable to its enemies'.[31] Achieving the lofty aims of effective governance required a new breed of ministers and administrators. The 'man of state' must be endowed with 'an exact knowledge of human nature, as well as being mature and reflexive'.[32] Government action, it was argued, should emanate from a combination of 'enlightened love of the nation [combined] with knowledge of the economy' in order that 'all political bodies prosper', for 'where civil philosophy thrives, order and harmony exist, and progress advances'.[33] Knowledge of these principles, Almodóvar contended, would empower the monarchy to eradicate 'inveterate errors authorized by custom, which throw off course the true direction of mankind'.[34]

As elsewhere in Europe during the early modern period, politics and economics were indivisible in Spain. This lack of differentiation had important consequences for the Bourbon conception of public happiness.[35] Political writers focused on the political repercussions of commerce, particularly the 'augmentation and improvement of the arts, the increase and nourishment of the population, and the expansion of the comforts [of life]'.[36] The Crown's support for the advancement and diffusion of political economy intersected with its regalist ambitions, each buttressing the other. Regalism's older categories were infused with dynamic content whereas the emerging discipline of political economy was endowed with almost instant prestige through its association with the monarchy, seamlessly assimilated into its political fabric. The expressed object of regalist legislation was the 'preservation of the state, subsistence, public tranquility by means of adequate employment, and the defense of the nation by the expansion of wealth'.[37] The conservation of the monarchy, the preservation of public tranquility and the expansion of prosperity were the pillars of Caroline reform ideology. Public happiness, therefore, was inextricably linked to discourses of population and commerce in both the Old World and the New. The remainder of this section addresses population and commerce in peninsular Spain whereas Chapters 3 and 4 pursue these themes in Spain's American empire.

Preoccupation with population size was a standard feature of seventeenth- and eighteenth-century European political thought. Its growth was presumed to indicate a society's well-being, a benchmark of national vitality, usually presaging economic development. In the seventeenth century, Colbert held that population growth was especially beneficial to a nation's balance of trade and conducive to the expansion of wealth and power. 'Every wise, just and mild government', Hume argued, would 'always abound most in people, as well as in commodities and riches'. Population decline, contrapuntally, was diagnosed by Montesquieu as an almost 'incurable ill' arising from the 'internal vice of bad government'.[38]

Spanish political writers accepted Montesquieu's and Hume's basic claims. 'The power of a state is always judged by the number and wealth of its inhabitants. Population determines greatness',[39] one prominent commentator succinctly put it. Arriquibar contended that 'population or depopulation is the sole measure of the power or weakness of a kingdom, because only people enrich it and defend it'.[40] Normante y Carcavilla noted that 'all princes should procure by whatever means the multiplication of their citizen, in which consists the dignity of sovereignty; by the same token, the lack of inhabitants in a country contributes to the ignominy of he who governs, who has, as his inseparable companion, unhappiness'.[41] Drawing on these ideas, policymakers sought to increase the number of inhabitants throughout the Spanish empire.

Steadily rising from 9.3 million to 11.5 million between 1749 and 1797, fear of depopulation and stagnation in peninsular Spain remained impervious to the upward shift registered by various censuses.[42] Political writers transformed population into a benchmark for overall economic performance and good governance. In this sense, their ideas converged with those of the French physiocrats and other political thinkers across Europe. For Quesnay, 'the population of a state increases in proportion to the nation's revenue, because the revenue procures well-being and gains by which men are maintained and attracted'. In his 1768 *Political Testament*, Frederick the Great proclaimed that it was 'the first, most generally valid and truest principle of government that the real force of a state lies in a numerous population'.[43]

This goal demanded the state's active intervention. 'Population is one of the cares to which the entire nation attends', a leading Spanish periodical stated in 1786, 'in order to make it flourish and become dominant over the other [states] ... no civilized and wise nation has ignored this phenomenon, which supports the force and power of the state'.[44] Population thus became a barometer of the wisdom of public policy, particularly with regard to agriculture. 'A wise agricultural policy avoids depopulation, revives nations, and raises up those who find themselves ruined and destroyed',[45] a prominent commentator explained.

Though the identification of a monocausal explanation of demographic growth eluded them, Spanish prescriptions for population increase may be grouped into four categories: first, 'the surest measure to increase population is the introduction of industry'. Restrictions on the size of the clergy and disincentives for joining the religious orders in the first place were proposed to promote this objective;[46] second, observers detected a feedback mechanism by which 'commerce attracts population and this increase spurs commerce';[47] third, the state's security was a key feature of population debates, for the depopulated state was considered to be more vulnerable to invasion: 'the security of the state depends on the preservation of the population, which is the nerve of this wealth and happiness';[48] fourth, some advocated a laissez-faire approach to population. To increase population, only 'Nature [*naturaleza simple*]' would be required. It merely was necessary to remove the 'obstacles which impede its operation ... if subsistence is the means to [increase] population, then reciprocally population facilitates and increases the means of subsistence'.[49] In this way, the pursuit of population growth usually overlapped with other state goals, particularly the encouragement of commerce.

The first eighteenth-century Spanish political economist of international repute, Gerónimo Uztáriz (1670–1732), linked economic prosperity and population. A more populous Spain, he contended, could generate greater tax revenue and thus enhance the power of the state by providing it with the fiscal resources necessary to pursue new projects at home and abroad. 'As the country is rendered more populous by means of manufactures', he argued, 'there will ensue an increase of revenue, arising out of the more frequent sales and larger consumption of commodities and fruits'. Uztáriz maintained that population and prosperity complemented one another and suggested that the former could be augmented through immigration: 'as soon as trade begins to flourish and people are sure of employment, there always will be a large and constant supplies of Catholics from abroad, who are skillful in the fabricks [sic] and their marrying and settling in Spain with their families, is a sure and safe method to increase the inhabitants considerably'.

Uztáriz refuted the widespread assumption that colonies drained the population of the metropole. Policy blunders, he argued, not colonial possessions *per se*, had caused Spain's precipitous population decline: 'the Indies are not the thing that enervates and dispeoples Spain, but the commodities by which foreigners have drained us of money, and destroyed our manufactures at the same time that our heavy taxes remain'. For Uztáriz, neither reliance on gold nor territorial expansion caused depopulation. Instead, he lamented Spain's uncompetitive economy, misgovernance, and failure to encourage maritime trade as the underlying causes of demographic decline. The expansion of Spanish maritime commerce, he wrote, would usher in an era of economic prosperity and burgeoning population.[50] The link made by Uztáriz between population and commercial growth reverberated in Spanish political thought throughout the century. 'Civil economy is the science by which the state attempts to procure the greatest population possible', Normante y Carcavilla, the first holder of the university chair in political economy at Zaragoza, noted, 'as well as the maximum perfection, wealth and power which it is capable of attaining'.[51]

An admirer of Colbert, Uztáriz envisaged economic resurgence deriving from state support for peninsular manufactures. He contended that economic backwardness could be overcome rapidly through export-oriented trade.[52] The benefits of commerce, in his view, did not depend on whether it was practiced by trading companies or individual merchants, but, rather, the use of domestic manufactures.[53] Uztáriz promoted the revival of an 'extensive and profitable commerce' constructed on the edifice of differentiated manufactures, 'bolstered by indulgences and exemptions from duties' by an actively interventionist state, and bemoaned Spain's unfavourable balance of trade. Such themes would structure the priorities of subsequent Spanish political writers for the next half-century.

Spanish political economists came to embrace the liberalization of the domestic economy. This notion encompassed an array of policies which aimed to eliminate deep-seated obstacles to agrarian growth, including restrictions on the internal grain trade, the end of the disruptive transhumance stemming from the *Mesta* privileges, and the moratorium on further acquisition of property by the Church. Agriculture, Danvila wrote, 'should be the first concern of a civilized nation'. Domestic commerce should be freed of the 'exclusive privileges and exactions' which only served to 'destroy, perturb and annihilate' economic growth. A 1765 royal order abolished controls on grain prices and mandated its unregulated shipment throughout peninsular Spain.[54]

Not all of these agricultural economic reforms met with success. The reform of the *Mesta*, for example, only partially succeeded, as the Crown relented in the face of opposition from landowners who benefited from the ancient authorization to permit their livestock to devastate private and common pastures. Similarly, the sale of confiscated Jesuit properties did not generate great profits for the state as disentailment directly profited larger landowners capable of purchasing estates.[55] Agrarian reform, then, remained woefully incomplete in the decades preceding Napoleon's occupation of

Spain. The nation composed of small farmers, envisaged by Olavide and Campomanes, never came into existence.

Commerce, never pursued for its own sake, also was considered an instrument to augment state power. 'Spanish commerce is obligated', Campomanes often repeated, to 'conform to the spirit of patriotism'.[56] In this manner, official attitudes reflect the central tenets of Cameralism, conceiving of economics as an administrative technology to harness natural and human resources and further the political and social aims of the state. Cameralism made no distinction between the police and economic functions of the state. The process of regulation was not conceived in terms of state intervention in the economy since the state and the economy had no independent existence.[57] Social regulation and welfare, in this framework, were legitimate objectives of government policy. Such a 'well-ordered police state' would preserve the hierarchical structure of society and, at the same time, encourage the active, enterprising, unfettered, and creative individual citizen to promote material wealth and progress as well.[58]

By the twilight of Charles III's reign, the link between state power, population, and commercial development was well established. 'I am entirely persuaded', a 1782 *real cédula* declared, that the 'protection of commerce and industry is the cause which most influences the power, wealth and prosperity of a state'.[59] In spite of the percolation of more advanced economic doctrines in the greater Atlantic World, Madrid's policymakers clung to older mercantilist assumptions about the long-term harmony of power and wealth.[60]

Nevertheless, a backlash to this political economy of reform arose from the ecclesiastical establishment. In an attack on Normante, a Cordoban priest derided the Aragonese professor's claim that 'ecclesiastical laws and observances are contrary to the population and multiplication of mankind'. Normante's views, Cabra bluntly stated, 'contradict the Truth of the Evangelist' and dismissed him as 'a cruel enemy of both the *patria* and religion ... the only secure and true happiness of a Nation is God'.[61]

For the vast majority of the participants in these debates, both lay and ecclesiastic, however, religious conviction, political enquiry into population growth, and advocacy of economic reform were compatible. They sought to conjoin the precepts of political economy with those of Catholicism. In his translator's preface to Genovesi's *Lezioni*, for example, Villava boasted that he had excised 'several unfortunate passages of Genovesi's work which touch on the government of the Church, its leader and his authority'.[62] In subsequent essays, he extended this argument, contesting the view that Enlightenment and faith were antithetical: 'the impious attribute [the growth of] despotism and ignorance to our sacred religion and, contrapuntally, attribute liberty and enlightenment to the advancement of impiety'. Against these positions, Villava defended a central place for religion in politics on two grounds: first, 'morality and laws without the support of religion would be weak and the bonds which unite society would break, unable to continue without them'; second, 'the nobility and the ecclesiastical state are the two counterweights which balance absolutism, and, without them, the balance would fall entirely toward despotism'.[63] Suspicious of both despotism and the dissipation of religious bonds, Villava captured the prevailing ethos of the reformers who cautiously, yet comprehensively, sought to effect fundamental change without perturbing core cultural values. Public happiness, constructed on the edifice of populationist and commercial arguments, was transformed into a key weapon in the intellectual arsenal of regalist ministers.

Church–State relations in Spain before Charles III's accession

Caroline regalism concerned the demarcation separating the jurisdictions of Church and State. The centralizing tendencies of Spain's early modern monarchs encountered resistance from ecclesiastical institutions reluctant to relinquish their accumulated economic resources and political–legal privileges. By the eighteenth century, many Crown officials believed that the Church's wealth, especially its land holdings, represented a major obstacle to the economic development of Spain.

This complaint about the Church's wealth was a long-standing grievance, rooted in the medieval past. As Christians in Spain battled against Muslims in the twelfth and thirteenth centuries, the Bourbon regalists lamented, the Curia unleashed its centralization programme. The inaugural moment in this process was Gregory VII's declaration of the Papacy's complete authority within the Church, not subject to secular authority. With an increasing number of appeals to Rome and the imposition of a regular taxation of the clergy, the Papacy corroded the autonomy of local dioceses through the system of provisions and the reservation of benefices. This assertion of fiscal authority was the first thrust of a three-pronged attack. Its second facet was the Papacy's gradual assumption of the right to appoint to major ecclesiastical offices and, in 1305, Clement V decreed that patriarchates, archbishoprics and bishoprics would be disposed of by the Holy See.[64] The third element was the process by which papal law was established, rigorously separated from secular law, and conceptually unified as canon law which became the *ius commune*, the body of law common to all Christian territories, superceding customary law everywhere.

Canon law regulated criminal and civil causes arising out of sin and breach of faith, maintaining jurisdiction over clerics and Church property. Royal law claimed competence to deal with criminal and civil cases arising from seisin of freehold land and breaches of civil peace, with jurisdiction over freeholders, felons, and matters pertaining to the Crown and its property. The boundary separating canon from civil law, however, was highly permeable as both types depended so heavily upon one another. Thus, for centuries, they coexisted without major conflict.[65]

According to the Gregorian theory of 'consonance', however, canon law came to signify precisely that which did not contradict the decrees of the Pope.[66] The principle of dualism had not been excised fully from the discourse, but had been 'so fundamentally conditioned by another axiom, the superiority of the spiritual power, that it was in effect replaced with a unitary view of the two powers'.[67] The transformation of the notion of legitimacy to include temporal power required a concomitant change in the conception of the Christian world. The transformation of *ecclesia* to *christianitas* broadened the scope to include independent Christian kingdoms dissatisfied with overlapping jurisdictions which undercut their territorial sovereignty.[68] They sought to define ecclesiastical authority more narrowly, groping for some concrete basis of royal power. They found it in property and material possessions. These theorists of *regalia* argued for the exclusive rights of the king with regard to 'temporalities' and denied ecclesiastical authority over them. These royal rights associated with temporal goods, houses, and estates received the name of *regalia*, rights that were considered to be inalienable.[69]

For this reason, all was not lost for the Spanish monarchy: the *Reconquista* of Muslim Spain, and the subsequent colonization of the New World, provided a grand opportunity to wrest authority away from the Curia. A 1486 Bull granted the Crown the right of universal patronage—the power to nominate or present a cleric for installation in a vacant benefice—for all territory conquered in the kingdom of Granada and conceded in perpetuity the *diezmos*, or tithes, which the converted Muslims paid to the Church. In the New World, three further Alexandrine Bulls, known collectively as the *Real Patronato*, of 1493, 1501, and 1508, respectively, conceded tremendous new authority to the Spanish Crown: the *donación pontifica*, or dominion of the Indies, along with the exclusive right to proselytize the indigenous population; the *diezmos*; and the *patronato universal*, the right of universal patronage over the Church. Though the *fuero eclesiástico*, or the clergy's right to trial in ecclesiastical courts, remained unmodified until a 1578 Bull, the Council of the Indies enjoyed legal jurisdiction over most matters in the Americas. In addition to fiscal benefits, the Spanish King obtained further advantages from the *Patronato Real*. These included the *pase regio*, or the royal consent, permit, or license for all documents or appointees originating in Rome and pertaining to either a Spanish subject or an ecclesiastical official within the Crown's territory. A second institution was the *placet* and its partner the *exequatur*. The *placet* expressed royal agreement with specific proposals generated by the Curia whereas the *exequatur* granted permission for their performance.[70] The expansion of royal power in American Church affairs reached its apogee in a 1765 *cédula* which declared the legitimacy of royal interference in most formerly ecclesiastical affairs.[71]

If the Spanish monarch was 'God's Vicar' in the New World, his status in the peninsular Church was less exalted. The king retained substantial rights of patronage: his Royal Council could evoke cases from the ecclesiastical courts and the Inquisition and all papal bulls required his approval before taking effect in Spanish territory. In spite of this authority, the king's authority was circumscribed. He could not alter the jurisdiction of the Inquisition without soliciting the Pope's approval.[72] He neither could make ecclesiastical appointments, nor tax the clergy, nor dispose of Church land.[73]

The Church's control over land in the Iberian Peninsula was a particularly acute problem for the Crown. In 1749, the Church owned 15 per cent of the landed property in Castile, from a low of five per cent in Galicia to a high of 27 per cent in Zamora. Its share of agricultural wealth, moreover, was discernibly greater than the proportion of land it owned: the Church received 21 per cent of the Castile's overall annual income.[74] Most problematic was that Church land was held in mortmain, for canon law forbade the Church to sell, give away, or bequeath property once acquired. Crown policymakers would declare that mortmain was one of the primary obstacles to the efflorescence of peninsular Spain.

The wealth of the peninsular Church was not entirely inaccessible to the Crown. In addition to the *dos novenas*, the Crown's 2/9 share of the Church's tithes, the Crown extracted three subsidies, *tres gracias*, with papal sanction: the *cruzada*, a tax levied on papal indulgences; the *subsidio* on clerical incomes; and the *excusado*, the tithe from the richest estate in each parish.[75] Yet these potential revenue streams paled in comparison with the Crown's virtually untrammelled authority in the New World. These limitations necessarily resulted in the interdependence of Church and State in peninsular Spain. According to one eminent scholar, 'Church and king were the two common elements in the disparate and fragmented Spanish monarchy; and religious uniformity, enforced by the king, Church and Inquisition, was the guarantee of continuing political order and stability'.[76]

Yet by the mid-eighteenth century, the monarchs of Southern Europe came to believe that this long-established interdependence was responsible for disorder and instability. They sought a new arrangement, more advantageous to the state, which would give them unprecedented control over the Church. The monarchs exploited the relative weakness of the Papacy to demand the authorization to appoint bishops, determine the protocols of Church discipline, and regulate the founding and governance of new seminaries. The future Charles III of Spain, for example, took advantage of the Church's relative weakness, beginning with the 1729 Treaty of Seville which secured his right to succeed to Parma and Plasencia without pontifical investiture. His feuds with the Papacy, while reigning in Naples (1734–59), resulted in the 1741 Concordat. The benefits achieved were sweeping: the number of religious holdings was reduced; the Crown wrested control over the appointment of bishops; the number of convents and the number of new entries into the regular orders were decreased; the possibility of auditing and then taxing clerical property; and the Neapolitan Church's formerly broad fiscal powers were diminished.[77]

Charles III's victories in Naples presaged Ferdinand VI's success in securing the Concordat of 1753 in Spain. Whereas in 1715 two-thirds of all appointments to the Church in Spain were made in Rome, under the terms of the new Concordat, the Crown gained near-universal patronage over most major ecclesiastical benefices after 1753.[78] These concessions, however, were merely one part of a much broader programme of state control which would reach its apogee with Charles III's accession to the Spanish throne in 1759. His ministers perceived the Church as a corporation ripe for reform and plunder.[79] They sought an ideology to justify their efforts. In regalism, they encountered what was required.

The aims of Bourbon regalism

Before analysing regalist political thought, its central tenets must be distinguished from those of Jansenism. Describing regalists as 'Jansenists', 'heterodox encyclopedists' or *'afrancescado'* often has served to denigrate them, thus leading to a failure to engage with their ideas and aspirations. The regalists themselves often insisted on the orthodoxy of their religious beliefs. One leading regalist, for example, professed to know nothing about Jansenism: 'I confess my ignorance that I do not know what [Jansenism] is, and up until now I didn't know that to be a Jansenist implied anything more than to profess one of the condemned opinions of Jansen, and that this name has been given to those who are the enemies of the Jesuits, but I do not know anything more'. This disavowal and plea of ignorance notwithstanding, this same regalist declared that his first loyalty was to the Spanish monarchy. 'I would sell my conscience, my religion, and faith what, by divine and human law, I owe to my king and master', he said, if 'I were not to defend the authority and independence of his jurisdiction and of the rights that God has given to him'.[80] It is exigent, therefore, to differentiate regalism from Jansenism.

Regalism may be likened to Jansenism due to its concern with jurisdiction, authority, and power, on the one hand, and with encouraging change, outward and inward, among both laymen and clergy, on the other.[81] In Spain, Jansenism was synonymous with opposition to excessive papal power. By pitting episcopal authority against ultramontanism, the Jansenist controversy revived Tridentine disagreements over the scope of episcopal power.[82] Spanish Jansenism, therefore, was more of a 'current of opinion rather than a party, in which there figured moderates, zealots and place-men ... united only by the spiritual and intellectual culture of the baroque, post-Tridentine Catholicism'. Regalists and Jansenists both articulated a 'secular, utilitarian spirit'.[83] For the purposes of this monograph, notwithstanding their overlapping features, regalism is distinguished from Jansenism because the former was less concerned with metaphysics than power politics, less with the Church's welfare than the state's political and economic advancement.

In addition to Campomanes and Floridablanca, the leading regalists from c. 1760–1800 were Francisco de Carrasco, *fiscal* at the Treasury; José de Gálvez, Minister of the Indies; Manuel de Roda, Secretary of State for Grace and Justice; José Nicolás de Azara, Spanish Representative in Rome; and Antonio de Porlier, a leading figure on the Council of the Indies. There were other eminent figures, but the ideas purveyed by these men, who occupied the highest posts in government, are not merely representative of the entire movement, but also those which most decisively influenced government policy. Though Campomanes and Azara receive the lion's share of the attention in this section due to the voluminous and engaging nature of their writings, the exposition and analysis of their ideas equally applies to the other leading regalists due to the homogeneity of their basic sentiments.

The regalist-inspired policymakers are best conceived of as an intelligentsia. While they dabbled in metaphysics and jurisprudence, they did not engage in these pursuits for their own sake, but rather as part of a larger quest. This broader objective was the expansion of state power in order to modernize Spanish society, which they considered uncompetitive in relation to other European states. The ambitions of the regalist intelligentsia are captured by the periodical *El Pensador*'s purportedly first-hand account of a *tertulia* composed of the 'most famous politicians of the Court'. *El Pensador* mockingly reported that 'each participant proposed methods to remedy everything and return Spain to the pre-eminent status which it had attained in other epochs, again making it a universal monarchy, claiming that such a project is neither as difficult nor as chimerical as many believe'.[84] In spite of this parody of their views, the regalists believed that concrete steps could be taken in domestic affairs to reverse Spain's geopolitical fortunes.

There were three overarching facets of Caroline regalism with relation to the Church. The first was the Crown's attempt to control it through the nomination of higher-ranking officials amenable to expanded state authority. The second was a pro-active refusal to permit the Roman Curia to intervene in Spanish ecclesiastical affairs. The third was an effort to increase state intervention in ecclesiastical affairs, effectively effacing the demarcation separating temporal from spiritual power.[85]

The regalists sought to transform these convictions into policy using four tactics. First, they radically re-formulated the distinction between temporal and spiritual authority, slanting the preponderance of power towards the former. Second, they sought to demonstrate how state control over the Church was consistent with the dictates of public happiness. Third, they appealed to patriotism to insinuate how the allegiance of ecclesiastics, especially Jesuits, to Rome posed a security threat. Fourth, they sought to demonstrate that harnessing the Church's wealth was critical to the resurrection of Spain's economy and, by extension, its geopolitical fortunes.

One of the major intellectual battles waged by the regalists concerned the relation of temporal and spiritual authority. The respective scope of each power constituted a focus of many eighteenth-century regalist tracts and the definitions of temporal and spiritual authority were a battleground of the persistent conflict. The spiritual domain, they contended, 'never should extend beyond its proper sphere'.[86] Since the 'object of the priesthood is to fortify morals by supernatural means, its authority lies in its faculty to administer to religious souls, penalties and recompense of a spiritual nature ... When neither the liberty, nor security, nor property of a person is violated, the sovereign does not have any right to determine the sacerdotal functions'.[87] Temporal authority encompassed 'all which pertains to the present life; and the subjects of this authority are men, at least while their bodies participate in this life and they enjoy worldly goods ... the establishment and maintenance of peace, good order, public tranquility, and the preservation of the rights which each [person] possesses, is the jurisdiction of temporal authority'. The attempt, therefore, to endow spiritual authority with the 'power [to use] force, and coercion, is entirely heretical'.[88]

Azara was preoccupied with this boundary between spiritual and temporal authority. The trajectory of his thought embodies regalism's evolution from a narrower concern with Church–State affairs into a broader language of governance. His biographical details are representative of the regalist policy elite: in addition to friendships with leading ministers and intellectuals, especially Roda, Muñoz, and Almodóvar, he reportedly enjoyed and 'merited the strictest confidence' of Catherine the Great whereas Frederick the Great 'held him in the highest esteem'.[89] Azara's library boasted 1,800 books from the eighteenth century alone, including the regalist tracts of Giannone and Febronius, alongside the Encyclopedists, Montesquieu, Mandeville, Paine, and Filangieri, not to mention those of his compatriots, Uztáriz, Almodóvar, and Ulloa.[90] In addition to his loquacious and entertaining despatches, he penned the introduction to the Spanish translation of Mengs's writings on aesthetics. He was, in short, a man of many interests and wide experience.

Due, perhaps, to his service as Spain's Ambassador to Rome for several decades, Azara's primary intellectual preoccupation involved the proper scope of temporal power. 'It never could have been [the Pope's] intention', he reasoned, to 'authorise rebellions, strip vassals of the obedience and fidelity they owe to their princes, and to nullify laws promulgated by legitimate authorities'. The antiquity of practices and the embeddedness of custom was no justification, in Azara's view, because it was predicated on an initial transgression. 'If the usurpations of the Popes in Italy were even one hundred centuries old', he claimed, 'I would not venerate them as sacred; in the temporal dominion, the Pope possesses nothing with a greater right than Mohammed II claimed when he pillaged Constantinople'.[91] Azara asserted that the regalists no longer needed to acquiesce to such usurpations. He implored his fellow ministers to take action: 'the arrogance, avarice and the rest of the vices [of the Papacy] are intolerable in a century in which, by the grace of God, we are not as weak as before ... the time has arrived for the king to liberate us from this tyranny'.[92] Armed with the writings of canon jurists and newfangled doctrines drawn from political economy, the regalists sought to diminish Rome's influence in peninsular political, juridical, and economic life.

They strove to replace this 'tyranny' with a new model of interdependence with the state in the leading role, one which would conform to the requirements of public happiness. Regalists contended that Church–State interdependence was indispensable in order for both institutions to flourish: 'reciprocity binds them together and they move [together] like a perfectly concerted machine'.[93] Arguments for state supremacy, then, usually were expressed as pleas for harmonization. Reformers purportedly aimed not to 'exaggerate civil authority at the expense of the ecclesiastical', but, rather, to encourage Spaniards to 'respect spiritual authority in its proper function in the same manner that in temporal affairs the king and his ministers are respected, because each is independent and sovereign in its respective sphere'. Though 'distinct in their actions and jurisdiction', Church and State 'should mutually help and defend one another'.[94]

When regalists stressed interdependence, however, a robust conception of the state's function in overall society always was implicit. The monarch was entitled, they asserted, to 'contain' ecclesiastical power whenever 'its exercise could perturb public tranquility'.[95] They argued that the 'king and the kingdom are the same thing ... the king can impede his vassals who contract or dispose of their goods to their own disadvantage and to the harm of the sovereign'.[96] They refused to recognize limits to civil jurisdiction, defining temporal power as 'everything which pertains to civil society [*sociedad civil*], to the extent that it is a civil affair, temporal happiness and the tranquility of mankind'.[97] The centralization of authority was defended as the precondition for the full realization of public happiness.

Armed with an amplified conception of civil power, Caroline regalists strove to eliminate clerical autonomy; to subject ecclesiastics, as fully as lay subjects, to royal authority; and to attenuate the bonds to Rome which shackled royal authority.[98] They reserved special disdain for two privileges established by canon law: first, the *fuero* which exempted ecclesiastics from judicial proceedings besides ecclesiastical tribunals; and second, the protection of ecclesiastics from arrest and imprisonment for criminal behaviour.[99] Additional regalist objectives in the same sphere included the limitation on the right to asylum, the *exequatur*, and the suppression of certain practices deemed overly superstitious.[100] Campomanes captured the prevailing regalist sentiment when he disparaged ecclesiastical immunity as 'certainly destitute of sense in civil society'.[101]

The regalists faced the problem, however, of articulating their views without appearing anti-clerical and impious. In this regard, patriotism proved a useful device. The regalists resorted to a political language of patriotism which depicted the clergy as aliens within the realm and inimical to its interests. This hostility is discernible at the highest levels of government. 'Friars belong to no nation', Grimaldi informed Tanucci, 'from the moment they take vows they should be looked upon as foreigners, or rather enemies of the state in which they were born. In their maliciousness, the Popes have struck upon this secret of maintaining [power]'.[102] This sentiment was diffused throughout the regalist intelligentsia. Azara recognized the subversive potential of such formulations: 'having been born vassals to one sovereign, they pledge blind allegiance to another, which makes them independent and insolent, and it is the state which suffers and pays the price. It is difficult to fathom that such an arrangement still exists in the eighteenth century'.[103]

A related rhetorical strategy was to ignore the concept of spiritual power altogether and to consider the Papacy solely in its capacity as a sovereign political state. This verbal sleight of hand enabled Azara to claim that clerics 'pass effectively to the service of another prince, as if he were the king of Prussia, because the prelate dedicates his service to the Pope and not to the Church itself'.[104] In 1781, this allegation was enshrined in legislation when Charles III determined that Bishops in the Indies must swear obedience not only to the pontiff, but also take an additional oath of allegiance to the Spanish monarch.[105]

The rising tide of regalist political thought did not mean, however, that its proponents sought to exclude the Church from public life. While mistrustful of the clergy, the regalists recognized, and valued, its sway over the populace. In their view, it was an under-exploited vehicle for the implementation of policy. 'The enlightenment of the clergy', Floridablanca argued, 'is essential for the realization of all of these important projects ... a secular and regular clergy, informed by good studies, would know the fundamental limits which separate ecclesiastical and royal power'.[106] Regalists thus expected a great deal from the Church. As one eminent scholar has written, it was to be 'powerful but subordinate; resourceful but pliant; and enlightened but pious'.[107] The regalists had discovered, and were now employing, a formula, grounded in the languages of patriotism, political economy, and grand strategy, which made their views palatable and lent their cause political traction.

The intellectual origins of Caroline regalism

The regalists' proposed reform of the Church was firmly rooted in both foreign and Spanish juridical traditions. The theoretical foundations of Caroline regalism were profoundly pan-European. The most influential foreign writers were Bossuet, Giannone, Van Espen, and Febronius.

Bishop Bossuet sought to legitimize the expansion of temporal government by buttressing it with scriptural evidence. He asserted that the 'whole world began with monarchies; and almost the whole world has preserved itself in that state, as being the most natural'. Bossuet (1627–1704) rejected the bifurcation of the two realms and argued that 'princes act as ministers of God, and His lieutenants on earth ... the royal throne is not the throne of a man, but the throne of God himself'. While asserting the compatibility of princely authority with religious precepts, he refused, in a clear echo of Jean Bodin, to countenance interference with the prince's exercise of his authority. 'If there is in a state an authority capable of stopping the course of public power, or of hampering its exercise, no one is safe', Bossuet postulated, for 'it is necessary that authority be invincible, and that nothing can overwhelm the ramparts, under whose shelter the public repose and the safety of individuals are protected'. Bossuet repudiated the notion of ecclesiastical interference in state affairs: 'when Jesus said to the Jews: "Render unto Caesar that which is Caesar's", He did not examine how the power of the Caesars had been established: it was sufficient that He found them established and reigning, and he intended that the divine order and the foundation of public peace should be respected in the form of their authority'. Bossuet enumerated the types of affairs in which scriptural authority is inapplicable and impertinent: 'Religion does not enter into the details of establishing the public taxes'. For these and other pronouncements, Bossuet's doctrine would be employed by reformers across Europe who sought to enhance royal authority at the Church's expense.

Yet Bossuet stopped short of sanctioning princely pre-eminence and, instead, stressed the mutual reliance and common ultimate source of Church and State:

the priesthood in the spiritual [realm] and the empire in the temporal depend only on God. But the ecclesiastical order recognizes the empire in the temporal [sphere] as kings, but in the spiritual [realm], recognize themselves as the humble children of the Church. Every state in the world turns on these two powers. This is why they owe each other mutual help.[108]

In Bossuet's scheme, the king existed in an 'exalted sphere above all interests' and, because the monarchy is absolute, he can strive 'single-mindedly' towards the general welfare of the state.[109] Bossuet's massive impact in the Hispanic World, suggested by three separate translations and editions of his *Politics* in 1743, 1768, and 1789, demonstrates the resonance of his ideas in Caroline conceptions of monarchical power.[110]

Pietro Giannone's *The Civil History of the Kingdom of Naples* (1723) promulgated a more radical brand of *giurisdizionalismo* which advocated the separation of Church and State and the independence of the local churches from Rome. Giannone's narrative traced the encroaching authority of the Papacy over civil jurisdiction in Naples.[111] He lamented that the corrosive, retarding, and preponderant influence of the Church in the development of Naples. Echoing Bossuet's thesis on the potential synergy of amicable

Church–State relations, Giannone predicted that 'if the empire assist the priesthood with its power, in order to support the Honour of God, and if the priesthood, in return, tie and unite the affection of the people to the obedience of the Prince, the whole state will flourish and be happy'. In Naples, to his chagrin, the opposite had transpired, precipitating 'confusion and ruin; out of which the many disorders which have happened on that account in this our kingdom are flagrant testimonies'. Giannone speculated that 'fear that their unbounded sovereignty might degenerate into irregularity and tyranny' served to preserve the fragile equipoise. The current predicament of Naples was attributable to vast, unchallenged ecclesiastical privilege which remained 'the evident cause of our misery'. Giannone warned that 'if a stop be not put to it, the ecclesiastics in a short time will not only purchase the whole city of Naples, but within the space of an age will be masters of the whole kingdom'.[112]

These late seventeenth- and early eighteenth-century regalist views were reinforced and revivified in the mid-eighteenth-century writings of Bernard Van Espen (1646–1728), Nicholas Von Hontheim (1701–90) (alias 'Febronius'), and the António Pereira de Figueiredo (1725–97), canonists who sharply criticized the Papacy, defining its absolutist pretensions as a medieval abuse which undermined the rightful authority of national episcopates and Church councils. This conviction spurred them to emphasize the Tridentine decrees which enhanced the jurisdiction of the bishops.[113] According to Febronius, bishops were not subjects of the Pope, but, like the pontiff himself, appointed by divine right as successors of the apostles. The Curia, therefore, exercised no jurisdiction which competed with that of the bishops.[114]

Advocates of a national, or at least more autonomous, Spanish Church found such ideas tremendously appealing. A leading regalist contended that Spain's exposure to authors such as these would presage beneficial shifts in attitude. 'What a divine change Spain would undergo in such a brief span', Azara speculated, 'if two or three books on this subject were published here; in a single year, Spain would be enlightened forever', and he specifically cited Giannone, Febronius, Pereira, and Bossuet.[115] Contact with these authors was not merely desirable, he asserted, but indispensable for national regeneration. 'The dissemination of excellent books is the first step needed in order for Spain to progress; for without this preparation, it will be founded on unsteady ground'.[116] For Azara and his peers, intellectual change would prefigure and underpin institutional transformation. Exposure to new currents was vital if the Catholic Church's position in Spanish politics was to be refashioned and downgraded.

The embrace of foreign juridical writers always was tempered by the fragility and interdependence of Church–State authority. Nor were they universally lauded: Febronius's writings were denounced by Spanish ecclesiastical authorities as a 'schismatic and perturbative doctrine, disturbing the peace of the Church and producing polyarchy, or even anarchy, caused by not determining a visible head for this body, nor settling upon the form of its government'. His theories were derided, therefore, as equally applicable to undermine princely authority as to assert the primacy of Bishops over the Pope:

> By these same ancient laws, one can fear greater upheaval in the political realm. Kings will not be secure in the possession of their sceptres or crowns due to the [intellectual] weaponry deployed by the author to deprive the Pope of the supreme power which he wields in the Church. These same arguments could in the future be used against the King to negate his power as supreme monarch and legislator.[117]

Even Pereira's books were disallowed because they threatened the delicate equilibrium between Church and State. Pereira's notion of episcopal 'absolute, unlimited and supreme power' made a translation untenable: his doctrine explicitly contradicted 'the definition of faith which has been established' by the Concordat of 1753 and a Spanish edition would 'deprecate the authority of the Holy See'.[118] Fear of the unintended consequences of adopting Febronius's and Pereira's doctrines, combined with fear of accusations of impiety, caused policymakers to embrace them tepidly or to express their views anonymously.

Many leading policymakers, however, believed that the positive effects of the diffusion of such foreign ideas outweighed the risks involved. The arch-regalist Campomanes, for example, recommended against the publication of a book of epistles from a minor religious writer critical of Febronius, stating that the author was 'naturally disaffected with royal authority ... his writings are designed to disturb the public peace' and introduce 'disputes with pernicious consequences'.[119] Febronius, then, was perceived by Campomanes as favouring, not endangering, the fortification of royal authority. The flood of foreign regalist texts into Spain continued unabated through numerous channels, including the reform of the university curriculum. By 1776, Van Espen's *Ius Ecclesiasticum Universum* was a required text in the law faculties at the Universities of Valladolid, Alcalá, Valencia, Salamanca, Oviedo, Zaragoza, and Granada.[120]

Spanish regalists did not rely on foreign ideas alone, but also identified peninsular precedent for their proposed reforms. Caroline regalists found comfort in both the seventeenth-century regalist writers and in a romantic conception of Church–State relations during the Visigothic period. Spanish political and philosophical writers had not always asserted the equality of civil and ecclesiastical power, let alone the former's superiority. In the sixteenth century, there had been a lively debate on this matter. On the one hand, Francisco Suárez argued that 'ecclesiastical power is not only nobler in itself, but also is superior, and the civil power is subordinate and subject to it'. Francisco de Vitoria, on the other hand, had contended that 'temporal power is not entirely dependent upon spiritual power', but instead was 'complete and perfect in itself and directed towards its own immediate end'.[121]

The intellectual shift in favour of the regalist conception of secular authority became apparent in the late seventeenth-century. Juan Luís López, for example, rejected the notion of a divinely sanctioned ecclesiastical right to material goods: 'no divine law exists which exempts ecclesiasts in matters that are not purely spiritual, but merely profane and temporal'.[122] Castillo de Bovadilla, whose seventeenth-century tract was reprinted often in the eighteenth century, never explicitly referred to the demarcation between Church and State. He rather appealed to the benefits derived from obedience in all affairs and asserted the plurality of powers: 'there are many varieties of authority and principalities and each must be obeyed according to its origin and type'.[123] Pre-Caroline regalists stressed the Crown's function as the main 'protector of the Church', striving to 'preserve the purity of religion' and enforcing ecclesiastical discipline. They argued that this role was rooted in canon law which 'recognizes this title, and even encourages the concession and use of this protection'.[124] This type of reasoning would inspire the Bourbon regalists.

The Caroline contribution to the discourse was its peculiar use of, and pre-occupation with, historical precedent. In Chapter 1 of this book, the Caroline intelligentsia was shown to be infatuated with the defence of the conquest and colonization of the Americas from the vituperation of foreign authors. This same cohort displayed a comparable affinity with the Visigothic period (AD 456–711) of Spanish history. The idealization of the Visigothic period by regalist ministers became a crucial component of their defence of monarchical aggrandizement. As shall be suggested in this section, the strength of the King vis-à-vis the Church in the Visigothic period attracted them while the near-complete independence of the bishops from Rome appealed to those disgruntled with papal oversight. In this way, historical scholarship was transformed once more into a political tool to advance regalist political aims.

The pervasiveness of the Visigothic model for purportedly 'enlightened reformers' complicates the traditional depiction of the eighteenth century as heterodox, materialist, newfangled, and anti-Hispanic. As suggested in Chapter 1, the Bourbon policy elite was self-consciously backward-gazing. They looked not only to the now-decayed opulence of Philip II's reign, but to a post-Roman, pre-Islamic past, when a united peninsula flourished, free from external entanglements and impediments.[125] The tendency to envisage an idealized Visigothic past had antecedents. Seventeenth-century reformers advocated a 'return to the primeval purity of manners and morals; a return to just and uncorrupt government; a return to the simple virtues of a rural and martial society ... [through] a programme of national regeneration and rededication'.[126] The Bourbon fascination with the Visigoths, then, should be understood as an extension of these earlier tendencies. The fascination with the Visigoths did not mean that Roman imagery disappeared. Charles III still avidly received detailed reports from Tanucci concerning the excavations at Herculaneum. For political and legal reformers, however, the Roman inheritance increasingly became more of a hindrance than an inspiration. The persistence of Roman law, in particular, was troublesome. While praising it as a 'perfect and sufficient body of law according to the state and circumstances of the Roman empire', jurist Juan Francisco de Castro argued that it did not 'accommodate' Spain's contemporary customs, particularly in its 'mutilated' condition. Roman law, then, was 'nothing more than a pile of disunited and various fragments which serves for nothing except to provoke great perturbations'.[127]

Although the historian Muñoz deprecated it as an age of 'little light [*de poca luz*]', the Bourbons overwhelmingly lauded the Visigothic period of peninsular history. Prominent scholars, including Gregorio Mayans, Francisco Manuel de la Huerta, and Martín de Ulloa, extolled various aspects of the Visigothic kingdom in histories published before 1750. In his maiden speech to the Royal Academy of History in 1748, Campomanes lamented that the Islamic conquest 'obscured the glory of the Goths'. Campomanes subsequently transmitted this favourable judgment to a broader audience in his *Educación Popular* (1775). While admitting that the Goths failed to introduce 'important arts' to the Iberian Peninsula, he argued that they 'conserved, at the same level, those used under the Romans' and 'maintained, if not improved, the customs of the Romans'.[128] 'Under their dominion', another historian claimed, the 'laws were re-established, and thereafter [the inhabitants of Iberian peninsula] breathed again and thus formed a great empire'.[129]

The regalists incorporated the Visigoths into a broader narrative which showed how royal power, formerly robust, had been slowly encroached upon, and hence weakened, by the Church. In the sixth and seventh centuries, the Visigothic king possessed the indisputable right to appoint bishops and, during any gap in the appointment, to purloin Church property. The Church evolved into a national institution, unusually centralized and closely associated with the court. While nominally recognizing the primacy of Rome, Spanish bishops rarely communicated with the Eternal City, and the metropolitan of Toledo achieved a *de facto* primacy within the realm. Within the peninsular Church itself, the king exercised authority over all aspects of ecclesiastical life. When it pleased him to summon one, a plenary council met, but it only discussed public affairs brought to its attention by the king. In this way, the Councils functioned as a support for, and not a check on, secular power. Conciliar measures neither possessed the character of civil law nor were enforceable by judges in Visigothic Spain. Instead, kings were regarded as divinely authorized to regulate ecclesiastical affairs.

Bishops and the clergy were subject to the civil laws of the kingdom. The monarch's pre-eminence in religious affairs was exemplified by his right to excommunicate a subject for a breach of civil laws.[130]

The absolute power enjoyed by the Visigothic kings naturally inspired Bourbon reformers who felt that their monarch's power was circumscribed by the accumulated abuses of a bevy of ecclesiastical and civil corporations. Visigothic Spain thus represented a golden age, one which had been torn asunder by the Muslim conquest of the eighth century. Between the dissolution of the Visigothic kingdom, its vestiges preserved only in the mountain villages of Asturias, and the ultimate victory of the *Reconquista* in 1492, the regalists regarded with disdain what they perceived as the Curia's encroachment on royal jurisdiction.

The Bourbon regalists' admiration for Visigothic Church–State relations suggests that they saw it as a model for emulation in the eighteenth century. Sempere y Guarinos recalled with fondness an all-too-distant epoch in which the 'sacerdocy and the empire, far from sparring over their respective rights, were very much in accord'. Sempere hoped to cultivate 'better appreciation for our primitive law codes, whose study would undermine the dominance' of ultramontane jurisprudence, with its 'subtleties and sophisteries', which had 'altered ancient legislation' to the detriment of Spain.[131] Guided by a similar spirit, Campomanes sought to institutionalize regalist principles through his 1771 reform of the University of Salamanca. He castigated the canon law faculty for its curriculum, contending that it overemphasized modern jurisprudence and neglected that of late Antiquity, particularly the Visigothic period. He argued that, in the first eight centuries of the Church's existence, 'we see represented the most pure discipline ... whose restoration has always been desired'.[132] For Sempere y Guarinos and Campomanes, then, the revival of Visigothic jurisprudence, which could be hastened by its incorporation into the university curriculum, offered a long-term solution to Church–State jurisdictional disputes.

Employing the Visigothic past as a precedent for the renovation of politics in their own time, Caroline regalists disputed the validity of an original ecclesiastical jurisdiction over what had become, by the eighteenth-century, Church property:

> It is certain that the Popes, after the final division of the [Roman] empire, began to accumulate power due to the weakness or absence of the emperors ... amplifying their jurisdiction in the states of other princes and their entitlement to ecclesiastical liberty, they attempted to exercise temporal dominion over them ... [faced with] uneducated emperors and princes who wielded but little power, the pontiffs, vigilant and well-educated, knew how to take advantage of the occasion to pass from a mere spiritual power to a temporal one, expanding ecclesiastical liberty and jurisdiction, in order to achieve the *grandeza* which they now enjoy.[133]

By means of such manipulative manoeuvres, the regalists argued, the Church attained a degree of control over temporal affairs, unmandated by scripture, that it originally had not possessed. 'At the founding of the Church', Antonio Porlier claimed, 'the Church had no possessions and revenue other than the offerings of the faithful'.[134] Asserting that this state of affairs persisted until the end of the *Reconquista*, Manuel Abad y la Sierra claimed that these kings

> founded, instituted and endowed, at their own expense and from their personal fortunes, the monasteries and chapels of their *real patronato*. The ground, the buildings, the rents and the jurisdiction accumulated by the Church had pertained [originally] to the prince ... the prince's jurisdiction and free disposition came into existence with the kingdom, along with his state, goods and vassals ... the royal chapels were entirely beyond episcopal jurisdiction, and all other ecclesiastical and secular powers, uniquely dependent on the king's jurisdiction ... The present monarch should take back those fundamental powers originally possessed by the earlier kings.[135]

The regalists claimed that the medieval kings had weakened themselves in their zealous defence and rehabilitation of the Church both during and after the *Reconquista*. Their deeper aim, of course, was to demonstrate that Church property was, intrinsically and originally, royal property, subject to regalias which were inalienable. Any temporal property possessed by the Church, according to this view, was of merely derivative jurisdiction and might be reacquired legally by the Crown. Spain's economic weakness, therefore, could be attributed to pious, if misplaced, generosity. Appealing to dubious precedent, the Bourbon regalists called for a recalibration of the purported imbalance which had led to the Church's allegedly preponderant position in temporal affairs.

The regalists assumed *a priori* that any Church institution that produced pernicious consequences for the Crown, or obstructed its efforts, resulted from a medieval papal usurpation. Drawing on their nebulous theory of Church–State interdependence, all disputes were presumed to arise from the perturbation of a primordial and natural equilibrium. 'Our divine master', the *fiscal* of the *Audiencia* of Seville argued in 1776,

> established the Church without the intention of subverting the throne, without extinguishing its power, splendour, or its decency; without diminishing its territory, without depriving it of the proper obedience owed to it by its vassals, reserving for the Church only that which is purely spiritual and of a supernatural order ... demarcating a line between both powers in an unmistakable manner. We can attribute any dispute, therefore, to either the ambition or the unmeasured desire to extend the limits prescribed to each authority.[136]

The regalists perceived themselves, then, as counteracting a historical trend towards ecclesiastical usurpation which 'began in the eighth century, accelerated until the thirteenth, and continued unabated until the Council of Trent'.[137] In this manner, regalists sought to return papal power to its early limitations, purveying a glorified vision of a Visigothic past in which the monarch, assisted by the bishops he appointed, governed a Church which enjoyed considerable autonomy from Rome.[138]

The fusion of regalism and public happiness

Foreign ideas and Visigothic precedent helped to fortify regalism's intellectual underpinnings. It was in public happiness, however, that the Bourbon reformers encountered the key justification for the state's infringement on ecclesiastical wealth and property. 'It is a certain principle', Campomanes announced at the outset of his *Tratado de la Regalía de Amortización* (1765), that 'the greatest happiness of a Republic consists in being very populated because a large population is the greatest wealth that a Kingdom can desire'.[139] Carrasco, Campomanes's senior colleague, noted that the 'lands that are amortized could be the most cultivated, produce the most fruit, and be most useful to the state. To impede access to this land is tantamount to depriving the population of its wealth, which ensures its happiness'.[140] The regalists thus converted public happiness into a weapon in their struggle against the Church. It provided a new justification for a long-standing regalist objective: the encroachment on Church property and autonomy by the state.

The Bourbon regalists first took aim at the Jesuits, whose oath of loyalty was to the Pope, not to the secular ruler in whose territory they operated. In Spain and its overseas empire, the Jesuits numbered 3,000 in 1765, but the Order exerted a disproportionate and highly visible influence. It administered the secondary education of the nobility as well as 117 colleges, including the prestigious *Colegio Imperial* and *Seminario de Nobles* in Madrid.[141] Another major source of hostility towards the Jesuits was the existence of a virtually autonomous Jesuit state in Paraguay where the Order was accused of exploiting the indigenous population, forbidding Spaniards to trade, and failing to recognize the authority of the royal courts. The Jesuits' refusal to pay the full ecclesiastical tithe on the produce of its American *haciendas* was particularly onerous. By a special arrangement, obtained in 1750, the Jesuits surrendered a mere 1/30 of their produce. The effect was to reduce the income of the bishops and cathedral chapters, who were maintained by the tithe, and to reduce the Crown's income from its share of the *dos novenas*.[142]

This autonomy and preponderant influence resulted in resentment towards the Jesuits, which culminated in their expulsion from the Portuguese, French, and Spanish empires by 1767. Subterranean for decades, Spanish hostility towards the Jesuits erupted in the wake of the *motín*, or riot, of Esquilache in 1766. The expulsion of the Jesuits and the movement, led by Madrid, to compel Rome to suppress the Order linked the Catholic Monarchies in a common political struggle.[143] This coalition of Catholic kings against Rome's extensive power in their own realms was a prelude to more direct attempts at control over Church property.

The fusion of the languages of regalism, public happiness, patriotism, and economic prosperity became discernible in the crisis that erupted between the Duchy of Parma and the Pope in 1768–9. In the mid-eighteenth century, Parma was cross-fertilized by Spanish, French, and Neapolitan culture. Charles III briefly ruled there in the 1730s and, until the 1760s, it was governed by Charles's younger brother Philip, until the latter abdicated in favour of his son, Ferdinand, in 1765. The engine of reform was the chief minister Guillaume Du Tillot. He attempted to impose strict curbs on the privileges and immunities of the Church, directing his ambitions at the regulations which permitted the accumulation of lands in mortmain and, thus, their exemption from ducal taxation. In 1760, Du Tillot wrote to Roda expressing his conviction that the Church bore direct responsibility for Parma's economic stagnation. He blamed the 'inexpressible damage' to the clergy's privileges and immunities, describing them as 'irregular and of scandalous excess'.[144] He also denounced the clergy's 'buying, acquiring and inheriting everything' to the 'great detriment' of the 'poor subjects'. According to his estimate, religious institutions controlled 'two-thirds or more' of Parma's cultivable land.[145] Stoking the flames of discontent, Roda advised Du Tillot to disregard the Pope, who 'only possessed a mere spiritual jurisdiction, and even that is narrower than he alleges'. As a temporal prince, Roda contended, the Pope 'only merits the attention due to any other sovereign, and perhaps even less owing to the small size of his dominions and [armed] forces'.[146] Leading Spanish regalists, therefore, condoned and encouraged Du Tillot's incendiary ambitions.

Buoyed by their support, Du Tillot, in the Duke of Parma's name, forbade the future transfer into mortmain of any property in a pragmatic issued in October 1764. Du Tillot then took the matter a step further, ordering the Church to pay retroactive taxes on property acquired since 1560. He also issued an edict banning appeals by the clergy to Rome without the Duke's consent and declared all papal bulls and briefs invalid unless they carried the ducal signature.

Madrid's involvement in this proxy battle derived from deeper motives than dynastic loyalties and power politics. Spanish regalists had long held mortmain in contempt due its tendency to reduce overall cultivation and thus diminish revenue. Eleven *Cortes* in the sixteenth century requested a law to restrict it, and, on four occasions in the late seventeenth century, the Council of Castile proposed a similar measure. The parallel situation in Parma tempted Spanish regalists to pursue an ambition which was frustrated on their own peninsula, a pattern which would be repeated, as shall be seen in Chapter 3, in Spain's American empire.

Buttressed by Madrid and personally convinced of his action's public benefit, Du Tillot boasted that the amortization programme would enable 30,000 families 'to escape from the oppression which threatens them with an imminent and extreme poverty'.[147] In a letter to Roda, Azara expressed enthusiasm for Du Tillot's policies, noting the 'marvellous effect' that the entire affair had produced: the reputation of the *Infante* had undergone a tremendous 'metamorphosis', who 'today passes for a hero, a great prince who defends his sovereignty and the independence of his state, whereas a few months ago he was considered a mere imbecile'.[148] In correspondence with ranking Spanish ecclesiastics, Grimaldi justified the support as Charles III's 'effort to protect and support the Duke of Parma. The Duke cannot forsake the protection which he owes to his vassals'.[149] While dynastic allegiance was formally invoked, the requirements of public happiness also featured prominently in this defence.

The brazen actions of the Bourbons coincided with the resurgence of the Papacy. In contrast to the pliant and benign policies of Benedict XIV in the 1740s and 1750s, Clement XIII's 1758 accession signalled the advent of a reinvigorated Church, resistant to reforms which threatened to erode Rome's political clout.[150] The Papacy and the Bourbon regalist informers thus clashed in a proxy battle in Parma.

The Curia rejected Spain's justification for its support and the Pope condemned the entire reform programme as heretical in a *Monitorio de Parma*, which nullified the Parmese edicts and excommunicated the ministers involved. These actions, in effect, reasserted Rome's sovereignty over the Duchy. They also instigated the formation of a coalition of European courts against the Roman Curia, leading directly to France's occupation of Avignon and Naples's military incursion into the Benevento. The coalition interpreted Clement's attack on Du Tillot's programme as more than an isolated incident, but rather as the opening salvo of a broader assault on similar laws that were being drawn up across Europe.[151]

The Spanish Crown intervened by forbidding the publication of the monitorium and sponsored Campomanes (albeit anonymously at first) to draft *Juicio Imparcial*, subsidizing its publication in 1768.[152] This work surpassed the terms of its commission and became Caroline regalism's most coherent manifesto, though some passages propounded ideas more radical than the majority of regalists would have countenanced publicly. In *Juicio Imparcial*, Campomanes repudiated ecclesiastical privileges which collided with the exercise of royal authority: 'our proposition is that the privileges and immunities enjoyed personally by ecclesiastics in temporal affairs are not derived in any manner from canon law'.[153] Ecclesiastical privileges, therefore, became subordinate to the Monarch's responsibilities to promote public welfare.[154] Temporal and spiritual authority no longer maintained an equilibrium, as all powers were subordinated to the Crown.

In Campomanes's view, the pliable notion of public happiness justified the incursion of royal power into spheres previously beyond its purview. 'Our monarchs', he contended, are 'considered under the same obligation to care for and promote both ecclesiastical and secular affairs'.[155] Campomanes argued that 'the social compact [*pacto social*] in any system of government has reserved to the judgment of the sovereign the necessity, utility and convenience of the establishments therein so that they are directed toward the public happiness of all classes of subjects'.[156] Campomanes thus de-legitimized papal interference in Parma: 'each [king] in his kingdom is the true vicar of God and the Pope has no faculty whatsoever to annul nor derogate the edicts, laws or constitutions, like those which were published in Parma or in any other state or kingdom, even where such edicts apply to ecclesiastics as citizens and members of the state'.[157] Campomanes maintained the legitimacy of state intervention in spheres previously pertaining exclusively to the Church based on the calamitous results wrought by ecclesiastical control, especially poor harvests. He claimed that the Church's role in secular affairs had been deleterious, particularly its 'incessant acquisitiveness [which] enervates the authority and treasury of the sovereign'.[158] On this foundation, he advocated a law to restrict amortization, contending that such a measure would regenerate Parma's (and Spain's) countryside and encourage the emergence of a flourishing class of small farmers.[159] According to Campomanes, a prince wields 'all power necessary to do that which the demands of public welfare and utility dictate ... in this dominion, then, its use is pre-eminent, architechtonic and paternal'.[160] Public happiness and Crown responsibility for general welfare were used to justify this long-standing regalist policy goal.

The publication of the *Juicio Imparcial* provoked vehement protests which compelled the Crown to order its revision. Supervised by five regalist-leaning bishops, and edited by the future Count of Floridablanca, its most incendiary passages, concerning strict limitations on papal power and derogations of the Church's lax discipline, were tempered or excised. The revised version, however, retained an uncompromising defence of the Duke of Parma's unimpeachable sovereignty and the regalian rights promulgated in Campomanes's original document.[161] Some moderate voices faulted the audacity of the original *Juicio Imparcial*: one anonymous writer bluntly remarked that it demonstrated a 'lack of political sense to cite Febronius's works because it is impossible to convince Rome [of its error] by relying on such an author'.[162]

Notwithstanding the criticisms which his book endured, Campomanes's attitude was consistent with the regalist intelligentsia's hostility to the ubiquitous vestiges of corporate privilege which retarded Spain's economy and hindered its international competitiveness.[163] Under the banner of 'the utility of the nation', Campomanes declared that the 'first obligation of [all] sovereigns is to ensure the public prosperity of the state, which depends on distributing goods among the vassals, such that poverty does not oppress in order to superfluously enrich some communities'.[164] The political vocabulary of regalism, therefore, could be adapted to confront other challenges confronting the Crown. 'By the same [principle] that the Church within the state should enjoy those rights which are not denied to the rest of the citizenry', Carrasco reasoned, 'it is necessary to observe that [ecclesiastical] acquisitions are ruinous to the public'.[165] Carrasco's logic, echoed in myriad contemporary documents, facilitated treatment of the Church as an ordinary corporation, discarding the notion of special status conferred by its religious function. As shall be suggested in Chapter 3, arguments with a similar rhetorical structure were deployed against the monopoly held by colonial trading companies during precisely the same period.

In the final 30 years of the eighteenth century, Spanish regalists sought to deprive the Church of the property that it gradually had acquired, and to prevent further acquisitions, without provoking a dispute on the scale sparked by Du Tillot's Parmese amortization scheme. The ultimate aim of the regalists, to expand the state's sway in perceived power vacuums, is well illustrated by the arguments proffered to assert royal jurisdiction over ecclesiastical property during lapses in appointments. Since regalists also intended for such appointments to be certified by the king, the *fiscales* sought to strip the Church of certain holdings without flagrantly disregarding canon and civil law. During vacancies, Álvarez de Abreu claimed, 'it is understood that the Crown may distribute revenues as it deems fit'.[166] Antonio Porlier, *fiscal* of New Spain's *Audiencia* in the 1780s, elaborated on this argument, contending that during a vacancy 'the Crown is empowered to manage and distribute goods' and such power emerges primarily from the law's silence, for 'neither law, nor canon nor disposition exists which prescribes the effective application and distribution of the *espolios*' before the new prelate was installed. 'By the absence of this appointment the revenues do not belong to the Church nor does it have a right to them; instead, they remain in the Treasury, as patrimony of His Majesty, and have no other master'.[167] This argument suggested a broader design to expand Crown authority on the basis of purportedly pre-existing and under-utilized regalian rights. A second, related strategy was to claim that a regalian right had either fallen into disuse or was the victim of papal usurpation. The *Real Patronato*, for example, 'today [in 1781] is found quite disfigured'.[168] The regalists strove to revive and enforce these lapsed rights in the face of vigorous ecclesiastical opposition.

Although he defied the Pope over Parma and eventually compelled Rome, temporarily at least, to suppress the Jesuit Order, Charles III's audacity could not prevent amortization in his own realm. Regalist ideas were ascendant, but their political efficacy was muted by the resistance of powerful entrenched interests, the political miscalculations of their ministerial proponents, and fear of socio-political destabilization. The confiscation of Jesuit properties, as noted previously, failed to bring the anticipated results.

No buyers existed for the highly priced, newly expropriated lands. Thus, they were sold at a fraction of their estimated value, hardly resulting in the windfall revenue expected by the Crown.[169] Both Charles III and Charles IV indirectly discouraged mortmain by stripping ecclesiastical property of its tax-exempt status and by adding an amortization levy of 15 per cent. These actions constituted a prelude to the sweeping 1804 decree, issued during the war with Britain which had triggered fiscal collapse, which compelled the Church to alienate all property belonging both to its charities and pious works.[170]

This legislation not only attenuated Church–State relations, but also demolished the fragile alliance between the two, a blow which not even the most rapacious regalists had envisaged. The struggle against mortmain, according to one anonymous critic, 'broke the lovable and precious peace which united the Church and the empire and brought with it discord and enmity', a fracture 'all the more lamentable because such legislation alone cannot restore the nation to its ancient wealth, power and splendour'.[171] The fleeting 'regalist moment' thus did not revolutionize government and lead to Spain's prosperity as its proponents had hoped. This failure would have been inconceivable to Charles III's coterie of ministers who strove to 'put everything upside down, to open that which is now closed, and to close that which is now open'.[172]

Though the explicitly stated regalist programme may have weakened by 1788, and withered by 1808, both its goal of Crown supremacy over corporate bodies and its notion of public happiness as inextricably linked to economic growth survived. Regalist arguments became disentangled from the Church–State jurisdictional debates from which they first emerged and thereafter breathed new life into reform initiatives which sought to curb the autonomy of privileged corporate bodies. Regalism infused, for example, the internal colonization scheme in the Sierra Morena and galvanized attempts to overhaul ultramarine legislation.

Regalism in practice: the *Nuevas Poblaciones* and the *Novíssima Recopilación de las Leyes de Indias*

On the same day that he expelled the Jesuits from the Spanish Empire in 1767, Charles III also issued a *cédula* establishing the *Nuevas Poblaciones*, an internal colonization scheme in the depopulated, arid zones of the Sierra Morena. This act created a new juridical regime, distinct from all other Spanish territory.[173] The *Nuevas Poblaciones* explicitly drew inspiration from Prussian and Russian internal colonization precedent, particularly Catherine the Great's 1763–4 effort to persuade Germans to settle the Russian steppes. These new colonies, supervised by Pablo de Olavide, were designed to attain three objectives: to populate deserted zones, to ensure security and public order along the route from Seville to Madrid, and to form a model society.

The *Nuevas Poblaciones* indicates that the ideology of Caroline governance resulted from two convergent and complementary processes: first, foreign models provided a new impetus to older, pre-existing national practices; second, these models were modified upon contact with Spanish ideas, of which regalism was the most decisive. This interplay of exogenous–endogenous constituted the primary intellectual dynamic of the epoch.

The founding *cédula* of 1767 stipulated that 6,000 Flemish and German Catholic recruits would be induced to settle in the Sierra Morena, in places judged by Olavide to be 'healthy, well-ventilated and without stagnant water'. Each *población* would consist of a community of 15, 20, or 30 houses and each familial unit would receive 50 *fanegas* of land. Each male colonist was responsible for remaining and steadily cultivating the allotted land for ten years or else suffer the penalty of conscription.[174] Olavide evinced great faith in the scheme that he administered: 'today these [lands] are despised as useless, but they will flourish with an infusion of manure and sweat'.[175] If the origin and organization of the scheme drew on European precedent, the role of the Church in the new settlements was decidedly limited, in accordance with the precepts of regalism: the *diezmos*, the *cédula* emphasized, 'pertained absolutely to the Crown by virtue of its regalian rights and in remuneration for its initial outlay of funds'.[176] In this novel jurisdiction, the Crown precluded competition and all revenue was claimed by the Treasury. There would be no haggling over sovereignty in these new internal colonies.

Determining the ultimate success of the *Nuevas Poblaciones* poses numerous conceptual challenges. Many of the towns founded by the original *cédula* survive until the present day, so the initiative cannot be characterized as a failure in the strict sense. Contemporary foreign observers, however, conjectured differently: arriving in the capital La Carolina, Swinburne described an 'agreeable sensation at the sight of this absolute creation, this new world risen out of the very heart of desolation and solitude; everything seems so alive, so green, neat and thriving'. His excitement later was tempered upon visiting the settlement of La Carlotta where there was 'great reason to apprehend that this colony will prove one of those ephemeral productions which so often spring up in monarchical governments and almost immediately after their birth sink into their original nothing'.[177] An Austrian diplomat confirmed this latter premonition after a visit in 1770: 'Spain always remains stuck in the old system. The German colonists in the Sierra Morena wish to return [to their native country] due to the absolute poverty from which they suffer'.[178] The *Nuevas Poblaciones* did not fulfil, therefore, their initial promise. This result, however, did not discourage further initiatives on both sides of the Atlantic.

In spite of the monarchy's relatively firm control over ecclesiastical affairs in America, regalist precepts also shaped its revamped ultramarine legislation. All books circulated in Spanish America, for example, were subject to the

Council of the Indies' approval. Books containing religious themes, in particular, were evaluated by a regalist litmus test. Some, such as Pedro José de Parras's *Gobierno de los Regulares de la América*, secured approval, not solely because it contained nothing 'contrary to the *Real Patronato*, jurisdiction and *regalías*' of the king, but also for its 'wise choice of including documents which demonstrate the prerogatives of the Crown'.[179] Books concerning political economy underwent similar scrutiny: Muñoz's *Economía Política* (1769) was approved for publication and distribution upon finding that it contained nothing 'against the maxims of our religion or the regalian rights of His Majesty'.[180]

Regalist precepts almost were extended to New World governance in a more fundamental, sweeping way through the unrealized effort of the special *Junta del Nuevo Código*, formed in 1776 to revise the *Nueva Recopilación de las Leyes de Indias* of 1680. Since jurisprudence was considered to be 'science of governing states and directing public affairs', legal reform was a crucial aspect of Bourbon ultramarine governance.[181] Long before Charles III's accession, there were murmurs in the Council of Castile regarding the need to update the *Recopilación*. This body of laws, approved and promulgated by Charles II, consisted of nine books containing 5,515 laws. It remained in force until the end of Spanish rule, but it was amended frequently. Every *cédula* issued was, in theory, supposed to be enforced in the same manner as the laws codified in the *Recopilación*. But the *cédulas* never were collected into a comprehensive document and, as they proliferated, enforcement, and even clerical upkeep of new legislation, emerged as a serious challenge.

In 1755, a *fiscal* recommended the formation of a junta in order to 'judge the usefulness of the existing laws and to determine the convenience of adding to them'.[182] In the late 1750s, José de Gálvez also stressed the exigency of reforming the laws of the Indies. Even greater than the threat posed by foreign nations, 'the greatest disorder', he claimed, was the 'exorbitant' acquisitions of the Church in Spanish America. To bolster his arguments, which he claimed were consistent 'with the ancient prohibition which most justly established the law of the Indies', he cited examples of foreign historical figures who imposed the same limits: Charles the Great in France, Edward III in England, Frederick II, the Dukes of Savoy and Milan, the Kings of Poland, Austria, and Hungary, Portugal and Spain since the reign of Alonso 'the Wise'.[183] An updated legal code, Gálvez contended, would 're-establish ancient laws' and reform those laws which neither were 'useful nor adaptable' to modern circumstances. It would thus create a new 'clear and decisive' body of law to replace the 'notable confusion and disorder'.[184] Consistent with the spirit of emulation described in Chapter 1, legal codes from rival powers were studied and a translation was undertaken of Czarina Catherine II's code (from French) for consideration by the *Junta de Leyes*.[185]

The members of this special junta were nominated in mid-1776, headed by Juan Crisóstomo Ansotegui, a *fiscal* of the Council of the Indies. The proposed revised code received support from the peninsular-born attorneys of the colonial *Audiencias*. Some colonial jurists urged a new code out of sheer necessity, for there was a scarcity of available law codes in the New World. Each city, one *fiscal* argued, possessed but a single copy which 'few have seen and most ignore'.[186] This problem was remedied partly by the frequent republication of the 1680 *Recopilación* in the second half of the eighteenth century. The underlying problem was, however, much graver: an *oidor* of Mexico's *Audiencia* asserted that 'many laws are not in use, nor would it be useful to enforce some of them, whereas others require reform, still more needed further clarification, and many new ones are required especially in relation to matters of government'. He urged a *recopilación*, declaring that 'laws in the political body perform the same functions that the soul does in the human body. Without laws, therefore, the political body is little more than a corroding and miserable corpse'.[187] A genuinely new document was required and it would be inadequate to merely 'transfer royal orders [*cédulas*] into legal codes'. A digest was required which would 'discard all that is not essential'.[188] This task would later be entrusted to the special junta.

In 1778, Ansotegui assured Gálvez that he had begun 'without losing an instant and continued to carry out his arduous responsibility with the same tireless effort' to ensure that a draft would be prepared within a year for presentation to the Council of the Indies. He declined numerous solicitations from colonial *fiscales* to assist him, claiming that, since they possessed only the *cédulas* and dispatches pertinent to their own viceroyalty, they lacked the documentation necessary to 'organize a body of universal legislation for both Americas' which 'by its very nature should be common for all of the kingdoms of America'.[189] This final statement reveals a great deal about the motives underlying the *Novíssima Recopilación*: the streamlining, centralization, and codification of Bourbon power. The *Novíssima Recopilación* was intended to superimpose legal uniformity on a changing colonial order and to codify basic principles of Caroline reform. Circumstances had evolved and the laws were in desperate need of overhaul.

In the introduction to his commentary on the proposed *Novíssima Recopilación*, Manuel de Ayala conveyed the staunch regalism which animated the Junta's work. He noted that the 'Church considers sovereigns as its tutelar angels [*angeles tutelares*], and its orations have for their object the conservation and prosperity of the monarchy ... the Church recognizes that the hands of Eternity have established and sustain the throne of the kings [and that] their power is derived directly from God'. Similarly, it should not appear odd that a king 'exhorts and demands that his vassals profess and defend' religion, for the sovereign is its 'protector and custodian; beneath the shelter of its authority and power, the sovereign conserves, extends and keeps watch over its progress'.[190] The regalists were still at work on the peninsula, but their reforming gaze now also encompassed America. There, too, they sought to extend 'the shelter of [the Crown's] authority and power'. Practical politics, however, prevented the *Novíssima Recopilación* from taking effect anywhere in the Spanish Atlantic World.

The failure could not be blamed on the Junta's indolence. In accordance with his promise, Ansotegui delivered the first book of the *Novíssima Recopilación* to Charles III in September 1780 and it was forwarded to the Council of the Indies for approval. The Council did nothing and nine years elapsed before the first approved book was presented to Charles IV, by which time Ansotegui and several other junta members had died. In 1792, the king acknowledged it as law but, curiously and inexplicably, forbid its publication, promulgation, and enforcement. It never, therefore, took effect in the Indies. Ferdinand VII briefly revived the Junta in 1814, but it was suppressed before it could re-open the matter. In this way, the *Novíssima Recopilación*, like so much in the Caroline era, remained a mere project, unknown to the general populace, and never enforced. In spite of the ardent efforts of reforming legislators, the New World remained governed, by and large, by the antiquated Habsburg legal code.[191]

Judged solely on the basis of its results, nonexistent as these were, the *Novíssima Recopilación* was an utter failure. Such an interpretation bolsters the theses of scholars inclined to view the Bourbon reforms as a litany of unrealized proposals. The *Nuevas Poblaciones,* too, might be dismissed as easily, though its *fuero* remained in effect well into the nineteenth century. Nevertheless, these two projects offer key insights into the Bourbon official mind. Each suggests how regalism informed, and in some cases propelled, reform initiatives in areas beyond its traditional sphere.

The *Nuevas Poblaciones* and *Novíssima Recopilación* were not isolated initiatives. The Crown would employ similar justifications to diminish the autonomy of various corporations and individuals deemed a threat to state power. For example, in 1791, new instructions ordered foreigners who wished to remain in Spain indefinitely for the purposes of exercising the 'liberal arts or mechanical offices' to swear obedience to the Church, to the sovereign, and to Spanish law. Royal officials justified this measure as a royal prerogative, thus transforming the rules governing naturalization, formerly determined by local communities, into a regalian right.[192]

The political language of regalism, then, began to permeate debates tangential to Church–State disputes. One eminent historian of ideas has noted that the 'surest sign that a group or society has entered into self-conscious possession of a new concept is that a corresponding vocabulary will be developed, a vocabulary that can be used to pick out and discuss the concept with consistency'.[193] This statement holds true for Bourbon

Spain where a somewhat esoteric conception about state jurisdiction moved into the mainstream and structured political discourse in multiple spheres. Incubated for centuries in both Iberian and broader European thought, the coincidence of a reinvigorated monarchy enabled regalism's maturation and facilitated its meteoric ascendance. This development was fortified by parallel trends in political thought, particularly notions of the state's responsibility to promote public happiness, which made incumbent its unprecedented intervention in social and economic affairs.

From this caldron emerged a new concoction: a flexible political idiom of governance and reform. The new vocabulary was derived, though now detached, from the disputes out of which it initially arose. Regalism, broadly construed, provided a framework for conceptualizing politics which could be applied effortlessly to topics unrelated to jurisdictional clashes between Church and State.

3
Imperial Governance and Reform: Ideas and *Proyectos*

By the mid-seventeenth century, it was common for Spanish political writers to lament that foreigners 'destroy us and steal all of our gold and silver, and it is with this [wealth] that the customs, language and number of people in these countries expand, leaving us with nothing'. These *arbitristas* recognized that Spain had been reduced to a passive factor in the imperial chain of production. They sought to identify, devise, and implement measures to reduce smuggling, spur peninsular growth, revive the royal navy, and fortify colonial ports.[1] Paralleling these practical reforms was a discourse of national regeneration and rededication.[2] Complaints of wrongful dispossession and decline had, by the mid-eighteenth century, given way to a more desperate effort to comprehend and counteract the forces which enabled competitor nations to outstrip Spain. Gandara observed that the 'spirit of commerce has spread among the modern nations ... its study, application, and insights have opened their eyes, they who slept when Spain's candle burned brightly; yet today, it is we who slumber while they pass the night in fervent activity'.[3]

This observation anticipated the tremendous flurry of reform initiatives that coincided with Charles III's accession and Spain's underperformance in the Seven Years' War. From the mid-1760s, the state became the main protagonist of the economic arena and, armed with precepts of regalism and European political economy, aspired to absolute dominance of political and social spheres as well.[4] 'Political commerce is the nerve of the state', Campillo y Cosío observed, 'it is the blood which invigorates the entire monarchy'.[5] Enamoured of what Adam Smith would famously disparage as the 'mercantile system', the Caroline policy intelligentsia sought to expand state power by harnessing the resources of both its peninsular and ultramarine kingdoms. They naturally turned their reforming gaze to America, which always had been a crucial dimension of Crown policy. For the Bourbon reformers, Spanish America assumed an even greater importance: between 1763 and 1783, revenues from the Indies accounted for approximately 15 per cent of the Madrid treasury's revenues, a figure which reached 25 per cent by 1790 and had skyrocketed, in the midst of the French revolutionary wars, to 40 per cent in 1804.[6]

This chapter traces and analyses metropolitan debates concerning the reform of colonial administration and commerce on the imperial periphery. Like the preceding chapters, it is concerned with the state's enlarged role in economic and social affairs and how this expanded scope resulted from the intermingling of foreign and Spanish thought. Unlike previous scholarly accounts of metropolitan debates, it argues that a significant discrepancy existed between discourses of trade, governance, and population growth in Madrid-based circles and the political sentiments and ideas proffered by 'men-on-the-spot'; that is, the governors, intendants and their subalterns who administered the vast overseas empire. Such a demarcation, it shall be argued, enables historians to probe Bourbon political ideas concerning empire more effectively.

The first part of this chapter examines the major ultramarine institutions, the competing conceptions of trade, agriculture, and population which circulated within the government bureaucracy, and efforts to revivify stagnant institutions. It focuses mainly on metropolitan administrators and peninsular political writers. The second part of the chapter treats these same institutions and ideas, but from the perspective of the 'men-on-the-spot', especially colonial viceroys, captain-generals, and other ranking provincial officials. It concludes with a case study of governance and reform in the Spanish Caribbean in order to describe how institutional structures and the ideology of empire functioned in practice.

In pursuing these themes, there are few references to the two jewels in Spain's imperial crown—Peru and New Spain—and the emphasis is on the 'imperial periphery'. The imperial periphery represented an opportunity for ambitious reformers. Its dynamic economy, burgeoning population, and relatively fluid administrative structures provided an opening to enact reforms perilously pursued on the peninsula or amidst the deeply entrenched hierarchies of New Spain and Peru. The term 'imperial periphery' is not mere shorthand to encompass all of Spanish America except those two grand viceroyalties. It designates the emerging, yet still relatively undeveloped, regions which enticed the reforming lust of the Bourbon bureaucrats.

The term 'imperial periphery' summarizes and draws attention to three historical phenomena: the first phenomenon is the absence of fiscally self-sufficient administration in most of Spanish America. The *situado*, transfer, of Mexican silver kept much of the Spanish Caribbean afloat. In 1793, currency-strapped Havana, Puerto Rico, Trinidad, Santo Domingo, Florida, and Louisiana still depended on substantial bullion transfusions to finance basic expenses. While not technically a deficit operation, the viceroyalty of the Río de la Plata barely broke even in 1790, returning a paltry surplus to the depleted Madrid treasury.[7] The remittances sent by the treasury in New Spain to Caribbean colonies tended to surpass the value of the royal silver transferred annually to the metropolis.[8]

The second significance of the term 'imperial periphery' is its reflection of the region's relative economic weakness, notwithstanding its rapid modernization and emergent prosperity. This condition is suggested by exports from Cádiz: whereas New Spain and Peru received a staggering 57.1 per cent of total exports to Spanish America from 1785–96, Louisiana and Florida jointly received 0.1 per cent of the total, the entire Caribbean 7 per cent, Honduras and Campeche a combined 6.7 per cent, New Granada 8.2 per cent, Venezuela 10.1 per cent, and the Río de Plata 10.8 per cent.[9]

The third phenomenon to which 'imperial periphery' refers is the condition wrought by, depending on the colony in question, geographical isolation, small size of the population, and belated economic development.[10] These helped to inspire a new, flexible, and authentically Bourbon mode of governance which flourished in such places. Such experiments were less constrained by long-existing, firmly entrenched elites and intervention was less likely to arouse the ire of prosperous local creoles. The Spanish Crown sought to find ways to exploit the resources of the periphery. It sponsored numerous scientific expeditions—including Malaspina's famous voyage of 1789–94—to learn more about the flora, fauna, and geography of its less-developed provinces. While animated by scientific curiosity, these initiatives were underpinned by a quest for useful knowledge which could be harnessed to augment the size of the treasury. The periphery, then, played a key role in the political imagination of the Bourbon policy elite.

It is not suggested, however, that Peru and New Spain are secondary characters in this drama; on the contrary, many of the reforms and institutions studied here originated in those principal colonies. Because of their politico-economic pre-eminence, and the existing wealth of scholarship concerning them, however, New Spain and Peru tend to outshine their peripheral counterparts. This prejudice rightly reflects the economic and demographic disparities and dependencies sketched above.

What remains less certain is whether it accurately describes the political and cultural–intellectual dynamics: for example, did the Spanish American periphery function as a dim, secondary receptor of European cultural light which first passed through the core colonies? Were the reform proposals in Havana and Santiago de Chile, for instance, merely generic versions of those enacted in Lima and Mexico City? This chapter suggests that the imperial periphery was not inert intellectually but rather vibrant, governed by a bevy of 'enlightened administrators' who applied newfangled ideas to the formulation and implementation of policy.

Colonial reform from metropolitan perspective

Eighteenth-century Spaniards, as suggested in the preceding chapters, were obsessed with their nation's place in the annals of empire. Campomanes devised a simple taxonomy to classify colonial powers: he labelled the first type of empire as 'militaristic', placing the Celts, Romans, and Arabs in this category; the second variety, he named 'mercantile and peaceful', a cohort which included the Phoenicians and Greeks. Campomanes considered the former 'odious, as they were instituted to deprive free nations and peoples of their liberty', whereas the latter was 'estimable because, without depriving people of their natural rights, they provided a vent for their products and instructed them about commerce and shipping, thus achieving mutual utility'. Applying this set of criteria to modern imperial powers, he classified the Spanish and Portuguese empires as 'military', but noted, as an extenuating circumstance, that the nations subdued by the *conquistadores* otherwise 'would have remained mired in their idolatrous barbarism and their lands without agriculture'. By contrast, he contended, rival European nations, especially France and Britain, established colonies 'purely mercantile in nature, [marked by] a reciprocal and continuous commerce with the metropole'.[11]

Campomanes's contemporary and friend, Antonio de Ulloa, however, dissented from the characterization of rival empires as 'mercantile and peaceful'. 'The discovery of America and its wealth', he argued, 'awoke emulation in the nations and with it the desire to acquire part of those abundant treasures. [Emulation] ... was the chief motive driving the expansion of *armadas*'.[12] But whether the militaristic path chosen by Spain was unfortunate or inevitable, the assertion that its empire's *grandeza* had faded was a less contentious proposition.

All political writers concurred that other European nations had surpassed Spain. No political writer, however, portrayed the deficit of wealth and power as insurmountable. Campillo y Cosío trumpeted the specific advantages enjoyed by Spain's colonies over those of its European rivals: it boasted the most extensive lands, the richest mines and precious fruit, and 'a vast empire with thousands of obedient vassals'.[13] The challenge which ministers faced was the reform of the fiscal and administrative structures in the colonies in order to exploit their natural endowment through a comprehensive overhaul of commercial regulations and administrative structure.

A brief sketch of the institutions of government in the eighteenth-century Spanish empire will situate the attempted reforms in their proper context.[14] At the accession of Charles III in 1759, policy was formed in royal councils and through the five Secretariats. These Secretariats were State [*Estado*], Treasury [*Hacienda*], Indies [*Indias*], Grace and Justice [*Gracia y Justicia*], and Navy and War [*Marina y Guerra*]. The Councils were numerous, but the two most salient were those of Castile and the Indies. The power of the Secretaries increased steadily at the expense of the Councils towards the end of the Caroline era.[15] In 1787, the *Junta Suprema de Estado* was established. The secretaries served on this Junta and jointly advised the king. A further reconfiguration occurred in 1787: the Secretary of the Indies' responsibilities were divided between two ministries. A minister for Treasury and War and one for

Grace and Justice, both especially for the Indies, were established in the same year. These bodies were integrated into a *Consejo de Estado* in 1792.

No legislative process existed in Spanish America. Laws, created by the Council of Castile, were enforced by colonial government officials. Additional royal commands were sent out, not irregularly, as *cédulas*. The *Recopilación de Leyes de Indias* (1680) compressed nearly 400,000 such *cédulas* into 5,500 laws. The laws governing the Indies, then, were a hodgepodge of the codified *Recopilación* and the *cédulas* issued after 1680. Efforts to revise the *Recopilación*, chronicled in the final section of Chapter 2, and to incorporate the *cédulas* into a single legal code never materialized.

The viceroy stood at the apex of the colonial government. He issued proclamations [*bandos*] and measures [*ordenanzas*], but not laws in the strict sense. His authority was constrained by an elaborate system of checks and balances. The greatest limitation on viceregal authority was imposed by the *Audiencia*, the highest court of Spanish America, of which 13 had been established by 1661.[16] The judges [*oidores*] of the *Audiencia*, appointed directly by the king, were empowered to correspond directly with Madrid on all matters and especially on the behaviour of the viceroy. The *Audiencias* also retained attorneys [*fiscales*] responsible to the king for all things pertaining to the treasury. The *Audiencias* were subdivided into districts, variously called *corregimientos*, *alcaldías mayores*, and *gobernaciones*. At a local level, the *cabildo*, or town council, was an important institution, and it relied on the rent or lease of town property and local judicial fines as its sources of revenue. The *cabildo*, sometimes called the *ayuntamiento*, exercised police functions and handled municipal revenues as well.

Although subject to an increasingly greater degree of oversight, the colonial treasury was administered by the viceroy.[17] Viceregal fiscal autonomy was checked by the *Residencia*. At the expiration of his term of service, each official underwent this evaluation of his conduct. Such a review, it was hoped, would serve as a deterrent to graft and excess on the part of the viceroy. Later Bourbon reforms further fragmented viceregal power. The *Visitor General* and the *Intendant*, in particular, both encroached on viceregal jurisdiction. The creation of colonial *Consulados*, discussed in Chapter 4, empowered to collect certain minor levies on commerce and to petition Madrid, further siphoned off municipal power at the end of the colonial period. The imperial structure was not, however, immutable and numerous debates about the optimal institutional arrangement proliferated. These debates generally concerned the best manner to maximize two goals: population increase and commercial growth.

As in peninsular Spain, Madrid sought to spur population growth in the colonies from exogenous sources, enticing foreign immigration to its overseas dominions. Royal decrees stipulated that such invitations were conditional on religious homogeneity: 'all foreigners originating from powers and nations which are friends of mine, who seek to establish themselves, must demonstrate that they profess the Roman Catholic religion and if they do not meet this indispensable condition, they will be unable to settle'.[18] The influx of 'true Catholics [*verdaderos católicos*] would increase population without cost to the Treasury or the peninsula'.[19] In a similar spirit, Gálvez balked at the Council of Castile's proposal to deport Spanish gypsies to the New World. 'Their bad example and pernicious customs' would 'pervert' other colonists, he claimed, and Spain would 'suffer from the grave evil' plaguing Britain, which unwisely populated its colonies with 'errant and delinquent men who lacked even the smallest measure of goodness'.[20] With these caveats in mind, ministers sought to enlarge the population of the colonies.

Policymakers strove to replenish depopulated, and to populate desolate, frontier zones, those most vulnerable to foreign penetration or raids by indigenous peoples. The magnitude of the challenge did not escape the reformers. In the late 1700s, for example, independent, unsubjugated Indians effectively controlled at least half of the territory of continental Spanish America, accounting for at least 1/5 of the total population. These areas were rife with contraband, where European smugglers traded with Indians and thus injected products into the colonial economy. They also represented potential beachheads for foreign invasion. In the 1780s, faced with these threats, both real and exaggerated, the Spanish Crown sought to re-colonize its far-flung territories, bringing them under firmer state control. Colonists were sent to the peripheries of empire—the Mosquito Coast, Patagonia, Easter Island, and Northern California—to extend and consolidate dominion.[21] Population policy, then, lay at the intersection of economic and geopolitical stratagems to achieve the imperial resurgence envisaged by ambitious ministers.[22]

Deficient population was merely one of many impediments to economic growth. Existing fiscal, manufacturing, and trade policies also were considered detrimental to the colonial economy. Political economists sought to diagnose and cure Spain's economic ailments. In the 1720s, Uztáriz portrayed Spain's overseas kingdoms as a potential bastion of national strength if 'the fabricks are revived and augmented, and our taxes [become] less heavy'. He therefore favoured an 'active, and not passive', export-oriented trade, on the British model, carried out with Spanish manufactures on Spanish vessels.[23] Uztáriz's vision of an insular colonial trade by, with, and for peninsular Spaniards became one of Madrid's foremost imperial goals.

Bernardo de Ulloa, slightly modifying Uztáriz's analysis of colonial commerce in his *Restablecimiento de las Fábricas, Tráfico y Comercio Marítimo de España* (1740), did not identify depopulation as the primary obstacle to a flourishing economy. Instead, he blamed Spain's 'grave laziness'.[24] Ulloa contended that the main remedy for economic distress consisted in expelling, not admitting, foreigners and vigilantly eliminating contraband.[25] A revivified Spanish manufacturing sector, now smothered by the surfeit of Northern European textiles, could emerge. Ulloa argued that this conjectured scenario assumed several policies were enforced, including consolidated internal taxes, tax exemptions, and protective tariffs designed to block the export of raw materials, and raised duties on imported manufacturers.[26] All Spanish political writers concurred with Ulloa that colonial economic activity should be confined to the production of raw materials for export and should not be permitted to foment manufactures. In Danvila's formulation, colonies should be 'dedicated to agriculture, and must not duplicate peninsular products and increase competition'.[27] In this respect, early eighteenth-century political economists endorsed standard tenets of European mercantilism.

The insights of these earlier political writers were broadened by José Campillo y Cosío, Minister of War and Finance under Philip V, who advocated 'economic governance [*gobierno económico*]'. 'Commerce is not a mystery', Campillo argued, 'we have before us the experience of Europe's greatest men who, in the last century and a half, have perfected this branch of political science'.[28] Drawing heavily on Campillo's ideas, Bernardo Ward contended that 'in America, where commerce is constrained, nothing can be produced save economic illness and political disaster ... [it is necessary] to open this commerce, or else to permit the establishment of manufactures in America ... the surest way to increase population is the same in America as it is elsewhere. It consists in introducing the spirit of industry'.[29]

The most persistent debate among Spanish political economists, however, concerned who should be permitted to conduct transoceanic commerce. The organization of colonial trade was among the most contentious topics in the Spanish Atlantic World. Two great systems of monopoly operated simultaneously in the late eighteenth century: first, the colonial system by which each empire sought to exclude the merchants of all other nations; second, a system of exclusive companies by which imperial states attempted to exclude all merchants other than those of a single, privileged company.[30] From the advent of its dominion in the New World, the Spanish Crown had zealously guarded its American colonies from foreign penetration through the use of both of these systems of monopoly. Foreign commercial ships were, legally at least, prohibited from entering Spanish American ports. Until 1720, all merchant ships were compelled to call at Seville, and, between 1720 and 1765, at Cádiz, whose merchants virtually monopolized the American trade.

The formation of exclusive, privileged trading companies in the first half of the eighteenth century partially abrogated the monopoly enjoyed by the merchant oligarchies of the Andalusian ports. The legitimacy of trading companies, in turn, would be undermined by the rise of regalist precepts concerning the proper scope of royal power and intrinsic distrust of autonomous corporate bodies within the realm. Before tracing the decline of trading companies, however, their rise must be fully understood.

The early eighteenth-century Spanish political economists endorsed both Spain's absolute monopoly and the virtues of privileged trading companies. They attributed Spain's economic stagnation to the composition of its foreign and domestic trade and to its poor shipping facilities, both of which caused otherwise reducible outflows of precious metals. Privileged companies, it was hoped, could help to improve Spain's lagging position, overcome the mercantile superiority of other nations, and foment commerce in less developed parts of the empire where the absence of Spanish trade had engendered rampant contraband.

The public benefits produced by a trading company's activities justified, at least in theory, its monopoly: the building of forts and garrisons; its function as a proxy for the state against external aggression; and its management of relations with, or subjugation of, indigenous populations.[31] Primarily organized with capital from Catalonia and the Basque provinces, Spanish chartered companies received special privileges for, if not a complete monopoly over, trade with the peripheral and undeveloped areas of the empire.[32] These companies, moreover, were entrusted to spur the production of colonial exports, such as the *Compañía Guipúzcoana's* role in fomenting Venezuelan cocoa, and to militarily defend the distant, vulnerable, and economically less vibrant provinces.[33] Spanish companies, however, never wielded the sovereign or military power exercised by, for instance, the English East India Company. Furthermore, they were granted exclusive rights for a fixed number of years only, and were forbidden from operating in the lucrative mining colonies (such as New Spain). In spite of such restrictions, the companies blossomed and accounted for 20 per cent of Spain's transatlantic shipping by the mid-century.[34]

By the second half of the eighteenth century, Spanish opinion had turned against privileged trading companies. They had failed to lower prices, improve the quality of goods, introduce new methods, and establish a stable and secure commercial system. This uncompetitiveness heralded their eventual dismantlement, with the demise of the French *Compagnie des Indes*, a harbinger of things to occur south of the Pyrenees.[35] In 1755, the Cádiz monopoly was denounced as a 'skeleton' which merely served to protect and veil the interests of foreigners, the Caracas and Royal Havana Companies remained alarmingly stagnant, and Madrid contemplated major institutional change which promised to disrupt, if not regenerate, the old system of monopoly. The commercial malaise, critics of companies argued, allowed foreigners to extract greater benefits from America than Spain itself.

Trading companies, nevertheless, were not rejected altogether though most policymakers continued to deride their penchant for underperformance. A *proyecto* proposed in the 1750s proposed permitting additional peninsular ports to trade in the New World, even 'dividing the commerce of America among all of the provinces of Spain ... so that each port pursued its own happiness, and each of them will strive to surpass the others in greatness'.[36] One of Ferdinand VI's advisors promulgated a similar idea, proposing the creation of 12 companies, emanating from various regions of peninsular Spain, each responsible for trade with a particular ultramarine province. While monopoly was under attack, however, policymakers had not yet shunned the usefulness, necessity, and convenience of companies.[37] Arguments in their favour not only would persist, but largely prevail until the end of the colonial period.

The expansion of companies was checked, however, by the political disputes which they engendered. The potential establishment of a Bilbao company for trade with Buenos Aires in the late 1740s, for example, was blocked by the obstinate opposition of the Cádiz merchants.[38] By 1765, the *Real Compañía de la Habana* had been stripped of its exclusive status.[39] The attack upon, but incomplete victory over, trading companies gave rise to a chaotic situation. There were multiple and overlapping monopolies in Spain's American trade and the relation between the respective actors was both unharmonious and often undefined.

The move away from companies was prompted both by subtle ideological shifts and the waning of Cádiz's political influence. By the late 1750s, many Spanish political writers openly condemned exclusive companies. 'All private privilege', one administrator wrote concerning trade in Campeche and the Yucatán, 'is hateful'.[40] Gandara's arguments epitomized the emerging hostility to monopoly trade: no 'better, more useful or dignified' company could exist, he contended, 'than the entire nation', arguing that such 'barriers to trade oppress liberty and deplete the well-being of the people'.[41] Campomanes asserted that 'it is bad politics for a single company to control the exclusive commerce of a province because this makes commerce stagnate ... this is repugnant to the spirit of sovereignty'.[42] He pointed to English colonies in which 'everything is permitted ... and [by this means] they come to have strong vassals'.[43] The tide, it seemed, had turned against monopoly companies.

If companies were, at least temporarily, in disfavour, Spanish policymakers also suspiciously viewed the prospect of commerce open to merchants of all nations. Apart from the exigencies of war, when limited trade with neutral countries was reluctantly permitted, this notion never received serious consideration, in spite of the crescendoing number of requests by disenchanted and desperate merchants. To Crown officials, commercial reform was needed not for private enrichment, but in order to buttress the resurgence of political–military power.[44] The winter of mercantilism had not yet begun to thaw.

By the mid-1760s, the mood shifted. Bourbon reformers became disillusioned with the Cádiz monopoly in particular and privileged trading companies in general. The anachronistic use of fleets, the limitations on the number of ships licensed to trade, the high duties on exports and imports, and the antiquated method of taxation on volume of goods without reference to value also were lamented.

These nascent attitudes became manifest in the policies recommended by a 1764 colonial commercial reform commission. This body produced a report (issued in February 1765) detailing potential methods to further the 'increase, prosperity and preservation' of Spanish America while, simultaneously, extracting its wealth and defraying the burgeoning costs which its defence and administration entailed. Since hefty taxation would 'destroy' and lighter levies would fail to generate sufficient revenue to recover overhead expenses, it was 'necessary to seek other methods'. Among these, none was as 'easy and certain' as the expansion of commerce and navigation to satisfy the metropolitan market. As commerce sprouted, the commissioners reasoned, the colonial population of workers, artisans, sailors, and construction labourers would increase. The commission referred to this policy as the 'method which foreigners adopted in their American acquisitions to populate and defend their colonies' whereas Spain, 'by our current method, follows a completely contrary practice'.[45] The 1765 *comercio libre* decree, which opened the Spanish Caribbean to eight additional peninsular ports besides Cádiz, resulted directly from the commission's recommendations.

Contemporary scholars have been sceptical of the motives underlying this shift towards freer trade for several reasons. First, even though limited liberty to several peninsular ports in order to pursue reciprocal commerce was granted, deregulation neither was full nor general, leaving vast regions excluded from the new trade regime.[46] Second, Charles III's commercial reforms were designed to reclaim control of trade within the empire, which had been eroding steadily.[47] Third, the *comercio libre* decree was a desperate response to burgeoning British contraband trade.[48] Fourth, *comercio libre* policy was not particularly original, following the model of the Dutch free port at St. Eustatius (1737), the Danish example in St. Thomas and St. John (1763), and French experiments in Martinique and Guadeloupe (1763–5). Its implementation, moreover, barely preceded the long-anticipated British Free Port Act (1766). These considerations cast doubt on the claim that free trade ideas had fully penetrated the Caroline policy elite's approach by the mid-1760s.

The critical attitude towards both the Cádiz monopoly and privileged companies, however, appears to have penetrated the upper echelon of government by 1770 and made the prospect of less-regulated trade within the empire a more tempting proposition. In his rejection of a proposal by Galician and Asturian merchants for exclusive trade with the Yucatán, Grimaldi explained that 'a kingdom flourishes when all of its provinces have an opportunity to enrich themselves ... but not privately for the benefit of two, but rather for all the kingdoms' of peninsular Spain.[49] The rolling back of existing, and the reluctance to sanction additional, trading companies after 1770 represented, then, a manifestation of the fusion of ascendant principles of political economy with precepts which bear a strong rhetorical and structural resemblance to regalism. The Crown refused to relinquish the state's authority in the imperial periphery to corporations not directly controlled by Madrid and whose quasi-sovereignty could diminish its capacity to dictate policy and extract revenue.

It is plausible that Madrid's policymakers concluded that the privileges and protection demanded by provincial peninsular merchants, who sought exclusive trade with one of the less developed ultramarine zones, threatened the Crown's sovereignty and, moreover, promised few guaranteed benefits. An examination of a rejected 1767 proposal to establish a Bilbao-based company for trade with Louisiana corroborates this argument. The principals offered to form a company in order to:

fortify, populate, augment, and protect the colony of Louisiana ... to establish an arsenal, capable of arming, in necessary cases, five or six thousand Indians or Blacks ... to recruit, ship and bring to the colony three thousand Catholic families of all types of professions appropriate to the land and the cultivation of the country ... to introduce 20,000 African slaves, should they be necessary, for wealth and increase depend much on their labour ... to employ all [of the company's] power for the advancement and progress of agriculture, commerce and population, thereby making this colony flourish.[50]

In exchange for these pledges, however, the merchants of Bilbao demanded that the Spanish government grant 'exclusive privileges for thirty years, without disturbance, troubled by no pretext whatsoever'. The petitioners also demanded the right to confiscate property, to distribute land and to enjoy the exclusive ownership of any minerals unearthed in the colony. Furthermore, in case of war, they demanded that Spain 'assume its responsibilities and relieve the colonists, with troops and naval forces, at [the state's expense], so that they may be combined with those of the company ... furthermore, the Crown would pay for the transport of the families in its frigates'.[51] In an age of re-awakened regalism, this proposal was rejected as Madrid's policy elite contemplated strategies to encourage economic growth without the transfer of sovereignty for indefinite periods. The Crown would seek to control the flow of trade, somewhat paradoxically, by expanding access to it.

The 1778 decree of *comercio libre* represented a broader effort to achieve this goal. Amplifying its 1765 predecessor, it effectively abolished the monopoly of Cádiz and reaffirmed Spain's trade monopoly, to the exclusion of other nations. Charles III declared that only '*comercio libre* can re-establish in my kingdoms agriculture, industry and population to their old vigor'.[52] In practice, however, free trade was not free of taxes as 3 per cent was charged on Spanish goods and 7 per cent on foreign ones.[53] The 1778 decree sought to accomplish four goals: first, to increase royal revenue from the Americas by boosting the overall volume of trade; second, to encourage the development of agricultural exports from the colonies which peninsular intermediaries could then introduce to Europe; third, to stimulate the growth of peninsular manufactures by opening colonial markets formerly obstructed by high taxes; and fourth, to reduce the pervasive contraband, which had led to the leakage of New Spain's silver to non-Spanish agents, resulting in an irreparable loss of Crown revenue.[54] In these respects, the new commercial code differed little from those of other maritime powers which similarly protected national shipping and impeded foreign penetration.[55]

Bourbon reformers were not embracing nascent economic liberalism, but rather pursuing standard mercantilist aims. Trade policy represented a concerted attempt to augment state revenues and to sideline contraband traders who exploited Spain's impotence to enclose its colonial commerce and to defend its porous borders. Far from 'free' to both the merchants who paid steep customs duties and the majority of Spaniards who remained excluded altogether from transoceanic commerce, the reformers sought to protect the ultramarine economy from foreign interference in order to expand the benefits derived from imperial trade for the Crown.[56]

Bourbon reformers strove to eliminate agents who undermined Crown authority and detracted from its much-needed revenues. For this reason, contraband traders of all nationalities were despised. Smugglers were disparaged as 'sloppy, evil men, who have nothing to lose ... who look with indifference upon religion, king and nation'. Peninsular commentators were shocked that the contrabandist 'enjoys the open protection of the governors and ministers. The coasts of Cartagena and Tierra Firme and Buenos Aires are the principal places where they unabashedly and insolently practice this wrong-doing'.[57] Regardless of whether administrators provided inducements to contraband trade, it continued unabated. As a *fiscal* of the *Audiencia* of Charcas (modern Bolivia) complained jocularly: 'in Italy, one expects to encounter a statue of St. Peter beneath the Column of Trajan; here it is quite common to find, near or even inside a chapel, a smuggler or a merchant'.[58] In the ensuing decades, Spanish policymakers adhered to the notion that prosperity, abundance, and low prices, not the vigorous enforcement and creation of new punitive measures, could eradicate smuggling. 'The abundance of goods and lower prices would slowly extinguish contraband', one anonymous commentator noted, 'for centuries we have combated this hydra with prohibitions, punishments, laws and coast guards. Have we made any advances? Not one'.[59] In practice, then, *comercio libre* was neither a panacea for smuggling nor a solution to the structural problems of belated industrialization and colonial undersupply.[60]

Far from a commitment to *laissez-faire, comercio libre* represented a belated effort to forestall colonial economic collapse, placate internal opposition, and stymie foreign interlopers. It was a drastic response to scarce resources and an attempt to harness the wealth of the rapidly expanding imperial periphery. The pragmatic, not dogmatic, approach of the Caroline reformers is suggested by the following anecdotes: *ad hoc* arrangements permitting limited trade with foreign colonies often continued side-by-side with regulations which strictly forbid such activity. In Caracas, for instance, from 1777 until independence, merchants enjoyed legal sanction to trade non-cacao products with foreign markets in exchange for slaves and currency.[61] The advent of free trade did not stem the tide of contraband trade. Commerce with foreign colonies accounted for 19 per cent of Venezuela's total trade in 1791 whereas trade with other Spanish colonies hovered at a mere 8 per cent.[62] Madrid was not ideologically wedded to low tariffs, one of the pillars of *comercio libre*. In 1792, the effective commercial tax rate in colonial trade was 15.7 per cent, but by 1805, after more than a decade of war, it had soared to 32.8 per cent.[63] The frequent exceptions made to rules and the chronic vacillation of policymakers suggests that increased revenue, military exigencies, and enhanced sovereignty animated the ultramarine commercial reforms of the late eighteenth century.

Madrid's policymakers experimented with combinations of freer trade and privileged companies in the hopes of discovering a formula for lasting prosperity. Valentín de Foronda defended the utility of monopoly companies under certain circumstances, but feared the reproach of 'the lovers of liberty of commerce [*libertad de comercio*], that enchanting deity to whom I give my adoration with all of my heart, who are exasperated by even hearing the word "privileged company."' More alarming, however, than the privileged company-free trade debate, for Foronda, was the present state of colonial commerce which had fallen into 'the hands of our rivals'. On this basis, he praised the Caracas Company whose administrative territory previously had languished as a 'dense forest when its cultivation was first undertaken', but had been transformed into a 'populated province with abundant cacao, tobacco and brimming with wealth'.[64]

But there was lively debate and the ideas articulated by Foronda were hotly contested. Francisco de Saavedra, the intendant of Caracas, expressed greater ambivalence, considering privileged companies as useful only at the inaugural stage of colonization and economic development. He analogized the efficacy of a company to a small child's use of a walker which 'up to certain age is necessary, but afterward harms the same end for which it was originally employed'.[65] The governor of Caracas in the 1790s went further still, claiming that the persistence of a monopoly company aroused 'the tedium, aversion and disaffection' of the populace who believed it to be 'the main source of their ills'.[66]

While these debates were important to the long-term fate of the colonial system, in the 1780s and 1790s proponents of trading companies still occupied influential governmental posts. Almodóvar's lobbying for a Philippines company, discussed in Chapter 1, found a receptive ministerial audience in the 1780s. They concurred that such an entity could 'renovate the bases of economic sustenance of colonial power'. It would accomplish this goal by 'supplying America with the goods of Asia in exchange for their surplus produce', a course of action 'dictated both by wise policy and prudent economics'. Such a company would soon be entrusted with a monopoly trade between those Pacific islands and the rest of Spain's empire, receiving a royal charter in 1785.[67]

Proponents of the company predicted that the archipelago was destined to become the 'emporium of Asian commerce', aiding Spain's balance of trade by substituting Asian products for those currently received from France, Germany, and Switzerland. The company also would become the exclusive supplier of African slaves in the Spanish Indies. Supporters argued that the merchant marine would flourish, paving the way for the traffic of African slaves, thus reducing dependence on European suppliers.[68] Since the company was formed out of the remnants, and took over the functions of, the defunct Caracas Company, it was granted the right to carry 40 per cent of Spain's exchange with Caracas as well, effectively excluding the colony from the *comercio libre* regime operating in the rest of the Caribbean until 1789.[69]

Free trade and privileged companies, then, existed side-by-side, and often overlapped, until the eve of Spanish American independence. Neither idea achieved unrivalled predominance. Many exceptions and exclusions were made by administrators in response to local exigencies. Though Spain never resembled Britain's 'ledger-book empire of ships, ocean routes, of naval bases and entrepôts',[70] Spanish policymakers experimented with a variety of approaches and ideologies whose apparent incoherence masked a consistent commitment to the increase of revenues and the concentration of power.

Bourbon reformers reached a tacit consensus that privileged companies were permissible, perhaps desirable, in the distant extremities of empire, such as the Philippines and Venezuela. Though potentially lucrative, the stretched Madrid treasury could not spare the enormous fixed costs that such endeavours entailed either in terms of subsidies to encourage migration, salaries for officials to administer (or soldiers to protect) the imperial periphery, or financial incentives to spur desirable economic activity. As José de Gálvez admitted in 1779, 'to supply all the troops, military supplies and fortifications that Spain and its colonies seem to require would be an impossible enterprise, even if the king of Spain might have at his disposition all the treasures, the armies and the storehouses of Europe'.[71] Ministers thus remained receptive to the intervention of quasi-state entities, including privileged companies, to do the work which restraints on royal personnel and finances precluded.

Closely linked to the imperial solvency and control over distant provinces was a related idea, also emerging from national chauvinism and mercantilist precepts. Self-sufficiency became a key rallying cry of reformers. The circulation of goods was merely one component of intra-imperial commerce. The supply of forced labour was a second, and mounting, concern for reformers committed to self-sufficiency and agricultural prosperity. The economic advances of the Danes, Dutch, English, and French were incorporated into an argument for a 'free slave trade principle'—the free importation of African slaves by Spaniards and foreigners alike—in the Spanish Atlantic World. 'If the prodigious spectacle of [foreign] prosperity should make us want the same thing for our possessions', a disgruntled governor of New Granada urged, 'we can do even better using the same methods which other nations followed', referring in particular to increasing the influx of slaves. Similar arguments were propounded by members of Madrid's Economic Society: 'it would be very easy and even an indispensable necessity, if Spaniards want to give their lands value, like the foreign nations have done, to introduce slaves that will cultivate them'.[72]

Madrid pursued self-sufficiency by reducing its dependence on competitor nations for the fundamental factors of production, including slave labour. The challenges inherent to this course of action are well illustrated by the paradox of its increasing dependence on African slave labour in the swiftly expanding imperial periphery (Cuba, New Granada, and Caracas) and its exclusive reliance on slave traders from rival European states. The rise of Cuba's sugar economy, in particular, was predicated on forced labour, guaranteeing a steady high demand for slaves. Between 1766 and 1771, the *Compañía Gaditano de Negros* brought 9,143 slaves to Cuba whereas between 1773 and 1779, 13,864 slaves were introduced, ghastly figures which do not account for the substantial clandestine supply, especially from Jamaica. Nor was the dramatic increase in slavery confined to Cuba. Between 1761 and 1810, 300,000 Africans were imported as slaves into Spanish America.[73]

There was, however, one major problem: Spain was prohibited under international law from directly engaging in the slave trade on the western coast of Africa. Under the Treaty of Alcáçovas (1479), Spain had renounced its right to establish outposts or factories in Africa. For this reason, the introduction of African slaves into its colonies had been conducted by other European powers. Spain was reliant on foreign nations for its slaves. The privilege of supplying slaves to Spain's colonies was called the *asiento* and was 'one of the most highly-coveted and bitterly-contested plums of international diplomacy'.[74] Under the terms of the Treaty of Utrecht, 1713, the *asiento* went to the British South Seas Company 'at a rate of 4,800 *piezas de India* [slaves] in each of the said thirty years'.[75] The War of Jenkins' Ear effectively ended this monopoly, but the problem of supplying enough slaves to meet the burgeoning demand, without deregulating the trade and opening it up to merchants from other European nations, had reached epic proportions.

Under the terms of the Treaty of San Ildefonso of 1778, brokered by the Duke of Almodóvar, Portugal ceded two islands off the Guinea Coast to Spain along with the right to use them as a base for the slave trade. Ministers entertained no fantasies of a vast African empire. The sole object of the acquisition of Fernando Po and Ano Bom, Count Floridablanca reminded the Brigadier Conde de Argelejos, leader of the expeditionary force sent to the islands, was neither to 'acquire possessions nor well-established settlements' but, 'with great cost and effort', to provide Spain with the 'commerce of [African slaves] which only we do not possess, for we need this trade more than any other nation'. All that was necessary to remedy this deficiency was 'the cession of some sovereign who possesses those rights ... without which all of the nations will resist our entrance, having forbidden us navigation in those seas'.[76] The Portuguese treaty, then, appeared to solve the problem for it would allow Spain to supply slaves to its American empire without recourse to foreign intermediaries.

The Crown planned to survey its new acquisitions and then establish an outpost from which to conduct the slave trade. The expedition began inauspiciously, however: Ano Bom turned out to be merely 'a small island with arid and sterile terrain', inconveniently located far from the coast. Fernando Po represented a more promising slave trade entrepôt, capable of supporting cultivation and located near the mouths of rivers leading into Africa's interior. The Spanish force complained bitterly, claiming that their nation had been tricked by Portugal in accepting the island, which they had believed to be pacified, well-fortified and self-sufficient.[77] One of the ranking members of the expeditionary force, Josef Varela y Ulloa, warned that 'whatever project is undertaken here will be very time-consuming, require a great number of workers and amount of materials, in addition to other assistance which is not to be found' in the Gulf of Guinea. He also observed additional 'great difficulties', not the least of which was the intransigent refusal of the indigenous people, who 'considered themselves free and independent', to recognize nominal Portuguese sovereignty, let alone its transfer to Spain. This situation, Varela y Ulloa feared, could not be resolved 'without employing force and spilling some blood'.[78] Unable to resort to violence due to meagre numbers and ammunition, a comical scene, which demonstrates the flexibility and flimsiness of the term 'sovereignty' in such colonial ventures, ensued:

> The Brigadier [Argelejos] proclaimed Your Majesty to be the Sovereign of Fernando Po, erecting on that isle the Spanish flag, which we saluted with seven cheers of 'Long Live the King'. Even though the instructions permitted me to further celebrate this event by firing three canon shots, it seemed to me a better decision to not make use of this permission, so that we should not terrorize the inhabitants who, even without this motivation, will leave this island now that we have arrived.[79]

Yet it was the Spaniards, not the inhabitants of Fernando Po, who departed ignominiously. Floridablanca responded angrily to their retreat, reiterating 'the object is not to conquer, nor to possess new lands, nor vassals (especially not of this variety), but solely to acquire posts which benefit the slave trade. Other nations, with fewer advantages and fewer rights, had 'acquired this object through 'hard work and constancy'.[80]

The expeditionary force debacle aside, foreign observers were unsurprised by Spain's failure to achieve self-sufficiency for structural reasons. As a French slave trader resident in Havana explained in 1781, 'there is inadequate infrastructure here for a direct [slave] trade', adding that beyond the sheer absence of 'necessary knowledge' to carry out such a scheme, aspiring Spanish American traders lacked the 'ships, mariners, credit, and desirable goods' required to succeed along the Guinea Coast.[81] This frustrated imperial venture was succeeded by other comparably failed schemes, including the Philippine Company's ill-fated effort to supply the Americas with a sufficient number of slaves to satisfy demand. While certain viceroys, most notably Caballero y Góngora in New Granada, openly defied the order from 1786 onwards, proponents of a 'free slave trade' rejoiced when a 1789 *real cédula*, which applied to Cuba, Santo Domingo, Puerto Rico, and Caracas, granted their long-frustrated wishes.[82]

The Crown, nevertheless, never forsook its fantasy of an entirely self-sufficient slave trade. A 1793 Royal Order sought to stimulate Spanish slave voyages by exempting them from export duties on goods shipped for this purpose from any port in Spain or the Indies. In a similar spirit, a 1794 statute authorized subjects who originally went to foreign colonies to acquire slaves to import agricultural machinery duty-free if they were unable to purchase the forced labour they initially had sought.[83] In 1796, the recently founded Havana *Consulado* enviously discussed the 'advantages' accrued by England and Portugal through their slave outposts off the West African coast. Yet even without such outposts, or at least effective exploitation of them, the number of Africans sold into bondage continued to crescendo, especially in Cuba, where 13,830 slaves were imported in 1802 alone.[84]

Just as the search for new sources of slave labour did not imply colonial economic prosperity, the creation of new institutions and the promulgation of new laws did not portend a successful overhaul of Spanish colonial administration. Retrograde ideas and interloping contrabandists represented but two of the restraints. The rampant corruption that corroded all public institutions was the most pervasive problem that slowed the implementation and undermined the efficacy of the Bourbon reforms. This phenomenon, of course, was not new. In the late 1640s, the Bishop of Puebla, Juan de Palafox, predicted that the 'proliferation of sins, cruelties and tyrannies' inevitably would result in colonial revolt. In their originally secret and privately circulated report describing the egregious abuses of government in Peru, written a century after Palafox's prophecy, Antonio de Ulloa and Jorge Juan recorded lurid stories of disreputable *corregidores* who flagrantly manipulated the tribute system, the *mita* and the *repartimiento de comercio*, all of which precluded the state's unified management over colonial society and economy.[85] The dismal situation was attributable partially to the fact that the highest-ranking posts were coveted for their potential illegal income, further exacerbated by the Crown's policy of raising revenue by selling and taxing bureaucratic posts. This mode of government paved the way for widespread corruption.[86]

In order to combat this corruption, the Bourbon reformers developed several major innovative policies to improve the management, revenue collection, and security of the Atlantic Empire. These innovations especially impacted the rapidly modernizing periphery, which they hoped to bring under more direct Crown control. The earliest, and perhaps most effective, change of policy was the formation of the *Intendant* system, a French invention transplanted in Spain originally in 1721 and re-introduced in 1749. Each intendant was responsible for the general administration of his respective province and wielded police powers, whose exercise was designed to revive the enervated colonial economy. The intendant significantly decreased the autonomy of the viceroy and was directly responsible to the Crown, thus making the implementation of Madrid's policies more direct. The modicum of success achieved by the centralizing measure on the peninsula prompted its extension overseas, initially in Cuba in 1764–5, and subsequently throughout Spanish America.[87] In Peru, for example, the benefits of improved management included reduced fraud and corruption in the collection of revenue, more strenuous efforts to compile economic and demographic data, and the modest development of public works.[88]

The intendancy presaged a grand revision of the basic administrative units of the empire. In 1776, the viceroyalty of the Río de la Plata was created, carved out of Peru, which was further truncated when Chile gained autonomy and was governed by its own Captain-General from 1778. By 1777, the half-dozen provinces along the northern coast of South America were refashioned into the *capitanía general* of Venezuela. In 1776, the northern part of New Spain was transformed into a virtually autonomous *comandancia general*, known as the Interior Provinces of New Spain. This reconfiguration coincided with a vast expansionist project as long-neglected borderlands were garrisoned, from Patagonia to Northern California. While they sprang from myriad local circumstances, these changes reflected the increased economic importance of the periphery, the Crown's desire to consolidate control over its ultramarine provinces at the expense of the older viceroyalties, and a new, vigorous approach to imperial defence.

The Bourbons also developed a new approach to the unsubdued indigenous populations of the periphery. Traditionally, the missions had taken the lead, pursuing conversion as a prelude to the fuller integration into colonial society and economy. The Spanish Crown became increasingly sceptical of ecclesiastical intentions, however, and sought to break missionaries' monopoly over the land and labour of mission Indians and, consonant with precepts of regalism, to reduce their responsibilities to the care of spiritual lives. The hostility towards the virtual autonomy of the Jesuit state in Paraguay, which led to their eventual expulsion from the Spanish empire in 1767, marked the advent of the new policy. The Crown subsequently sought to convert missions

into self-supporting parishes whose members would come under civil authority and lose the exemption from taxes, tithes, and other fees, thus making
them, as Felíx de Azara put it, both 'useful vassals and sociable men'.[89]

Smaller innovations also yielded tremendous benefits, particularly the
creation of the state-owned postal service, the *Correo Marítimo*, which greatly
improved communications between Spain and Havana (1765) and, subsequently, was extended to Buenos Aires (1767).[90] This postal service was cele-
brated as emblematic of the state's increased capacity to monitor its distant
possessions: 'an uprising in a remote province of a contiguous, active and
ambitious nation ... requires promptitude and shortness in the communication of news and orders'.[91] The post promised to improve communication
networks whose slowness had proved damaging in the Seven Years' War. In
establishing the postal service, Charles III's royal order explicitly recognized
and lamented the 'lack of frequent communication' which had occasioned
the 'delay in the compliance' with his wishes. The postal service, therefore,
heralded the beginning of 'regular contact' between the Old and New
Worlds.[92] It symbolized Caroline attempts to bridge the distance separating
scattered dominions, a pivotal step in bringing the far-flung parts of the realm,
which enjoyed varying degrees of *de facto* autonomy, under central control.

The reform of state monopolies, particularly of liquor, playing cards, and
tobacco led to the transfer of their administration from private contractors to
direct management by royal officials. In New Granada, for example, the Visitor
General unified the management of all levies in a new central office in Bogotá
to direct, coordinate, and account for revenue raised from these taxes.[93] A
closely related aim was the rationalization of fiscal administration. The collection of the tax receipts which financed the Armada de Barlovento, for instance,
was reorganized in order to conform to a 'general and uniform method'.[94]

Redrawing the boundaries of viceroyalties, the imposition of new taxes,
military overhaul, the creation of intendancies, and the reorganization of
the Council of the Indies all represented major breaks from past practice.
Spasmodic efforts towards freer trade, improved communications, and
streamlined administration, however, remained subordinate to the defensive modernization of Spanish America. This effort was marked by immense
fortification projects, the unification of civil and military authority, the
increase of soldiers stationed overseas, and policy innovations designed to
identify and protect newfound sources of wealth.[95] Their benign impact,
combined with a respite from acute conflict with other European powers
between 1763 and 1778, ushered in an era of unprecedented prosperity.

Enlightened governance on the imperial frontier: population, commerce, and agriculture

In addition to the specific administrative measures they devised, the architects
of imperial reform also wrestled with the questions of who should govern

and what constituted the background of the ideal colonial administrator. According to José de Gálvez, Creoles needed to be excluded entirely. He proposed a modification to the *audiencia* structure to prevent them from serving in their home *audiencia*, a measure aimed to dissipate the 'spirit of partiality' which he claimed dominated those bodies. He also recommended removing Creoles altogether from the upper ranks of the military, replacing them with 'commissioned [peninsular-born] officials of sound conduct and known disinterest, moreover, trained in the army, who will thereby know the importance of royal service and the conservation of their honor'. Creole administration of the colonial treasury, Gálvez complained, suffered from 'notable backwardness and embezzlement due to the absence of good administration'.[96] After his elevation to Minister of the Indies in 1776, Gálvez implemented elements of his vision, purging the *audiencias* of Creoles and replacing them with peninsular military officials.[97]

Not all high-ranking officials concurred that Gálvez's was the most efficacious means of improving administration or of securing Creole affection. In his farewell 1796 *relación* from New Granada, Viceroy Ezpeleta lamented that the terrible state of the colonies was due, in 'no small amount, to the ignorance of the viceroys in political and economic affairs'. Accustomed to 'the military spirit', they treated their subjects with 'more harshness than they would a regiment'. Instead, he argued, colonial bureaucrats should be chosen from the diplomatic corps, men who were 'perspicacious in matters relating to commerce and navigation'. Emulation played a central role in his rationale: Ezpeleta claimed that a diplomat's experience in 'advanced and industrious nations' would ensure that he would 'doubtless attempt to encourage the same ideas in America'. Furthermore, having observed firsthand the 'methods by which these nations extract great riches from their colonies', this new breed of administrators could 'raise Spain's empire to the same level of opulence' as its rivals. Men accustomed to 'observing usable roads, well-managed ports, easy navigation and flourishing agriculture' would respond to the desires of the 'sacred voice of humanity and the wellbeing of their people' to pursue similar projects in the viceroyalties which they governed.[98]

The second part of this chapter addresses the political attitudes and ideas of the administrators, the 'men-on-the-spot', who were responsible for enacting and enforcing Madrid's initiatives. The discussion will be confined largely to the Río de la Plata, Chile, and the greater Caribbean. In the 1760s and early 1770s, Buenos Aires, previously a 'backwater' and 'entrepôt for contraband', became a bastion of trade and was transformed into the 'fulcrum of a modernizing empire', its newfound importance epitomized by the creation of the Viceroyalty of the Río de la Plata in 1776.[99] Between 1767 and 1785, moreover, the civil bureaucracy of Buenos Aires swelled from four agencies employing 14 men to ten agencies with 125 employees.[100] Reforms in Chile undertaken during the *Visita General* during almost the same period (1778–86), animated by a similar spirit, aimed to create an efficient fiscal system and to endow the colony with new bureaucratic institutions—a *Tribunal de Minería*, a University, a *Consulado*—designed to strengthen Crown control.[101] The imperial periphery experienced rapid demographic growth as well: Chile's population jumped from 184,000 to 583,000 between 1775 and 1810 whereas Venezuela's rose from 330,000 to 780,000 between 1780 and 1800.[102]

This rapid expansion of the imperial periphery was overseen by a new breed of administrators. Though many hailed from military backgrounds, as Gálvez favoured, others were steeped in newer modes of thought, as Ezpeleta proposed. The political sentiments and attitudes of the ultramarine governing elite deserve examination. An analysis of their dispatches to superiors in Madrid provides a new and under-appreciated insight into 'enlightened absolutism', exploring the varied uses (and abuses) of new ideas in overseas administration. Previous historians have focused almost exclusively on the pronouncements of Madrid's policymakers. When they study colonial administrators at all, they tend to discuss the viceroy and neglect the lower-ranking officials who actually implemented policy. These often-ignored, yet vitally important, voices help to develop a more nuanced understanding of reform.

The majority of Spanish governors stationed at remote outposts had little time for, or inclination towards, abstract thought. Conditions were difficult and aroused complaints. Serving as an administrator on the periphery, a loquacious governor in provincial Chile complained, is 'a hard slavery, an unsupported and mortal task ... in such a destroyed and disfigured machine, closer to utter ruin than you can imagine'.[103] Such harsh conditions were not conducive to political thought even if such an inclination had existed in the first place. Often it did not and administrators remained interested chiefly in self-enrichment. Another Chilean governor requested exemption from the *alcabala*, sales tax, which he promised would serve as a 'new stimulus to dedication and to the defence and preservation' of the province.[104] Such requests were common and reflect the ethos of graft and sinecure-seeking which prevailed in the administrative ranks.

There were other colonial administrators, however, who professed to govern in accordance with loftier principles, merging the pursuit of 'the happiness of the people' with the 'advantages of the metropolis and the increased share for the king'.[105] Some administrators entertained grandiose visions of their colony's future development. From New Orleans, Ulloa wrote to Grimaldi that he aspired to found a 'new military and commercial city which could be established with more regular and managed customs, to diminish the [moral] laxity which reins in this kingdom ... and the excesses [here] would become moderated by the example of our city [and the] inhabitants would apply their energies to useful and advantageous activities'.[106] Yet even the highly regarded Ulloa never enjoyed the opportunity to construct such a utopia and was compelled to content himself soliciting minor and piecemeal changes from Madrid.

In official correspondence, however, administrators cloaked their frustration in the language of public happiness, improvement, and population growth. A subsequent administrator in Louisiana would claim that the 'primary and principal object which should be pursued is the foment of population within a short period of time ... it seems that the only thing that can bring this about is free commerce with the French colonies and with France'.[107] In many cases, including this one, such requests often sought to make *de jure* what already existed *de facto*.

Such an interpretation may produce the unintended consequence of distracting from what might be termed 'enlightened governance' on the imperial periphery. Sympathy for the plight of colonists was articulated in official correspondence, though it often borders on hyperbole. Lamenting Chileans' inability to export surplus commodities, the governor of Chiloé claimed that this 'unhappy people' and 'poor province' were like 'the inhabitants of Asia and Africa' who realize neither the 'extent of the iniquity nor the depth of the oppression from which they suffer'.[108] On the island of Trinidad, the chief administrator noted that Madrid's new policies 'calmed the spirits' of its inhabitants, who until then had 'seemed fully given up to chance', made them 'work more steadily', and encouraged 'rich people' in neighbouring colonies to emigrate in order to reap its advantages.[109] Such reports leave the impression that 'enlightened governance' was not merely fashionable, but reflected a more genuine shift of attitude towards responsible administration.

Administrators often lamented that they were incapable of implementing directives from Madrid. Their protests differed, however, from the famous 'I obey but do not execute' non-compliance apology which typified Spanish imperial administration from its inception. Reform projects were stymied, according to one provincial official in New Granada, by the inadequate size of the population: 'commerce, agriculture and population are like the three links, or rings of a chain which must be unified and connected ... but the basis of all prosperity always must be the increase of population and much more so in America where the primary object should be to give value to the great extension and fertility of its lands'.[110] Lacking prerequisite conditions, he argued, little could be accomplished. Meeting these minimal conditions was considered indispensable because, as a Crown official in Chile extrapolated, from 'the state of population and commerce the state of the arts may be easily inferred'.[111]

Population growth was depicted by colonial administrators as a panacea for other politico-economic ailments, and its absence was demonized as the 'true cause' of 'decadence'. The *Visitor General* of New Granada argued that it was merely necessary to 'respond to the problem of the lack of population' and 'put in motion internal traffic' to escape from this condition.[112] Other colonial officials thought the causal relation went in the opposite direction. The governor of Valdivia, Chile, for example, held that the 'great unhappiness, poverty and few inhabitants' was attributable to the failure of the territory to provide the 'species and fruits most necessary for the preservation of human life'.[113] To the extent that population and state power were correlated, Trinidad's governor advocated recruiting foreigners away from neighbouring islands or from more secure parts of Spanish America. Such a scheme would ensure 'increase at the expense of the rest of the enemy states'.[114]

Nevertheless, population growth was encouraged so long as the means employed did not contradict deep-seated values. A scheme to populate immense stretches of coastline in Guatemala called for the forced migration of gypsies, who 'live as vagrants' in Spain, in order to 'make them useful by interspersing them [in communities of] colonists'.[115] Gálvez rejected this proposal, as noted earlier in this chapter, maintaining that gypsies were unsuitable colonists, whose supposedly indolent habits would infect the existing colonists, instead of the other away around. Immigration had to guarantee the entry of morally sound new subjects: in Trinidad, a plan was hatched to admit Irish settlers who were 'active and docile' and whose 'industry and example undoubtedly will be a powerful influence to the emulation and activity which the current inhabitants lack ... they are less infected than the French with regards to the pernicious doctrines of modern philosophers'.[116] Population growth, like commerce, was never divorced from ideological factors.

If colonial administrators met some success in stimulating population growth, their efforts to foment commerce encountered further obstacles. Some officials contended that little intervention was needed: 'commerce asks for nothing but protection and liberty [*protección y libertad*]', one governor contended.[117] Other officials less enthusiastically embraced proto-liberal notions: Ulloa claimed that it was 'not possible to know whether a privileged company could flourish [in Louisiana] or not'.[118] Most administrators agreed that the expansion of commerce entailed facilitating the export of colonial products, regardless of their destination. 'To increase the commerce of this kingdom, which is in a deplorable state', New Granada's viceroy argued, in 1790, 'there is no more appropriate method than to facilitate the export of its products'.[119] This viceroy would have endorsed the intendant of Caracas's contention that there existed a correlation between commercial and agricultural growth: 'it is a political as well as natural axiom that, lacking commerce, agriculture should be considered destroyed. It is inaccurate declare that if one of these ceases to exist then the other can flourish'.[120]

Yet, however confidently they repeated such axioms, the 'men-on-the-spot' recognized, to a greater degree than their superiors in Madrid, the limit to the speed and scope of change that governmental action could produce in the ultramarine provinces. They accepted, some more reluctantly than others, that their actions were constrained by larger geographic, demographic, and economic forces. While still governor of Concepción, Chile, Ambrosio O'Higgins, future Captain-General of Chile and Viceroy of Peru, argued that in an 'open country', contraband was inevitable. However, smuggling could be reduced considerably if, like Cuba, Chile was granted the right to export some portion of its annual harvest to other parts of Spanish America, a change which would benefit Chileans, bolster other colonial markets, reduce contraband, and increase royal receipts.[121] In a similar spirit, Chiloé's governor endorsed the notion that the 'exit and easy sale or consumption of goods' was the 'chief care' of 'a politician who seeks to foment industry'.[122] Similar challenges were faced in the Caribbean. 'The continuous correspondence between [Trinidad] and all foreign [colonies]', its governor insisted, 'would satisfy reciprocal needs, [such as] the prompt exit of the harvest, early payment for produce, exactly what we currently practice and it is indispensable that it continue'.[123] While professing loyalty to official trade policy, colonial administrators recognized that compliance was impossible given the restraints imposed by local conditions.

In addition to acknowledging the limitations on state action, administrators noted that the widening chasm separating legally sanctioned commerce and what occurred in practice had reached absurd proportions, particularly during wartime. The scarcity of Spanish goods necessitated trade with merchants from neutral nations. In Caracas, 'more than an entire year passed without the arrival of even a single mailship. In a word, we are isolated'.[124] This situation, indeed, formed part of a broader trend of the declining number of ships from Spain caused by war with Britain: between 1793 and 1796, 138 ships entered Caracas's harbour, whereas only 50 entered between 1797 and 1800.[125] As shall be suggested in Chapter 4, it was the utter collapse of this mercantile system, revealed starkly by trade with neutral nations during times of war, which would lend force to Creole yearnings for independence from Spain.

Because commerce was subject to the vicissitudes of geopolitical conflict, colonial administrators shifted their gaze to agricultural improvement, an area less vulnerable to the whims of British smugglers.[126] Agricultural improvement inevitably involved slavery. As Trinidad's governor reported to the Minister of the Indies:

> agriculture is the thing that has elevated the islands of Barlovento to the state of splendor in which they are now found ... that caused their population to increase ... but these same lands, which have until now been the foundation of wealth, demand more labor every day ... the most essential thing is to speed the acquisition of slaves.[127]

The growing reliance on slave labour, particularly in the greater Caribbean, appeared with greater frequency in gubernatorial correspondence towards the end of the eighteenth century. This occurred, in part, because of the demands of increasingly powerful colonial interests.

Cuban planters, most notably, desperately wanted new slaves. Seeking to mitigate the potential for social calamity, one influential observer contended that a rapid influx of slaves would not trigger unrest, claiming that the likelihood of revolt was 'quite remote and very easy to avert'. He declared that, under 'our system, obedience is surer than in the English one' since it has 'fewer principles favourable to liberty'.[128] As sugar's preponderance in the Cuban economy increased, colonial officials unabashedly recognized its reliance on slave labour. More than an 'efficacious means', it was portrayed as the 'only chance' for the Cuban economy. Without African slaves, Ezpeleta conceded, 'there cannot be agriculture' and without that, neither 'happy inhabitants nor comfort nor wealth' would be found in Cuba. Faced with such forced labour scarcity, planters could only extract 'a hundredth part' of their island's wealth.[129]

The embrace of enlightened ideas, then, never could upset the stability of Spanish America or detract from revenue collection. In 1802, Caracas's intendant informed Madrid of the 'disturbances' in Saint Domingue and throughout the French Caribbean. He maligned the 'despotic hand' of Toussaint l'Ouverture and his 'artificial criminal system, destroyer of societies, the observance of laws and supreme governments'. Yet while dismissing the 'pretexts of love of country [*patria*] and adhesion of humanity' as 'the veil of usurpation poorly concealed', the governor conceded the 'danger' which this 'pernicious and insolent example' posed to 'all of the colonial dominions' of the European empires. He especially feared attempted 'emigration' by slaves 'attracted and corrupted by false promises'.[130]

By 1800, then, the themes dominating the correspondence of imperial administrators resembled the demands of the most powerful colonial mercantile and agrarian groups. This phenomenon, which shall be examined further in Chapter 4, should not be attributed to the fact that they represented the interests of these classes, but rather that mutual advantage was recognized. Colonial governors enforced the regalist-inspired policies promulgated in Madrid, but came to understand that the end to which they were designed would require new means. Colonial merchants and planters benefited from increased wealth while the Crown received enlarged revenues to support the voracious fiscal–military state.

Case study: governance and reform in the Spanish Caribbean

When it surrendered to Lord Albemarle's forces after a protracted amphibious siege in 1762, Havana boasted nearly 40,000 inhabitants, the third most populous city in Spanish America, behind Mexico City and Lima, and its most strategic port. In the year of its capture, Campomanes referred to the city as 'the bulwark of our America'. Albemarle had been instructed to make a 'speedy and effectual impression of the Spanish colonies in the West Indies' and then to proceed to Florida or VeraCruz, but the stubborn resistance of the *Habaneros* slowed the execution of his design, limiting him to the conquest of Havana.[131] Waiting confirmation of this debacle at his country palace in Aranjuez, Charles III wrote to Tanucci, 'I strongly hope that God will help me also in those parts' of the empire.[132]

Fate was unkind and Havana's capture devastatingly revealed Spain's maritime weakness and Britain's naval supremacy. In the ensuing peace settlement, Britain stripped Spain of Florida while France transferred Louisiana to Spain as compensation for its ill-fated adherence to the Family Compact. In accepting Florida, British administrators recognized that 'Spain had no revenue from Florida', but blamed the 'indolence of the Spaniards [which] affords but few instances of what the soil and climate are capable of producing'. Furthermore, they recognized the 'proximity to Havana' for contraband during peacetime and its 'great utility in distressing His Majesty's enemies during war'.[133]

Precisely because they concurred with their British counterparts concerning the Gulf of Mexico's military value, Madrid's policymakers overlooked Louisiana's dubious economic value and embraced it as a frontier province or quasi-borderland, a protective barrier against British ambitions.[134] Florida, according to Arriaga, was 'not a profitable dominion, but neither is it excessively dispensable' whereas 'Louisiana did not produce a considerable utility during the time that France possessed it'. Florida and Louisiana, in his view, would not 'merit greater defense than the Island of Margarita, Trinidad and many other possessions', for they would only be 'taken by enemies in wartime and it will be necessary to recover them in the subsequent peace'.[135] Cuba was quite different, however, for it was considered to be among Spain's most valuable colonies.

Contemporary scholars based in Cuba reject the British occupation as a historical watershed.[136] Prior to the 1959 Cuban Revolution, however, the British occupation was interpreted as *the* key event which heralded the fall of colonial commercial monopoly and the advent of *comercio libre*, the 'source of the island's prosperity' in the subsequent one hundred years.[137] The contemporary consensus, among historians working outside of Cuba, regarding the nine-month occupation is that it proved 'more beneficial than harmful'.[138] While post-1959 Cuban accounts of this period rightly direct scholarly attention to the reforms and innovations occurring before 1762— the creation of an arsenal (1725), the founding of the University (1728) and the shift of the Armada from Vera Cruz to Havana (1748)[139]—they also obscure the capture's significance in the eyes of Spanish policymakers who strategically assessed Cuba's military and productive capacities in the context of the entire Caribbean region.

In the wake of Britain's withdrawal, Esquilache's government sent Alejandro O'Reilly to survey the damage wrought and to recommend policies for

Cuba's renewal. O'Reilly, however, reported that the British conduct, far from deleterious, had demonstrated 'the infinite advantages' possible from the 'expansion of commerce', marvelling at the wealth accrued by the British during their nine-month occupation.[140] In a report submitted three years later, Agustín Crame, the engineer who accompanied O'Reilly, bluntly stated that the Albemarle's conquest had 'opened [Cuban] eyes', awakening its inhabitants from a 'remarkable ignorance'. Crame clearly was referring to the 4,000 African slaves introduced during the British period, a figure which dwarfed the total number of slaves sold into bondage there during the preceding five years, and who had supplied the forced labour necessary for the sugar industry's take-off.[141] Other metropolitan voices concurred: Cuba's 'commerce would increase if it enacted policies like those of the English in the nine months that they were masters of but a single port ... if Spain were to continue this policy, there would be considerably less clandestine trade introduced in the island'.[142] While deploring the temporary loss of Havana, Crown officials discerned its benefits and urged that certain British policies should be retained.

Though O'Reilly's report praised Cuba's 'great fertility' and prospects for 'advancement', it also warned that the island's current tax revenues would fail to defray the expense entailed by an expanded army and marine, new fortifications, and a reformed administration of justice. O'Reilly observed that Cuba's 'slowness' was attributable to 'the absence of justice, the scarcity of [African slaves] ... the total lack of commerce to trade surplus products'. These problems would dissipate gradually, O'Reilly predicted, with the expansion of Cuba's wealth and he argued that the sugar industry's development was, by far, the most important consideration, 'meriting the full protection of the King'. Though its 'quality was much better than that of the Portuguese, English and French', Cuban production costs remained higher due to the abundance of slaves in those other colonies and high customs duties on Cuban products.[143] O'Reilly believed that a semi-liberalized system of trade would undercut contraband, stimulate economic growth, fortify the treasury, and underwrite a sizeable military presence.[144]

Such sentiments hardly constituted an epiphany. Since 1741, Cuban sugar had struggled to penetrate the Spanish, let alone European, market due to foreign, especially Brazilian, competition, the shortage of ships and the inherent impediments of the galleon and *flota* systems. In 1760, for example, Cuba annually produced a mere 5,500 metric tons of sugar. Its Caribbean neighbours, Saint Domingue and Jamaica, produced 56,646 and 39,841 metric tons, respectively.[145] Cuba was the 11th ranking sugar producer in the Americas, behind not only Jamaica and Saint Domingue, but also Dutch Guiana, Guadaloupe, and Barbados.[146] Imperial rivalry and profit motive often proved indistinguishable and, on the cusp of the nineteenth century, colonial officials professed that their 'ultimate aim' was not only to 'favor commerce and agriculture' and to promote the 'happiness' of the colonists, but also to 'make [Cuba] preponderant among the neighboring foreign colonies'.[147] Surrounded by formidable, hostile potentates, colonial officials and subjects confronted the means by which these goals could be achieved, a debate which led to a revaluation of the Spanish empire's restrictive trading system.

For this reason, Cuba's stagnant population growth preoccupied numerous reformers. O'Reilly's report diagnosed its meagre size as an obstacle to development and called for the recruitment of non-Spanish settlers whose 'industry and diligence' would buoy Cuba's efflorescence. He pointed to the British practice in recently ceded Florida which had 'more foreigners than subjects ... [Britain] has brought Germans to Pensacola and will continue to do so until [the colony] flourishes'. Population distribution posed as much of a problem as its scarcity, and the cities of Nueva Filipinas (modern-day Pinar del Río), Mariel and Manzaniello were founded to anchor sparsely populated and strategically vital areas after 1750.[148] The agricultural transformation envisaged stalled due to Cuba's 'lack of manpower' which rendered it necessary, 'before all else, to foment population'.[149] In spite of this acute need, Cuban population discourse rarely was race-neutral, and the priority remained the enlargement of Cuba's white population. This is suggested by an official policy that facilitated the emigration of white families, including 4,000 Spaniards resident in Santo Domingo, dislocated by the conflict which culminated in the Haitian Revolution between 1795 and 1808. 'It is of the utmost importance to the happiness and security of this island', a member of the *Consulado* argued, 'to increase its population with white families that might be brought from Santo Domingo'.[150]

Regardless of the harshness of their methods in domestic affairs, the correspondence of colonial officials in the decade following the Seven Years' War is saturated with aversion for international hostility and imbued with the hope that Spain could strengthen its military force during a peaceful interlude. This attitude was manifest even at the highest levels of colonial government and articulated by the most belligerent officials. Given British designs, Esquilache told the architect of Cuba's reform, the Count of Ricla, that he was 'persuaded that the precautions necessary to fortify the most exposed outposts should not be delayed'.[151] O'Reilly described his 'infinite satisfaction' with the 'amicable' settlement reached with Britain to his friend, and future viceroy of New Spain, Antonio Bucareli. 'Each year we will be in a better state', he wrote, 'the plazas and fortifications and troops improve daily'. If several years without war ensued, he predicted, Spain would possess the capacity to 'counteract a state as powerful' as Britain and to defend its 'vast and distant dominions'.[152]

Cuba possessed certain advantages which made it an ideal laboratory for accelerated reform. These advantages included a social structure, composed of a small, homogenous Creole elite dependent on peninsular manufactures, an uncomplicated economic structure, centred primarily on tropical produce, and the notable absence of an indigenous population. The organs of Spanish authority, firmly established since the sixteenth century, were a captain-general, responsible for military matters, and a governor, who oversaw the maintenance of public order and overall police functions. The primary innovation, made in response to O'Reilly's report, was the nomination of an intendant responsible for boosting royal receipts, eliminating fraud and contraband, and administering a wide array of military expenditures.[153]

Some observers, nevertheless, remained unconvinced that the proliferation of public offices would propel economic growth, let alone enhance the island's security. On the contrary, many commentators urged less public interference in Cuban economic life. To a greater extent than O'Reilly, Crame was enamoured of freer trade and contended that diminished government oversight would not induce lapsed political loyalty. As he phrased it, 'never have I heard of a prosperous people rebelling, [because] men in all places love their happiness'.[154] The Crown heeded Crame's advice, incorporating his insights into new policies. It would be inaccurate to exaggerate, however, the degree to which such reforms produced substantive departure from earlier practices. Creoles chronically complained that 'regulatory laws were created at a certain time and under circumstances which have not remained the same. They now require a reform, even if they were excellent and pertinent in the sixteenth century when American was discovered'.[155] Out of this dissatisfaction, a consensus emerged concerning commercial policy. Following the 1765 *comercio libre* decrees, which effectively sanctioned *de jure* the less-restricted commerce enjoyed *de facto* during the occupation, *Habaneros* lamented the 'pure inaction' which caused 'agriculture to remain backward'.[156]

The Caroline reforms met indubitable success in Cuba, even if the spike in revenue—almost 60 per cent between 1765 and 1773—is attributable mainly to merchants' reporting previously withheld receipts.[157] Mercantile growth paralleled the sugar industry's takeoff. Between 1760 and 1792, Cuba's production increased three-fold while the revolution that engulfed Saint Domingue augured further market opportunities.[158] The sudden nature of this change deserves emphasis. In the mid-1750s, Cuba was a settler community of small-scale agricultural enterprises. As late as 1774, the total population of *La Isla* did not exceed 171,620. Most crucially, the injection of capital for the construction of new fortifications—particularly Havana's massive San Carlos de la Cabaña, which still guards the approach to the harbour—enriched Havana's merchants, providing them with the capital necessary to finance the burgeoning sugar industry. Between 1770 and 1790, large-scale agriculture triumphed and the size of the average *ingenio* expanded from 134 to 670 acres.[159] The implementation of the *alcabala*, however, which eventually would account for more than 40 per cent of tax receipts generated on the island, never produced revenue sufficient to defray the full costs required for the veteran garrison, militia, and improvements to fortifications.[160] The spectacular expansion of the neighbouring Mexican mining economy, however, spared Cuba the dilemmas a shortfall would have precipitated, permitting Madrid to transfer massive subsidies from VeraCruz to Havana to defray the costs of projects which the island's own fiscal infrastructure could not support.[161]

Without commercial and fiscal reform, nothing could abate the illegal trade with foreigners which drained Spain's prospective revenue. Controlling, or at least reigning in, rampant contraband constituted a chief administrative objective, but, in private epistles to Esquilache, Conde de Ricla acknowledged that he would 'forever insist that illicit commerce will survive so long as its legal counterpart does not expand'. The collusion of colonial officials with smugglers and high tariffs on imported goods constituted additional barriers to the elimination of contraband.[162] Towards this goal of profitability, Madrid showered the region with beneficial legislation, including permitting foreign iron machinery to enter duty-free, liberalized the African slave trade, and freed the smaller ports of numerous fiscal constraints.[163]

If Cuba was a Bourbon success, Louisiana and Florida fared less well. Louisiana's governor, Antonio de Ulloa, predicted that 'it is conceivable that the commerce the French currently enjoy here will not continue under our rule. Sharing a frontier with the English will require much at every instant to combat them, spending great sums and employing many military men, who could serve in other places'. Notwithstanding this challenge, he pledged to 'maintain this country and govern with gentleness and sweetness'.[164] Complicating this intention, Ulloa revealed, were British machinations on the frontier: 'our neighboring nation is ambitious of glory and territory; its intention is to command and extend unlimited commerce everywhere: Louisiana is a short-term object for its ambition; [therefore] the conservation and defence of this colony must be the goal of our government'.[165] From the outset of his administration, then, defensive considerations were the chief objective.

Across the border in British West Florida, governor George Johnstone strove to convince his superiors in London that Pensacola could become the 'seat of extensive commerce within a few days' sail of the richest cities in the world ... [and] bids fair to be the emporium of the New World'. Johnstone audaciously sought to persuade Ulloa that, notwithstanding the regulations prohibiting trade between the British and Spanish empires, their two provinces should strive to establish 'reciprocal assistance ... unmingled with any of the jealousies which have often infected neighboring states'.[166]

Ulloa politely ignored these overtures, but noted in official correspondence with Madrid that Spanish Louisiana could be flooded by British American commerce. With preservation and defence as the foremost goals of his administration, stabilization through military fortification was Ulloa's chosen formula. As he warned Grimaldi, 'if these projects are not undertaken, the colony will remain defenseless ... a nation like England, ambitious of conquests, seeks to be the sole arbiter of the Mississippi'.[168] Responding to Ulloa's fears and precautionary measures, Grimaldi sympathized with the 'difficulties which have occurred', but clarified that 'the king is neither disposed to maintain large armed forces there, nor to construct large fortifications; instead, he believes that the population and its interests will constitute its best defence. For this reason, a species of liberty of commerce has been permitted that no other American colony enjoys, and the king is convinced that this measure alone will enable our goals to be realized'. In Madrid's view, costly military defences were unnecessary for a colony which possessed modest economic value. By permitting freer trade, policymakers reckoned, the profitability of smuggling could be undermined. Unable to comply with this policy directive, Ulloa signalled that Louisiana would perish unless its commerce with France was 'left entirely free'. The inhabitants 'cannot subsist', he confessed, and would 'seek recourse with the English ... [and] it will be easy for that nation to expand its settlements' up to the border of New Spain. The less regulated commerce offered by Madrid was deemed inadequate to ameliorate the situation. Though Ulloa played on Madrid's greatest fears—colonial depopulation, British mercantile advantage, and the strategic vulnerability of New Spain—his pleas went unheeded. The austere measures implemented by Ulloa triggered an uprising in New Orleans, subsequently crushed by O'Reilly, who was granted 'extensive powers' to overhaul the province's administration. In strident fashion, he imposed traditional Spanish legal institutions, extended Louisiana's trade with Cuba while cracking down on British contraband, established a militia, and reorganized land grant procedures.[168]

In the wake of the uprising against Ulloa, significant metropolitan debates ensued concerning the utility of Louisiana's retention as a colony. Two influential ministers unequivocally proposed its recession to France, provided the impossibility of its further transfer to any rival nation. A third official disagreed, arguing for the symbolic necessity to 'repress whatever intent against what is due to his Majesty', regardless of the wayward colony's ultimate fate. Conde de Aranda contended, however, that it was 'indispensable to maintain [Louisiana] at all costs'. Regardless of its potential fertility and economic viability, he argued, the 'principle reason' for its retention was its extension of New Spain's border to the Mississippi River, 'a natural and recognized frontier', thus forming a 'unmistakable barrier' with Britain's colonies.[169] Aranda's reasoning carried the day, but subsequent measures, however, failed to resolve the crisis that threatened Louisiana's survival, prompting impassioned pleas for a dramatic shift in policy:

The colony will return to being a desert, overturning all of the advantageous projects and privileges which have been conceded to transform it into a barrier between British America and the Mexican empire. Spanish

merchants are scared away by the continuous losses that they suffer here
and are attracted by pleasing visions of encountering more secure profits
on the coasts of Peru, Chile and the banks of the Río de la Plata. This
province needs either to maintain contraband trade or else to suffer
depopulation.[170]

On the imperial periphery, therefore, trade rules remained more flexible than
in the more lucrative core colonies. Even after repressing the rebellion in New
Orleans, O'Reilly admitted that Louisiana could not subsist without illicit commerce. He argued that freer communication between New Orleans and Havana
would bring mutual advantages: timber for the construction of naval ships, for
example, could come from Louisiana.[171] The Minister of the Indies recognized
that commerce was the 'only available measure to re-establish public happiness', but this conviction did little to promote the colony's development.[172]

If Louisiana proved more of a burden than a bounty, Spanish fortunes in
Florida were even more dismal. Abbé Raynal mused that Spain had neglected Florida, because it discovered neither the fountain of youth nor gold
there. British observers disagreed and asserted that Florida's fertility, combined with the 'same latitude as Persia', promised that the 'colony would
raise some similarly valuable commodities, in particular silk'. They approv-
ingly heralded that 'both the Floridas are in climate better adapted to such
cultivation than any other colony upon the continent'. Accordingly, these
same enthusiasts predicted, 'numbers will never be wanting to settle countries, where the immediate subsistence from the soil so certain'.[173] Spain's re-
annexation of the lower Mississippi Valley in 1781, coupled with the virtual
elimination of the British menace in North America after 1783, encouraged
some Spaniards to share Raynal's appraisal. 'Louisiana', one official declared,
is 'destined by Nature to become the most powerful and fertile province of
America'.[174]

The Floridas and Louisiana, however, never were indispensable to Spanish
designs. According to British sources, even their champion, Count Aranda,
routinely offered them in exchange for Gibraltar in negotiations with
Britain, remarking that they were not 'limbs of Spain', a designation he
reserved for Cuba, Puerto Rico, and South America.[175] The re-acquisition of
Florida in the peace settlement of 1783 provoked oscillating optimism and
pessimism in the administrators appointed to govern it: 'East Florida has
been uncared for for many years and not very much is known about it, nor
is it considered to have much strategic value'.[175] Several years after the new
trade regulations had taken effect, conditions had not improved dramatically
in Florida: 'there is no commerce here, no agriculture ... no money circulates
and there is no stimulus to industry'.[177] Some commentators argued freer
trade had been detrimental: 'the extension of [less restricted] commerce,
more than liberating, has sown disorder'.[178] By 1791, however, Spain had yet
to ameliorate Florida's and Louisiana's predicament while the persistence of

older problems, and the tedious reiteration of earlier proposals for reform, fostered mounting desperation:

> I believe that it would be advantageous to concede this colony complete liberty of commerce with foreign nations ... in a country naturally inclined to contraband, it is necessary to close all of the doors to clandestine greed and to open wide the doors of legitimate commerce. In this manner, this land will achieve a level of commerce which corresponds to its capacity.[179]

But such conviction rarely prompted metropolitan authorities to act decisively and policy proceeded spasmodically. Governance in Louisiana and the Floridas, in one prominent historian's judgement, was an 'utter failure' insofar as it aimed to render those colonies it profitable to Spain, to prevent contraband and to foment a large and loyal population.[180] Cuba benefited from considerable largesse to be sure, but its population and agriculture had begun their prodigious growth before the inauguration of the Bourbons reforms.

A more satisfactory explanation situates policy in the Gulf of Mexico in both regional and hemispheric context. In Chile, for example, the fiscal reforms and administrative restructuring, both of which stimulated growth in Cuba but failed to stir slumbering Florida, created corporations and layers of bureaucracy which previously were nonexistent, yet it did not produce the result heralded by reform.[181] One exasperated official called for the overhaul of the colonial system. In order for reform to succeed, he believed, it would be 'necessary to overcome the laws and the entire system of government in these dominions'.[182] His frustration differed little from his counterparts in Madrid. 'Our experience', Gardoqui wrote, 'should oblige us to shift and follow an entirely new path ... when a nation has no capacity to trade, all attempts at reform become useless'.[183] At both ends of the Bourbon era, and on both shores of the Atlantic, from north to south, from the highest to the lowest echelons of power, ministers and merchants bemoaned the decadence which fettered the state. The prosperity envisaged by the architects of reform was slowly coming into being, but the state's capacity to harness this growth remained incomplete.

This chapter analysed the theory and practice of Bourbon reform on the imperial periphery. Population, commercial and administrative policies in the less developed regions of Spain's American empire were studied, revealing connections between debates concerning colonial affairs and the themes addressed in Chapter 1 and Chapter 2. Above all, this chapter sought to show how the revised notion of state power, derived from regalism, was applied to ultramarine policy. The assertion is not that this application was effective in practice, but rather that policymakers operated in an intellectual milieu influenced by the tenets of regalism, the insights of political economy, and the demands of keeping pace with international rivals.

The present chapter also described the ideas and attitudes underpinning reform from both metropolitan and local administrative perspective, in an effort to complement traditional scholarly accounts of institutional change which focus, almost exclusively, on the policy which emanated from Madrid. Examination of local officials' correspondence with their metropolitan superiors suggests that policy was not a process of commands received and implemented faithfully by provincial administrators. Local exigencies, the inapplicability of certain policies due to local circumstances, and the impact of personal preferences conspired to frustrate Madrid's Bourbon intelligentsia.

Chapter 4 carries this analysis one step further. It recounts and analyses how the Bourbon reforms were received, and responded to, by Creole landowning and mercantile elites. To no institutions were commerce, population, agriculture, and public happiness more crucial than the colonial *Consulados* and Economic Societies, whose rise and impact on policy are examined in the next and final chapter.

4
Colonial Elites and Imperial Governance

This chapter examines the main ideas which animated the intellectual and political activities of the *Consulados* and Economic Societies in three major cities of Spanish America—Buenos Aires, Santiago de Chile, and Havana—between 1785 and 1810, though some attention is devoted to Caracas, Cartagena de Indias, and VeraCruz as well. *Consulado* documents, in particular, provide insight into the colonial response to the Bourbon reforms and suggest how policymaking within an absolutist empire remained subject to, and restricted by, complex negotiation and compromise between the metropolitan decision-makers and the elites of Spanish America.

These elites, operating in state-sanctioned civil society institutions, did not pursue independence from Spain. Initially, at least, they sought licensed privilege and moderate, incremental reform within the structures of Old Regime. Working through the *Consulados* and Economic Societies, the intelligentsias of the imperial periphery shaped metropolitan objectives and solidified their socio-economic pre-eminence. Ultimately, but by no means immediately, the limited self-determination exercised in *Consulados* enhanced Creoles' sense of belonging to a separate, perhaps imagined, political community and helped to incubate a vibrant civil society in the primordial polities that replaced the defunct Spanish empire after 1808.[1]

At mid-century, however, this ultimate result was far from easily envisaged or anticipated. In their *Voyage to South America* (1748), Antonio de Ulloa and Jorge Juan derided the 'innate sloth and indolence' of the Americans which prevented them from 'cultivating the gifts of Nature'.[2] They bemoaned the attitudes and institutions which, they maintained, corroded the sinews of the expanding colonial state. Such disparagement of the New World and its inhabitants, both indigenous and Creole, was symptomatic of a broad, pervasive discourse of civilization and barbarism in eighteenth-century Europe.[3]

Yet in spite of the low regard in which they were held in metropolitan circles, Bourbon reformers recognized that the flora, fauna, mines, and men of Spanish America were instrumental to their geopolitical ambitions. Since the sixteenth century, Madrid had colluded with selected elites in colonial society in order to establish and maintain effective control. As a result, Creoles had gained access, especially between 1640 and 1760, to decision-making positions within the American bureaucracy, though this was an informal rather than an institutionalized arrangement.[4]

From 1760 until 1780, as the first three chapters of this book have sought to describe, royal reformers reversed course and sought to fashion subservient colonies out of what had once been considered equal and integrated parts of the Spanish Crown. Armed with regalist precepts of governance and deep-seated antipathy for corporate privilege, the Bourbon reformers sought to demolish the autonomy of the American elites, severely restricting their right to hold office and tightening peninsular control over colonial trade.[5] They believed that these measures would produce economic growth which, in turn, could be siphoned to meet the burgeoning requirements of the Spanish state. Building on limited victories over privileged corporations, including the Church, as described in Chapter 2, Bourbon reformers sought to deprive the *Consulados* of Cádiz, Lima, and Mexico City, obstacles to a more powerful state, of the stranglehold they collectively exercised over colonial commerce. The successive free trade decrees, especially those of 1765, 1778, and 1782, and the creation of privileged trading companies in which the Crown invested heavily were among the measures devised to undercut the entrenched mercantile oligarchies and to make the Spanish empire more uniformly prosperous.[6]

In spite of its growing prosperity of the late eighteenth century, Bourbon attempts to raise revenue through administrative and fiscal centralization helped to spark widespread disaffection and resistance throughout Spanish America.[7] Creoles, now deprived of the ancient liberties which they believed that they possessed by natural right, continued to conceive of themselves as members of a composite monarchy at a time when this notion had become anathema to Crown.[8] In the wake of the revolts of the 1780s, the Bourbon reformers shifted strategy and recognized that metropolitan government must at least placate, and perhaps collaborate with, discontented and restless colonial elites.[9] This awareness became acute in the late 1790s as the wars sparked by the French Revolutionary Wars triggered an imperial crisis. The combined force of internal resistance and external threats did not dissolve Bourbon contempt for privileged corporations and semi-autonomous provinces. It did, however, compel compromise, bargaining, and mutual concessions.[10]

In the 1780s and 1790s, both Crown reformers and political writers attempted to envisage a new relationship between the peninsular and ultramarine kingdoms which, in spite of the ruptures caused by global conflict, would mollify Creoles and retain for Madrid the advantages of dominion. 'America', the enlightened reformer Victorián de Villava prophesied in 1797, 'due to its size, its distance and great wealth, is not naturally governed from Europe'. He proposed a re-organisation of colonial government on a federalist model, the dismantlement of the viceroyalties, and the empowerment of Creole-dominated *Audiencias*. Through decentralization and refashioned administrative institutions, Villava suggested, the dissolution of the Spanish empire could be delayed, if not averted.[11] Other officials rejected the voluntary dismemberment of empire, but acknowledged the urgent need to 'tighten the bonds' uniting the peninsula with America in order to 'preserve perpetually their union'.[12] Creole loyalty could be fostered, another reformer proposed, by 'transplanting' young men from America to the Iberian Peninsula, reserving scholarships in the *colegios* for them, and, ultimately, employing them in tribunals.[13] The Crown thus embraced limited concessions and endeavoured to reinvigorate attenuated cultural bonds in order to guarantee the security and to promote the longer-term prosperity of its American empire.

Yet more sceptical commentators failed to accept the logic by which better governed ultramarine provinces and cultivated fondness for Spain would satiate those American subjects dissatisfied with the overall frameworks of commerce and politics which overwhelmingly favoured the metropole. One political writer mocked Madrid for treating Spanish America like a 'sheep that should be affectionate for cutting its wool and lapping up its milk'.[14] As a particularly candid colonial administrator conceded, on the eve of the French Revolution, government policy could achieve little with a 'small population, miniscule industry, and limited agricultural activity'.[15] The ultimate objective, then, became the economic development of the colonies, a goal bound to satisfy potentially recalcitrant mercantile and agrarian elites. This wealth, in turn, eventually could be harnessed to further the Crown's geopolitical objectives.

Spain's strenuous effort to control the flow of precious metals, curb contraband, and implement new revenue-enhancing mechanisms thus led to innovative alliances with American elites on the imperial periphery which stressed mutual interest. The Crown devolved a small degree of authority to new *Consulados*, Creole-controlled administrative and deliberative bodies, in the rapidly developing fringes of the empire. It empowered new elites on the expanding periphery, attempted to disempower those entrenched in the core colonies of Peru and New Spain, and simultaneously bolstered its own objectives in the Old World and the New.

As war crippled Spain's oceanic commerce during the incessant wars against France (1793–6) and, subsequently, against Britain (1796–1802, 1804–8), the Crown increasingly would depend on these nascent civil society institutions[16]—which shared its goal of greater prosperity—to stave off the atrophy and, ultimately, the collapse of its trade regime.[17] The requirements of revenue and imperial defence, then, softened traditional regalists' hostility towards corporate privilege and permitted alliances based on mutual interest to develop.[18] Colonial elites, for their part, enthusiastically cooperated with the Bourbon state and contented themselves with the exercise of licensed privilege and moderate, incremental reform within a revivified, socio-economically stable Old Regime.[19] Through nascent civil society institutions, they participated in the reform process and influenced both the formulation and implementation of the commercial and agricultural policy. This collaboration, marked more by cooperation than conflict, prefigured what contemporary sociologists now describe as 'state-society synergy'; that is, a situation in which civic engagement strengthens state institutions which, in turn, foster an environment conducive to civic engagement.[20]

The dynamic imperial periphery enticed Bourbon reformers with its potential windfall revenues for the Crown. Since material betterment both would permit Spain to better realize its fiscal–military ambitions and mollify restless colonial elites, symbiotic collaboration proved irresistible.[21] Indeed, the 'dismal' situation lamented by Ulloa in the 1740s had metamorphosed remarkably a few decades later. In 1781, the intendant of Caracas reported that the Creoles 'today are in a very different state than that of some years ago. They have been enlightened greatly in a short time. The new philosophy is making much more rapid progress here than in Spain'.[22] By all accounts, the late colonial period witnessed the efflorescence of scientific, literary, and academic culture in Spanish America.[23] Scientific and botanical expeditions, patronized by the Crown, multiplied (at least 28 embarked between 1777 and 1807), leading Alexander von Humboldt to remark with admiration that 'no European government had sacrificed greater sums than that of the Spanish to advance the knowledge of plants'.[24] The emergence of a periodical press, furthermore, attests to the multiple avenues for literate, social, and intellectual exchange which flourished in Spanish America at the turn of the nineteenth century.[25]

This spirit of improvement and patriotic intellectual enquiry was best embodied in two civil society institutions which the Crown sanctioned and elevated to a quasi-official status: the Economic, or Patriotic, Societies and the *Consulados*. These associations promoted the advancement of technical methods and the dissemination of 'useful' knowledge which would, in turn, stimulate improvements in agriculture, industry, and commerce.[26] Public education, scientific experiments, and the exploration of little-known wilderness were seized upon as modes of improving commerce and mercantile affairs. As the leading member of Cartagena's *Consulado* observed, 'knowledge of the earth is the first step, the very foundation, of a flourishing agricultural system. We have better knowledge of China's terrain than we do of the land which we inhabit'.[27] The rest of this chapter, then, will examine the ways that members of the *Consulados* and Economic Societies engaged with, and in some cases manipulated, the Bourbon reform programme in order to overcome this deficit and achieve local objectives.

The rise of the new *Consulados* of the Spanish empire

Since the thirteenth century, the *Consulado* functioned as a maritime tribunal and guild in Spain and its empire, directing its energies to the protection of property rights, ships, and cargo against piracy and other depredations.[28] Three *Consulados* dominated Spanish oceanic trade from its inception: Seville (founded 1543), Mexico City (1594), and Lima (1613). Together with the *Casa de Contratación*, Seville's *Consulado* arranged the outfitting and dispatch of the fleets to America, largely controlled the size of cargoes, and effectively determined the prices of goods in America. In Mexico City and Peru, the *Consulados* functioned as a chamber of commerce, adjudicating disputes over contracts and bankruptcy while administering the *alcabala*, sales tax, and other duties.[29] These corporations, enjoying a special mercantile *fuero* and possessing considerable autonomy from the Crown, became the bulwark of Spain's commercial monopoly in America and, over the centuries, steadily accumulated financial and political power.

In the wake of the 1765, 1778, and 1782 *comercio libre* decrees, which increased the number of ports permitted to trade with the Americas, Charles III created new peninsular *Consulados* in La Coruña, Santander, and Málaga in 1785.[30] These new mercantile bodies further undermined the grip of the *Consulado* of Cádiz which, in 1720, had assumed Seville's exalted position in the American trade. Less than a decade later, *Consulados* on the imperial periphery were established: Caracas and Guatemala (1793), Buenos Aires and Havana (1794), and Cartagena[31], Santiago de Chile, Guadalajara, and Veracruz (1795). The Crown's decision to charter additional colonial *Consulados* was underpinned by two factors: first, the regalist intention to supplant the entrenched corporations of its American empire with institutions more amenable to metropolitan manipulation; second, the recognition of mutual interest uniting the metropolitan state and the emerging elites of the imperial periphery. *Comercio libre* legislation and new *Consulados*, then, were two mechanisms by which the Crown planned to wrest control of its American markets and supersede monopoly corporations that thwarted its aims.[32]

Established in the wake of the modifications to viceregal jurisdiction of the late 1770s, the new American *Consulados* further eroded the dominance of the established *Consulados* of Lima and Mexico City.[33] In many ways, their creation was the culmination of earlier Bourbon policy. From the early 1750s, Madrid actively sought to curb Creole participation in public affairs, especially in the *Audiencias*, in Mexico and Peru, substituting *peninsulares* in their place.[34] In 1754, the lease on tax farming enjoyed by Mexico's *Consulado* was terminated and its administration placed firmly under Crown control. By 1779, all leases for taxation in New Spain had been recalled in favour of direct royal administration. In 1795, when the *Consulado* of VeraCruz received its charter, Mexico City's merchants complained bitterly and called for the Crown to abolish its new rival for New Spain's commerce.[35] New civil society institutions, bestowed with the same name but possessing fewer privileges than the antecedent corporations, were established to counterbalance the accumulated authority of the old, siphoning away their previously unchallenged dominance.[36]

By creating *Consulados* both in the less developed parts of the empire and on the periphery of the core viceroyalties, then, the Crown adopted a more flexible approach to governance, a trend which gained momentum after the outbreak of war in the early 1790s. Colonial officials on the frontier, overwhelmed by increasing responsibilities engendered by expanding commerce, agricultural output, and population in their jurisdictions, were prepared to codify informal alliances with elites out of sheer necessity.[37] Though their creation required some limited dispersal of political authority, the creation of *Consulados* in peripheral regions promised three irresistible benefits to the Crown: economic growth, efficient administration, and the eradication of contraband.

The improvement of agriculture and commerce, the intendant of Caracas reassured the Minister of the Indies, was the 'source of [creole] happiness and the principal link of [their] indissoluble union with the metropolis'. A *Consulado*, composed of landowners and merchants, he continued, would recognize and codify this 'reciprocal encouragement' which would 'promote and influence happiness'. Until this institution was established, the colonists would continue to conceive of their 'happiness' as 'dependent solely on the action, and perhaps despotism, of the chiefs of the province'.[38] A viceroy of New Granada concurred, praising the potential 'utility and necessity' of the *Consulado* which 'surely will foster the opulence and prosperity' of the colony. Not solely a tribunal of convenience, he envisaged the *Consulado* as a 'body of zealous patriots who promote public happiness'.[39] One of his successors recommended establishing a *Consulado* in Bogotá, praising that city's merchants for 'bringing together their faculties and *las luces* for the good of the state. They are very useful and granting one for this capital is highly necessary'.[40]

The creation of a commercial court would free Crown officials from the tedium of adjudicating mercantile disputes and improve the conduct of commerce. Because the majority of the backlogged judicial cases involved 'debts and mercantile contracts whose judgment should be rendered as summarily as possible', the governor of Trinidad commented, the creation of a *Consulado* was recommended. Its absence, he argued, meant that 'bad faith invents numerous subterfuges disguised by [the pretext of] law'.[41] A commercial court could resolve such conflicts, Caracas's intendant stated, 'rapidly and summarily, consonant with the new style of commerce' whose previous delays 'resulted in the complete ruin of several very useful vassals'.[42]

To economic growth and expeditious justice, the advocates of *Consulados* noted a third potential benefit: the eradication of contraband. Merchants,

Caracas's intendant mused, always 'know what contraband is being carried out, who introduces it, of which goods it consists, as well as the actors, the accomplices, and the participants', but failed to inform the authorities for fear of antagonism or 'staining [their reputations] with the mark of an informer'. A *Consulado*, he claimed, 'would reduce the need to fret over this prospect and would guard most vigilantly against clandestine trade. Not even the officials of the Royal Treasury are as interested in the extinction of contraband as these merchants are'.[43]

Bourbon aims coincided, in this instance at least, with those of colonial merchants and planters. This confluence facilitated the growth of quasi-governmental bodies on the imperial periphery which institutionalized previously informal collaboration. The creation of *Consulados* normally received the support of municipal government as well. The endorsement of the Caracas *Cabildo*, for example, employed the same rationale and language as that of the intendant.[44] Merchants themselves strove to emphasize this mutual advantage, contending that the *Consulado* would pursue not merely the 'particular' interests of its constituent members, but rather the 'universal public good'. 'Our ideas', New Granada's merchants pledged before their *Consulado* was chartered, 'would unite individual interests with public happiness'. In this way, this 'patriotic body of good citizens' would 'stimulate and breathe life [into the economy] with prizes awarded for the cultivation of the fields, the discovery of precious things, and the exportation of provincial produce'.[45]

As stipulated by its royal *cédula*, a *Consulado* was designed to achieve two purposes: its primary function, discussed earlier in this chapter, delegated to a tribunal, guaranteed merchants a swift and quasi-independent judicial procedure to handle their professional disputes. *Consulados* heard cases relating to bankruptcy, demands for the payment of debts, cession of goods to creditors, sales of property at auction arising from such cases, the administration of wills and effects of deceased merchants, merchants suspected of smuggling and, for those convicted, supervised the dispersal of their confiscated goods.[46] The second function of a *Consulado*, delegated to its *Junta Económico y de Gobierno*, concerned the 'protection and encouragement of commerce'. This responsibility entailed:

[To use] all possible means for the advancement of agriculture, the improvement in the cultivation and benefit of its products, the introduction of the most advantageous machines and tools, the facilitation of the internal circulation [of goods]; in sum, whatever seems most conducive to the growth and extension of all branches of cultivation and commerce.[47]

The *Consulado* discharged this duty by founding schools of commerce, assuming custodial duties at maritime ports, introducing and experimenting with newfangled agricultural techniques, and undertaking infrastructural improvements to expedite the transport of agricultural products from the hinterland to the port cities.[48] This economic development function ensured that membership was not only to merchants, but to planters as well, membership being limited to property-owners of sufficient status.[49]

In default of adequate provision within colonial budget to finance these initiatives, the *Consulados* were empowered to collect a small tax to defray the capital expenditures that infrastructure and education projects entailed. This tax, known as the *avería*, was an import–export duty determined directly by the Crown, fluctuating between 0.5 per cent and 1.5 per cent.[50] Santiago's *Consulado* was permitted to collect a 0.5 per cent *avería* on exports and imports in Chile in order to finance its projects, the vast majority of its income deriving from commerce transacted in Santiago and at the neighbouring port city of Valparaiso. In 1796, the paltry sum collected barely covered its meagre salaries and overhead costs, causing Santiago's *Consulado* to lament its 'impoverished condition'. Without an increase, the *Consulado* claimed, it could not 'protect and foment' commerce, introduce machines and tools into Chile, or provide public instruction to merchants and farmers, 'the most efficacious method to promote agriculture'. The *Consulado* of Buenos Aires initially levied the same level of *avería*. Even after an increase to 1 per cent, however, the *Consulado* continued to operate at a loss and many of its grandiose projects failed to materialize.[51]

The improvement of infrastructure—the extension of roads, the maintenance of ports, and the construction of bridges—was deemed by the *Consulados* a precursor to economic growth. The burgeoning interest in public works in Spanish America paralleled developments elsewhere in Europe. Most notably, the French physiocrats demonstrated concern for the improvement of transport facilities. Dupont de Nemours, for example, maintained that 'society needs to have as many public works carried out as possible, at the least expense'.[52] In Spain itself, as early as the 1720s, Uztáriz called for the state to invest in infrastructure on both sides of the Atlantic through an extensive public works programme, contending that agricultural improvement, expanded trade, and manufacturing growth were inconceivable without such projects.[53] In America the situation was more desperate: even in the late eighteenth century, river and land communication was unreliable, hazardous, and extremely slow. In New Granada, for example, the journey from Cartagena to Bogotá could last up to two months.[54] Calls for highways linking the remote interior with coastal cities, the 'making navigable those rivers' currently unfit for commerce, and other 'public works of urgent and well-known utility' are recurrent in colonial *Consulado* reports to the Crown.[55] In most parts of America, public investment in the economy remained negligible and colonial officials busied themselves with extracting resources and shipping them to Spain, instead of undertaking long-term projects.[56] By the early 1780s, this neglect had become unsustainable as increased revenues from America were judged the best way to fund Spain's geopolitical ambitions.

Inadequate infrastructure was berated universally as an impediment to commerce. In Cuba, for example, the most widespread complaint concerned the scarcity of suitable roads for the transport of agricultural products from the hinterland to the coastal metropolis. This absence, it was claimed, stymied economic activity.[57] In the Río de la Plata, the proponents of a *Consulado* emphasized the long-neglected 'relations between the provinces' and dedicated themselves to devising a 'means of facilitating communication, by means of roads, canals and rivers'. They sought to eradicate the 'obstacles which impede the easy communication of the provinces with one another'.[58] Public works, Trinidad's governor argued, 'were not pursued with the same rapidity as [colonists'] imagination conceived of them and necessity required'. Roads and bridges were necessary before the island could be properly inhabited and cultivated. The colonists suffered due to this absence, he asserted, and 'remained inactive'.[59] In Mexico, the viceroy endorsed the *Consulado* of VeraCruz's intention to build a road linking it with the capital, a 'dignified object [of attention]' to facilitate the 'reciprocal communication between these admirable and opulent provinces', for which 'nothing had been done' in 200 years. He focused on the 'export of [mineral] wealth and precious produce which mutually revives and supports Old and New Spain'.[60]

Public works garnered praise not only for their economic benefits, but also as a symbol of good government. 'The wharfs of London and Amsterdam are dignified monuments for posterity of what commerce creates when buttressed by government support', a member of VeraCruz's *Consulado* declared.[61] One of his colleagues elaborated:

> In the eyes of the well-seasoned traveller, public roads preview the large and delectable avenues of the city. They provide a glimpse of the beauty of great cities, thereby suggesting the majesty of the state. Their construction and preservation, therefore, are linked with the interests of the state. The most celebrated nations of antiquity never neglected them.[62]

If public works indicated efficacious and commendable governance, then, their disrepair was nothing short of an embarrassment. 'By an incomprehensible misfortune, we see abandoned roads and rivers without bridges throughout the kingdom', New Granada's viceroy groaned in 1796, 'everything is found pitifully uncared for and this issue begs the most serious attention of the government'.[63] In order to redress these deficiencies, the *Consulados* sometimes pursued public projects in conjunction with their counterparts in other colonies. A proposed road from Santiago to Mendoza, for example, generated avid interest in the *Consulados* of both Santiago and Buenos Aires around 1800, but failed to yield concrete results.[64]

While the improvement of infrastructure and the foment of economic growth were heralded as mutually beneficial to both the Crown and the Creole elite, *Consulado* projects often provoked conflicts with both royal officials as well as other privileged groups within colonial society. The *Consulados* enjoyed, to be sure, a modicum of autonomy, but they ultimately operated at the mercy of Crown officials who conceived of these institutions as a buttress to their authority. Antagonistic relations soon developed in Cartagena de Indias, for example, where the governor suspended the *Consulado* in 1795. He declared that it had 'caused confusion and disorder, pursuing activities which surpassed the limits determined by its charter', asserting itself to be superior to the 'chiefs and tribunal of this place, disturbing public tranquility, and causing great anxiety among all the people. [The *Consulado*] even prescribed methods, rules and norms for the best fulfillment of my own obligations as governor'.[65] In 1806, Cartegena's *Consulado* was embroiled in a dispute with the viceroy over its request for a new printing press. The request was rejected, the viceroy argued, because it would have been 'exposed to abuses', particularly the 'introduction of dangerous writings and pamphlets' inconsistent with the overall 'goal' of the *Consulado*.[66] As their prestige and influence grew, however, the *Consulados* jealously guarded their newfound autonomy against the usurpation of Crown officials. Particularly irksome was intervention in mercantile disputes. In 1808, the Chilean *Consulado* complained of the 'unjust desire' of the Captain-General to meddle in the 'private and particular affairs' of the *Consulado*, an act that it claimed would 'despoil' the law of the kingdom.[67]

Since the new *Consulados*, by definition and membership, usually pursued the interests of the planter and merchant community in the city in which they were founded, they also entered into conflicts with groups from other regions, with whose interests their activities collided. The Cartagena *Consulado*, for example, was criticized harshly by economic elites of the interior who complained that the coastal *Consulado* did nothing to advance or protect their interests. Similar disputes, between the 'newer' merchants of VeraCruz and the 'older' merchants of Mexico City, occurred in New Spain. As their power and ambition increased, then, *Consulados* were assailed both by rival groups within Creole society and colonial officials who once confidently had heralded their utility.[68]

In spite of these disputes, the *Consulados* pursued initiatives which dovetailed with the aims of Bourbon reformers. The emphasis on public works epitomized the mutual advantage which was openly acknowledged. The expansion of transportation links, the construction of canals and bridges, and the improvement of maritime facilities promised to generate improvements in trade, general welfare, and tax revenues. If the goals were common and means were beyond the dispute, however, the ideas which led to this consensus differed. For Madrid's regalists, robust state action alone would bring about the desired result. For the *Consulados*, by contrast, state power would be strictly defined and limited. For most *Consulado* members, the commitment to the principles of political economy implied recognition of the limits which they set on politics. Laws would rule society and the state merely would serve as their guardian.[69] Nevertheless, the most important convergence was the priority assigned to economic growth by both the *Consulados* and Crown reformers, a priority which minimized the likelihood of confrontation and made civil society-state interdependence a pillar upon which prosperity could be erected.[70]

The political and economic ideas of the American *Consulados*

The *Consulados* did not always fulfil their extravagant promises concerning the economic prosperity that their activities would produce. The *Consulado* of Cartagena, for example, according to one eminent scholar, 'failed to become a beacon for promoting economic development' in New Granada.[71] Regardless of their ultimate success in facilitating mercantile affairs or the completion of the infrastructure projects they undertook, the *Consulados*, together with the Economic Societies with which they often shared members, served as a key conduit through which new political and economic concepts infiltrated policy. *Consulados* endowed Creoles with a modicum of self-government and directly encouraged economic development by diffusing economic ideas and technical knowledge.

The extensive activities of the *Consulado* of Buenos Aires support the view that these bodies helped to galvanize intellectual life in the colonies. Manuel Belgrano (1770–1820), destined for a premature death as a general in the wars of independence, articulated his political and economic ideas in his capacity as secretary of Buenos Aires's *Consulado*. Beginning in 1794, Belgrano presented an annual *memoria* which disseminated—in abridged and rather loose translations—the ideas of, among others, Quesnay, Dupont de Nemours, Galiani, and Genovesi. Echoing Quesnay's and Mirabeau's tract *Rural Philosophy* (1763), Belgrano proclaimed that free trade could be a motor of revival and asserted that land was the unexploited patrimony of the colony. He contended that 'agriculture is the true destiny of mankind ... everything depends and results from the cultivation of land; without it, the primary products for the arts would not exist and, consequently, industry would have nothing to which to apply itself, and thus commerce would be impossible. In an agrarian state, any other type of wealth is precarious'.[72]

Belgrano's embrace of physiocracy was shared by the merchants of Buenos Aires who contended that 'the principal source of wealth' is 'cultivated land'.[73] This formulation enabled them, as a leading scholar has indicated, to 'query components of mercantilism without overturning the architecture of a highly controlled and regulated commerce'.[74] Belgrano thus espoused political and economic ideas which did not explicitly undermine the Spanish colonial trading system. Instead, he called for changes in policy which could be accommodated within the present trade and political regime. In this way, Belgrano and other colonial *Consulado* figures were simultaneously patriotic and cosmopolitan in their approach to ideas: cosmopolitan in their engagement with political economy regardless of its provenance; patriotic in their commitment to using the knowledge encountered to improve their own society.[75]

Assertions of the primacy of agriculture and its intimate connection to commerce also may be found in Caracas and Santiago. The Caracas *Consulado* described 'the intimate link between agriculture and commerce, the one creates and supplies the other ... [agriculture] is the primordial seed of the abundance of states'.[76] This enthusiasm for agriculture was shared by Manuel de Salas (1754–1841), *síndico* of Santiago's *Consulado*, who lamented Chile's over-reliance on mineral extraction and asserted that agriculture, if developed, could become the guarantor of prosperity. 'I believe that the decadence [of Chile]', he argued, is due to a 'defect of its constitution, as has been the case in other lands solely dedicated to mining'.[77] A discernible conviction in agriculture's primacy animated his *memorias* to the Chilean *Consulado*: 'no nation [*nación*] that encourages agriculture has not enjoyed a large population, or improved industry, or has failed to establish an advantageous commerce'.[78] Many obstacles blocked this efflorescence. Merchants lamented that under-population precluded genuine development of abundant resources, leaving the colonies with 'treasures that we cannot cultivate due to the absence of labour'. Population was lauded as the 'greatest treasure and true wealth of a state' and its increase was actively encouraged through a series of both prudent and outlandish schemes.[79] Deficient population, combined with faulty agricultural techniques, led the *Consulado* to conclude that previous policy had proved a colossal failure: Chile, 'the most fertile [colony] in America and the most adequate for human happiness', lamentably stagnated and remained 'the poorest of Spain's dominions'.[80]

The *Consulados'* fascination with political economy intersected with their explicit invocation of foreign practices as models of reform for Spanish Americans to emulate. Belgrano argued that colonial societies required exposure to foreign economic ideas for such 'principles are constant and the happy state that England, France, Germany and Italy have achieved is well-known. Some [peninsular] writers have observed the usefulness and advantageous consequences of their methods'.[81] In spite of this adulation of foreign and peninsular practices, Belgrano cited few specifics, asserting only that his propositions were imbued with such insights. Agricultural improvement depended, the Chilean *Consulado* contended, on the acquisition and adequate dissemination of scientific knowledge, and he praised the 'great influence' of the Academies and Economic Societies of France, Berne, London, and Spain in the 'progress of the happiness of the human species' through their 'brilliance and research'.[82] Nevertheless, even in the mid-1790s, only a smattering of documentary evidence for engagement with newfangled ideas is evident in the *Consulado* minutes, though Britain routinely was praised, in vague terms, for the 'beautiful *luces* which illuminate its sciences'.[83]

The entry of foreign ideas and practices helped to transform attitudes towards commerce still dominant in the Spanish Atlantic World. Belgrano, for example, participated in efforts, initiated by Campomanes's treatises on popular industry, to remove the stigma associated with commercial activities and to invest them with honour.[84] In order to realize this aim, Belgrano suggested that 'honour and prizes' are the 'motors of the human heart which ensure that the spirit of man does not slumber'. He cited the 'great' Antonio Genovesi, the Neapolitan political economist, to bolster his argument that performance incentives should be adopted by 'enlightened governments', on the basis that they are 'drawn from Nature and human history'.[85]

The scarce diffusion of such foreign ideas, however, was a source of frustration for the local American intelligentsias. 'Commerce, a profession subject to rules and principles', an exasperated Salas berated his fellow members of the Santiago *Consulado*, 'here has solely been the art of buying cheap and selling high'. But this primitive approach may have been due less to obstinate ignorance than to unfamiliarity with newer modes of thought. As one astute commentator noted in the early nineteenth century, 'Guatemala, founded in 1524, has not contemplated the teachings of political economy for nearly three centuries'.[86] The mere arrival of European ideas could not by itself transform colonial society which remained 'neither agrarian, nor industrious, nor commercial'. On the eve of independence, Santiago's *Consulado* announced that Chile 'only required enlightenment', and this could be acquired by the establishment of an Economic Society in the capital.[87]

Even when these institutions—the University, *Consulado*, and Economic Society—were established, however, *Consulado*-affiliated intellectuals resigned themselves to the apathetic reception of the ideas they disseminated by culturally inert colonists. This pessimism is exemplified by Chilean Juan Egaña's exhortation to draw inspiration from 'great men' such as Condillac, Uztáriz, Genovesi, and Filangieri who 'inspire us with their *luces* and example so that we can profit from their work and cease being the humiliation of humankind'. He lamented that colonial 'literary establishments languish in mediocrity' instead of benefiting from these 'shining models [offered by] wise and generous Europe'.[88] In Cartagena, Jose Ignacio Pombo expressed a similar frustration that his contemporaries had 'wasted time translating [foreign] novels which can only corrupt good taste and sound customs', complaining that to such misplaced priorities must be attributed the failure to translate Adam Smith's *Wealth of Nations* (1776) into Spanish until 1794.[89]

Whereas most of the South American *Consulado* documents reveal frustration with the slow diffusion of foreign, purportedly 'enlightened' ideas due to a faith in their efficacy, Havana's *Consulado* firmly believed that the state should bring about Cuba's collective prosperity by any means necessary, whether through the introduction of newfangled ideas or special preferential measures. The expanding wealth of Cuba's sugar-planting patriciate nourished its conviction in the state's responsibility for the promotion and protection of its interests. 'The class that at all times and in all countries', one *Consulado* document declared, 'has been, and will be, the most valuable, the foundation of the state, on which it relies in the most urgent times, the masters of agriculture'.[90] By the mid-1760s, a new understanding had developed between the Crown and the American elite. The former indulged the latter with unprecedented special commercial privileges, more titles of Castile, new opportunity for military rank and a hefty *fuero* for the militia.[91] These concessions indicate that a dynamic partnership between Cuban elite and Crown flourished, an alliance predicated on government policy conducive to the expansion of Cuba's wealth.

Chartered during the gubernatorial tenure of Luís de las Casas in the early 1790s, Havana's *Consulado*, like those of Santiago and Buenos Aires, assumed responsibility for the 'protection and encouragement' of agriculture and commerce.[92] Often defining the contours of the *Consulado* debates was its *síndico* and *asesor* Francisco Arango y Parreño (1765–1837) who, like Belgrano in Buenos Aires, delivered orations which claimed to utilize the 'discoveries' of European political economy in order to solve local policy conundrums.

After returning from Spain, where he, like Belgrano, studied civil law, Arango, in his maiden speech to the *Consulado* in 1794, asserted that Havana's agriculture was a 'victim of an exclusive monopoly company that shackled its industry'. While paying lip service to the 'tragic surrender to the English' in 1762 in the closing moments of the Seven Years' War, he lauded the unintended, yet beneficent, consequences of the occupation, which brought 'considerable wealth' to the island. Arango argued that, 'with their [African slaves] and free commerce, [Britain] accomplished more [in nine months] than we had in the previous seventy years'.[93] In 1794, employing similar arguments, Havana's *Sociedad Patriótica* eulogized the 1765 Bourbon *comercio libre* decrees as the grand moment when Cuba

broke free from its ancient shackles [...] [which] suppressed a multitude of possibilities, imprisoned our industry, and enervated activity; with a single action, it made all of us happy, destroying that detestable monopoly which enriched, at most, four people to the detriment of the rest of the colony [...] from this happy metamorphosis, our *patria* has been converted into a cultured, brilliant, and populous city.[94]

The unregulated, plentiful entry of slaves and the removal of mercantile restrictions in 1762–3, then, greatly benefited Havana's sugar planters. Though these laws were repealed with the return of Spanish administration, Havana's sugarocratic intelligentsia recognized the *comercio libre* decrees of the mid-1760s also had, though to a lesser degree, benefited their interests. The revival of these 'English' policies and the deepening of *comercio libre* constituted the main pillars of the commercial reforms sought by Havana's *Consulado* and Economic Society.[95]

In subsequent orations, Arango purveyed a vision of the *Consulado* as a catalyst of economic expansion. He criticized the first *Consulados* which had been organized in a 'defective manner' and, subsequently, had 'degenerated significantly' through a monumental failure to exercise their commercial functions, and thus perfunctorily acted 'like an ordinary judicial tribunal'.[96] Arango contended that the *Consulado* should play a more dynamic role in exploiting the island's economic potential, which, he believed, could best be accomplished through emulation of the successful practices of rival European states. Far from mere intellectual fashion, Arango described the urgency imposed on Cuban agriculture by imperial rivalry. It was necessary to 'transplant to our soil the advantages achieved by foreign nations by means of their greater knowledge'. In view of the 'great advances which the English have achieved in their establishments in Sierra Leone', he warned, 'we must not lose a single moment'. In the mid-1790s, Arango journeyed to Spain, Portugal, England, Barbados, and Jamaica, at the *Consulado's* request, in order to acquaint himself with techniques potentially applicable to Cuba. Arango marvelled at the 'comfort which [Portugal and Britain] enjoy in relation to the supply of [African slaves]' and implored his colleagues to find a 'means by which we may enjoy similar advantages'.[97]

Like many of his contemporaries in the Spanish Atlantic World, Arango heaped eulogiums on Britain's 'opulence', the 'beauty of its countryside', the 'perfection of its cultivation'. Unlike many of his contemporaries who contented themselves with vague and effusive praise, however, he praised specific institutions. 'Why don't we shift our gaze to wise England?', Arango frequently implored. With regard to colonial agriculture, the quality and 'low price of machines and tools' which British colonial planters employed impressed him most. He reported that these same devices, if widely distributed, could be indispensable to the accelerated growth of Cuba's sugar industry. In Jamaica, he praised the 'methods which in all times have been employed to increase the population of white [colonists]', identifying the roads which had been constructed, and the discipline and 'division of labour' imposed on the slaves as the two chief policies to be emulated.[98] Neither tax structures nor land use practices evaded his observation. In Britain, he reported, a land tax was imposed and collected without causing disruption, still at a considerable benefit to the Treasury. In its Caribbean colonies, however, Britain did not collect this tax. This dual policy, suited to the peculiar circumstances of each location, formed the basis for Arango's favourable comparison of British with Spanish colonial governance. 'We continue to do the inverse', he lamented, for 'we want to test out in the colonies a type of tax which our wise government has not even been able to collect successfully in [peninsular] Spain'.[99] Arango's glowing appraisal of British practices was shared by Havana's Economic Society, whose members admired the 'progress of [England's] agriculture by indefatigable constancy' and 'continued relish for the perfection of rural practices' which had brought 'abundance to that kingdom'. The Economic Society also lauded England's 'foreign commerce, which had increased prodigiously and [enabled England to] amass wealth and population'.[100] The *Consulados* and other enlightened Creoles, then, sought to obtain and disseminate 'useful' knowledge, developed locally and abroad, to encourage agricultural improvement as well as commercial expansion.

Ultramarine Economic Societies, intellectual exchange, and colonial development

The backwardness denounced by the *Consulados* was the impetus behind the *Sociedad Económica*,[101] or Economic Society, an institution that flourished throughout the Spanish empire in the late eighteenth century. Seventy societies were created on the peninsula and 14 were founded overseas between 1770 and 1820. The Economic Societies encouraged what may be anachronistically termed 'best practices', sponsoring essay prizes to stimulate innovation, particularly new agricultural techniques.[102] Composed mainly of wealthy Creoles, these societies also compiled libraries of Spanish and foreign books (often dominated by technical subjects) and sponsored schools and institutes for instruction in agriculture, the natural sciences, and various manual arts. Applied knowledge, which would lead to economic improvement, was decidedly the emphasis of these ventures. In New Granada, one prominent intellectual summarized this pervasive instrumental orientation towards knowledge when he declared that the study of astronomy proved a 'fruitless activity' unless it 'improves our geography, our roads and our commerce'.[103]

The antecedents of the Economic Societies were the agricultural improvement organizations which flourished throughout Europe at mid-century. The societies of Dublin, Zurich, Florence, and Bern were especially influential.[104] Modelling itself on Basque precedent, the first Cuban *Sociedad Patriótica*, founded in 1787 in Santiago, met sporadically in 1790, but ceased to function altogether by 1792, the same year in which its counterpart in Havana began to swell in size, prestige, and political clout. From its inception, Havana's *Sociedad Patriótica* claimed its mission was to eradicate the impediments to the 'free circulation of the sciences and the arts', thereby facilitating '*el comercio de las luces*', and contributing 'efficaciously to the abandonment of the vain knowledge of the schools'.[105] In Guatemala, petitioners seeking royal permission to found an Economic Society argued that its projects would yield practical results. The collapse of houses during earthquakes, they suggested, was attributable to 'having known neither the rudiments of geometry nor architecture' and pledged to 'prefer those branches of learning which open new roads, construct cities, defend ports and infinitely facilitate' the colony's economy. By 1810, Economic Societies had been established in VeraCruz, Havana, Lima, Quito, Buenos Aires, Caracas, and Guatemala.[106]

Commercial education was a chief concern of merchants on both sides of the Atlantic. The statutes for proposed mercantile academies varied, but all stressed that the same minimum knowledge and essential skills were to be imparted: arithmetic; language acquisition (particularly French, English, and Dutch); and double-entry book-keeping. Endowed with this training, it was hoped, the young apprentices would develop into 'perfect merchants, good consuls, wise judges, and, ultimately, vassals capable of undertaking important projects'.[107]

In the late 1790s, Havana's *Consulado* and *Sociedad Patriótica* jointly sought to found an institute for *Ciencias Exactas y Naturales para la Educación de la Juventud* to 'diffuse in all minds a love of the sciences, an inclination that produces the happiest effects', claiming that such an institution could be 'the instrument of happiness of the people'. It could 'banish inaction', they asserted, in idle young men. Furthermore, the natural sciences would help Cuba achieve its greatest 'prosperity, robustness and greatness'. Although the governor thought it 'recommendable' to 'enlighten the nation by the progress of letters', the petition was rejected, without explanation, by the Crown.[108] The *Sociedad Patriótica*, undeterred, reiterated its conviction in the immediate benefit to be derived from such schools, proposing a training programme in botany and chemistry so that agriculture might 'attain closer communication with those sciences'.[109] Although the principal expressed aim of these schools would be to 'promote public enlightenment', it is apparent that their primary virtue lay in their anticipated benefit to the island's sugar industry.[110] Similar proposals proliferated elsewhere, often tailored to local exigencies. Modelling themselves on the Santander *Consulado*'s successful petition for an *Escuela de Náutica y Dibujo* in 1792, both the Havana and Buenos Aires *Consulados* aspired to establish similar academies, whose mission would be to 'train good sailors'. To the absence of such an academy, it was said, 'a series of losses may be attributed' for its existence would make 'many youths useful to the state'.[111]

In spite of Havana's status as the capital of the pearl of the Antilles, the most vibrant city in the Spanish Caribbean, its inhabitants remained cognizant of their distance from the epicentres of European intellectual activities, as their efforts to replicate Old World institutions, such as the nautical and drawing school, suggest. Aware of the paucity of individuals qualified to teach Chemistry, for example, a member of the *Sociedad Patriótica* bemoaned:

the distance which separates us from the Old World and the cruel necessity of acquiring everything from there, our communication having been
disrupted by a prolonged war, the scarcity of native professors, and the
difficulties entailed in recruiting a foreign one, oblige us to solicit the
most remote regions in order to begin the study of a science shamefully
unknown in our country.[112]

Not all projects met similar frustration, however, particularly when pertinent to the lucrative sectors of the economy. The most commonly pursued
objective concerned the improvement of sugar cane cultivation. *Habaneros*
sought to familiarize themselves with foreign practices and to diffuse them
widely. The *Consulado* and *Sociedad Patriótica* subsidized translations of
prominent technical manuals which had 'enabled the cultivation of sugar to
achieve the highest grade of perfection'.[113] There was a creative thrust gal-
vanizing these efforts, which would 'awaken not only an investigative spirit,
but also lead to the discovery of new laws from which the progress of
unknown or forgotten branches of knowledge will arise'. For this reason, the
proposed translation of French sugar manuals would be accompanied by a
'succinct exposition of the method which we currently employ, with the
aim that we will be able to compare one with the other and thus deduce
which system works better'.[114] The ultimate goal of these endeavours was
the achievement of a 'perfect system of agriculture that will facilitate the
greatest harvest at the least possible cost. France and England have not lost
sight of this maxim, following it in all of their colonies in America'.[115]

Not all of the Havana intelligentsia's efforts should be dismissed as
merely instrumental to economic aims, as anecdotal evidence for less
immediately remunerative cultural pursuits may be gleaned from lists of
foreign books purchased by the *Consulado* for its library. One such shipment in 1811 revealed, among others, John Marshall's *Life of George
Washington*, Alexander Hamilton's complete works, Thomas Jefferson's
Notes on the State of Virginia, and Alexander von Humboldt's *Political Essay
on the Kingdom of New Spain*.[116] Other *Consulados* also sought to introduce
their members to European texts. In 1801, the VeraCruz *Consulado's* leader-
ship requested that its agent in Madrid procure 'the best works on political
economy, in all the branches most pertinent to the prosperity of the
monarchy in general and to the institution of the *Consulado* in particular'.
In response, the agent suggested eight sixteenth-century political writers,
including Castillo de Bobadilla, Gutiérrez de los Ríos, López Madera, and
Pérez de Herrera. Seventeenth-century mercantilists also feature prominently, including Moncada and Zevallos. Uztáriz, Bernardo de Ulloa, Ward,
and Campomanes are among the eighteenth-century writers cited. Among

contemporary foreign writers, the agent passed over available translations of Hume, Quesnay, and Galiani; instead, the works of Steuart, Forbonnais, and Necker were included. The few extant catalogues of other colonial libraries reflect a similar range of titles.[117]

The drive for useful knowledge in the Americas, as in Spain itself, gleaned from foreign sources was not an indiscriminate obsession with the exotic. On the contrary, a member of Havana's Economic Society clarified, 'it never will be advantageous for one to copy another. In each country there are a number of unique factors determined by its circumstances, its temperament, government, the state of its industry and agriculture, whose effects greatly influence which establishments may be organised'.[118] Such a spirit led not to xenophobia and cultural stagnation, but rather impelled new intellectual projects. Havana's *Sociedad Patriótica* complained, for example, of the failure of Creoles to write their own histories and eschewed continued reliance on European accounts. One attempt to redress this absence was a project to compile a 'Provincial Dictionary' of Cuba. 'What a gift we shall give to the literary world', José María Peñalaver marvelled, 'and those who seek to write the history of this island ... will not be able to replace our creole voices with peninsular ones'.[119]

An eminent Cuban scholar argued that, due to the activities of the Economic Societies, the Spanish American '"kingdoms" turned into "countries" which were converted into *"patrias"*, each with its own consciousness apart from that of Spain'.[120] This conclusion, however, is not incontrovertible. It is unnecessary to concur that the Economic Societies spawned national consciousness in order to grasp that they, in conjunction with the *Consulados*, galvanized colonial intellectual life during the late Bourbon period. Until the late 1790s at least, the majority of colonial intellectuals pursued licenced privilege within the contours of Old Regime instead of outright sovereignty.[121] This attitude gradually changed, but did not disappear, in the final decade of the century as external shocks to Spain's transatlantic trading system produced economic grievances which corroded the legitimacy of Spain's claim to be the linchpin of public happiness in America.[122]

The *Consulados*, war, and the dilemma of neutral commerce

The rapid development and maturation of colonial political-economic thought is best demonstrated in the reactions of the *Consulados* and Economic Societies to the commercial regulations issued by Madrid between 1790 and 1810. Major naval defeats to Britain, first at Cape St. Vincent (1797) and, eight years later, at Trafalgar (1805) made Spain's communication with America decreasingly frequent and its commerce scarce. The British fleet's blockade of Cádiz further disrupted Spain's transatlantic trade networks, prevented Madrid from supplying the Spanish American market, and triggered a precipitous decline in imperial commerce. The commercial crisis in the fast-growing imperial periphery was particularly debilitating due to its perishable export commodities and its reliance on imported manufactures.[123] In Buenos Aires, for example, exports in 1797 plummeted to a mere 1/16 of their 1796 level while the prices of foreign-made goods doubled.[124] These events and their consequences, replicated throughout the empire, compelled Madrid to modify existing trade regulations.

In the agrarian colonies, many commentators contended that colonial monopoly required greater flexibility well before the outbreak of war crippled oceanic commerce. Steady economic growth, Havana's *Consulado* maintained, had accompanied the removal of most of the restrictions on Cuba's economy during and in the aftermath of the Seven Years' War. Though the amplification of the market attracted supporters, no advocate of freer trade would have lobbied for the legal admission of foreign merchants into the Spanish Atlantic economy. Colonial merchants pursued outlets for their commodities within the existing architecture of Spanish American trade. The *comercio neutral*, neutral trade, decrees of 1797 and 1801 were a last-gasp measure when deprivation wrought by war necessitated alternative trading outlets.[125] Neutral trade is a vital topic not solely because it reveals the fissures of the Spanish empire that appeared in the years preceding the outbreak of the wars of independence, but also because it demonstrates how elites sought to reconcile their ambitions with the aims of the Crown's priorities even during the most severe crises. *Comercio neutral*, first sanctioned by Charles IV in November 1797, ostensibly responded to the 'stagnation' which threatened Spanish America with scarcity, permitting merchants of nations not at war with Spain to supply Spanish American markets with products which the peninsula could not supply.

The merchants of Santiago and Buenos Aires initially were vehemently opposed to opening channels of trade, even during periods of extreme, war-produced scarcity, to non-Spanish merchants. As Caracas's intendant had predicted in the 1780s, most *Consulados* proved vigorous champions of colonial monopoly. A leading historian recently noted that 'abandoning the securities and safeguards of sheltered trade would have exposed guild merchants to greater competition' and thus provided the *Consulado* members with 'an interest in shoring up the archaic structures of market life in the colonies'.[126] When trade with neutral nations was legalized, some *Consulados* continued to contest the wisdom of this expedient. The merchants of Buenos Aires justified their opposition because it was 'impossible to execute [the neutral trade decrees] without causing great harm to the state, the treasury and commerce (...) this [new regulation] is insufferable and scandalous and the *Consulado* finds it abominable'.[127] Less regulated trade within the empire, then, was desirable whereas the penetration by foreign merchants of colonial markets, regardless of exigencies, was deemed deleterious.

The Crown soon came to share this judgment. In April 1799, a royal order suspended *comercio neutral* because 'far from achieving these favourable effects, it resulted in great harm to the state and increased the industry and commerce of [Spain's] enemies, putting at their disposal the most powerful force to continue the war'. In revoking *comercio neutral*, Madrid instructed administrators in Spanish America to 'repair the damage that had been caused' and to enforce the order immediately, 'accepting neither excuses nor pretexts' for non-compliance.[128]

By this point, however, the frailty of Spanish America's self-enclosed commercial system to all of its participants had become apparent, even those merchants who had objected at first to the neutral trade decrees. Colonial merchants protested that, given the 'grave necessity and urgency beyond comparison', neutral ships should be allowed to 'rescue' the colonists from their plight.[129] The Crown and colonial merchants realized that their interests were irreparably adrift, but they still sought to evade open confrontation. In response to a further royal order in 1803, which demanded a vigilant stance against contraband, Havana's *Consulado* confessed that the 'deplorable situation in which the war has left us' necessitated non-compliance with traditional imperial commercial regulations. While paying obligatory lip service to its 'impatience to re-establish the natural links' between Cuba and metropole, the *Consulado* did not disguise the 'total decadence of commerce' which made unsanctioned trade with neutral nations a 'necessity'.[130] 'The obstruction of commerce between this island and Spain', remarked an anonymous letter to the intendant, 'permits, in moments of necessity, an abrogation of the old laws which restrict the entry of foreign goods'.[131] The *Consulado* clamoured for renewed licence to trade with neutral nations in the 'unfortunate and all-too-probable case of war' because of the 'misfortunes which threaten the sugar [producing] islands' when war prevented regular communication with Europe.[132]

Neutral commerce proved critical for agrarian and livestock-exporting colonies like Cuba, Río de la Plata, and Venezuela whose agricultural exports represented a significant percentage of its overall trade.[133] Bullion still accounted for the majority of the overall cargo value of imports into Spain from Spanish America, mainly from Peru, New Spain, and New Granada.[134] Trade of the imperial periphery, by contrast, was composed overwhelmingly of agricultural produce. In Caracas, for example, cacao and indigo accounted for 95 per cent of all exports in 1795.[135] In these colonies whose livelihood depended on perishable commodities, the disruption of trade portended disaster. 'The state of commerce is deplorable here', the Buenos Aires *Consulado* announced, the 'war has interrupted the circulation [of goods] without which none of the three branches of public happiness can flourish'.[136] This condition led *porteño* merchants to seek markets in neighbouring Brazil and even in Mauritius for their commodities.[137]

The *Consulado* of Cartagena reached a similar conclusion: given 'the current circumstance of being entirely cut off from the Metropolis, in order to avoid damage to industry, agriculture and commerce which may result from lack of commerce', the export of commodities to neutral nations was exigent.[138] Scarcity provoked fears for survival, which then drove the mercantile and agricultural elites of the periphery to deviate from the regulations which had long structured Spanish America's commerce. They sought to justify this deviation by resorting to the pliable rhetoric of public happiness. The Caracas *Consulado*, for example, claimed that, according to the 'principles of political economy', *comercio neutral* was the only way to rescue its agriculture, ruefully remarking 'if only these were not true principles!'[139] The synergy which had previously characterized state's relations with civil society began to lose its force. The Bourbon state, in previous decades hailed as a beacon of economic and moral improvement, lost its lustre and came to be viewed, increasingly, as an arbitrary power by the local colonial intelligentsias.

American merchants and planters were not alone in their efforts to circumvent existing trade restrictions. Colonial administrators also claimed that compliance with the ban on neutral trade was both impractical and undesirable. In 1799, the viceroy of New Granada, who, just two years earlier, had refused to authorize neutral trade in spite of a royal order legalizing it, reversed his judgment. He remarked that such a prohibition would merely encourage contraband, the 'inevitable' result of a 'complete absence' of communication with the peninsula. 'The gain compensates for whatever risk is involved and interest makes illusory all precautions', he claimed, 'the law of necessity is superior to all other laws'. Indeed, only eight ships from Spain reached Cartagena between 1796 and 1801, making recourse to contraband unavoidable.[140]

Provincial officials concurred with their superiors, contending that contraband would flourish were the order to abolish neutral trade enforced. Anti-smuggling policy would entail a massive coast guard operation, certain to be both outnumbered and overmatched by superior British vessels. Imperfect as it was, the superintendent of Cumaná argued, *comercio neutral* at least guaranteed that the royal treasury collected some taxes and that trade was conducted primarily with neutral nations, instead of with Britain. In addition to these considerations, he argued, there existed a graver danger: the 'poverty, suffering, discontent, and desperation' he foresaw from the suspension of *comercio neutral* could incite an uprising which would irreparably harm the war effort and trigger political chaos with unpredictable consequences.[141]

Colonial merchants sought to replace disrupted commerce with the peninsula not only with neutral trade, but also to offset it by strengthening links between the various colonial economies of Spanish America. They stood ready to operate within, and profit from, the regional specialization that prevailed. Creoles formed pan-American networks of trade, particularly during the wars of 1796–1802 and 1804–14. The chronic shortages wrought by incessant war, the slowly expanding networks of communication, and the emergence of the export commodity industries converted provincial merchants to embrace intercolonial trade. Whereas in 1790 only four ships departed Montevideo for Havana, 14 followed the same route in 1796.[142] Contemporaries reported that the majority of the 159 vessels arriving at Cartagena in 1799 set sail from other Spanish colonies, confirming the assertion that intercolonial trade boomed.[143]

Intra-imperial trade, then, offered the prospect of respite from the war-induced disruption of trans-oceanic trade with peninsular Spain. Montevideo's *Consulado*, for example, contacted its Havana counterpart, bewailing its 'isolation caused by political convulsions' and the attempts of 'foreigners to oppose the progress of [our] industry, commerce and shipping, the declared enemies of our prosperity'. Havana's *Consulado*, in turn, was enamoured of the 'great reciprocal advantages of commerce' with the Southern Cone, noting the benefits of exchanging 'our tropical fruit' for the 'meat which we lack'. Similar arrangements were sought with Buenos Aires's merchants, whose commerce was likewise considered 'reciprocally advantageous'.[144]

Consulados, however, more often pursued trade with foreigners than intra-imperial trade, leading to acrimonious exchanges. The policies pursued by one colony's merchants sometimes clashed with the interests of another. Reliance on neutral trade intensified friction, then, between various regions of Spanish America.[145] Havana's merchants, for example, were infuriated by rumours that, during a period marked by 'our reduced agriculture', Luso-Brazilian traders 'continue to introduce liquor into the Kingdom of La Plata to the great detriment of our own'.[146] The deleterious effect of such illicit commerce was to prevent 'natural connections' among Creoles on both sides of the equator who 'find themselves abused by this competition with foreign goods'.[147] The Havana *Consulado*, in turn, was censured by VeraCruz's for its booming war-time trade with the neutral United States. Havana's aim, it claimed, was 'individual interest and the growth of that colony, without consulting the general well-being of the nation'.[148] According to one disgruntled British observer, neutral trade gave Cuba 'not only protection, but advantages before unknown. The infancy of agriculture in Cuba, far from being checked, is greatly aided in its portentous growth during the war'.[149]

Whereas *comercio neutral* and expanded inter-provincial trade were stop-gap measures to stave off the collapse of the old colonial system, the *comercio libre* decrees and new institution of the *Consulado* were aimed to satiate the rising demands of mercantile and agrarian elites on the imperial periphery. For the most part, these measures failed to meet the expectations which they fostered. But their relative failure did not impel colonial merchants and planters to seek independence from Spain. Instead, colonial elites sought to portray divergence from official policy as a temporary expedient to attain the goals which they shared with the peninsula: flourishing commerce, enhanced public works, agricultural improvement, and efficacious governance. The *Consulados* were considered to be loyal, patriotic institutions by the Crown. This confidence is reflected, for example, in the 1805 royal order which entrusted the *Consulados* with the collection of a *subvención de guerra* duty to subsidize the war effort.[150] The calls for less regulated trade, therefore, were neither a harbinger of independence nor an embrace of free trade ideology, but rather an attempt to harmonize, modernize, and recalibrate a system of benefits for both the Crown and largely collaborative colonial elites.

The intellectual vibrancy of late colonial Spanish America is beyond dispute. Creole intellectuals modified the ideas they obtained from Europe, contributed original concepts, and creatively adapted ideas to the peculiar circumstances of the New World. Though Spanish Americans certainly drew heavily on Europe, they succeeded in 'creating an intellectual tradition that was original, idiosyncratic, complex, and distinct from any European model'.[151] Colonial intellectuals drew on an 'eclectic range of sources to create a "mobile rhetoric" of reform'.[152]

But the spirit of reform, as this chapter has affirmed, was not necessarily a precursor to political schism. The Enlightenment in Spanish America, as in Europe, was often not a subversive movement, but rather 'developed within and in support of the established order, not outside and against it.'[153] Though conflict occurred and tensions sometimes ran high, the relations between the Spanish Crown and the ultramarine *Consulados* and Economic Societies were, in fact, amicable and mutually supportive.[154] The rhetoric invoked by American intellectuals was largely one of licensed privilege, not indignant demand, operating within the framework of empire.[155] An array of clashing political ideas was utilized, but most of them tended to repair, not further tear, the bonds uniting the peninsula with the colonies. Subversive ideologies often remained subordinate to colonial elites' long-standing commitment to incremental reform and collaboration with metropolitan reformers. In their joint pursuit of expanded commerce, improved public works, newfangled agricultural techniques, and good governance, civil society and state actors had greater incentives to cooperate than to enter into conflict. It was only in the absence, not the exercise, of royal authority, triggered by Ferdinand VII's abdication in 1808 after Napoleon's invasion of the peninsula, that instigated the crisis which led the various provinces of the Spanish empire to confront the now unavoidable problem of sovereignty.[156]

If political independence proved to be the ultimate solution to the power vacuum in the Spanish Atlantic World after 1808, it is clear that the republican and separatist ideas normally associated with the struggle for sovereignty did not enjoy hegemony before that fateful year, and perhaps not until the intransigent attitude towards American affairs adopted by the peninsular delegates to the *Cortes* of Cádiz from 1810. The political languages which dominated the colonial *Consulados* and Economic Societies did not advocate, initially at least, a full release from the bonds of empire. It must be acknowledged, of course, that exposure to the Bourbon discourse of reform provided a source of opposition to the Old Regime after 1808: the political language of public happiness could metamorphose into an idiom of opposition to Spanish rule.[157] The *Consulados* and Economic Societies thus incubated the political writers and actors who eventually laid the intellectual groundwork for political emancipation from Spain. Nevertheless, it is instructive to emphasize that these same political writers, operating within the institutions chartered by the Crown, were nourished on, and clung to, instead of rejected, the ideals and policies promulgated by Bourbon reformers. These now half-forgotten origins of independence political thought are, perhaps, discomfiting to traditional, nationalist historiography and suggest the crucial need to reconsider the causal relation between the Bourbon reforms and Spanish American independence.

Conclusion: Enlightenment, Governance, and Reform in Spain and its Empire: A Reconsideration

> Ancient historians [were] more inclined to speak of battles, sieges, revolutions and other strange events, that make noise in the world, than to transmit to the public measures in favour of commerce and other policies of government.[1]

This book sought to supplement the existing historiography of the Bourbon reform epoch. It emphasized changing conceptions of governance and reform in Spain and its American empire, with a special focus on their intellectual origins and dramatic transformation in response to domestic and geopolitical exigencies. Four aspects, it was argued, have received insufficient attention from previous scholars: first, the impact of international rivalry on the governing ideology of the Spanish empire; second, the role of juridical ideas, especially regalism, in the reconceptualization of the monarchy and its relation to the economy, the Church, and, broadly speaking, corporate privilege; third, the transformation of major ultramarine institutions and the decisive part played by local administrators in this process; and fourth, the intellectual activities of the colonial elites which affected, to a hitherto underappreciated extent, the formulation, implementation, and efficacy of the Bourbon reform programme. Analysis of these four aspects led to the following conclusion: regalist jurisprudence, political economy, and the critical emulation of foreign institutions and legislation were the main intellectual pillars upon which the edifice of Bourbon reform was erected.

Any study that seeks to examine the link between ideas and politics will never be able to arrive at a neat conclusion; on the contrary, an appreciation of the chaotic and contingent nature of these connections is required. This monograph sought to emphasize the turbulent coexistence of often competing ideas and the Bourbon officials, on both shores of the Atlantic, and colonial actors who used them. Emulation of foreign models always was tempered by patriotic priorities and the dictates of local circumstances. These factors necessarily resulted in intellectual hybridity. Far from an

152

absence of 'sentiments more liberal and enlarged',[2] the idiosyncratic and uneven nature of policy resulted from the diversity, not paucity, of competing ideas which the Spanish Crown sought to implement, often simultaneously, in various colonies, confronting a kaleidoscopic range of circumstances in an empire distinguished by its topographical, demographical, and economic heterogeneity.

The failure to appreciate sufficiently this eclecticism led previous commentators to conclude that the Bourbons were 'simply pragmatic nationalists administering a fragile state and a porous empire', who 'merely proliferated traditional structures' in order to shore up the 'gothic edifice' of the imperial system.[3] Instead, this book has suggested, it is more accurate to view this 'pragmatism', the range of policies without an apparent 'master plan', as a manifestation of two phenomenon: first, the widely divergent ideological underpinnings of the reformers themselves, which pulled policy in multiple, often mutually exclusive, directions; and second, the modifications in policy which necessarily occurred in response to local exigencies, specifically the maintenance of relatively harmonious relations with local elites. This perspective, it is hoped, might help to re-frame the relationship between the Bourbon state and increasingly dynamic American elites on the eve of independence.

In addition to making a specific contribution to the historiography of the Bourbon reform period, this monograph aimed to demonstrate the relevance of three tendencies in contemporary historiography for the study of Spain and its overseas empire: first, the study of networks of intellectual exchange and transnational cultural transmission in imperial perspective; second, the study of Spanish America as an integral, not parallel, part of Iberian History;[4] and third, the enlargement of primary sources deemed pertinent to the study of the history of political thought. In addition to published texts, historians should consider official correspondence and the minutes of government and civil society institutions, both colonial and metropolitan, in order to probe the ideas, sentiments, and attitudes of a historical period.

This study of the Bourbon reform period, then, endeavoured to open, and contribute to, new avenues of research. While remaining aware, as indicated in the introductory chapter, of the paradigms and priorities which have guided previous researchers, it argued for an interpretation of the Bourbon period which would emphasize regalist precepts of governance and the emulation of foreign practices in the context of imperial rivalry. In stressing the loftier political concepts which guided reformers, this monograph did not offer an apology for Bourbon government's indelibly dubious legacy in both the Old World and the New, but rather sought to recount and analyse the myriad efforts of Crown officials, political and economic writers, local administrators, and merchant intellectuals to make their kingdoms, in Campomanes's phrase, 'vigilant, awake, and instructed in the arts of war and peace'.[5]

Abbreviations

AEA	*Anuario de Estudios Americanos*
ACC	Archivo de Conde de Campomanes (Madrid, Spain)
AGI	Archivo General de Indias (Seville, Spain)
AGN	Archivo General de la Nación (Buenos Aires, Argentina)
AGS	Archivo General de Simancas (Simancas, Spain)
AHDE	*Anuario de Historia del Derecho Español*
AHN	Archivo Histórico Nacional (Madrid, Spain)
AHU	Arquivo Histórico Ultramarino (Lisbon, Portugal)
AN (Havana)	Archivo Nacional de Cuba (Havana, Cuba)
AN (Santiago)	Archivo Nacional de Chile (Santiago, Chile)
ANH	Academia Nacional de Historia (Buenos Aires, Argentina)
BL	British Library (London, England)
BN	Biblioteca Nacional (Madrid, Spain)
BNJM	Biblioteca Nacional José Martí (Havana, Cuba)
BPR	Biblioteca del Palacio Real (Madrid, Spain)
BRAH	*Boletín de la Real Academia de la Historia*
EEH	Escuela de Estudios Hispanoamericanos (Seville, Spain)
HAHR	*Hispanic American Historical Review*
JLAS	*Journal of Latin American Studies*
PRO	Public Records Office (Kew, London, England)
RAH	La Real Academia de la Historia (Madrid, Spain)
RI	*Revista de Indias*

Notes

Introduction

1. AGI Indiferente General 2436, 'Informe de la extensión que ha tenido el comercio de Indias por un efecto de la libertad', 26 January 1788.
2. See plate 1 for the full version of Giambattista Tiepolo's study, 'The Wealth and Benefits of the Spanish Monarchy under Charles III' (1762), upon which the fresco is based.
3. The year 1700 marks Philip V's accession to the throne, but it was only after the Treaty of Utrecht of 1713, which concluded the War of Spanish Succession, that his reign was uncontested.
4. Among the leading works contributed by historians in the English-speaking world are Jeremy Adelman, *Republic of Capital: Buenos Aires and the Legal Transformation of the Atlantic World* (Stanford, 1999) and *Sovereignty and Revolution in the Iberian Atlantic* (Princeton, 2006); Kenneth Andrien, *The Kingdom of Quito, 1690–1830: The State and Regional Economic Development* (Cambridge, 1995); Jacques Barbier, *Reform and Politics in Bourbon Chile, 1755–1796* (Ottowa, 1980); David Brading, *Miners and Merchants in Bourbon Mexico, 1763–1810* (Cambridge, 1971); Richard Herr, *The Eighteenth-Century Revolution in Spain* (Princeton, 1958); Allan Kuethe, *Cuba, 1753–1815: Crown, Military and Society* (Knoxville, 1986); John Lynch, *Bourbon Spain, 1700–1808* (Oxford, 1989); Anthony McFarlane, *Colombia Before Independence: Economy, Society and Politics Under Bourbon Rule* (Cambridge, 1993); P. Michael McKinley, *Pre-Revolutionary Caracas: Politics, Economy and Society, 1777–1811* (Cambridge, 1985); Stanley Stein and Barbara Stein, *Apogee of Empire: Spain and New Spain in the Age of Charles III, 1759–1789* (Baltimore and London, 2003); and David Weber, *Bárbaros: Spaniards and their Savages in the Age of Enlightenment* (New Haven and London, 2005). Among the leading works by Spanish and Latin American historians are: Antonio Álvarez de Morales, *Pensamiento Político y Jurídico de Campomanes* (Madrid, 1989); José Carlos Chiaramonte, *La Ilustración en el Río de la Plata: Cultura Eclesiástica y Cultura Laica Durante el Veirreinato* (Buenos Aires, 1989); Antonio Domínguez Ortiz, *Sociedad y Estado en el Siglo XVIII Español* (Barcelona, 1976) and *Carlos III y la España de la Ilustración* (Madrid, 1988); Ricardo García Cárcel, ed., *Historia de España Siglo XVIII: La España de los Borbones* (Madrid, 2002); Agustín Guimerá, ed., *El Reformismo Borbónico: Una Visión Interdisciplinar* (Madrid, 1996); Francisco Sánchez-Blanco, *El Absolutismo y Las Luces en el Reinado de Carlos III* (Madrid, 2002); and Jean Sarrailh, *La España Ilustrada de la Segunda Mitad del Siglo XVIII* (Mexico City, 1957).
5. See plate 2 for Goya's portrait of 'Charles III as a Hunter' (c. 1788).
6. J.H. Elliott, 'A Europe of Composite Monarchies', *Past and Present*, 137 (1992): 48–71 passim.
7. J.H. Elliott, *Empires of the Atlantic World: Britain and Spain in America, 1492–1830* (New Haven and London, 2006), 307–8.
8. Jaime E. Rodríguez O. argued convincingly that, under the Habsburg's, 'Spanish America was not a colony of Spain but an integral part of the Spanish Monarchy'

and that 'New World discourse was based on the belief that the American realms were not colonies but equal and integral parts of the Spanish Crown' in *The Independence of Spanish America* (Cambridge, 1998), xii, 2; Anthony Pagden made a similar claim: 'the Spanish-American dominions were not colonies—that term is never used to describe any of the Habsburg possessions—but discrete parts of the crown of Castile. As early as the 1560s they had come to be seen by their inhabitants as quasi-autonomous kingdoms, part of what came to be called "Greater Spain" no different, whatever the realities of their legal status, from Aragon, Naples or the Netherlands.' See Pagden, *Spanish Imperialism and the Political Imagination: Studies in European and Spanish American Social and Political Theory, 1513–1830* (New Haven and London, 1990), 91.

9. These lines liberally take their inspiration from Eric Stokes, *The English Utilitarians and India* (Oxford, 1959), xii–xiii. I thank Richard Drayton for bringing this connection to my attention.

10. Henry Swinburne, *Travels Through Spain in the Years 1775 & 1776* (2nd edn, London, 1787), vol. II, 170.

11. The author remains cognizant of J.H. Elliott's observation that 'excessive concentration' on ritual, ceremony and artistic propaganda is 'liable to distract attention from other and possibly more potent weapons in the armory ... the exercise of power is, after all, something more than the manipulation of images' in 'Power and Propaganda in the Spain of Philip IV', in Sean Wilentz, ed., *Rites of Power: Symbolism, Ritual and Politics Since the Middle Ages* (Philadelphia, 1985), 146.

12. Jacques-Benigne Bossuet, *Politics Drawn from the Very Words of Holy Scripture* (Cambridge, 1999), 109; on Bossuet and other French theorists of absolutism, see Nannerl O. Keohane, *Philosophy and the State in France: the Renaissance to the Enlightenment* (Princeton, 1980).

13. Valentino Crivellato, *Tiepolo* (London, 1962), 65; in addition to the Throne Room, Tiepolo also completed two additional frescos in the *Sala de Guardias* and *la Saleta*; for a description of these frescos, see F.J. Sánchez Canton, *J.B. Tiepolo en España* (Madrid, 1953), 10–16 passim; Catherine Whistler, 'G.B. Tiepolo at the Court of Charles III', *Burlington Magazine*, 128 (1986): 203; Jesús Urrea Fernández, *La Pintura Italiana del Siglo XVIII España* (Valladolid, 1977), 125; Michael Levey observed that Tiepolo never enjoyed great popularity in Paris, Venice, or Rome. He noted that 'the places where [Tiepolo] was sought are revelatory of his art. Milan under the Austrians, Stockholm and Madrid ... his own art was deeply *ancien régime*, anachronistic of its century' in *Rococo to Revolution: Major Trends in Eighteenth-Century Painting* (London, 1967), 91.

14. These manuals would have been Cesare Ripa's *Iconologia* and Vincenzo Cartari's *Imagini Degli Dei*; Fabre confessed that 'I have experienced no small difficulty in understanding [the frescos' imagery] ... this type of allegory is not linked easily to types and models [*tipos y modelos*] ... it is necessary to seek recourse to the imagination in order to execute the assignment' in Francisco José Fabre, *Descripción de las Alegorías Pintadas en las Bóvedas del Real Palacio de Madrid* (Madrid, 1829), 130, 117; Fabre, however, could have relied, at least in part, on Ripa's *Iconologia*, as it provides useful clues. See plate 3, 'Glory of the Prince', for instance, whose influence is reflected clearly in Tiepolo's sketch for the Throne Room fresco.

15. William L. Barcham, *Giambattista Tiepolo* (London, 1992), 45; to a certain extent, Tiepolo's Throne Room fresco repeats the formula he had employed in earlier depictions of royalty, particularly in 'Maecenas Presenting the Arts to

Augustus' painted for Augustus II of Poland and in the 'Investiture of Bishop Herold' for the Würzburg *Kaisersaal*.

16. See plates 4 and 5 for details of Tiepolo's sketch for the Throne Room fresco.
17. Leslie Jones, 'Peace, Prosperity and Politics in Tiepolo's *Glory of the Spanish Monarchy*', *Apollo*, 114 (1981): 221, 226, 224.
18. On the concept of 'Cis-Atlantic' history, see David Armitage, 'Three Concepts of Atlantic History' in Armitage and M.J. Braddick, eds, *The British Atlantic World, 1500–1800* (London, 2002), 15.
19. Mengs was recruited to replace the Neapolitan painter Giaquinto who had occupied the post of *Primer Pintor* from 1753–62 after Queen Maria Amalia became enamoured of the altarpieces Mengs had painted for King Augustus in Dresden. Charles spent the staggering sum of 1, 250, 514 *reales de vellón* to recruit Mengs and, subsequently, paid as much for Tiepolo's services. See Whistler, 'G.B. Tiepolo', 199.
20. *The Works of Anthony Raphael Mengs. Published by Don Joseph Nicholás Azara*, 2 vols (London, 1796), 2; originally published as *Obras de Don Antonio Rafael Mengs, Primer Pintor de Camara del Rey* (Madrid, 1780); there is no direct evidence that Charles III read any of Mengs's writings on aesthetics in the 1760s. As Thomas Pelzel noted, '[Charles III] had hired Mengs not as a reformer of the art of painting, but as a reliable work-horse' in *Anton Raphael Mengs and Neoclassicism* (New York and London, 1979), 127.
21. Mengs, Works, vol. I, 35.
22. Mengs, *Works*, vol. II, 106; Winckelmann, Mengs's most famous and influential interlocutor-collaborator, stated in 1765: 'to original ideas, we oppose copied, not imitated ones. Copying we call the slavish crawling of the hands and eyes after a certain model; whereas reasonable imitation just takes the hint, in order to work by itself' in Johann Winckelmann, *Reflections on the Painting and Sculpture of the Greeks* (London, 1999), 256, 189; Pelzel argued that Mengs maintained that 'the emulation of the Greek taste for ideal beauty, rather than the passive borrowing of prototypes, which constituted the true imitation of the antique' in *Mengs and Neoclassicism*, 116.
23. See plate 6 for Mengs's portrait of Campomanes.
24. Pedro Rodríguez de Campomanes, *Discurso Sobre la Educación Popular de los Artesanos y su Fomento* (Madrid, 1775), 110–11.
25. *Informe* from 1 March 1769, reproduced in Juan Carrete y Parrando, 'Pedro Rodríguez de Campomanes: Informes Sobre la Real Academia de Bellas Artes de San Fernando', *Revista de Ideas Estéticas*, 137 (1977): 88.
26. Campomanes, *Noticia Geográfica del Reyno y Caminos de Portugal* (Madrid, 1762), dedication.
27. G.W. Pigman, 'Versions of Imitation in the Renaissance', *Renaissance Quarterly*, 33:1 (1980): 4, 22, 25, 32.
28. Daisy Rípodas Ardanaz, *Refracción de Ideas en Hispanoamérica Colonial* (Buenos Aires, 1983), 35.
29. While favouring an Atlantic perspective, however, it is prudent to remain cognizant of the intellectual context and geo-strategic perspective of the reformers themselves. In their worldview, peninsular Spain was both distinct from other European states and from Spain's overseas dominions. It remained a crucial actor in the Mediterranean world, especially in southern Italy and North Africa, during the Bourbon epoch. While maintaining that imperial considerations merit higher priority among historians of Europe, an over-estimation of the role of empire in continental politics is avoided in this book.

30. For two masterful overviews which place Bourbon affairs in broader context, see Paul Schroeder, *The Transformation of European Politics, 1763–1848* (Oxford, 1994) and H.M. Scott, *The Birth of a Great Power System, 1740–1815* (Harlow, 2006).

31. This insight is adapted from John Robertson's brilliant analysis of Franco Venturi in *The Case for the Enlightenment: Scotland and Naples, 1680–1760* (Cambridge, 2005), 38.

32. This framework is adapted from contemporary political science. Kurt Weyland, 'Introduction', in Weyland, ed., *Learning from Foreign Models in Latin American Policy Reform* (Washington, DC, 2004), 21; as Weyland indicated, imitation of foreign models is not without pitfalls: the 'desire to copy promising practices in order not to fall behind ... can expose policy makers to untested "fads and fashions" that hurt the quality of policy outputs'. Furthermore, 'people learning [from foreign models] need not process information correctly, draw valid inferences, nor improve diagnosis and policy recommendation'; see Weyland, 'Introduction', 5, 23; in employing Weyland's framework, I remain aware of James Lockhart's useful warning to Latin American historians that 'social science can bring in rigid concepts from a different intellectual context, which correspond to nothing ... [becoming] nothing but an amusing intellectual game', in his 'The Social History of Colonial Spanish America: Evolution and Potential', *Latin American Research Review*, 7 (1972): 33.

33. A modification of the framework proposed by Colin Bennett, 'What is Policy Convergence and What Causes it?', *British Journal of Political Science*, 21:2 (1991): 215–22 passim.

34. Regalism is a type of jurisdictionalism. Jurisdictionalism signifies a system of relations between two or more powers characterized by their distinction and simultaneous coordination. In this sense, it differs markedly from both theocratic and separatist doctrines. This definition relies on Álvarez de Morales, *El Pensamiento Político y Jurídico de Campomanes*, 29.

35. On Olivares, see J.H. Elliott, *The Count-Duke of Olivares: The Statesman in an Age of Decline* (New Haven and London, 1986); on the *arbitristas*, see Stanley Stein and Barbara Stein, *Silver, Trade and War: Spain and America in the Making of Early Modern Europe* (Baltimore and London, 2000).

36. Charles Noel noted that regalism's very malleability ranks among its defining features: 'one of the most significant aspects of regalism was the vagueness of its aims. Regalism was an approach more than a definable programme with universally recognizable goals ... Regalism should probably be understood as a weapon, wielded by individuals who each had somewhat different purposes'. See Noel, 'Campomanes and the Secular Clergy in Spain, 1760–1780: Enlightenment vs. Tradition' (PhD Dissertation, Princeton University, 1969), 6.

37. R.J.W. Evans, *The Making of the Habsburg Monarchy, 1550–1700: an Interpretation* (Oxford, 1979), 448–9; I am grateful for David Brading's suggestion that I consult Evans's book in relation to my argument.

38. Franco Venturi went so far as to note that Floridablanca's ministry 'seemed to follow in the footsteps of Joseph II', but did not elaborate further on this connection, in his *The End of the Old Regime in Europe, 1776–1789. Vol. I: The Great States of the West* (Princeton, 1991), 299.

39. José Antonio Maravall, *Culture of the Baroque: an Analysis of a Historical Structure* (Minneapolis, 1986), 145, 138.

40. Elliott, *Empires of the Atlantic World*, 133, 319–24, 364–5.

41. In the Andean colonies alone, there were at least 92 separate insurrections between 1750 and 1781. In New Granada, the *Comunero* revolt (1781) galvanized

15–20, 000 individuals. Nevertheless, with few notable exceptions, none of these movements sought political change beyond the redress of basic grievances: reduction in level of taxation, abolition of certain royal monopolies, and the dismissal of unusually obnoxious officials. See Peter Bakewell, *A History of Latin America* (Oxford, 1997), 282–7 passim.

42. Fifteen years ago, Kenneth Maxwell noted that 'while much has been achieved by the emphasis on conjunctural economic analysis and social history, it has unquestionably also led to the almost total exclusion of detailed examinations of elites, institutions and, above all, intellectual life and policy', in 'The Atlantic in the Eighteenth Century: a Southern Perspective on the Need to Return to the "Big Picture"' *Transactions of the Royal Historical Society*, 6th series (London, 1993): 210; to a certain extent, fortunately, this lacunae has been filled. This book, therefore, engages in dialogue with the following works which responded to Maxwell's plea: Lauren Benton, *Law and Colonial Cultures: Legal Regimes in World History, 1400–1900* (Cambridge, 2002); Adelman, *Republic of Capital*; not to mention Maxwell's own *Pombal: Paradox of the Enlightenment* (Cambridge, 1995).

43. In this effort, the argument responds directly to, and is inspired by, Richard Drayton's stimulating hypothesis about the trans-European origins of a turn toward an active 'crown imperialism' in the contemporary Georgian British Empire. See Drayton, *Nature's Government: Science, Imperial Britain and the 'Improvement of the World* (New Haven and London, 2000), from about fn. 139 of chapter 3 through chapter 4.

44. For a pioneering comparative study, see Anthony Pagden, *Lords of All the World: Ideologies of Empire in Spain, Britain and France, c. 1500– c. 1800* (New Haven and London, 1995).

45. As McFarlane rightly put it, with reference to New Granada, 'in the end it was to be Spain's vertiginous collapse in 1808 that would create the conditions for [the] separation of the parent power, rather than the ideas or projects of heroic or far-sighted Creole "precursors"' in *Colombia Before Independence*, 307.

46. As Jorge I. Domínguez explained, 'the neopatrimonial model stresses the centrality of the monarch who dispenses favors; openings for capitalism exist, but they have a political orientation. Economic elites petition the public authority for favors to further their private advantage'. See Domínguez, *Insurrection or Loyalty: The Breakdown of the Spanish Empire* (London and Cambridge, MA, 1980), 82.

47. My approach to the relation between the public sphere and the state is informed by T.C.W. Blanning, *The Culture of Power and the Power of Culture: Old Regime Europe, 1660–1789* (Oxford, 2002), 13.

48. This book employs the term 'civil society' in a slightly anachronistic sense, drawing on J.L. Cohen and Andrew Arato's definition, as a sphere of social interaction between economy and state, composed of the sphere of associations, social movements, and forms of public communication. See Cohen and Arato, *Civil Society and Political Theory* (London, 1992), ix; this understanding is different from what Anthony Black described as the pre-Hegelian understanding of *societas civilis*. See Black, 'Concepts of Civil Society in Premodern Europe', in Sudipta Kaviraj and Sunil Khilnani, eds, *Civil Society: History and Possibilities* (Cambridge, 2002), 33–6 passim.

49. R. Robinson and J. Gallagher, *Africa and the Victorians: The Official Mind of Imperialism* (London, 1961), 19, 25.

50. Stanley J. and Barbara H. Stein, *The Colonial Heritage of Latin America: Essays on Economic Independence in Perspective* (New York, 1970), 68.

51. This definition relies heavily on that of R.O. Keohane and J.S. Nye, quoted in Owen E. Hughes, *Public Management and Administration: An Introduction* (New York, 2003), 77.

52. Julián Marías, *La España Posible en Tiempo de Carlos III* (Madrid, 1963), 19; for an analysis of the most recent scholarship in greater detail than is possible in this book, see Gabriel Paquette, 'Enlightenment, Empire and Regalism: New Directions in Eighteenth-century Spanish History', *European History Quarterly*, 35:1 (2005): 107–17; for an extended review of the historiography, see Paquette, 'Governance and Reform in the Spanish Atlantic World, c. 1760–1810' (PhD Dissertation, University of Cambridge, 2006), esp. Chapter 1, 'Historiography'.

53. F. López, 'La Historia de las Ideas en el Siglo XVIII: Concepciones Antiguas y Revisiones Necesarias', *Boletín del Centro de Estudios del Siglo XVIII* [Oviedo] 3 (1975): 12.

54. Andrés Muriel, *Gobierno del Señor Rey Don Carlos III, o Instrucción Reservada Para Direccion de la Junta de Estado* (Madrid, 1839), 79.

55. Antonio Ferrer del Río, *Historia del Reinado de Carlos III en España* (Madrid, 1856), vol. I, xxi.

56. Richard Herr, 'The Twentieth-century Spaniard Views the Spanish Enlightenment', *Hispania*, 45:2 (1962): 184.

57. Marcelino Menéndez Pelayo, *Historia de los Heterodoxos Españoles* (Madrid, 1992), vol. II, 674, 700.

58. Herr, *The Eighteenth-Century Revolution in Spain*, 437–8.

59. Jean Sarrailh, *La España Ilustrada de la Segunda Mitad del Siglo XVIII* (Mexico City, 1957), 373, 711.

60. Marías, *La España Posible*, 126.

61. Anna María Rao, 'Carlos de Borbón en Nápoles', *Trienio*, 24 (1994): 31; Roberto Fernández, *Carlos III* (Madrid, 2001), 112; for broader perspectives on Naples during Charles's reign there, see Harold Stone, *Vico's Cultural History: the Production and Transmission of Ideas in Naples, 1685–1750* (Leiden and New York, 1997); and Girolamo Imbruglia, ed., *Naples in the Eighteenth Century: The Birth and Death of a Nation State* (Cambridge, 2000).

62. Venturi, 'Spanish and Italian Economists and Reformers in the Eighteenth Century', in *Italy and the Enlightenment: Studies in a Cosmopolitan Century*, ed. Stuary Woolf and trans. Susan Corsi (New York, 1972), 289.

63. Adelman, *Republic of Capital*, 56; also see Allan Kuethe and Lowell Blaisdel, 'French Influence and the Origins of Bourbon Colonial Reorganization', *HAHR*, 71 (1991): 579–607.

64. Charles Jago, 'The Eighteenth-Century Economic Analysis of the Decline of Spain', in Paul Fritz and David Williams, eds, *The Triumph of Culture: Eighteenth-Century Perspectives* (Toronto, 1972), 336, 340.

65. Luís Perdices de Blas, *La Economía Política de la Decadencia de Castilla en el Siglo XVII: Investigaciones de los Arbitristas sobre la Naturaleza y Causas de la Riqueza de las Naciones* (Madrid, 1996), 194–5, 156.

66. Francisco Sánchez-Blanco, *La Mentalidad Ilustrada* (Madrid, 1999), 331.

67. Miguel Amunátegui, *Los Precursores de la Independencia Chilena* (Santiago, 1909), vol. I, 367.

68. O. Carlos Stoetzer argued that 'the increasing influence of the *philosophes* ... did not nullify the scholastic influence', in *The Scholastic Roots of the Spanish American Revolution* (New York, 1979), 77, 85; for similar argument, see Richard M. Morse, 'Toward a Theory of Spanish American Government', *Journal of the History of Ideas*, 15 (1954): 75, 77.

69. Jaime Eyzaguirre, *Ideario y Ruta de la Emancipación Chilena* (Santiago, 1991), 79, 83; Sergio Villalobos R. suggested that the Bourbon reformers 'presented a panorama filled with stimulating suggestions [for reform], perhaps less important than their counterparts in other European countries, but one that was more easily comprehended by Creoles and bore closer relation to their reality', in *Tradición y Reforma en 1810* (Santiago, 1961), 47.

70. Adelman, *Republic of Capital*, 57; Bernardino Bravo Lira, 'El Absolutismo Ilustrado en España e Indias Bajo Carlos III (1759–1788)', *Revista Chilena de Historia del Derecho*, 14 (1991): 11–34.

71. Arthur P. Whitaker, 'Changing and Unchanging Interpretations of the Enlightenment in Spanish America', *Proceedings of the American Philosophical Society*, 114:4 (1970): 257.

72. Ricardo Levene, *El Mundo de las Ideas y la Revolución Hispanoamericana de 1810* (Santiago, 1956), 261.

73. McFarlane, *Colombia Before Independence*, 4.

74. David Brading, *The First America: The Spanish Monarchy, Creole Patriots and the Liberal State, 1492–1867* (Cambridge, 1991), 5.

75. Adelman, *Republic of Capital*, 68; for a precursor to this argument, see Roque Gondra's description of the influences on Manuel Belgrano's political economy in his *Las Ideas Económicas de Manuel Belgrano* (Buenos Aires, 1927), 124.

76. Chiaramonte, *La Ilustración en el Río de la Plata*, 54.

77. The first explicit reference appeared in 1758 in an article published in the *Correspondance Literaire* by Grimm and was subsequently employed in the Milanese Giuseppe Gorani's *Il Vero Dispotismo* (1770); see Derek Beales, *Enlightenment and Reform in Eighteenth-century Europe* (London, 2005), 39–51.

78. At the 1928 Conference of the International Committee of the Historical Sciences in Oslo and subsequently elaborated by the *Commission pour l'étude du despotisme éclairé* which met throughout the 1930s.

79. Michel Lhéritier, 'Le Rôle Historique du Despotisme Éclairé, Particulièrement au XVIIIe Siècle', *Bulletin of the International Committee of the Historical Sciences,* 1 (1928): 601–12 passim; and 'Rapport General: le Despotisme Éclairé, de Frédéric II á la Révolution Française', *Bulletin of the International Committee of the Historical Sciences,* 9 (1937): 185–225.

80. John G. Gagliardo, *Enlightened Despotism* (New York, 1967), 81.

81. M.S. Anderson, *Historians and Eighteenth-Century Europe, 1715–1789* (Oxford, 1979), 120–2.

82. Ibid., 131.

83. T.C.W. Blanning, *Joseph II and Enlightened Despotism* (London, 1970), 19.

84. T.C.W. Blanning, *Reform and Revolution in Mainz, 1743–1803* (Cambridge, 1974), 34–7 passim; Blanning was, of course, referring to German states in his analysis, but his insights are more generally applicable.

85. H.M. Scott, 'The Problem of Enlightened Absolutism', in Scott, ed., *Enlightened Absolutism: Reform and Reformers in Late Eighteenth-Century Europe* (Basingstoke, 1990), 17–18.

86. John Lynch, *Bourbon Spain, 1700–1808* (Oxford, 1989), 247.

87. Joseph Townsend, *A Journey Through Spain in the Years 1786 and 1787* (London, 1792), vol. II, 226, 394, 252; on British travellers in late eighteenth-century Spain, see Ana Clara Guerrero, *Viajeros Británicos en la España del Siglo XVIII* (Madrid, 1990), 316, 342–5.

88. William Robertson, *History of America* (London, 1777), vol. III, book 8, 337.

89. Ibid., vol. III, book 8, 343, 349, 350.

90. Gaspar Melchor de Jovellanos, 'Informe de la Ley Agraria' (1795), in Ernest Lluch and Lluís Argemí d'Abadal, eds, *Agronomía y Fisiocracia en España, 1750–1820* (Valencia, 1985), 494.
91. Cayetano Alcázar Molina, 'El Despotismo Ilustrado en España', *Bulletin of the International Committee of Historical Sciences*, 5 (1933): 729, 750–1.
92. Luis Sánchez Agesta, *El Pensamiento Político de Despotismo Ilustrado* (Madrid, 1953), 107, 174, 178.
93. Herr, *Eighteenth-Century Revolution*, 437.
94. [Hugh Trevor-Roper], 'The Spanish Enlightenment', *Times Literary Supplement*, 15 March 1957: 154.
95. Antonio Elorza, *La Ideologia Liberal en la Ilustración Española* (Madrid, 1970), 36.
96. José Antonio Maravall, 'La Formula Política del Despotismo Ilustrado', in Mario di Pinto, ed., *I Borbone di Napoli e I Borbone de Spagna* (Naples, 1985), 27–8, 32–3, 21; subsequent historians have implied that Maravall overstated his case. Novales observed that the Spanish enlightenment 'was born with an accent on [public] service ... [it was] an enlightenment of bureaucrats and government employees'. See Alberto Gil Novales, 'Ilustración y Liberalismo en España', in *Del Antiguo al Nuevo Régimen en España* (Caracas, 1986), 57.
97. Sánchez-Blanco, *La Mentalidad Ilustrada*, 333.
98. Sánchez-Blanco, *El Absolutismo y las Luces en el Reinado de Carlos III*, 47, 52, 443; Brading argued that even in the cases of purportedly 'enlightened' figures, such as Campomanes and Jovellanos, 'the assimilation of the Enlightenment remained cautious and tentative, more obvious in the aesthetic sphere where renaissance precedent existed than in religion or politics', in *The First America*, 511.
99. Lluís Roura I Aulinas, 'Expectativas y Frustración Bajo el Reformismo Borbónico' in Ricardo García Cárcel, ed., *Historia de España Siglo XVIII: La España de los Borbones* (Madrid, 2002), 217.
100. Antonio Mestre Sanchis, *Apología y Crítica de España en el Siglo XVIII* (Madrid, 2003), 117.
101. C.H. Haring, *The Spanish Empire in America* (New York, 1947), 335.
102. Brian Hamnett, 'Absolutismo Ilustrado y Crisis Multidimensional en el Periodo Colonial Tardió, 1760–1808', in Josefina Zoraida Vázquez, ed., *Interpretaciones del Siglo XVIII Mexicano: El Impacto de las Reformas Borbónicas* (Mexico City, 1992), 69. I am grateful to David Brading for bringing this book, to which he contributed an important essay, to my attention.
103. Colin M. MacLachlan, *Spain's Empire in the New World: The Role of Ideas in Institutional and Social Change* (Berkeley, CA, 1988), 126–8.
104. Horst Pietschmann, 'Protoliberalismo, Reformas Borbónicas y Revolución: La Nueva España en el Ultimo Tercio del Siglo XVIII', in Zoraida Vázquez, *Interpretaciones del Siglo XVIII Mexicano*, 60–1.
105. Bernard E. Bobb, *The Viceregency of Antonio María Bucareli in New Spain, 1771–1779* (Austin, 1962), 15.
106. Geoffrey J. Walker, *Spanish Politics and Imperial Trade, 1700–1789* (London, 1979), 219.
107. Antonio García-Baquero González, *Cádiz y el Atlántico (1717–1778): El Mundo Colonial Español Bajo el Monopolio Gaditano* (Cádiz, 1988), vol. I, 85.
108. Stein and Stein, *Apogee of Empire*, 23; Stein and Stein, *Colonial Heritage of Latin America*, 92–3, 103–4.
109. Weber, *Bárbaros*, 278.

110. Peggy Liss, *Atlantic Empires: The Network of Trade and Revolution, 1713–1826* (London, 1983), 74.

111. Kenneth R. Maxwell, 'Hegemonies Old and New: The Ibero-Atlantic in the Long Eighteenth Century', in Jeremy Adelman, ed., *Colonial Legacies: the Problem of Persistence in Latin American History* (New York and London, 1999), 71.

112. Sempere y Guarinos, *Historia del las Rentas Eclesiásticas de España* (Madrid, 1822), quoted in Juan Rico Giménez, *De la Ilustración al Liberalismo: El Pensamiento de Sempere y Guarinos* (Alicante, 1997), 178.

113. Ferrer del Río, *Historia*, vol. II, 520–52; vol. IV, 554.

114. Agustino Manuel Miguélez, *Jansenismo y Regalismo en España* (Valladolid, 1895), 118, 277–8.

115. Ibid., 280–3 passim.

116. Rafael Olaechea, *Las Relaciones Hispano-Romanas en la Segunda Mitad del Siglo XVIII: La Agencia de Preces* (Zaragoza, 1965); Isidoro Martín, 'Panorama del Regalismo Español hasta la Vigente Concordato de 1953', *Revista de la Facultad de Derecho de la Universidad de Madrid*, 5 (1961): 280, 284; Vincente Rodríguez Casado, 'Iglesia y Estado en el Reinado de Carlos III', *Estudios Americanos*, 1 (1948): 6.

117. Herr, *Eighteenth-Century Revolution*, 36.

118. Teófanes Egido, 'El Regalismo y las Relaciones Iglesia-Estado en el Siglo XVIII', in Antonio Mestre Sanchis, ed., *Historia de la Iglesia en España. Volume 4: Siglos XVII–XVIII* (Madrid, 1979), 125, 200, 135.

119. Alberto de la Hera, *El Regalismo Borbónico en su Proyección Indiana* (Madrid, 1963), 18, 129.

120. Antonio Benlloch Poveda, 'Antecedentes Doctrinales del Regalismo Borbónico: Juristas Españoles en las Lecturas de los Regalistas Europeos Modernos', *Revista de Historia Moderna* [Alicante] 4 (1984): 313.

121. Virgilio Pinto Crespo, 'Una Reforma desde Arriba: Iglesia y Religiosidad', in Equipo Madrid, *Carlos III*, 186–7; according to Emilio La Parra, 'la politique règaliste borbonienne fut, avant tout, un moyen d'entreprendre diverses reformes dans le secteur clérical' in 'Le Règalisme Borbonien', in Gérard Chastagnaret and Gérard Dufour, eds, *Le Règne de Charles III: Le Despotisme Éclairé en Espagne* (Paris, 1994), 184.

122. Sánchez-Blanco, *El Absolutismo*, 217, 255, 347.

123. D.A. Brading, 'Bourbon Spain and its American Empire', in Leslie Bethell, ed., *The Cambridge History of Latin America* (Cambridge, 1984), vol. I, 395, 408.

124. Ibid., 439.

125. Andrien, *The Kingdom of Quito, 1690–1830*, 190–1; Andrien pointed out, however, that, in the long run, such 'predatory' policies 'disrupted business, trade and capital accumulation'.

126. Miles Wortman, *Government and Society in Central America, 1680–1840* (New York, 1982), 129, 170.

127. John Lynch, 'The Institutional Framework of Colonial Spanish America', *JLAS*, 24 (1992): 79.

128. J.R. Fisher, A.J. Kuethe, and A. McFarlane, 'Introduction', in their *Reform and Insurrection in Bourbon New Granada and Peru* (Baton Rouge and London, 1990), 1, 4.

129. McFarlane, *Colombia Before Independence*, 2–3, 119.

130. Adelman, *Republic of Capital*, 21, 29, 25.

131. Stein and Stein, *The Colonial Heritage of Latin America*, 92–3, 103–4; Stein and Stein, *Apogee of Empire*, 212.

132. Stein and Stein, *Apogee of Empire*, 26.
133. Bartolomé Yun-Casalilla, 'The American Empire and the Spanish Economy: An Institutional and Regional Perspective', *Revista de Historia Económica*, 16 (1998): 147.
134. John Coatsworth, 'The Limits of Colonial Absolutism: the State in Eighteenth-Century Mexico', in Karen Spalding, ed., *Essays in the Political, Economic and Social History of Colonial Latin America* (Newark, 1982), 36.
135. Richard Herr, *Rural Change and Royal Finances in Spain at the End of the Old Regime* (Berkeley and London, 1989), 44; this view is consistent with Venturi's verdict that the Caroline reformers confronted the 'crises of the Old Regime not with ideas but with techniques, not in putting in question the fundamental problems, but improving administration, assistance, education and preserving and protecting the religion inherited from the past'; see Venturi, *The End of the Old Regime*, vol. I, 299.
136. Antonio García-Baquero González, '¿De la Mina a la Plantación? La Nueva Estructura del Tráfico de Importación de la Carrera de Indias en la Segunda Mitad del Siglo XVIII', in his *El Comercio Colonial en la Época del Absolutismo Ilustrado: Problemas y Debates* (Granada, 2003), 102.
137. Troy S. Floyd, 'The Guatemalan Merchants, the Government and the *Provincianos*, 1750–1800', *HAHR*, 41:1 (1961): 109.
138. Brading, 'Bourbon Spain', 420.
139. Mauro Hernández Benítez, 'Carlos III: Un Mito Progresista', in *Carlos III, Madrid y la Ilustración: Contradicciones de un Proyecto Reformista* (Madrid, 1988), 8, 22.

1   The Intellectual Impact of International Rivalry

1. Charles de Secondat (Baron de Montesquieu), *The Spirit of the Laws* [1748] (Cambridge, 1997), 393, 396, 454; John Campbell, *A Concise History of Spanish America* [1741] (London, 1972), 79.
2. Juan Pablo Forner, *Oración Apologética por la España y Su Mérito Literario* [1788] (Badajoz, 1945), 24; García Cárcel, *La Leyenda Negra: Historia y Opinión* (Madrid, 1992), 172; on the 'patriotic epistemological discourse' provoked by the publication of Masson de Morvillier's entry, see Jorge Cañizares-Esguerra, 'Eighteenth-Century Spanish Political Economy: Epistemology of Decline', *Eighteenth-Century Thought*, 1 (2003): 295–314 passim.
3. José de Cadalso, *Defensa de la Nación Española Contra la Carta Persiana de Montesquieu* [1764] (Toulouse, 1970), 39, 11.
4. Pablo de Olavide, *Plan de Estudios para la Universidad de Sevilla* [1768] (Madrid, 1989), 85–6.
5. BPR II/2867, Josef del Río [Spain's Consul General in Portugal], 'Observación Sobre la Necesidad de Establecer Escuelas Patrióticas de Comercio en Madrid' (1776), fo. 319v.
6. BPR II/2867, Francisco Antonio de Bringas, 'Papel Sobre las Prevenciones que Deben Hacerse a Todo Joven Viajante que se Dedique al Comercio' (1786), fo. 337v.
7. Madrid Economic Society (1775), quoted in W.J. Callahan, 'The Crown and the Promotion of Industry in Eighteenth-Century Spain' (PhD Dissertation, Harvard University, 1964), 139. I am grateful to Professor Callahan for generously sending me the sections of his dissertation which relate to emulation and imitation.
8. Enlightened narratives, according to John Pocock, are histories that conflate narratives of 'state formation and the civilisation of commerce which combine

to produce philosophical history'; see Pocock, *Barbarism and Religion, Volume II: Narratives of Civil Government* (Cambridge, 1999), 20–1; for a study of Almodóvar, see Ovidio García Regueiro's excellent *'Ilustración' e Intereses Estamentales: Antagonismo entre Sociedad Tradicional y Corrientes Innovadoras en la Versión Española de la Historia de Raynal* (Madrid, 1982).

9. J. Huizinga, *Homo Ludens: A Study in the Play Element in Culture* (London, 1980), 187.

10. Sebastião José de Carvalho e Melo [later Pombal], *Escritos Económicos de Londres (1741–1742)* (Lisbon, 1986), 158; also quoted in Kenneth Maxwell's seminal article 'Pombal and the Nationalization of the Luso-Brazilian Economy', *HAHR*, 48:4 (1968): 608; such observations corroborate C.A. Bayly's recent thesis that modernity is a 'process of emulation and borrowing'; see Bayly, *The Birth of the Modern World, 1780–1914: Global Connections and Comparisons* (Oxford, 2004), 10.

11. This phenomenon was not, of course, unique to Spain. For French observers, the Spanish monarchy served as an example of financial and colonial mismanagement. See Paul Cheney's fascinating essay 'Finances, Philosophical History and the "Empire of Climate": Enlightenment Historiography and Political Economy', *Historical Reflections*, 31 (2005): esp. 148–54.

12. Istvan Hont, *Jealousy of Trade: International Competition and the Nation-State in Historical Perspective* (Cambridge, MA, 2005), 115–17.

13. John Iverson, 'Introduction: Forum on Emulation in France, 1750–1800', *Eighteenth-Century Studies*, 36:2 (2003): 218.

14. Quoted in Hont, *Jealousy of Trade*, 118 and 122; Drayton provided further evidence of this phenomenon and suggests how eighteenth-century English officials 'came to imitate the styles of government, copy the institutions and respond to the ideologies of their [continental] contemporaries', in *Nature's Government: Science, Imperial Britain and the 'Improvement' of the World* (New Haven and London, 2000), 68.

15. Adam Smith, *The Theory of Moral Sentiments* [1759] (Amherst, 2000), part 6, section 2, chapter 2, 335–6.

16. Hont, *Jealousy of Trade*, 120–1.

17. John Shovlin, 'Emulation in Eighteenth-century French Economic Thought', *Eighteenth-Century Studies*, 36:2 (2003): 226.

18. Juan Sempere y Guarinos, *Historia del Luxo y de las Leyes Suntuarias de España* (Madrid, 1788), vol. II, 167.

19. Ibid., 210.

20. Juan Pablo Forner, *Oración Apologética por la España y Su Mérito Literario* , 19.

21. BPR II/2829, Marqués de Llanos, 'Los Medios con que Puede Conseguir la Felicidad de la Monarquía' (1755), fo. 102v.

22. Gerónimo de Uztáriz, *The Theory and Practice of Commerce and Maritime Affairs* (London, 1751), vol. II, 423; the impact of French mercantilist writers in Spain is treated in Stanley Stein and Barbara Stein, *Silver, Trade and War: Spain and America in the Making of Early Modern Europe* (Baltimore and London, 2000).

23. Pedro Rodríguez de Campomanes, *Discurso Sobre la Educación Popular de los Artesanos y su Fomento* (Madrid, 1775), 79.

24. AGI Estado 86A, no. 2, [José de Gálvez], 'Discurso y Reflecxiones [sic] de un Vasallo Sobre la Decadencia de Nuestras Indias Españolas' n.d., fo. 23v.

25. Eduardo Malo de Luque [Duke of Almodóvar], *Historia Política de los Establecimientos Ultramarinos de las Naciones Europeas* (Madrid, 1784–90), vol. II, appendix, 6; this account is consistent with that of William Robertson who

argued that 'the growing power of Spain naturally turned the attention of mankind toward the importance of those settlements in the New World to which they were so much indebted for that preeminence'. Furthermore, Columbus's voyages had 'excited a vehement desire of emulating the glory of Spain'; see William Robertson, *The History of America* (London, 1777), vol. 9, book 31, 1–2.

26. AGI Mexico 1242, O'Reilly to Bucareli, 24 November 1770.
27. BPR II/2866, Josef Fuertes, 'Pensamientos, o Proyecto Sobre Volver a Reconciliar com la Madre Patria las Provincias Discolas de la América Meridional' (1781), fo. 249.
28. Bernardo Ward and Gaspar Melchor Jovellanos, both quoted in Blanco Martínez, *La Ilustración en Europa y en España* (Madrid, 1999), 201.
29. Pedro Rodríguez de Campomanes, *Reflexiones sobre el Comercio Exterior a Indias* (Madrid, 1762), 7.
30. Physiocratic ideas, for example, which were 'never followed strictly by any Spanish thinker', are a good example of this process of cultural hybridization: according to Puerto Sarmiento, interest in agriculture located its 'origins in the "agronomistas" of the seventeenth century, whose influence was never suffocated entirely ... physiocracy was neither the motor nor the principal reason behind [late eighteenth-century] Spanish scientific [botanical] expeditions', in Francisco Javier Puerto Sarmiento, *La Ilusión Quebrada: Botánica, Sanidad y Política Científica en la España Ilustrada* (Madrid, 1988), 80.
31. Campomanes, *Educación Popular*, 25.
32. This fusion has been recognized in other national contexts. On Naples and Scotland, for example, see John Robertson, *The Case for the Enlightenment: Scotland and Naples, 1680–1760* (Cambridge, 2005), 38.
33. Campomanes, *Educación Popular*, 19.
34. Antonio Juárez Medina, *Las Reediciones de Obras en Erudición de los Siglos XVI and XVII Durante el Siglo XVIII Español* (Bern, 1988), 99–177 passim.
35. Francisco Lafarga, 'La Traducción en La España del Siglo XVIII', in S.M. Santamaría, ed., *Traveses Culturales: Literatura, Cine, Traducción* (Vitoria, 1997), 39.
36. *Diario Pinciano* of Valladolid (1787), quoted in Callahan, 'The Crown and the Promotion of Industry in Eighteenth-Century Spain', 136.
37. Figures taken from Vicent Llombart, 'Traducciones Españolas de Economia Política (1700–1812): Catálogo Bibliográfico y una Nueva Perspectiva', *Cromohs*, 9 (2004): 1–14; last accessed 10 January 2005: http://www.cromohs.unifi.it/9_2004/llombart.html.
38. Callahan, 'The Crown and the Promotion of Industry in Eighteenth-Century Spain', 137; among the periodicals which furnished the Spanish reading public with instructions for various manufacturing methods developed abroad was the *Diario Estrangero* edited by Francisco Mariano Nipho. Among the articles of this type were: 'Lencería y modo de blanquearla de Harlem' and 'Operación para hacer el verde de Saxonia para teñir paños', both from 1763.
39. E. Lluch Martín, 'El Cameralismo en España', in Enrique Fuentes Quintana, ed., *Economía y Economistas Españoles. Volume 3: La Ilustración* (Barcelona, 2000), 727; Jordi Oliveras Samitier, *Nuevas Poblaciones en la España de la Ilustración* (Barcelona, 1998); Manuel Capel, *La Carolina, Capital de las Nuevas Poblaciones : Un Ensayo de Reforma Socio-Económica de España en el Siglo XVIII* (Jaén, 1970), 80; BPR II/2817, Nicolas Norton Nicols, 'El Comercio de Manila: las Conveniencias, Beneficio y Utilidad que las Islas Philipinas Deben Dar a S.M. como a sus Vasallos' (n.d., addressed to Charles III), fo. 258.

40. Campomanes, *Reflexiones*, 283, 302; Campomanes misrepresented Danish practices in the Caribbean. The royally chartered West India and Guinea Company had cultivated the islands and established routes and markets which paved the way for privatized Danish shipping and trade after 1759; see Ole Feldbaek, 'The Organizational Structure of the Danish East India and West India Companies in the Seventeenth and Eighteenth Centuries', in Blussé and Gaastra, eds, *Companies and Trade: Essays in Overseas Trading Companies During the Ancien Régime* (Leiden, 1981), 155–8; see also, Waldemar Westergaard, *The Danish West Indies Under Company Rule (1671–1754)* (New York, 1917).

41. Campomanes, *Reflexiones*, 95, 97; on Campomanes's opposition to privileged companies, see García Ruiperez, 'El Pensamiento Económico Ilustrado y las Compañías de Comercio', *Revista de Historia Económica*, 4 (1986): 538.

42. Campomanes, *Reflexiones*, 380.

43. AHN Estado 2927, no. 271, Francisco de Craywinckel, 'Utilidad que Podría Sacar España de su Desgracia Por la Perdida de la Habana', enclosed in a letter to Ricardo Wall, 12 November 1762, 23.

44. José de Campillo y Cossío, *Nuevo Sistema de Gobierno Económico Para América* (Oviedo, 1993), 108–9.

45. AGI Santo Domingo 2665, Navarro to Valdes, 16 April 1789, fos. 327–8.

46. Juan Egaña, 'Oración Inaugural Para la Apertura de los Estudios de la Real Universidad de San Felipe', 14 April 1804, in his *Escritos Inéditos y Dispersos* (Santiago, 1949), 14, 17.

47. AGI Caracas 443, Memoria, 26 December 1778.

48. AGI Estado 61, no. 13/2, Manuel de Guevara Vasconcelos to Secretary of State, 25 May 1801, fo. 21.

49. Almodóvar, *Historia Política*, vol. III, appendix.

50. AHN Estado 2927, no. 271, Craywinckel 'Utilidad que Podría Sacar España', 25.

51. AGI Estado 86A, no. 2, [Gálvez], 'Discurso y Reflecxiones [sic] de un Vasallo Sobre la Decadencia de Nuestras Indias Españolas', n.d., fo. 3v.

52. Kuethe and Blaisdell, 'French Influence and the Origins of Bourbon Colonial Reorganization', *HAHR*, 71 (1991): 607.

53. A key exception is J.H. Elliott who observed that 'it was one of the ironies of the 1760s that Spanish ministers should have taken Britain's commercial empire as a model for their own at a time when the British themselves were becoming increasingly attracted by the idea of a more centrally controlled empire on the model of the Spanish', in *Empires of the Atlantic World: Britain and Spain in America, 1492–1830* (New Haven and London, 2006), 303; John H.R. Polt also contended that 'the role played by English letters in eighteenth-century Spain has in the past been somewhat obscured by the more spectacular and undoubtedly more widespread influence of things French', in 'Jovellanos and his English Sources: Economic, Philosophical and Political Writings', *Transactions of the American Philosophical Society*, n.s, 54:7 (1964): 6.

54. Antonio Domínguez Ortíz, *Sociedad y Estado en el Siglo XVIII Español* (Barcelona, 1976), 53.

55. As the Steins indicated, a 'major restraint on policy-making during Charles III's administration was the predictable, forceful English reaction to Spanish attempts at protectionism in both the metropole and colonies'. See Stanley Stein and Barbara Stein, *Apogee of Empire: Spain and New Spain in the Age of Charles III, 1759–1789* (Baltimore and London, 2003), 23; on Anglo-Spanish conflict in the late 1700s, see Julius Goebel, *The Struggle for the Falkland Islands: A Study in Legal*

and Diplomatic History (New Haven and London, 1970); Warren L. Cook, *Flood Tide of Empire: Spain and the Pacific Northwest, 1543–1819* (New Haven and London, 1973), 206–17; and Stetson Conn, *Gibraltar in British Diplomacy in the Eighteenth Century* (New Haven, 1942), 27, 220–1.

56. Josephine Grieder, *Anglomania in France, 1740–1789: Fact, Fiction and Political Discourse* (Geneva and Paris, 1985), 117–19; on Scottish ideas in Germany, see Keith Tribe, *Governing Economy: The Reformation of German Economic Discourse, 1750–1840* (Cambridge, 1988), esp. chapter 7, 'The "Smith Reception" and the Function of Translation'; Fania Oz-Salzberger, *Translating the Enlightenment: Scottish Civic Discourse in Eighteenth-Century Germany* (Oxford, 1995); and Lazlo Köntler, 'William Robertson and his German Audience on European and Non-European Civilisation', *Scottish Historical Review*, 80:1 (2001): 63–89.

57. Previous commentators have recognized that 'the new spirit of the eighteenth century is the old spirit of the early seventeenth century, revived after an intermission of a hundred years' and that 'the seventeenth-century kindlers of the eighteenth-century Enlightenment, Hobbes and Locke, Petty and Newton' merited closer attention. See [Hugh Trevor-Roper] 'The Spanish Enlightenment', *Times Literary Supplement*, 15 March 1957: 154; while emphasising foreign influences, it remains crucial to recognize, as Llombart Rosa has, that Spanish political and economic writers were involved in 'active reception characterised by acceptance and selection ... of acclimation, modification ... [this produced] an added value which may be judged either favourably or unfavourably ... [eighteenth-century Spanish economists] imported many good ideas from a great many sources, but their thought was much more than a mere reflection'. See V. Llombart Rosa, 'El Pensamiento Económico de la Ilustración', in Fuentes Quintana, ed., *Economía y Economistas Españoles. Volume 3: La Ilustración*, 66–7.

58. There is little doubt, as Pocock argued, that the incorporation of Britain requires a 're-writing and pluralisation of the history to be termed European'. See Pocock, 'Enlightenment and Counter-Enlightenment, Revolution and Counter-Revolution: A Eurosceptical Enquiry', *History of Political Thought*, 20:1 (1999): 139; David Landes also made a strong case for the 'continental emulation' of Britain, though he does not refer to Spain explicitly. According to Landes, after c. 1750, Britain was 'the very model of industrial excellence and achievement ... all watched and visited and tried to learn', Landes, *The Unbound Prometheus: Technological Change and Industrial Development in Western Europe from 1750 to the Present* (Cambridge, 2003), 124.

59. AGI Indiferente General 2405A, Consulado of Santander to Valdés, 1 June 1790.

60. Azara to Roda, 15 November 1770, in *El Espíritu de D. José Nicolás de Azara Descubierto en su Correspondencia Epistolar con D. Manuel de Roda* (Madrid, 1846), vol. II, 94.

61. Melchor de Macanaz, quoted in Callahan, 'The Crown and the Promotion of Industry', 148–9.

62. Campillo, *Nuevo Sistema*, 110.

63. BPR II/2851, [Anon.], 'Reflexiones Sobre las Reglas y Medios Verdaderos de Adelantar nuestro Comercio y Notas y Reparos' (1787/88), fo. 299.

64. Francisco Álvarez, *Noticia del Establecimiento y Población de las Colonias Inglesas en la América Septentrional* (Madrid, [1778] 2000), 3.

65. Pablo de Olavide, *Informe Sobre la Ley Agraria*, in *Obras Selectas*, ed., Estuardo Núñez (Lima, 1987), 488–9; Olavide was a great admirer of English literature, ranking Samuel Richardson, Henry Fielding, and Daniel Defoe among his

favourite authors. See Luís Perdices de Blas, *Pablo de Olavide (1725–1803): El Ilustrado* (Madrid, 1993), 45.

66. Antonio de Ulloa, *La Marina: Fuerzas Navales de la Europa y Costas de Berberia* (Cádiz, 1995).
67. Ulloa to Grimaldi, 6 October 1768, quoted in Lawrence Kinnaird, ed., *Spain in the Mississippi Valley, 1765–1794: Translations of Material from the Spanish Archives of the Bancroft Library; Part I: The Revolutionary Period, 1765–1781* (Washington, DC, 1949), 73.
68. Almodóvar, *Historia Política*, vol. II, appendix, 12.
69. *Espíritu de Los Mejores Diarios que Se Publican en Europa*, no. 88, 24 January 1788, 798.
70. Vicent Llombart, *Campomanes, Economista y Político de Carlos III* (Madrid, 1992), 81, 82 fn. 46
71. John Reeder, 'Bibliografía de Traducciones, al Castellano y Catalán, durante el Siglo XVIII, de Obras de Pensamiento Económico', *Moneda y Crédito*, 126 (1973): 57–78 passim.
72. To my knowledge, no scholar has assessed how many Spaniards spoke English. It has been impossible for me to ascertain which of the political writers and policymakers studied in this book spoke or read English, though their knowledge of English books, often through French translations, is uncontestable. Eterio Pajares has called French the 'authentic cultural bridge between the languages and cultures of Spain and England'. See Pajares, 'Traducción Inglés-Español en el Siglo XVIII', in *El Mundo Hispánico en el Siglo de las Luces* (Madrid, 1996), 992.
73. Sánchez-Blanco, *El Absolutismo y las Luces en el Reinado de Carlos III* (Madrid, 2002), 24.
74. On Genovesi, see John Robertson, 'The Enlightenment Above National Context: Political Economy in Eighteenth-Century Scotland and Naples', *Historical Journal*, 40 (1997), 667–97.
75. See Sophus Reinert, 'Blaming the Medici: Footnotes, Falsification, and the Fate of the "English Model" in Eighteenth-Century Italy', *History of European Ideas*, 32:4 (2006): 430–55.
76. On Campomanes's economic thought, see D. Manuel Bustos Rodríguez, *El Pensamiento Socio-Economico de Campomanes* (Oviedo, 1982); Laura Rodríguez Díaz, *Reforma e Ilustración en la España del Siglo XVIII* (Madrid, 1975); and Llombart, *Campomanes*.
77. Campomanes, *Educación Popular*, 17–18.
78. Pedro Rodríguez de Campomanes, *Discurso sobre el Fomento de la Industria Popular* (Madrid, 1774), cxlix; there were many calls for Charles III to establish a chair of commerce as he had in Naples; see AHN Estado 3188, no. 377, Eugenio de Santiago Polomares, 'Establecimiento de una Escuela de Comercio en Madrid o Valencia', July 1786.
79. Campomanes, *Discurso Sobre el Fomento de la Industria Popular*.
80. Campomanes, *Reflexiones*, 233.
81. Concepción de Castro, *Campomanes: Estado y Reformismo Ilustrado* (Madrid, 1996), 69–70; in ACC 31–1 and 20–4.
82. Pedro Rodríguez de Campomanes, *Itinerario de las Carreras de Posta de Dentro, y Fuera del Reyno* [1761] (Madrid, 2002), 1.
83. Campomanes, *Industria Popular*, cxliii fn., cli fn.
84. V. Llombart, *Campomanes, Economista y Político de Carlos III*, 329–35 passim.
85. BPR II/2867, Josef del Río [Spain's Consul-General in Portugal], 'Observación Sobre la Necesidad de Establecer Escuelas Patrióticas de Comercio en Madrid' (1776), fo. 313v.

86. Quoted in Callahan, 'The Crown and the Promotion of Industry', 136.

87. Nicolás de Arriquibar, *Recreación Política: Reflexiones Sobre el Amigo de los Hombres en Su Tratado de Población Considerado con Respecto a Nuestros Intereses* (Madrid, 1779), vol. I, i–ii; according to Perdices de Blas, Campomanes and Arriquibar were the Spanish political writers 'most influenced by the English arithmetic political writers', in *La Economía Política de la Decadencia de Castilla en el Siglo XVIII: Investigaciones de los Arbitristas sobre la Naturaleza y Causas de la Riqueza de las Naciones* (Madrid, 1996), 153.

88. BPR II/2867, Francisco Antonio de Bringas, 'Papel Sobre las Prevenciones que deben hacerse a todo joven viajante que se dedique al comercio', October 1786, fo. 337.

89. Thomas Mun, *England's Treasure by Forraign Trade or, The Balance of our Forraign Trade is the Rule of our Treasure* (London, 1664). n.b. Mun's work was composed in the 1620s.

90. John Cary, *An Essay on the State of England, in Relation to Trade, its Poor, and its Taxes, for Carrying on the Present War against France* (Bristol, 1695), 66–7; Joyce Oldham Appleby, *Economic Thought and Ideology in Seventeenth-Century England* (Princeton, 1978), 136–8.

91. BPR II/2819, Manuel Leguinazabal, 'Tesoro de España: Discurso Sobre el Comercio de España con sus Américas ...' (1763–4), fo. 7; on aristocratic ideal and its relation to eighteenth-century political economy, see A.O. Hirschman, *The Passions and the Interests: Political Arguments for Capitalism Before its Triumph* (Princeton, 1997), 58.

92. William J. Callahan, *Honor, Commerce and Industry in Eighteenth-Century Spain* (Boston, 1972), 17, 33, 50–1, 59, 63.

93. William Petty, *Political Arithmetick, or a Discourse* (London, 1691), 1.

94. Charles Davenant, *Discourse on the Publick Revenues and on the Trade of England* (London, 1698), part I, 7–8; the term 'political arithmetick' originated with William Petty and was taken up by various subsequent writers, including Davenant.

95. Davenant, *Publick Revenues*, part II, 69.

96. Davenant, *Essays Upon Peace at Home and War Abroad* (London, 1704), part I, 205–6

97. [Josiah Child], *A Discourse about Trade* (London, 1668, 1690), 94–5; on seventeenth-century British attitudes toward empire, see David Armitage, *The Ideological Origins of the British Empire* (Cambridge, 2000).

98. Davenant, *Publick Revenues*, part II, 207.

99. Campomanes, *Reflexiones*, 242.

100. Campomanes, *Educación Popular*, 262 fn; for republished works of the *Arbitristas*, see the multi-volume appendices to this work.

101. Josef Alonso Ortíz, translator's preface, Adam Smith, *Investigación de la Naturaleza y Causas de la Riqueza de las Naciones* (Valladolid, 1794), vol. I; modern scholars corroborate this judgment: R.S. Smith argued that 'the last half of the eighteenth century produced no "school" of Spanish economics or any well-developed body of doctrines which the leading writers professed in common', in 'Economists and the Enlightenment in Spain, 1750–1800', *The Journal of Political Economy*, 63 (1955): 346; see also Smith's 'The *Wealth of Nations* in Spain and Hispanic America, 1780–1830', *Journal of Political Economy*, 65 (1957): 104–25.

102. ACC leg. 22–4, 8 April 1780.

103. Almodóvar, *Historia Política*, vol. II, appendix, 124.

104. AGI Santa Fe 758B, 'Idea de la Obra de los Escritos de Coronel Roberto Hodgson', 25 June 1784.

105. AGI Estado 86A, no. 2, Anon., 'Discurso y Reflecxiones [sic] de un Vasallo Sobre la Decadencia de Nuestras Indias Españolas', n.d., fo. 33.
106. AHN Estado 2927, no. 271, Craywinckel 'Utilidad que Podría Sacar España', 7–13 passim, 17, 25.
107. AGI Indiferente 2410, 'Dictamen de Grimaldi sobre la solicitude ... de Galicia e Asturias', 17 February 1770.
108. On history and historians in eighteenth-century Spain, see María Teresa Nava Rodríguez, 'Reformismo Ilustrado y Americanismo: La Real Academia de la Historia, 1735–1792' (PhD Dissertation, Universidad Complutense de Madrid, 1989); see also Eva Velasco Moreno, 'Las Academias de la Historia en el Siglo XVIII: Una Comparación entre Francia y España', in *El Mundo Hispánico en el Siglo de las Luces* (Madrid, 1996).
109. ARAH 11–3-1–8235, Miguel de Manuel y Rodríguez, Speech to Royal Academy of History, 17 August 1781.
110. Antonio Porlier y Sopranis [Marqués de Bajamar], Speech to the Council of the Indies (1804), in Marqués de Bajamar, *Discursos al Consejo de Indias* (Madrid, 2002), 169.
111. Campomanes to Jovellanos, 14 October 1777, quoted in Fernando Baras Escolá, 'Política e Historia en la España del Siglo XVIII: Las Concepciones Historiográficas de Jovellanos', *BRAH*, 191:2 (1994): 353.
112. On the Black Legend, see J.H. Elliott, *The Old World and the New, 1492–1650* (Cambridge, 1970), 94–7; Ricardo García Cárcel, *La Leyenda Negra: Historia y Opinión*; Pagden, *Lords of All the World: Ideologies of Empire in Spain, Britain and France, c. 1500–1800* (New Haven and London), 87, 116; Bejamin Keen, 'The Black Legend Revisited: Assumptions and Realities', in *Essays in the Intellectual History of Colonial Latin America* (Boulder, 1998); on the Spanish refutation of the Black Legend in the eighteenth century, see Paul J. Hauben, 'White Legend Against Black: Nationalism and Enlightenment in a Spanish Context', *The Americas*, 34 (1977): 1–19; and Javier Yagüe Bosch, 'Defensa de España y Conquista de América en el Siglo XVIII: Cadalso y Forner', *Dieciocho*, 28 (2005): 121–40.
113. *Correo de los Ciegos de Madrid*, #30, 19 January 1787.
114. On the self-conscious use in the Spanish court of the Roman analogy with regard to imperial affairs, see Miguel Artola, 'América en el Pensamiento Español de Siglo XVIII', *RI*, 115 (1969): 59; on the importance of classical Rome to Charles while in Naples, see Félix Fernández Murga, *Carlos III y el Descubrimiento de Herculano* (Salamanca, 1989), 123, 126.
115. Francisco José Fabre, *Descripción de las Alegorías Pintadas en las Bóvedas del Real Palacio de Madrid* (Madrid, 1829), 133, 147.
116. For an overview of historical scholarship in Bourbon Spain, see Roberto López-Vela, 'De Numancia a Zaragoza. La Construcción del Pasado Nacional en las Historias de España del Ochocientos', in Ricardo Gárcia Cárcel, ed., *La Construcción de las Historias de España* (Madrid, 2004).
117. The expeditionary force commanded by O'Reilly suffered casualties of 1,500 soldiers killed and 3,000 wounded in its feeble and failed attempt to lay siege to Algiers. See Charles Petrie, *King Charles III of Spain: An Enlightened Despot* (London, 1971), 157–9 passim.
118. ARAH 11–3-1–8234, 'Discurso Sobre la Legislación de España que Leyó Bernardo Joaquin Danvila y Villarrasa en Su Ingreso en la Real Academia de la History', 3 April 1778.

119. ACC 4–6, Campomanes, 'Reflexiones Históricas ... y las Razones con que el Rey Debe Reunir a la Corona los Países que Conquisten las Armas Españolas en Portugal', 1762.
120. Stein and Stein, *Apogee of Empire*, 26.
121. Elliott, *The Old World and the New*, 94.
122. Edward Gibbon, *The History of the Decline and Fall of the Roman Empire* (New York, 2001), 361–2.
123. Antonio Porlier y Sopranis [Marqués de Bajamar], Speech to the Council of the Indies (1804), 169–70.
124. AGI Santa Fe 758B, 'Idea de la Obra de los Escritos de Coronel Roberto Hodgson', 25 June 1784.
125. Félix de Azara, quoted in David Weber, *Bárbaros: Spaniards and their Savages in the Age of Enlightenment* (New Haven and London, 2005), 5.
126. Francisco Xavier de Viana, quoted in Weber, *Bárbaros*, 49.
127. The debates over the introduction of Robertson's *History of America* in Spain are not recapitulated here as they already have received thorough treatment by scholars. For a brilliant and pioneering treatment of the reception of Robertson's work in Spain in the context of its broader intellectual milieu, see Jorge Cañizares-Esguerra, *How to Write the History of the New World: Histories, Epistemologies and Identities in the Eighteenth-Century Atlantic World* (Stanford, 2001); for an analysis of Robertson's views on Spain, see David Brading, *The First America: The Spanish Monarchy, Creole Patriots and the Liberal State, 1492–1867* (Cambridge, 1991); on Robertson's positive appraisal in the broader context of British attitudes toward Spain, see Gabriel Paquette, 'The Image of Imperial Spain in British Political Thought, 1750–1800', *Bulletin of Spanish Studies*, 81:2 (2004): esp. 202–6.
128. Letter of Juan Bautista Muñoz to King Charles III, 8 June 1779, reproduced in RAH, *Catalogo de la Colección de Don Juan Bautista Muñoz: Documentos Interesantes para la Historia de América* (Madrid, 1956), vol. III, xli–xliii; for a treatment of Muñoz's participation in the various polemics of his epoch, see Carlos William de Onis, 'Juan Bautista Muñoz: Ensayista de la Ilustración' (PhD Dissertation, University of Colorado, 1980), esp. 83–126; the scope of his work, however, led Muñoz's friends, especially José Nicolas Azara, to question whether a cogent account would be possible due to the 'immense number of subjects, quite disparate, which are treated, and I do not know how it would be possible to bring them together in order to compose an interesting and unified narrative'; Azara quoted in Antonio Ballesteros Beretta, 'Juan Bautista Muñoz: La Creación del Archivo de Indias', *RI*, 2 (1941): 56; his propensity and aptitude for comprehensive collection served him better, however, when he spearheaded the movement to create the Archive of the Indies in Seville, thus realizing his ambition to endow future Spanish historians with a solid documentary foundation for their work: 'the true history of the Indies', he predicted in a letter to J.A. Mayans y Siscar in 1782, 'will only surface through an analysis of the authentic documents that have not yet been used', quoted in Cañizares-Esguerra, *How to Write*, 193.
129. Juan Bautista Muñoz, *Historia del Nuevo Mundo* (Valencia, 1990), 25; Anthony Tudisco, 'America in Some Travelers, Historians and Political Economists of the Spanish Eighteenth Century', *The Americas*, 15 (1958): 15; María Teresa Nava Rodríguez, 'Robertson, Juan Bautista Muñoz y la Academia de la Historia', BRAH 187 (1990): 435–56.

130. Speech of José de Guevara Vasconcelos to the Royal Academy of History, 10 November 1791, reproduced in RAH, *Catálogo de la Colección de Don Juan Bautista Muñoz*, vol. III, ci, cxiv; Cañizares-Esguerra portrayed Muñoz as a classical humanist, differentiating his document-based reconstruction of the past with the philosophical narratives which dominated the eighteenth century. As Muñoz told Gálvez in 1783, 'I have done what in the sciences those few who now deserve the name of inventors or restorers have practiced ... observing in painstaking detail every particular, drawing generalizations from induction, establishing solid and fecund foundations from whence the propositions of a perfect system will emerge'. Quoted in Cañizares-Esguerra, *How to Write*, 195–201 passim.

131. Almodóvar to RAH, 15 November 1791, reproduced in RAH, *Catálogo de la Colección de Don Juan Bautista Muñoz*, vol. III, cxvii.

132. Christon Archer, 'Spain and the Defence of the Pacific Ocean Empire, 1750–1810', *Canadian Journal of Latin American and Caribbean Studies*, 11 (1986): 24.

133. Nicolas Rodríguez Laso, 'Elogio Histórico del Excelentísimo Señor Duque de Almodóvar, Director de la Real Academia de la Historia' (Madrid, 1795), x.

134. On Spanish diplomats in the eighteenth century, see Didier Ozanam, 'La Elección de los Diplomáticos Españoles en el Siglo XVIII (1700–1808)', in J.L. Castellano, ed., *Sociedad, Administración y Poder en la España del Antiguo Régimen* (Granada, 1996), esp. 12–13.

135. AGS Estado 7290, Almodóvar to Grimaldi, 20 November 1767.

136. AGS Estado 7005, Almodóvar to Floridablanca, 25 May 1779.

137. García Regueiro, *'Ilustración' e Intereses Estamentales*, 51.

138. Almodóvar, *Historia Política*, vol. II, appendix, 5.

139. Almodóvar, *Historia Política*, vol. II, appendix, 6.

140. Abbé Guillaume-Thomas François Raynal, *A Philosophical and Political History of the Settlements and Trade of the Europeans in the East and West Indies*. Trans. J.O. Justamond, 3rd edn, 4 vols (Dublin, 1779), vol. I, book 2; vol. II, book 9, 537; vol. II, book 6, 167; Justamond completed the English translation of the 12th French edition in 1776. His translation was reviewed favourably in the British press for its accuracy and elegance. On Justamond, see Anthony Strugnell, 'La Réception de l' *Histoire des Deux Indes* en Angleterre au Dix-Huitième Siècle', in Hans-Jürgen Lüsebrink and Manfred Tietz, *Lectures de Raynal: L'Histoire des Deux Indes en Europe et en Amérique au XVIII Siècle* (Oxford, 1991), 256–8.

141. Raynal, *Philosophical and Political History*, vol. II, book 6, 150, 183, 202; vol. II, book 8, 428–34 passim, 449; for a stimulating recent analysis of the views of Raynal and Diderot on colonies, see Sankar Muthu, *Enlightenment against Empire* (Princeton, 2003), 106.

142. Raynal, *Philosophical and Political History*, vol. II, book 6, 222 and book 8, 424; vol. II, book 7, 305; vol. III, book 16, 114; vol. IV, book 19, 513; vol. III, book 14, 560; vol. II, book 8, 468–9; vol. IV, book 19, 493; and vol. II, book 8, 458.

143. Almodóvar, *Historia Política*, vol. I, v, vii; vol. II, viii.

144. For a diagrammatic account of the differences between Raynal's and Almodóvar's texts, see Antonio Truyol Serra, 'Nota Sobre la Versión Castellana de la Obra de Raynal', in *Homenaje al Prof. Carlos Ollero 'Estudios de Ciencia Política y Sociología'* (Madrid, 1972), 876–8; see also Manfred Tietz, 'L'Espagne et l' *Histoire des Deux Indes* de l'abbé Raynal', in Lüsebrink and Tietz, *Lectures de Raynal*; n.b. there may have been personal as well as political–intellectual reasons

for Almodóvar's omission of American affairs: he was fully aware that Muñoz had received a commission in 1779 to write a history of America. Fear of redundancy, combined with personal friendship with Muñoz, may help to explain this curious absence.

145. Almodóvar, *Historia Política*, vol. II, appendix, 8.
146. Almodóvar, *Historia Política*, vol. I, 380.
147. Almodóvar, *Historia Política*, vol. I, 192.
148. Almodóvar, *Historia Política*, vol. II, appendix, vii, 125, 209; additional contemporary Spanish writers criticized Britain for 'operating semi-tyrannies in its colonies ... [by which Britain] has subverted its empire in the Indies'; see BPR II/2866, Josef Fuertes, 'Pensamientos, o Proyecto Sobre Volver a Reconciliar con la Madre Patria las Provincias Discolas de la América Meridional' (1781), fos., 248–9 passim; in this way, these writers anticipated C.A. Bayly's analysis of British 'overseas despotisms' during this period which were 'characterised by a form of aristocratic military government supporting a vice-regal autocracy, by a well-developed imperial style which emphasised hierarchy and racial subordination'. See Bayly, *Imperial Meridian: The British Empire and the World 1780–1830* (Harlow, 1989), 8.
149. Almodóvar, *Historia Política*, vol. II, appendix, 4; Christopher Schmidt-Nowara made an excellent observation when he noted that 'with the turn toward Asia and Africa ... [Britain and other European imperial powers] built interventionist colonial regimes that not only regulated the economy more carefully but also sought to control and civilize the subject population, a mission whose contours resembled the supposedly archaic ambitions and strategies of the Spanish empire', in 'Introduction: Interpreting Spanish Colonialism', in Schmidt-Nowara and J.M. Nieto-Phillips, eds, *Interpreting Spanish Colonialism: Empires, Nations and Legends* (Albuquerque, 2005), 12.
150. Almodóvar, *Historia Política*, vol. III, appendix, 67.
151. Almodóvar, *Historia Política*, vol. III, appendix, 68; this view was shared by Almodóvar's contemporaries who enquired 'from where are bloody and costly wars between England and France if not from the emulation [*emulación*] which each has for the other's commerce?'; see BPR II/2817, Nicolas Norton Nicols, 'El Comercio de Manila: las Conveniencias, Beneficio y Utilidad que las Islas Philipinas Deben Dar a S.M. como a sus Vasallos' (n.d., addressed to Charles III), fo. 258v.
152. Juan Sempere y Guarinos, 'Eduardo Malo de Luque', in *Ensayo de Una Biblioteca Española de los Mejores Escritores del Reynado de Carlos III* (Madrid, 1786), vol. IV, 1.
153. Jovellanos quoted in Fernando Baras Escolá, 'Política e Historia en la España del Siglo XVIII: Las Concepciones Historiográficas de Jovellanos', *BRAH* 191:2 (1994): 351.
154. Almodóvar, *Historia Política*, vol. v, 54.
155. Ovidio García Regueiro, 'Intereses Estamentales y Pensamiento Económico: La Versión Española de la "Historia" de Raynal', *Moneda y Crédito*, 149 (1979): 88; in addition to the rapacity of which he accused them, Raynal contended that privileged companies never recovered, through the duties they levied, the money advanced to them; on this theme, see W.R. Womack, 'Eighteenth-Century Themes in the *Histoire Philosophique et Politique des Deux Indes* of Guillaume Raynal', *Studies in Voltaire and the Eighteenth Century*, 96 (1972): 129–263.
156. Almodóvar, *Historia Política*, vol. II, appendix, 23.

157. Bourbon economic debates, including those concerning privileged trading companies, are examined in Chapters 3 and 4.

158. Almodóvar, *Historia Política*, vol. V, 93, 382–3; for a fuller treatment of Almodóvar's hopes for a trading company, see Ovidio García Regueiro, 'Manila, Acapulco y Cádiz: Una Concepción del Comercio Español con Oriente en el Siglo XVIII', *Cuadernos Hispanoamericanos*, 409 (1984): 5–35.

159. Almodóvar, *Historia Política*, vol. v, 334; the originality of Almodóvar's scheme must not be exaggerated. In 1765, Francisco de Leandro de Viana had called for such a company to serve as a bulwark against Dutch and English competition in the Pacific. See W.L. Schurz, 'The Royal Philippine Company', *HAHR*, 3 (1920): 494.

160. BPR II/2879, Félix de Maquina, 'Informe Relativo al Estado de Aquellas Islas, su Fomento y Producciones' (1790), fo. 140v.; Stetson Conn, *Gibraltar in British Diplomacy in the Eighteenth Century* (New Haven, 1942), 220–1.

161. Josep M. Fradera, *Filipinas, La Colonia Más Peculiar: La Hacienda Pública en la Definición de la Política Colonial, 1762–1868* (Madrid, 1999), 87; BPR II/2851, 'Disertación Sobre las Utilidades que Logran los Franceses, Ingleses y Holandeses con su Comercio en el Continente de Asia y las que podrá conseguir la España con este Trafico', fos. 27, 30; Schurz, 'Royal Philippine Company', 498–9; Lourdes Díaz-Trechuelo, 'El Comercio de Filipinas durante la Segunda Mitad del Siglo XVIII', *RI*, 23 (1963): 463–85.

162. As Vicent Llombart has shown for texts of political economy, there was a rising tide of translations of foreign works into Spanish after 1760: whereas there were a mere nine translations during the 1751–60 period, the decade 1781–90 was marked by 49 translations. See his 'Traducciones Españolas de Economia Política (1700–1812): Catálogo Bibliográfico y Una Nueva Perspectiva', *Cromohs*, 9 (2004): 1–14 [http://www.cromohs.unifi.it/9_2004/llombart.html; accessed January 14, 2005].

2 *Felicidad Pública*, Regalism, and the Bourbon Ideology of Governance

1. Azara to Roda, 31 March 1768, in *El Espíritu de D. José Nicolás de Azara Descubierto en su Correspondencia Epistolar con D. Manuel de Roda* (Madrid, 1846), vol. I, 38.

2. BPR II/2847, Manuel de Abad y la Sierra, 'Discurso Previo Sobre las Iglesias, Monasterios y Capillas del Real Patronato en General', 1781, fo. 231.

3. BNJM, *Papel Periódico de la Havana*, no. 60, 26 July 1792, 339.

4. Luís Antonio Muratori, *La Pública Felicidad: Un Objeto de los Buenos Principes* (Madrid, 1790), 5, 13, 42, 57; on Muratori, see Isabel Roma Ribes, 'Libros de Muratori Traducidos al Castellano', *Revista de Historia Moderna* [Alicante], 4 (1984): 113–48; Muratori's precepts were consonant with the broader intellectual trends of his time. As Robertson remarked, 'what characterised the enlightenment from the 1740s onwards was a new focus on the betterment in this world, without regard for the existence or non-existence of the next'. See Robertson, *The Case for the Enlightenment: Scotland and Naples, 1680–1760* (Cambridge, 2005), 8–9.

5. Antonio Porlier y Sopranis [Marqués de Bajamar], Speech to the Council of the Indies (1796), in *Discursos al Consejo de Indias*, ed. Maria Soledad Campos Díez (Madrid, 2002), 52.

6. Richard Drayton, *Nature's Government: Science, Imperial Britain and the 'Improvement' of the World* (New Haven and London, 2000), 89; 'the happiness of the subjects as a goal of government brought with it an amplification of the

role of the monarch', according to Bernardino Bravo Lira, 'El Absolutismo Ilustrado en España e Indias Bajo Carlos III (1759–88)', *Revista Chilena de Historia del Derecho* [Santiago], 14 (1991): 32.

7. BPR II/2760, 'Consulta del Consejo de Castilla a motivo de Representación de Don Francisco Carrasco, Fiscal de la Hacienda ... acerca del restablecimiento o renovación de la Ley de Amortización', 18 June 1766, fo. 18v.; see Salvador de Moxó, 'Un Medievalista en el Consejo de Hacienda: Don Francisco Carrasco, Marqués de la Corona (1715–1791)', *AHDE*, 29 (1959): 609–68 passim.

8. Ibid., fos. 31v., 49.

9. Quoted in Manuel Capel, *La Carolina, Capital de las Nuevas Poblaciones: Un Ensayo de Reforma Socio-Económica de España en el Siglo XVIII* (Jaén, 1970), 33.

10. AGI Chile 219, Francisco Hurtado [Governor of Chiloé] to José de Gálvez, 25 October 1787.

11. AGI Estado 54, no. 2, Archbishop Antonio Caballero y Góngora to Floridablanca, 26 March 1789.

12. Francisco Cabarrús to Jovellanos in *Cartas Sobre los Obstáculos que la Naturaleza, la Opinion y las Leyes Oponen á la Felicidad Pública, Escrita por Conde de Cabarrús al Señor Don Gaspar de Jovellanos* (Madrid, 1808 [written 1792]), 71.

13. J.H. Elliott, *Empires of the Atlantic World: Britain and Spain in America 1492–1830* (New Haven and London, 2006), 133.

14. *Diario Curioso*, no. 176, 23 December 1786.

15. Almodóvar, *Historia Política de los Establecimientos Ultramarinos de las Naciones Europeas* (Madrid, 1784–90), vol. II, v; vol. III, 71.

16. Victorían de Villava, *Apuntes Para Una Reforma de España sin Trastorno del Gobierno Monárquico ni la Religión* (Buenos Aires, 1822), xviii; n.b. this document was written in the late 1780s or 90s.

17. Antonio Muñoz, *Discurso Sobre Economía Política* (Madrid, 1769), 3.

18. Pablo de Olavide, 'Informe Sobre la Ley Agraria', in *Obras Selectas* [1768] (Lima, 1987), 486.

19. AGI Chile 219, Hurtado to Gálvez, 25 October 1787.

20. Lorenzo Normante y Carcavilla, *Proposiciones de Economía Civil y Comercio* (Zaragoza, 1785), 23; Normante held the first royally established chair in political economy in Spain (in Zaragoza); on Normante's economic views, see Alfonso Sánchez Hormigo, *La Cátedra de Economía Civil y Comercio de la Real Sociedad Económica Aragonesa de Amigos del País (1784–1846)* (Zaragoza, 2003), esp. 151.

21. BPR II/2873, Santiago Josef López Ruíz, 'Propuesta Político-Moral Sobre Varias Reflexiones Dirigidas a que se Establezca una Sabia y Prudente Reforma para Contener los Desordenes Publicos' (1789), fo. 2.

22. BPR II/967, [Anon], 'Decimas al Mal Gobierno del Marqués de Esquilache', fo. 66.

23. BPR II/1389, [Anon.], 'Disertación, en que se Demuestra la Regalía, que Compete a todos los Soberanos, y con Especialidad a los Reyes de Castilla para Establecer en su Dominios la Ley de Amortización' (n.d., 1790–5?), fos. 252v., 259.

24. Cabarrús, 'Carta al Principe de la Paz [Godoy]', in *Cartas Sobre los Obstáculos que la Naturaleza, la Opinion y las Leyes Oponen a la Felicidad Pública*,16.

25. Juan Sempere y Guarinos, *Historia de los Vínculos y Mayorazgos* [1805] (Alicante, 1990), 216.

26. AHN Estado 2927, no. 271, Francisco de Craywinckel, 'Utilidad que Podría Sacar España de su Desgracia por la Perdida de la Habana', enclosed in a letter to Ricardo Wall, 12 November 1762, 20.

27. Romá y Rossell, *Las Señales de la Felicidad de España y Medios de Hacerlas Eficaces* (Madrid, 1768), quoted in Alejandro Diz, *Idea de Europa en la España del Siglo XVIII* (Madrid, 2000), 165.

28. BPR II/2666, Miguel Antonio de Gandara, 'Apuntes para Formar un Discurso Sobre el Bien y el Mal de España' (1759), fo. 146v.

29. Sempere y Guarinos, *Vínculos*, 219.

30. BPR II/2866, [Anon.], 'Discurso Sobre la Necesidad que hay de que el Soberano Tenga Fabricas de su Cuenta, para Beneficio de Estado y del Particular', n.d., fo. 75v.

31. Muñoz, *Discurso Sobre Economía Política*, 165.

32. [Almodóvar], *Década Epistolar Sobre el Estado de Las Letras en Francia* (Madrid, 1781), 174.

33. Normante y Carcavilla, *Discurso Sobre la Utilidad de los Conocimientos de Economía Civil*, 12–13.

34. Almodóvar, *Historia Política*, vol. v, 208.

35. On this important theme, see Emma Rothschild, *Economic Sentiments: Adam Smith, Condorcet and the Enlightenment* (Cambridge, MA, 2001).

36. Lorenzo Normante y Carcavilla, *Proposiciones de Economia Civil y Comercio* (Zaragoza, 1785), 64, 66–7.

37. Juan Sempere y Guarinos, *Historia del Luxo y de las Leyes Suntuarias de España* (Madrid, 1788), vol. II, 205–6.

38. J.J. Spengler, *French Predecessors to Malthus: a Study in Eighteenth-Century Wage and Population Theory* (Durham, 1942), 22; David Hume, 'Of the Populousness of Ancient Nations', in *Essays Moral, Political and Literary* (Indianapolis, 1987), 382; Montesquieu, *The Spirit of the Laws*, trans. and ed. A.M. Cohler, B.C. Miller, and A.S. Stone (Cambridge, 1997), 454; Sylvana Tomaselli, 'Moral Philosophy and Population questions in Eighteenth-Century Europe', in M.S. Teitelbaum and J.M. Winter, eds, *Population and Resources in Western Intellectual Traditions* (Cambridge, 1988), 9–15 passim; F.G. Whelan, 'Population and Ideology in the Enlightenment', *History of Political Thought*, 12 (1991): 57.

39. AHN Estado 2927, no. 271, Craywinckel 'Utilidad que Podría Sacar España', 2.

40. Nicolás de Arriquibar, *Recreación Política: Reflexiones Sobre el Amigo de los Hombres en Su Tratado de Población Considerado con Respecto a Nuestros Intereses* (Madrid, 1779), vol. I, xiii.

41. Normante y Carcavilla, *Proposiciones de Economía Civil y Comercio*, 9.

42. Francisco Bustelo García del Real, 'La Población Española en la Segunda Mitad del Siglo XVIII', *Moneda y Crédito*, 123 (1972): 56.

43. François Quesnay, quoted in R.L. Meek, *The Economics of Physiocracy: Essays and Translations* (London, 1962), 88–9; Frederick the Great, quoted in T.C.W. Blanning, *The Culture of Power and the Power of Culture: Old Regime Europe 1660–1789* (New York, 2001), 126.

44. *Correo de los Ciegos de Madrid*, no. 2, 13 October 1786, 5.

45. Vicente del Seixo, 'Reflexiones Sobre Los Progresos de Agricultura y Pastoría' (1797), in Lluís Argemí d'Abadal, *Agricultura e Ilustración: Antología del Pensamiento Agrario Ilustrado* (Madrid, 1988), 120.

46. José del Campillo y Cossío, *Nuevo Sistema de Gobierno Económico Para América* (Oviedo, 1993), 284, 96.

47. AGI Santo Domingo 2668, Zespedes to Marqués de Sonora [Gálvez], 12 May 1787.

48. AGI Santo Domingo 2667, Miro to Valdés, 1 April 1788.

49. Muñoz, *Discurso Sobre Economía Política*, 27, 34–5.

50. Gerónimo de Uztáriz, *The Theory and Practice of Commerce and Maritime Affairs* (London, 1751), vol. I, 38–9, 49; see also A.V. Castillo, *Gerónimo de Uztáriz— Economist* (Philadelphia, 1980).

51. Normante y Carcavilla, *Proposiciones de Economía Civil y Comercio*, 9.

52. Stanley Stein and Barbara Stein, *Silver, Trade and War: Spain and America in the Making of Early Modern Europe* (Baltimore and London, 2000), 164, 169; on the diffusion of Colbert's ideas in mid-eighteenth century imperial circles, see M. Artola, 'Campillo y las Reformas de Carlos III', *RI*, 12 (1952): 687–8; Fernández Durán, *Gerónimo de Uztáriz: Una Política Económica Para Felipe V* (Madrid, 1999), 265, 321.

53. Marcelo Bitar Letayf, *Economistas Españoles del Siglo XVIII: Sus Ideas Sobre la Libertad del Comercio con Indias* (Madrid, 1968), 80; it should be pointed out that the study of economics was conceived in Spain, as elsewhere in Southern Europe, as 'a tool for initiating the politics of renewal without, however, granting it genuine scientific status, with ironclad mathematical or "mechnical" laws' in Vincenzo Ferrone, *The Intellectual Roots of the Italian Enlightenment: Newtonian Science, Religion and Politics in the Early Eighteenth Century*. Trans. Sue Brothertone (Atlantic Highlands, 1995), 259.

54. Bernardo Joaquin Danvila y Villarrasa, *Lecciones de Economía Civil, o del Comercio Escrito para el Uso de los Caballeros del Real Seminario de Nobles* (Madrid, 1779), 64, 159–60; it must be remembered, as Emma Rothschild observed, that 'early exponents of commercial freedom proposed policies of selective government intervention ... Turgot and Condorcet show that commitment to free commerce is consistent with support for government intervention in other markets'; see Rothschild, 'Commerce and the State: Turgot, Condorcet and Smith', *The Economic Journal*, 102 (1992): 1197–210.

55. These developments are discussed fully in Richard Herr, *Rural Change and Royal Finances at the End of the Old Regime* (Berkeley, and London, 1989), 34–45 passim. While inspired by some of the economic features of French physiocracy, most Iberian regalists would have shuddered at its adjoining political demands for freedom of the press, an independent judiciary, and public conduct of all government business. See Elizabeth Fox-Genovese, *The Origins of Physiocracy: Economic Revolution and Social Order in Eighteenth-Century France* (Ithaca and London, 1976), 46–65 passim. In Spain, according to Ernest Lluch, physiocracy 'penetrated belatedly and superficially, less economically and more politically' in *Agronomía y Fisiocracia en España, 1750–1820* (Valencia, 1985), 100.

56. Campomanes, *Discurso Sobre la Educación Popular de los Artesanos y su Fomento* (Madrid, 1775), 389.

57. Keith Tribe, 'Cameralism and the Science of Government', *Journal of Modern History*, 56:2 (1984): 266.

58. Marc Raeff, *The Well-Ordered Police State: Social and Institutional Change through Law in the Germanies and Russia* (New Haven, 1983), 179; on cameralism, see Albion W. Small, *The Cameralists: The Pioneers of German Social Policy* (Chicago, 1909); there was not universal assent, however, that government action could achieve the desired result. In the debate over the establishment of a National Bank in the 1780s, Valentín de Foronda argued that 'to believe that government can direct [the economy], like a labourer guiding water in order to irrigate his land, paying close attention to everything that is required, is to demonstrate an ignorance of the complicated nature of the political machine'. See Valentín de Foronda, 'Cartas Sobre El Banco de San Carlos', in *Miscelánea, o Colección de Varios Discursos* (Madrid, 1787), 86.

59. AGI Santo Domingo 2665, 'Real Cédula Concediendo Nuevas Gracias Para el Fomento del Comercio de la Luisiana', 1782.
60. Jacob Viner, 'Power versus Plenty as Objectives of Foreign Policy in the Seventeenth and Eighteenth Centuries', in D.C. Coleman, ed., *Revisions in Mercantilism* (London, 1969), 71.
61. BN Caja Foll. 320 (16), Gerónimo Josef de Cabra, *Pruebas del Espíritu del Sr. Melon y de las Proposiciones de Economía Civil y Comercio de Sr. Normante. Examen Escrituristico-Theologico-Dogmatico de Ambas Obras* (Madrid), part I, 87; part II, 34; on the Cabra-Normante 'scandal', see Menéndez Pelayo, *Historia de los Heterodoxos Españoles*, vol. II (Madrid, 1992), 708–9.
62. 'Discurso Preliminar del Traductor', reprinted in Ricardo Levene, *Vida y Escritos de Victorián de Villava* (Buenos Aires, 1946), appendix, x.
63. Villava, *Apuntes Para Una Reforma*; José María Portillo Valdés, *Revolución de la Nación: Orígenes de la Cultura Constitucional en España, 1780–1812* (Madrid, 2000), 142–6 passim.
64. J.P. Canning, 'Introduction: Politics, Institutions, Ideas', in J.H. Burns, ed., *The Cambridge History of Medieval Political Thought, c. 350 – c. 1450* (Cambridge, 1988), 348.
65. H.J. Berman, *Law and Revolution: The Formation of the Western Legal Tradition* (London and Cambridge, MA, 1983), 516–17.
66. Lauren Benton, *Law and Colonial Cultures: Legal Regimes in World History, 1400–1900* (Cambridge, 2002), 37; I.S. Robinson, 'Church and Papacy', 266–7; James A. Brundage, *Medieval Canon Law* (London and New York, 1995), 176–7.
67. Canning, 'Introduction', 366
68. James Muldoon, '*Extra ecclesiam non est imperium*: the Canonists and the Legitimacy of Secular Power', in *Canon Law, the Expansion of Europe and World Order* (Aldershot, 1998), vol. I, 580.
69. Walter Ullmann, *The Growth of Papal Power in the Middle Ages: A Study of the Ideological Relation of Clerical to Lay Power* (London, [1955] 1962), 407–8, 411; see also Alan Harding, *Medieval Law and the Foundations of the State* (Oxford, 2002), 295.
70. J. Lloyd Mecham, *Church and State in Latin America: A History of Politico-Ecclesiastical Relations* (Chapel Hill, 1966); W. Eugene Shiels, *King and Church: the Rise and Fall of the* Patronato Real (Chicago, 1961), 170–6 passim.
71. Nancy Farriss, *Crown and Clergy in Colonial Mexico, 1759–1821: the Crisis of Ecclesiastical Privilege* (London, 1968), 7–8, 28.
72. I.A.A. Thompson, 'Castile', in John Miller, ed., *Absolutism in Seventeenth Century Europe* (New York, 1990), 82–4 passim.
73. Only under the terms of the Concordat of 1753 did Ferdinand VI obtain from Pope Benedict XIV patronage rights in the entire Spanish peninsula, not solely in Granada.
74. William J. Callahan, *Church, Politics and Society in Spain, 1750–1874* (London and Cambridge, MA, 1984), 39–41.
75. Helen Rawlings, *Church, Religion and Society in Early Modern Spain* (New York, 2002), 135; It should be noted that while the Spanish Crown usually could squeeze revenue from the Church, through the imposition of general contributions on the clergy (such as the *excusado, subsidios, decima* and *millones*), the price of this windfall was the acknowledgement of ecclesiastical immunity.
76. J.H. Elliott, 'Power and Propaganda in the Spain of Philip IV', in Sean Wilentz, ed., *Rites of Power: Symbolism, Ritual and Politics Since the Middle Ages* (Philadelphia, 1985), 152.

77. Félix Fernández Murga, *Carlos III y el Descubrimiento de Herculano* (Salamanca, 1989), 113–14; J.J. Vidal and E. Martínez Ruiz, *Política Interior y Exterior de los Borbones* (Madrid, 2001), 202; Anna María Rao, 'Carlos de Borbón en Nápoles', *Trienio*, 24 (1994), 23–5.

78. Richard Herr, The *Eighteenth-Century Revolution in Spain* (Princeton, 1958), 13; William J. Callahan, *Church, Politics and Society in Spain*, 3; many of these developments, naturally, had been in motion since the final sessions of the Council of Trent in 1563, when the authority of bishops was strengthened and restrictions made on clerical appeals to Rome, but the Bourbon monarchs took advantage of them in unprecedented ways. See R. Po-Chia Hsia, *The World of Catholic Renewal, 1540–1770* (Cambridge, 1998), 23.

79. David Brading, *Church and State in Bourbon Mexico. The Diocese of Michocán, 1749–1810* (Cambridge, 1994), 226.

80. Quoted in Antonio Ferrer del Río, *Historia del Reinado de Carlos III en España* (Madrid, 1856), vol. II, 519.

81. Charles C. Noel, 'Clerics and Crown in Bourbon Spain, 1700–1808: Jesuits, Jansenists and Enlightenment', in J.E. Bradley and D.K. Kley, eds, *Religion and Politics in Enlightenment Europe* (Notre Dame, 2002), 131–2.

82. Hsia, *Catholic Renewal*, 207; on seventeenth-century French Jansenism, see W.R. Ward, *Christianity Under the Ancien Régime, 1648–1789* (Cambridge, 1999), 27–9 passim; eighteenth-century Spanish and French Jansenism did not display all of the characteristics of its seventeenth-century French predecessor and namesake: Dale Van Kley suggested that, in the eighteenth century, Jansenism 'came to represent ... not an Augustinian Theology or an austere moral attitude, but a kind of opposition to papal or 'Italian' intrusion into France's internal affairs represented by the bull *Unigenitus* ... a kind of vague political front uniting all Frenchmen against foreign sacerdotal influences which were corrupting both court and episcopacy' in *The Jansenists and the Expulsion of the Jesuits from France, 1757–1765* (New Haven and London, 1975), 28.

83. Brading, *The First America: The Spanish Monarchy, Creole Patriots and the Liberal State, 1492–1867* (Cambridge, 1991), 500; for another formulation of this same view, see Brading, 'The Catholic Monarchy', in Serge Gruzinski and Nathan Wachtel, eds, *Le Nouveau Monde, Mondes Nouveaux: L'Expérience Américaine* (Paris, 1996), 401.

84. *El Pensador*, vol. II, 176; on the institution of the *tertulia* in eighteenth-century Spain, see Gloria A. Franco Rubio, *La Vida Cotidiana en Tiempos de Carlos III* (Madrid, 2001).

85. Antonio Luis Cortes Peña, *La Política Religiosa de Carlos III y las Ordenes Mendicantes* (Granada, 1989), 25–7.

86. BPR III/471, containing Juan Luís Lopez, Marqués de Regalía, *Discurso Legal-Theologico-Practico en Defensa de la Provision y Ordenanza de Gobierno* (Lima, 1684), 49.

87. BPR II/2851, [Anon.], 'Observaciones Filosóficas sobre la Operación del Emperador de Alemania Joseph II en Materias Eclesiásticas' (late 18th century), fos. 52, 55.

88. BPR II/2875, [Anon.], 'Principios Sobre la Esencia, Distinción y los Limites de las dos Potestades Espiritual y Temporal' (1784), fos. 186v., 202.

89. Fray Antonio de los Reyes, 'Retrato Histórico y Elogio Fúnebre del Cavallero Don Josef Nicolás de Azara', in F.J. León and M.V. Sanz Sanz, *Tratadistas Españoles del Arte en Italia en el Siglo XVIII* (Madrid, 1981), 340.

90. Gabriel Sánchez Espinosa, *La Biblioteca de José Nicolás de Azara* (Madrid, 1997), 30–33 passim; appendix.
91. Azara to Roda, 30 June 1768, in *El Espíritu de D. José Nicolás de Azara*, vol. I, 86.
92. Azara to Roda, 11 August 1768, in *El Espíritu de D. José Nicolás de Azara*, vol. I, 109.
93. Antonio Porlier y Sopranis [Marqués de Bajamar], Speech to the Council of the Indies (1794), in Marqués de Bajamar, *Discursos al Consejo de Indias*, 32.
94. Campomanes, *Tratado de la Regalía de Amortización* (Madrid, 1765), 7; Alfredo Martinez Albiach, 'Campomanes "Regalista"', *Burgense*, 35:2 (1994): esp. 467.
95. BPR II/2757, 'Dictamen de la Sala de Leyes del Consejo de Indias', 8 February 1783, fos. 16v., 21v.
96. Campomanes, *Tratado*, 33; the treatise's influence outside of Spain was enormous, particularly in Tanucci's Naples. See Álvarez de Morales, *El Pensamiento Político y Jurídico de Campomanes*, (Madrid, 1989) 46–7.
97. BPR II/2757, 'Dictamen de la Sala de Leyes del Consejo de Indias', 8 February 1783, fo. 16.
98. Noel, 'Clerics and Crown in Bourbon Spain, 1700–1808', 131–2.
99. Farriss, *Crown and Clergy in Colonial Mexico*, 6.
100. Cortes Peña, *La Política Religiosa*, 41; as noted previously, the *exequatur*, or *pase regio*, was the name of the process in which pontifical documents could not take force in Spain or be disseminated until they received royal approval.
101. [Campomanes], *Juicio Imparcial Sobre Las Letras En Forma de Breve, que Ha Publicado La Curia Romana, en que se Intentan Derogar Ciertos Edictos del Serenisimo Señor Infante Duque de Parma y Disputarla la Soberanía Temporal con este Pretexto* (Madrid, 1768), 114.
102. AGS Estado 6096, Grimaldi to Tanucci, 28 August 1764.
103. Azara to Roda, 21 September 1769, in *El Espíritu de D. José Nicolás de Azara*, vol. I, 332.
104. Ibid.
105. Ismael Sánchez Bella, *Iglesia y Estado en la América Española* (Pamplona, 1991), 174.
106. [Floridablanca], 'Instrucción', 123.
107. Noel, 'Clerics and Crown in Bourbon Spain'.
108. Jacques-Benigne Bossuet, *Politics Drawn from the Very Words of Holy Scripture*. Trans. and ed. Patrick Riley (Cambridge, 1999), 47, 58, 89, 92, 174, 354, 233.
109. Nannerl O. Keohane, *Philosophy and the State in France: the Renaissance to the Enlightenment* (Princeton, 1980), 256.
110. François-Xavier Guerra, '"Políticas Sacadas de las Sagradas Escrituras": La Referencia a la Biblia en el Debate Político (Siglos XVII-XIX)', in Mónica Quijada and Jesús Bustamante, eds, *Élites, Intelectuales y Modelos Colectivos: Mundo Ibérico (Siglo XVI–XIX)* (Madrid, 2002), 184; references to Bossuet abound, see BPR II/2875, [Anon], 'Principios Sobre la Esencia y Distinción y los Limites de las Dos Potestades Espiritual y Temporal' (1784), fo. 238; this is not an uncontentious view as Mario Góngora argued that in the Spanish World there never existed 'regalism of the Gallican or Anglican kind, still less philosophical regalism of the kind expounded by Dante or Marsilius of Padua. This juridical tradition combined a monarchism based on Roman law with Papalist canon law'. See Góngora, *Studies in the Colonial History of Latin America* (Cambridge, 1975), 39; on the opposition to Gallicanism in Spain, see Antonio Rubio, *La Crítica del Galicismo en España (1726–1832)* (Mexico, 1937), esp. 200–1.

111. J.G.A. Pocock, *Barbarism and Religion, Volume 2: Narratives of Civil Government* (Cambridge, 1999), 31; Battlori, 'La Expulsión de los Jesuitas y el Jurisdiccionalismo Antiromano: Raíces Napolitanas y Austracistas', in *Carlos III y la Ilustración* (Madrid, 1988), 237.

112. Pietro Giannone, *On the Civil History of the Kingdom of Naples* (London, 1729), vol. I, preface, ii; vol. I, book 1, chapter 11; vol. II, book 30, chapter 2, 475; vol. II, book 60, 848–9; see Benedetto Croce, *History of the Kingdom of Naples* (Chicago and London, 1970), 155.

113. Brading, *Church and State in Bourbon Mexico*, 11; Samuel J. Miller, *Portugal and Rome c.1748–1830: An Aspect of the Catholic Enlightenment* (Rome, 1978), 5–6; E.E. Hales, *The Revolution and the Papacy, 1769–1846* (London, 1960), 20–1. Hales noted the widespread diffusion of Van Espen's works evidenced by a ten-volume edition appearing in Naples in 1766–9 and four volumes in Madrid in 1792.

114. W.R. Ward, *Christianity Under the Ancien Régime, 1648–1789* (Cambridge, 1999), 186.

115. Azara to Roda, 10 March 1768, in *El Espíritu de D. José Nicolás de Azara*, vol. I, 26–7.

116. Azara to Roda, 16 November 1769, in *El Espíritu de D. José Nicolás de Azara*, vol. I, 359; Brading noted that 'the Gallican theses of Bossuet and the ecclesiastical history of the Abbé Fleury were most frequently read and cited', in *Church and State in Bourbon Mexico*, 11.

117. BPR II/2840, 'Informe Sobre el Libro de Justino Febronio acerca del Estado de la Iglesia y Legitima Potestad de Pontifice Romano ... con el Fin de Disminuir sus Facultades y Captar el Animo de los Obispos con el Aumento de Jurisdicción que les Promete', n.d., fos. 170v., 172.

118. BPR II/2895, Francisco de Caseda y Muro, 'Consulta del Consejo de Castilla sobre Peyrera [sic] ... acerca de la Potestad de los Obispos' (1800), fos. 60, 105v.

119. BPR II/967, Campomanes, 'Informe ... sobre la Introducción en España del Libro Intitulado "Epistolas de Thomas Maria Manaqui a Justinio Febronio", impreso el año 1776', fo. 230v.

120. Mestre Sanchis, *Apología y Crítica de España*, 311.

121. Suárez and Vitoria, both quoted in Bernice Hamilton, *Political Thought in Sixteenth-Century Spain: A Study of the Political Ideas of Vitoria, De Soto, Suárez, and Molina* (Oxford, 1963), 69, 84–5.

122. BPR III/471, containing Juan Luís López (Marqués de la Regalía), *Discurso Legal-Theologico-Practico en Defensa de la Provision y Ordenanza de Gobierno* (Lima, 1684), 51.

123. Castillo de Bobadilla, *Política Para Corregidores y Señores de Vassallos* [1704] (Madrid, 1978), vol. I, 498.

124. BPR III/471, contains Juan Luís López, 'Historia Legal de la Bula Llamada *In Coena Domini*' (Madrid, 1768 [1668]), prologue.

125. On the Visigothic kingdom as prefiguring the political unity of modern Spain, see J.M. Wallace-Hadrill, *The Barbarian West, 400–1000* (Oxford, 1997), 138–9.

126. J.H. Elliott, 'Self-Perception and Decline in Early Seventeenth-Century Spain', in *Spain and its World, 1500–1700: Selected Essays* (New Haven and London, 1989), 252.

127. Juan Francisco de Castro, *Discursos Críticos Sobre las Leyes y sus Intérpretes* (Madrid, 1765), vol. I, 192.

128. Archivo de RAH 11–3–1–8235, Juan Bautista Muñoz, 'Discurso Sobre las Dificultades que se Ofrecen Para Ilustrar la Historia Nacional y Algunos Remedios

Para Vencerlas', 6 January 1792; Pedro Rodríguez de Campomanes, 'Discurso a la Real Academia', 5 April 1748; Campomanes, *Educación Popular*, vol. IV, 18, 21; ACC 30–20, contains Campomanes's unpublished notes towards 'Prólogo a la Disertación Sobre el Primer Rey Godo que Domino en España'; for an overview of eighteenth-century historiography, see Enrique García Hernán, 'Construcción de la Historia de España en los Siglos XVII y XVIII', in García Cárcel, ed., *La Construcción*, 179.

129. ARAH 11–3-1–8234, 'Discurso Sobre la Legislación de España que Leyó Bernardo Joaquin Danvila y Villarrasa en Su Ingreso en la Real Academia de la History', 3 April 1778.

130. E.A. Thompson, *The Goths in Spain* (Oxford, 1969), 275–9; P.D. King, *Law and Society in the Visigothic Kingdom* (Cambridge, 1972), 17, 123, 127, 152–3; for additional studies of Visigothic Spain, see Roger Collins, *Early Medieval Spain: Unity in Diversity, 400–1000* (London, 1983) and J.F. O'Callaghan, *A History of Medieval Spain* (Ithaca and London, 1975), 65.

131. Sempere y Guarinos, *Vínculos*, 105, 149, 186; Sánchez-Blanco, 'Ilustración sin Ilustrados?' in Bello and Rivera, eds, *La Actitud Ilustrada* (Valencia, 2002), 191.

132. Campomanes, quoted in George M. Addy, *The Enlightenment at the University of Salamanca* (Durham, 1966), 114, 237; on university reform in general, see José Luis Peset, 'La Renovación Universitaria', in Antonio Lafuente et al., eds, *Carlos III y la Ciencia de la Ilustración* (Madrid, 1987).

133. BPR II/2827, [Anon.], 'Origen de la Antigua Subordinación de los Pontifices a los Emperadores Romanos ... Extensión Injusta de la Jurisdición Eclesiástica en perjuicio del Dominio Temporal' [n.d.; but found among eighteenth-century documents], fos. 159–71 passim.

134. Antonio Porlier, 'Discurso Jurídico', fo. 4.

135. BPR II/2847, Manuel de Abad y la Sierra, 'Discurso Previo Sobre las Iglesias, Monasterios y Capillas del Real Patronato en General' (1781), fos. 207, 217.

136. BPR II/2880, José García de León y Pizarro (*Fiscal* of the *Real Audiencia de Sevilla*), 'Exposición Fiscal en Defensa de la Regalía sobre que el Conocimiento Jurisdicional en Cofradías y Hermandades toca a la Potestad Política' (1776), fo. 19v.

137. BPR II/2757, Dictamen de la Sala de Leyes del Consejo de Indias, 8 February 1783, fo. 13.

138. The political function of the Visigoths was not confined to the regalist reformers. Paradoxically, whereas regalists invoked the Visigothic monarchy to argue for the expansion of the state's authority, the Visigothic precedent would be used during debates at the *Cortes* de Cádiz to call for limitations and restrictions on monarchical power. See Joaquín Varela Suanzes, 'Los Modelos Constitucionales en las Cortes de Cádiz', in F-X. Guerra, ed., *Revoluciones Hispánicas: Independencias Americanas y Liberalismo Español* (Madrid, 1995), 264–5.

139. Campomanes, *Tratado*, 2.

140. BPR II/2760, 'Consulta del Consejo de Castilla a motivo de Representación de Don Francisco Carrasco, Fiscal de la Hacienda ... acerca del restablecimiento o renovación de la Ley de Amortización', 18 June 1766, fo. 18v.

141. Callahan, 'The Spanish Church', in Callahan and Higgs, eds, *Church and Society*, 43; according to Hsia, in 1749 the Jesuits claimed 22,600 members and administered 669 colleges plus 176 seminaries worldwide, in *Catholic Renewal*, 32.

142. Brading, *Church and State*, 12, 15.

143. Miller, *Portugal and Rome*, 20; a plausible explanation for this complicated episode, recently put forward by H.M. Scott, is that the Jesuits were 'victims of power politics, of the alignments and exigencies of continental diplomacy', focusing on the prominent role played by the Duc de Choiseul, in Scott, 'Religion and *Realpolitik*: the Duc de Choiseul, the Bourbon Family Compact and the Attack on the Society of Jesus, 1758–1775', *International History Review*, 25:1 (2003): 37–9, 62.
144. BN Mss. 7227, Du Tillot to Roda, 19 November 1760.
145. AGS 5180, Du Tillot to Roda, 17 November 1760.
146. Roda to Du Tillot, 1 November 1764, quoted in Isidoro Pinedo, *Manuel de Roda: Su Pensamiento Regalista* (Zaragoza, 1981), 44.
147. BN Mss. 7227, Du Tillot to Roda, 28 October 1764.
148. Azara to Roda, 3 December 1778, in *El Espíritu de D. José Nicolás de Azara*, vol. II.
149. AHN Estado 2831–1, Grimaldi to R.P. Fr. Joaquin de Osma, 23 November 1764.
150. Franco Venturi, 'Church and Reform in Enlightenment Italy: the Sixties of the Eighteenth Century', *Journal of Modern History*, 48 (1976): 221–3.
151. Charles Noel, 'Campomanes and the Secular Clergy in Spain, 1760–1780: Enlightenment vs. Tradition' (PhD Dissertation, Princeton University, 1969), 366.
152. For a description of this process, see Charles Noel, 'Opposition to Enlightened Reform in Spain: Campomanes and the Clergy', *Societas* (1973): 33–4, 36–7.
153. Campomanes, *Juicio Imparcial*, 30; Campomanes's debt to Gallican and Jansenist writers is clear from his copious footnotes, with its multiple citations of Febronius, Bossuet, Fleury, as a well as of Grotius and Pufendorf.
154. Noel, 'Campomanes and the Secular Clergy', 395.
155. Campomanes, *Juicio Imparcial*, 42.
156. Ibid., 98.
157. Ibid., 82–3.
158. Ibid., 98; the Church's aid to the poor was neglected in Campomanes's sweeping polemic. Paradoxically, however, it fulfilled its charitable role effectively, as Callahan noted, because 'rising agricultural prices paradoxically increased the numbers of those requiring assistance while endowing religious institutions with the revenue to provide that help', in Callahan, *Church, Politics and Society*, 50.
159. Herr, *Rural Change and Royal Finances*, 155.
160. Campomanes, *Juicio Imparcial*, 143.
161. Laura Rodríguez Díaz, *Reforma e Ilustración en la España del Siglo XVIII* (Madrid, 1975), 99–100.
162. BPR II/2853, [Anon.], 'Reparos Occuridos al Tiempo de Leer el Juicio Imparcial Sobre el Monitorio de Parma' (1768?), fos. 223, 230v.
163. It must be conceded that several contemporary political writers had assumed more moderate, even conciliatory, stances on the Church's social and economic function. While acknowledging that ecclesiastical immunity was a 'type of obstacle' which 'limits absolute power', Bernardo Ward argued that it was the 'Church in Spain, more than the Parliament in England, by being a solid institution, trustworthy and inviolate', that was the foundation of credit. See Bernardo Ward, *Obra Pía, y Eficaz Modo para Remediar la Miseria de la Gente de España* 2nd edn (Madrid, 1767), 110–12.
164. Campomanes, *Juicio Imparcial*, 126–7.
165. BPR II/2760, 'Consulta del Consejo de Castilla a motivo de Representación de Don Francisco Carrasco, Fiscal de la Hacienda … acerca del restablecimiento o renovación de la Ley de Amortización', 18 June 1766, fo. 44, 50.

166. Antonio Joseph Álvarez de Abreu, *Víctima Real Legal, Discurso Único Jurídico-Histórico-Político Sobre las Vacantes Mayores y Menores de las Iglesias de las Indias Occidentales Pertenecerá a la Corona de Castilla y Leon con Pleno y Absoluto Dominio [1720]* (Madrid, 1769), 195.

167. BPR II/2656, Antonio Porlier, 'Discurso Jurídico Sobre la Origen, Aplicación y Distribución de los Bienes-Espolios y Diferencia entre los de España y de las Indias' (1783), fos. 145, 237v.; Porlier later became the Marqués de Bajamar and served as President of the Council of the Indies in the early nineteenth century.

168. BPR II/2847, Manuel de Abad y la Sierra, 'Discurso Previo Sobre las Iglesias, Monasterios y Capillas del Real Patronato en General' (1781), fo. 104.

169. Arnold Bauer, 'The Church and Spanish Agrarian Structure: 1765–1865', *The Americas*, 28:1 (1971): 82, 84.

170. Farriss, *Crown and Clergy in Colonial Mexico*, 106–7, 170.

171. BPR II/1389, [Anon.], 'Disertación, en que se Demuestra la Regalía, que Compete a todos los Soberanos, y con Especialidad a los Reyes de Castilla para Establecer en su Dominios la Ley de Amortización' (n.d., c.1805), fos. 220v., 276.

172. BPR II/2666, Miguel Antonio de Gandara, 'Apuntes para Formar un Discurso sobre el Bien y el Mal de España' (1759), fo. 118.

173. Amable-Angel Fernández-Sanz, 'Utopia y Realidad en la Ilustración Española. Pablo de Olavide y las "Nuevas Poblaciones"' (PhD Dissertation, Universidad Complutense de Madrid, 1990), 396; Cayetano Alcázar Molina, *Los Hombres del Reinado de Carlos III: D. Pablo de Olavide (El Colonizador de Sierra Morena)* (Madrid, 1927), 82, 114–15; Jordi Oliveras Samitier, *Nuevas Poblaciones en la España de la Ilustración* (Barcelona, 1998).

174. 'Real Cédula ... La Instrucción y Fuero de Población ... en la Sierra Morena' (Madrid, 1767); Marion Reder Gadow, 'Teoria y Realidad en la Aplicación del Fuero de las Nuevas Poblaciones', in *Actas VI Congreso Histórico Sobre Las Nuevas Poblaciones* (La Carlota, 1994), 147–8.

175. Quoted in Herr, *Rural Change and Royal Finances*, 67.

176. Real Cédula Sierra Morena'.

177. Swinburne, *Travels through Spain in the Years 1775 and 1776*, 2nd edn, (London, 1787), vol. II, 104, 50.

178. Peter Von Lago, 25 July 1770, quoted in Luís Perdices Blas, *Pablo de Olavide (1725–1803): El Ilustrado* (Madrid, 1993), 370.

179. AGI Indiferente General 1656, Informe of Antonio Porlier, 2 October 1781.

180. AHN Consejos 5530, doc. #48, Informe of Juan de Arabaca, 25 April 1769.

181. Pablo de Olavide, *Plan de Estudios para la Universidad de Sevilla* [1768] (Madrid, 1989), 136.

182. AGI Indiferente General 1652, *Fiscal* of Castile, 4 April 1755 [n.b. this *legajo* is badly damaged and therefore the name of the *fiscal* was illegible]; on 1680 *Recopilación*, see Ismael Sánchez Bella et al., *Historia del Derecho Indiano* (Pamplona, 1992), 100.

183. AGI Estado 86A, no. 2, [Gálvez], 'Discurso y Reflecxiones [sic] de un Vasallo Sobre la Decadencia de Nuestras Indias Españolas', n.d., fos. 56v.–57.

184. Ibid., fo. 61.

185. BPR II/2828, 'Instrucción Dada por Catarina II, Emperatriz y Legisladora de Todas las Rusias a la Comisión que esta Soberana ha establecido para Trabajar en la Formación de Un Nuevo Código de Leyes'.

186. On membership, see Eduardo Martiré, 'Guión sobre el Proceso Recopilador de las Leyes de Indias', in Francisco de Icaza DuFour, coord., *Recopilación de Leyes de los Reynos de las Indias. Estudios Histórico-Jurídicos* (Mexico City, 1987), 40; BPR

II/2827, Antonio de León, 'Discurso Sobre la Importancia, Forma y Disposición de la Recopilación de las Leyes de las Indias Occidentales' (late 1770s), fo. 78.

187. BPR II/2843, 'Representación que hizo en 27 Junio al Exmo Sr Joseph de Gálvez ... Balthasar Ladron de Guevara, Fiscal de la Real Audiencia de Mexico sobre los Defectos que Padece la Actual Legislación de Indias, y Necesidad de Adiccionarla y Corregirla, el Modo con que Debia Hacerse y Proporción que Tenia que Trabajarla', fo. 147–8.

188. BPR II/2827, León, 'Discurso Sobre la Importancia', fo. 89v.

189. BPR II/2843, Juan Christostomo de Ansotegui to Gálvez, 17 November 1778, fos. 156–158.

190. Manuel Josef de Ayala, *Notas a la Recopilación de Indias: Origen e Historia Ilustrada de las Leyes de Indias* [1787] Ed. Juan Manzano Manzano (Madrid, 1945), 7, 11.

191. On this process, see Antonio Muro Orejón, 'El Nuevo Código de las Leyes Indianas. Proyectos de Recopilación Legislativa Posteriores a 1680', *Revista de Ciencias Jurídicas y Sociales*, 12 (1929): 301–17 passim; on the Council of the Indies in the reign of Charles IV, see M.A. Burkholder, 'The Council of the Indies in the Late Eighteenth Century: A New Perspective', *HAHR*, 56:3 (1976): 404–23.

192. Tamar Herzog, *Defining Nations: Immigrants and Citizens in Early Modern Spain and Spanish America* (New Haven and London, 2003), 88–9.

193. Quentin Skinner, 'Language and Political Change' in Terence Ball et al., eds, *Political Innovation and Conceptual Change* (Cambridge, 1989), 8.

3   Imperial Governance and Reform: Ideas and *Proyectos*

1. Juan de Castro, *Medio Para Sanar la Monarquía de España* (Madrid, 1668), 3; Stanley Stein and Barbara Stein, *Silver, Trade and War: Spain and America in the Making of Early Modern Europe* (Baltimore and London, 2000), 7, 100; on the *arbitristas*' use of foreign models, see Luís Perdices de Blas, *La Economía Política de la Decadencia de Castilla en el Siglo XVII: Investigaciones de los Arbitristas sobre la Naturaleza y Causas de la Riqueza de las Naciones* (Madrid, 1996), 44.

2. J.H. Elliott, 'Self-Perception and Decline in Early Seventeenth-century Spain', in *Spain and its World, 1500–1700: Selected Essays* (New Haven and London, 1989), 252.

3. BPR II/2666, Miguel Antonio de Gandara, 'Apuntes para Formar un Discurso Sobre el Bien y el Mal de España' (1759), fo. 135.

4. On intervention in the economic sphere, see Kenneth Andrien and Lyman Johnson, 'Introduction', in *The Political Economy of Spanish America in the Age of Revolution, 1750–1850* (Albuquerque, 1994), 5.

5. José de Campillo y Cossío, *Nuevo Sistema de Gobierno Económico Para América* (Oviedo, 1993), 75.

6. Carlos Marichal, 'Beneficios y Costes Fiscales del Colonialismo: Las Remesas Americanas a España, 1760–1814', *Revista de Historia Económica*, 15 (1997): 478.

7. Of the Mexican *situado* in 1793, Cuba received 2,113,741 (pesos); Santo Domingo 724,891; Louisiana 555,137; Puerto Rico, 377,096; the Philippines 250,000; Trinidad 200,000; and Florida 151,031. Figures taken from Eduardo Arcila Farías, *El Siglo Ilustrado en América: Reforma Económica del Siglo XVIII en Nueva España* (Caracas, 1955), 274; Herbert S. Klein, 'Structure and Profitability of Royal Finance in the Viceroyalty of the Río de la Plata in 1790', *HAHR*, 53:3 (1973): 457; nonetheless, it should be noted that the *situado* was part of the price of security for the transit of silver (a high value commodity) back to Spain.

8. Carlos Marichal and Matilde Souro Mantecón, 'Silver and *Situados*: New Spain and the Financing of the Spanish Empire in the Caribbean in the Eighteenth Century', *HAHR*, 74:4 (1994): 587–616; the term '*situado*', as defined by Marichal and Mantecón, 'refers to the remittance or transfer of royal funds from one *caja* of the treasury to another to cover expenses of strategic importance', 588 fn.3, 611.

9. Figures compiled by J.R. Fisher, *Commercial Relations Between Spain and Spanish America in the Era of Free Trade* (Liverpool, 1985), 55.

10. The demographic disparity also must not be neglected: in 1800, 46.4 per cent and 8.7 per cent of Spanish America's total population of 12.6 million lived in Mexico and Peru, respectively. See Peter Bakewell, *A History of Latin America* (Oxford, 1997), 256–7.

11. Campomanes, 'Apuntaciones de lo que Importa' (1788) in *Inéditos Políticos* (Oviedo, 1998), 21.

12. Antonio de Ulloa, *La Marina: Fuerzas Navales de la Europa y Costas de Berbería* (Cádiz, 1995), 13.

13. Campillo y Cossío, *Nuevo Sistema*, 108–9.

14. The summary draws on the pioneering and lucid works of, among others, H.I. Priestley, *José de Gálvez: Visitor-General of New Spain (1765–1771)* (Berkeley, 1916); L.E. Fisher, *Viceregal Administration in the Spanish American Colonies* (Berkeley, 1926); C.H. Haring, *The Spanish Empire in America* (New York, 1947); J.H. Parry, *The Spanish Seaborne Empire* (Berkeley, CA, 1966); Laura Rodríguez Díaz, *Reforma e Ilustración en la España del Siglo XVIII* (Madrid, 1975); John Lynch, 'The Institutional Framework of Colonial Latin America', *JLAS* (supplement) 24 (1992): 69–81; and Ismael Sánchez Bella et al., *Historia del Derecho Indiano* (Madrid, 1992).

15. Mark Burkholder argued to the contrary that rather than 'declining, the Council [of the Indies]'s importance and prestige enjoyed a renaissance in the final decades of Old Regime Spain', in 'The Council of the Indies in the Late Eighteenth Century: A New Perspective', *HAHR*, 56:3 (1976): 405.

16. The Viceroy was president of the *Audiencia*. Although the *Audiencia* was the highest court, extraordinary cases could be appealed to the Council of the Indies.

17. Except between 1786–8, the first two years of the intendancies in Spanish America; the *Audiencias* also gained control over *espolios*.

18. AGI Caracas 443, Real Cédula 'El Reglamento Para la Poblacion y Comercio de la Isla de la Trinidad de Barlovento' (1783).

19. Pedro Rodríguez de Campomanes, *Bosquejo de la Política-Económica Española Delineado Sobre el Estado Presente de Sus Intereses* [1750] (Madrid, 1984), 152–9 passim.

20. BPR II/2898, 'Dictamen de Sr. D. Joseph de Gálvez ... Sobre la Proposición Hecha a SM por el Consejo de Castilla de Que se remitiesen a Indias los Gitanos que Vagaban por Estos Reynos Para Poblar Aquellos', Sept. 1777.

21. David J. Weber, *Bárbaros: Spaniards and their Savages in the Age of Enlightenment* (New Haven and London, 2005), 12, 202.

22. Francisco de Solano, 'Ciudad y Geoestrategia Española en América durante el Siglo XVIII', in *La América Española en la Epoca de las Luces: Tradición, Innovación, Representación* (Madrid, 1988), 57.

23. Uztáriz, *The Theory and Practice of Commerce and Maritime Affairs*, vol. I, 1, 6, 49; vol. II, 378, 390, 422; see also Anthony Pagden, 'Liberty, Honour, and *Comercio Libre*: The Structure of Debates over the State of the Spanish Empire in the Eighteenth Century', in *The Uncertainties of Empire: Essays in Iberian and Ibero-Atlantic History* (Aldershot, 1994), 4.

24. Bernardo de Ulloa, *Restablecimiento de las Fábricas, Tráfico y Comercio Maritimo de España* (Madrid, 1740), part I, 14; n.b. Bernardo was the father of Antonio de Ulloa.

25. Ulloa, *Restablecimiento*, part II, 24–5; Marcelo Bitar Letayf, *Economistas Españoles del Siglo XVIII: Sus Ideas Sobre la Libertad del Comercio con Indias* (Madrid, 1968), 105.

26. Stein and Stein, *Silver, Trade and War*, 215.

27. Bernardo Joaquin Danvila y Villarrasa, *Lecciones de Economía Civil, o de el Comercio Escrito para el Uso de los Caballeros del Real Seminario de Nobles* (Madrid, 1779), 165.

28. Campillo y Cossío, *Nuevo Sistema*, 113; on Campillo, see David Brading, *Miners and Merchants in Bourbon Mexico, 1763–1810* (Cambridge, 1971), 25; also see Josefina Cintrón Tiryakian, 'Campillo's Pragmatic New System: a Mercantile and Utilitarian Approach to Indian Reform in Spanish Colonies of the Eighteenth Century', *History of Political Economy*, 10:3 (1978): 233–57.

29. Bernardo Ward, *Proyecto Económico, en que se Proponen Varias Providencias Dirigidas à Promover los Intereses de España, con los Medios y Fondos Necesarios para Plantificacion* (Madrid, 1779), 229, 284, 306; Imaculada Arias de Saavedra Alías, 'Irlandeses en la Alta Administración Española del Siglo XVIII', in Maria Bergoña Villar García, ed., *La Emigración Irlandesa en el Siglo XVIII* (Malaga, 2000), 48–54 passim; Osvaldo Chiareno, 'Bernardo Ward', in *Noticias Bio-Bibliográficas Sobre Economistas Españoles del Siglo XVIII* (Genoa, 1962), 8–9; the imprint of these political writers on policy did not escape foreign observers, including the British ambassador Liston, who lamented that the 'greatest part' of Spain's notions on the subject of commerce came from Ward's *Proyecto Económico*, which was 'sanguine to excess' concerning Spain's 'illusive prospect of success' and 'plans of national improvement'. See PRO FO 72/10, Liston to the Marquis of Carmarthen, 30 June 1787.

30. Emma Rothschild, 'Global Commerce and the Question of Sovereignty in the Eighteenth-century Provinces', *Modern Intellectual History*, 1:1 (2004): 9.

31. Gary Anderson and R.D. Tollison, 'Apologiae for Chartered Monopolies in Foreign Trade, 1600–1800', *History of Political Economy*, 15:4 (1983): 555.

32. Lynch, *Spanish Colonial Administration, 1782–1810: The Intendant System in the Viceroyalty of the Río de la Plata* (London, 1958), 10.

33. R.D. Hussey, *The Caracas Company, 1728–1789: A Study in the History of Spanish Monopolistic Trade* (Cambridge, MA, 1934), 33; this company was based in Bilbao, financed with Basque capital, and was intended to benefit the peninsular periphery which was judged to have been stymied by the Cádiz monopoly.

34. Stein and Stein, *Silver, Trade and War*, 202; Ringrose, *Spain, Europe and the 'Spanish Miracle', 1700–1900*, (Cambridge, 1996), 109.

35. Niels Steensgard, 'The Companies as a Specific Institution in the History of European Expansion', 247, 251, 260; and Pierre H. Boulle, 'French Mercantilism, Commercial Companies and Colonial Profitability', 98, 116–17, both in Leonard Blussé and Femme Gaastra, eds, *Companies and Trade: Essays in Overseas Trading Companies During the Ancien Régime* (Leiden, 1981).

36. BPR II/2829, Marqués de Llanos, 'Los Medios con que Puede Conseguir la Felicidad de la Monarquía' (1755), fos. 111v.–12.

37. Miguel Artola, 'América en el Pensamiento Español de Siglo XVIII', *Revista de Indias*, 29 (1969): 74; Mariano García Ruiperez, 'El Pensamiento Economico Ilustrado y las Compañías de Comercio', *Revista de Historia Económica* 4:3 (1986): 542–3.

38. José M. Mariluz Urquijo, *Bilbao y Buenos Aires: Proyectos Dieciochescos de Compañías de Comercio* (Buenos Aires, 1981), 118.

39. Montserrat Garate Ojanguren, *Comercio Ultramarino e Ilustración: La Real Compañía de la Habana* (San Sebastián, 1993), 172, 361.
40. AGI Indiferente 2410, Muzquiz to Arriaga, 19 February 1769.
41. BPR II/2666, Gandara, 'Apuntes', fos. 120, 125v.
42. Campomanes, *Bosquejo de la Política-Económica Española*, 130–1.
43. Campomanes, *Reflexiones sobre el Comercio Exterior a Indias* (1762), ed. V. Llombart Rosa (Madrid, 1988), 80.
44. A.J. Kuethe, 'The Early Reforms of Charles III in the Viceroyalty of New Granada', in Fisher, Kuethe and McFarlane, eds, *Reform and Insurrection in Bourbon New Granada and Peru* (Baton Rouge and London, 1990), 25.
45. BPR II/2639, 'Consulta Hecha a Su Magestad en Junta Formada de su Real Orden por el Marqués de los Llano, Francisco Craywinkel, Simon de Aragorri, Tomas Ortíz de Landazuri y Pedro Goosens sobre el Comercio y Exterior de España con sus Colonias' (1765), fos. 6v.–7.
46. Eduardo Arcila Farías, *Fundamentos Económicos del Imperio Español en América* (Caracas, 1985), 84; Matilla Quizá, 'Las Compañias Privilegiadas en la España del Antiguo Régimen', in Miguel Artola, ed., *La Economía Española al Final del Antiguo Régimen. IV: Instituciones*, (Madrid, 1982), 390–1.
47. Jeremy Adelman, *Republic of Capital: Buenos Aires and the Legal Transformation of the Atlantic World* (Stanford, 1999), 28.
48. Allan Christelow, 'Contraband Trade with Jamaica and the Spanish Main, and the Free Port Act of 1766', *HAHR*, 22:2 (1942): 311; the creation of the British free port system certainly played a significant role in Spanish imperial thinking: the number of vessels annually entering the Jamaican free ports rose steadily from 53 in 1767 to 279 in 1777; see Frances Armytage, *The Free Port System in the British West Indies: A Study in Commercial Policy, 1766–1822* (London and New York, 1953), table B, 149.
49. AGI Indiferente 2410, 'Dictamen de Grimaldi sobre la solicitude ... de Galicia e Asturias', 17 February 1770.
50. AGI Santo Domingo 2585, 'Proyecto de la Compañía que se Intento Establecer en Bilbao para el Comercio de la Luisiana' (1767), unfoliated.
51. Ibid.
52. *Reglamento y Aranceles Reales Para el Comercio Libre de España a Indias, 12 Octubre 1778* (Seville, 1978), 1.
53. John Lynch, *Bourbon Spain, 1700–1808* (Oxford, 1989), 353.
54. Stanley J. Stein and Barbara H. Stein, *Apogee of Empire: Spain and New Spain in the Age of Charles III, 1759–1789* (Baltimore and London, 2003), 186–7; on the rising tide of British contraband in the Caribbean up to 1778, see Héctor R. Feliciano Ramos, *El Contrabando Inglés en el Caribe y el Golfo de México (1748–1778)* (Seville, 1990).
55. J.R. Fisher, *The Economic Aspects of Spanish Imperialism in America, 1492–1810* (Liverpool, 1997), 139.
56. Bourbon trade policy, as Allan Kuethe has shown, was 'confined inside the strictest system of *comercio libre* which consisted of nothing more than the adaptation of traditional mercantilism by the new exigencies imposed by the resurgence of the peninsular periphery'; see Kuethe, 'El Fin de Monopolio: Los Borbones y el Consulado Andaluz' in Kuethe, E. Vila Vilar, ed., *Relaciones de Poder y Comercio Colonial: Nuevas Perspectivas*, 57; on this issue, see also Antonio García-Baquero González, *Cádiz y el Atlántico (1717–1778): El Comercio Español Bajo el Monopolio Gaditano* (Cádiz, 1988), vol. I, 76–85 passim.

57. BPR II/2867, Tomas Ortiz de Landazuri, 'Papel Haciendo Presente los Medios que Conceptuaba Debian Ponerse en Practica para Exterminar el Contrabando de Indias, Especialmente el que se Hacia en las Costas de Cartagena, Tierra Firme y Buenos Ayres' n.d., fos. 50–50v.

58. AGI Charcas 445, Sebastian Antonio Foro to Minister of the Indies, 14 September 1789.

59. BPR II/2851, [Anon.], 'Reflexiones Sobre las Reglas y Medios Verdaderos de Adelantar nuestro Comercio y Notas y Reparos' (1787/1788), fo. 300.

60. Stein and Stein, *Apogee of Empire*, 208, 212.

61. P. Michael McKinley, *Pre-Revolutionary Caracas: Politics, Economy and Society, 1777–1811* (Cambridge, 1985), 45.

62. Juan Andreo García, 'Del "Libre Comercio" a la Quiebra de Sistema Colonial (1789–1796). El Comercio Exterior de Venezuela', *AEA*, 51:2 (1994): 30, 32.

63. Ringrose, *Spain*, 122.

64. Foronda, 'Sobre la Nueva Compañía de Indias Orientales', in *Miscelánea, o Colección de Varios Discursos*. Madrid, 1787, 31, 19 passim.

65. Quoted in Angel López Cantos, *Don Francisco de Saavedra, Segundo Intendante de Caracas* (Seville, 1973), 120.

66. Quoted in McKinley, *Pre-Revolutionary Caracas*, 104.

67. BPR II/2851, 'Disertación Sobre las Utilidades que Logran los Franceses, Ingleses y Holandeses con su Comercio en el Continente de Asia y las que podrá conseguir la España con este Trafico', fos. 27, 30; Josep M. Fradera, *Filipinas, La Colonia Más Peculiar: La Hacienda Pública en la Definición de la Política Colonial, 1762–1868* (Madrid, 1999), 87; W.L. Schurz, 'The Royal Philippine Company', *HAHR*, 3:4 (1920): 498–9.

68. AHN Estado 2927, no. 273, 'Memoria Sobre las Primeras Operaciones de la Real Compañía de Filipinas y Su Estado Actual', 17 July 1787.

69. In 1789, as a result of shifting ideology combined with the Company's failure to deter contraband and to introduce slaves in sufficient quantities, the clause guaranteeing the Company's share in Caracas was rescinded and its total annual commerce rapidly plunged, accounting for a mere five per cent of the total by 1795. McKinley, *Pre-Revolutionary Caracas*, 114.

70. V.T. Harlow, *The Founding of the Second British Empire, 1763–1793* (London, 1952), vol. II, 797.

71. José de Gálvez, quoted on Weber, *Bárbaros*, 162.

72. BPR II/2840, Antonio de Narváez y la Torre, 'Relación o Informe de la Provincia de Santa Maria y Rio de la Hacha por lo que Respecta al Estado Natural de su Comercio, Labranzas, Haciendas y Frutos ... los que pueden Cultivarse y Conviene Fomentar para su Aumento de su Comercio ... Causas de su Decadencia' (1778), fo. 202; Speech of Miguel Gijon, 7 May 1776, *Memorias de la Sociedad Económica* (Madrid, 1780–1805), vol. III, 275; for a general overview, see J.F. King, 'Evolution of the Free Slave Trade Principle in Spanish Colonial Administration', *HAHR*, 22:1 (1942): 34–56; Like many Caroline initiatives, the 'free' slave trade drew on French precedent, most notably Choiseul-Praslin's creation of Castries and Mole St Nicolas as free ports in order to increase the inflow of slaves needed to promote agricultural improvement. I thank Richard Drayton for bringing this French precedent to my attention.

73. Pablo Tornero, 'Emigración, Población y Esclavitud en Cuba (1765–1817)', *AEA*, 44 (1987): 236; Burkholder and Johnson, *Colonial Latin America*, 5th edn, (New York and Oxford, 2002), 323.

74. Eric Williams, *Capitalism and Slavery* (Chapel Hill and London, 1994), 33.

75. The terms of the *asiento*, reproduced in Geoffrey Symcox, ed., *War, Diplomacy and Imperialism, 1618–1763* (New York, 1972), 289.
76. AGI Buenos Aires 41, Floridablanca 9 January 1779; n.b. Fernando Po and Ano Bom later became Equitorial Guinea, a Spanish colony until the late 20th century. The island Fernando Po is now known as Bioko; on the Treaty of Alcáçovas, see Burkholder and Johnson, *Colonial Latin America*, 133; on Luso-Spanish rivalry and the treaty of San Ildefonso, see Dauril Alden, 'The Undeclared War of 1773–1777: Climax of Luso-Spanish Platine Rivalry', *HAHR*, 41 (1961): 55–74.
77. AHU (São Tomé) Cx. 16, doc. 63, 30 November 1778. According to this same dispatch, when Count Argelejos returned to São Tomé, he contracted a fever and died shortly thereafter.
78. AGI Buenos Aires 41, Josef Varela y Ulloa to Gálvez, 12 March 1779.
79. Ibid.; Varela y Ulloa also wrote a manual for aspiring Spanish slavetraders entitled 'Sucinta Descipción de la Costa de Africa desde el Cabo de Monte hasta Onis, y Methodo con que los Extrangeros Hacen el Comercio de Esclavos, en los Diferentes Puertos de la Misma Costa'. This document may be found in the *legajo* cited above.
80. AGI Buenos Aires 41, Floridablanca to Gálvez, late March 1779.
81. Quoted in Pablo Tornero, 'Emigración, Población y Esclavitud en Cuba (1765–1817)', *AEA*, 44 (1987): 236–7; on Cuban attempts to initiate a trade with Fernando Po, see AGI Cuba 1257, letter directed at Navarro, 20 October 1778.
82. James Ferguson King, 'Evolution of the Free Slave Trade Principle in Spanish Colonial Administration', *HAHR*, 22:1 (1942): 34, 46, 49, 50; not all colonial administrators embraced this decision as sound policy. In New Granada, Viceroy Ezpeleta noted that 'the inhabitants of this kingdom are not disposed to take advantage of the freedom ... it has only served as a pretext for contraband'. Ezpeleta, October 1794, quoted in J.A. Barbier, 'Commercial Reform and *Comercio Neutral* in Cartagena de Indias, 1788–1808', in Fisher, Kuethe and McFarlane, *Reform and Insurrection*, 103.
83. King, 'Evolution of the Free Slave Trade Principle', 54.
84. AGI Estado 5B, 'Puntos que Ha Tratado ... Arango en su Relación, fo. 1v.; Pablo Tornero, 'Emigración, Población y Esclavitud en Cuba (1765–1817)', *AEA*, 44 (1987): 245.
85. Kenneth J. Andrien, 'The *Noticias Secretas de America* and the Construction of a Governing Ideology for the Spanish American Empire', *Colonial Latin American Review*, 7 (1998): 185.
86. Anthony McFarlane, 'Political Corruption and Reform in Bourbon Spanish America', in Walter Little and Eduardo Posada-Carbó, eds, *Political Corruption in Europe and Latin America* (London, 1996), 52–3.
87. Luís Navarro García, *Intendencias en Indias* (Seville, 1959), 12–15 passim; on the major differences between the French and Spanish models of Intendancy, see Ricardo Rees Jones, *El Despotismo Ilustrado y los Intendantes de la Nueva España* (Mexico City, 1983), esp. 199–200.
88. J.R. Fisher, *Government and Society in Colonial Peru: The Intendant System, 1784–1814* (London, 1970), 236–7. Nevertheless, the reforms did not meet universal approbation and some sectors even called for a return to older models of viceregal governance: Josef Fuertes recommended that the Viceroys 'regain their former authority, brilliance and splendour'. See BPR II/2866, Josef Fuertes, 'Pensamientos, o Proyecto Sobre Volver a Reconciliar com la Madre Patria las Provincias Discolas de la América Meridional' (1781), fo. 251.
89. This brief summary of Indian policy relies heavily on Weber, *Bárbaros*, 104–19 passim. As Weber points out, the Bourbon reformers were determined to prevent

a repeat of the Jesuits virtual autonomy in Spanish America. Floridablanca distributed the 30 Guaraní missions equally among the Franciscans, Dominicans, and Mercedarians, believing that the 'mendicants' vow of poverty and self-abnegation made them less threatening' to Bourbon policy aims, 119.

90. Ringrose, *Spain*, 109.

91. BPR II/2866, Josef Maria Zuaznavar, 'Memoria Sobre la Utilidad que Producen en el Reyno los Correos y Postas' (1791), fo. 283.

92. AGI Estado 86A, no. 7/1, 'Real Cédula Sobre el Establecimiento de un Correo Marítimo de España a las Indias Occidentales', 26 August 1764, fo. 1; the transatlantic postal system underwent but slight modification after its establishment in spite of calls for the expansion of direct links between peninsular Spain and VeraCruz, Cartagena and Caracas. See AHN Estado 3188, no.378, Antonio Albuerme to Count Floridablanca, 29 October 1792.

93. Anthony McFarlane, *Colombia Before Independence: Economy, Society and Politics under Bourbon Rule* (Cambridge, 1993), 203–4, 212.

94. AGI Santa Fe 660, Juan Gutierrez de Piñeres to Gálvez, 31 January 1781.

95. On these developments, see Juan Batista González, *La Estrategia Española en América durante el Siglo de las Luces* (Madrid, 1992), 135, 142.

96. AGI Estado 86A, no. 2, [Gálvez], 'Discurso y Reflecxiones [sic] de un Vasallo Sobre la Decadencia de Nuestras Indias Españolas' n.d., fos. 62–4 passim; on the changing composition of the colonial *Audiencius*, see M.A. Burkholder and D.S. Chandler, *From Impotence to Authority: The Spanish Crown and the American Audiencias, 1687–1808* (London, 1976); on Gálvez's views, see B.R. Hamnett, *Politics and Trade in Southern Mexico, 1750–1821* (Cambridge, 1971), 40–2.

97. For a sceptical, illuminating take on the efficacy of Gálvez's reforms, with a focus on New Spain, see Linda Salvucci, 'Costumbres Viejas, "Hombres Nuevos": José de Gálvez y la Burocracia Fiscal Novohispana (1754–1800)', *Historia Mexicana*, 33:2 (1983): 224–64.

98. BPR II/2896, 'Relación del Gobierno del Exmo. Sr. D. Josef de Ezpeleta ... a su Succesor el Exmo. D. Pedro Mendinueta' (1796), fos. 321–2.

99. Adelman, *Republic of Capital*, 20, 25–6.

100. Susan Socolow, *The Bureaucrats of Buenos Aires, 1769–1810: Amor al Real Servicio* (Durham and London, 1987), 27.

101. Jacques A. Barbier, *Reform and Politics in Bourbon Chile, 1755–1796* (Ottawa, 1980), 114–5, 191.

102. Burkholder and Johnson, *Colonial Latin America*, 321.

103. AGI Chile 219, Francisco Hurtado to Gálvez, 6 September 1787.

104. AGI Chile 219, Pedro Gregorio de Echenique [Gov. of Valdivia], 30 June 1784.

105. AGI Caracas 478, Saavedra to José de Gálvez, 28 June 1784.

106. AGI Santo Domingo 2585, Ulloa to Grimaldi, 18 September 1766.

107. AGI Santo Domingo 2666, Manuel de la Heras to Floridablanca, 9 January 1779.

108. AGI Chile 219, Francisco Hurtado to Gálvez, 25 October 1787.

109. AGI Caracas 152, José María Chacón to Antonio Valdés, 25 January 1788.

110. BPR II/2840, Antonio de Narváez y la Torre, 'Relación o Informe de la Provincia de Santa Maria y Rio de la Hacha por lo que Respecta al Estado Natural de su Comercio, Labranzas, Haciendas y Frutos ... los que pueden Cultivarse y Conviene Fomentar para su Aumento de su Comercio ... Causas de su Decadencia' (1778), fos. 190v., 195v.

111. AGI Chile 443, Anon. to Gardoqui, 10 January 1796.

112. AGI Santa Fe 660, Juan Gutiérrez de Piñeres to Gálvez, 30 June 1780.

113. AGI Chile 219, Pedro Gregorio de Echenique, 30 June 1784.

114. AGI Caracas 152, José María Chacón to Antonio Valdés, 25 January 1788; During Chacón's tenure in office, utilizing such techniques, the population surged from a meagre 2,763 inhabitants in 1783 to 11,716 in 1788. See Josefina Pérez Aparicio, 'La Perdida de la Isla de Trinidad', *AEA*, 22 (1965): 40.

115. AGI Estado 48, no. 1 Anon. [written from Guatemala], 12 December 1792; one governor endorsed the emigration of such 'vagrants', whom he contended would make ideal colonists, in a similar scheme in Chile; see AGI Chile 219, Hurtado to Gálvez, 4 October 1786.

116. AGI Caracas 443, Joseph de Abelos [Intendant of Caracas] to Gálvez, 23 December 1778.

117. AGI Chile 219, Hurtado to Gálvez, 25 October 1787.

118. AGI Santo Domingo 2585, Ulloa to Grimaldi, 8 September 1767.

119. AGI Santa Fe 957, Ezpeleta, 19 September 1790.

120. AGI Estado 61, no. 13/2, Manuel de Guevara Vasconcelos, 25 May 1801, fo. 5.

121. AGI Chile 219, Ambrosio O'Higgins to Marqués de Sonora [Gálvez], 23 April 1787; on O'Higgins's tenure as Intendant and Captain-General, see D.H. Edwards, 'Economic Effects of the Intendancy System in Chile: Captain-General Ambrosio O'Higgins as Reformer' (PhD Dissertation, University of Virginia, 1973).

122. AGI Chile 219, Hurtado to Gálvez, 25 October 1787.

123. AGI Caracas 152, José María Chacón to Antonio Valdés, 25 January 1788.

124. AGI Estado 61, no. 13/2, Manuel de Guevara Vasconcelos to Secretary of State, 25 May 1801, fo. 7v.

125. AGI Estado 62, no. 26/1, 'Testimonio de la Calificación ... de Real Ayuntamiento [de Caracas] de la Necesidad ... de Comercio con las Naciones Neutrales y Amigas Durante la Guerra con la Nación Britanica' (1801), fos. 8–9, 12–13.

126. For the pioneering treatment of agricultural improvement as a key theme in the enlightened imperial reform program in Georgian Britain, see Drayton, *Nature's Government: Science, Imperial Britain and the 'Improvement' of the World* (New Haven and London, 2000), esp. chapters 3 and 4.

127. AGI Caracas 152, José María Chacón to Antonio Valdés, 25 January 1788.

128. BPR II/2827, Agustín Crame, 'Discurso Político Sobre la Necesidad de Fomentar la Isla de Cuba' (1768), fo. 242v.

129. AGI Indiferente 2823, 'Nota al Consejo de las Indias al Informe del Virrey', 19 December 1791, quoted in Pablo Tornero Tinajero, 'El Suministro de Mano de Obra Esclava en Cuba: Estado Español y Oligarquía Criolla (1765–1820)', in Naranjo Orovio, ed., *Cuba: La Perla de las Antillas* (Madrid, 1994), 317.

130. AGI Estado 59, no. 17/1, Manuel de Guevara Vasconcelos to Madrid, 29 January 1802, fos. 1–6 passim; the intendant's fear was accurate for slave insurrections and conspiracies increased in the Spanish Caribbean between 1790 and 1810; on the pattern and frequency of slave revolts in the Caribbean, see D.P. Geggus, 'Slavery, War and Revolution in the Greater Caribbean 1789–1815', in Geggus and D.B. Gaspar, *A Turbulent Time: The French Revolution and the Greater Caribbean* (Bloomington, 1997), 9.

131. A.J. Kuethe, 'Havana in the Eighteenth Century', in F.W. Knight and P.K. Liss, *Atlantic Port Cities: Economy, Culture and Society in the Atlantic World, 1650–1850* (Knoxville, 1991); Campomanes, *Reflexiones*, 70; PRO 117/1, Egremont to Albemarle, 18 February 1762; on the broader implications of this event in

European politics, see R.L. Gold, *Borderland Empires in Transition: The Triple Nation Transfer of Florida* (Carbondale, 1969).

132. Carlos III to Tanucci, 28 September 1762, in *Carlos III: Cartas a Tanucci (1759–1763)* (Madrid, 1988), 352.

133. PRO CO 5/540 Gov. James Grant to the Earl of Halifax, September 1763; CO 5/541, Grant to the Board of Plantations, 26 April, 1766; on British East Florida, see C.L. Mowat, *East Florida as a British Province, 1763–1789* (Berkeley, 1943), 10–29 passim.

134. A.P. Whitaker, 'The Commerce of Louisiana and the Floridas at the End of the Eighteenth Century', *HAHR*, 8:2 (1928): 195; J.F. Bannon, *The Spanish Borderlands Frontier, 1513–1821* (New York, 1970), 191.

135. AGI Santo Domingo 2585, Arriaga to Grimaldi, 29 January 1767, fo. 932.

136. 'Bourgeois' historians, Pruna Goodgall wrote, converted the event into 'something akin to the third day of creation', thereby dismissing the 250 preceding years of Cuban History as 'mystification, barren, inanimate and dark'. See Pedro M. Pruna Goodgall, *Los Jesuitas en Cuba hasta 1767* (Havana, 1991), 1.

137. José Manuel de Ximeno, 'El Juicio de los Historiadores Sobre la Toma de la Habana por los Ingleses', *Boletín del Archivo Nacional* [Havana] 61 (1962): 101; Argentine historiography has a similar debate on the influence of the 1806 English invasion and capture, led by Home Popham, of Buenos Aires. See Luis Roque Gondra, *Las Ideas Económicas de Manuel Belgrano* (Buenos Aires, 1927), xxvi.

138. Celia María Parcero Torre, *La Pérdida de la Habana y las Reformas Borbónicas en Cuba (1760–1773)* (Madrid, 1998), 168–71 passim.

139. Pedro J. Guiteras, *Historia de la Conquista de la Habana por los Ingleses* (Havana, 1962), 42; for a recent reiteration of this earlier view, see César García del Pino, *Toma de la Habana Por los Ingleses y Sus Antecedentes* (Havana, 2002), esp. 153.

140. BPR II/2819, A. O'Reilly, 'Descripción de la Isla de Cuba' (1764), fo. 334v.; on O'Reilly's report, see Eduardo Torres-Cuevas, 'El Grupo de Aranda en Cuba y los Inicios de una Nueva Época', in Benimeli, ed., *El Conde de Aranda y su Tiempo* (Zaragoza, 2000), esp. 330–1; and Stein and Stein, *Apogee*, 57.

141. BPR II/2827, Agustín Crame, 'Discurso Político Sobre la Necesidad de Fomentar la Isla de Cuba' (1768), fos. 237–8; Manuel Moreno Fraginals, *El Ingenio: Complejo Económico Social Cubano del Azúcar* (Havana, 1978), 35.

142. BPR II/2819, Manuel Leguinazabal, 'Tesoro de España: Discurso Sobre el Comercio de España con sus Américas ...' (1763–1764), fo. 38 v.

143. A. O'Reilly, 'Descripción de la Isla de Cuba' (1764), fo. 334v.

144. A.J. Kuethe, 'The Early Reforms of Charles III in the Viceroyalty of New Granada, 1759–1776' in Fisher, Kuethe and McFarlane, eds, *Reform and Insurrection*, 26.

145. BPR II/2819; Levi Marrero, *Cuba: Economía y Sociedad, Volume 7: Del Monopolio hacia la Libertad Commercial (1701–1763)* (Madrid, 1986), 11; Manuel Moreno Fraginals, *El Ingenio: Complejo Económico Social Cubano del Azúcar*, 40–1.

146. Bakewell, *A History of Latin America*, 263.

147. AN (Havana), Asuntos Políticos, leg. 255, doc. 30, 1 September 1799.

148. BPR II/2819, A. O'Reilly, 'Descripción de la Isla de Cuba' (1764), fo. 337v.; Solano, 'Ciudad y Geoestrategia', 45.

149. Juan José de Espada y Fernández de Landa, (1808) in Obispo de Espada, *Papeles* (Havana, 2002), 211.

150. AN (Havana), Real Consulado, leg. 184, doc. 8926, Marqués de Somezuelos, 'Expediente Sobre la Conveniencia de Trasladar a esta Isla Familias Blancas de Santo

Domingo', 24 February 1801; on this issue, see Mercedes Valoro González, 'La Comisión de Guantánamo: Escenario para un Análisis de los Intereses Peninsulares y Criollos', in L.J. Aruca Alonso et al., eds, *La Real Comisión de Guantánamo en la Isla de Cuba, 1797–1802* (Havana, 2003), 77; and Consuelo Naranjo Orovio, 'Medio Siglo de Política Poblacionista en Cuba, 1790–1840', in M.J. Sarabia Viejo, ed., *Europa e Iberoamérica: Cinco Siglos de Intercambios* (Seville, 1992), vol. I, 326–8; Geggus affirmed that there were between 10,000 to 18,000 French in Santiago de Cuba alone in 1803. See his 'Slavery, War and Revolution', 25.

151. AGI Indiferente General 1629, Esquilache to Ricla, 20 September 1763.
152. AGI Mexico 1242, O'Reilly to Bucareli, 24 February 1771; for similar sentiments, see an earlier letter of 24 November 1770.
153. Juan B. Amores Carredano, 'La Elite Cubana y el Reformismo Borbónico', in Pilar Latasa, ed., *Reformismo y Sociedad en la América Borbónica* (Pamplona, 2003), 136–7; Amores, *Cuba en la Época de Ezpeleta (1785–1790)* (Pamplona, 2000), 285–7; A.J. Kuethe, *Cuba, 1753–1815: Crown, Military and Society* (Knoxville, 1986), 70; for a recent examination of social and economic factors, see Sherry Johnson, *The Social Transformation of Eighteenth-Century Cuba* (Gainesville, 2001).
154. BPR II/2827, Agustín Crame, 'Discurso Político Sobre la Necesidad de Fomentar la Isla de Cuba' (1768), fo. 237.
155. AN (Havana), Real Consulado, leg. 101, doc. 4990, José Ignacio Echegoyen, 20 February 1798.
156. BNJM, *Papel Periódico de la Havana*, no. 54, 5 July 1792, 213
157. Parcero Torre, *La Pérdida de la Habana*, 269.
158. Manuel Moreno Fraginals, *El Ingenio: Complejo Económico Social Cubano del Azúcar*, 41; on Saint Domingue sugar production, see D.P. Geggus, *Slavery, War and Revolution: the British Occupation of Saint Domingue, 1793–1798* (Oxford, 1982), esp. 382.
159. F.W. Knight, 'Origins of Wealth and the Sugar Revolution in Cuba, 1750–1850', *HAHR*, 57:2 (1977): 232, 243. Johnson contested the view that the Crown was entirely favourable towards the planter elite and hostile to other agricultural sectors. She cited a number of decrees—including the 1771 prohibition of cedar trees for sugar boxes and the 1779 permission granted to ship tobacco, but not sugar, on royal ships—as evidence. See Johnson, *Social Transformation*, 56–7.
160. A.J. Kuethe and D.D. Inglis, 'Absolutism and Enlightened Reform: Charles III, the Establishment of the *Alcabala* and Commercial Reorganization in Cuba', *Past & Present*, 109 (1985), 142; Stein and Stein, *Apogee*, 353.
161. On subsidies from Mexico, see John J. Tepaske, 'La Política Española en el Caribe durante los Siglos XVII y XVIII', in *La Influencia de España en el Caribe, la Florida, y la Luisiana, 1500–1800* (Madrid, 1983), 72; and Marichal and Mantecón, 'Silver and *Situados*', 587–616 passim.
162. Ricla to Esquilache, 8 April 1764, quoted in Parcero Torre, *La Pérdida de la Habana*, 256; A.W. Quiroz, 'Implicit Costs of Empire: Bureaucratic Corruption in Nineteenth-Century Cuba', *JLAS*, 35 (2003): 477.
163. Jacques A. Barbier, 'Imperial Policy Toward the Port of Vera Cruz, 1788–1808: The Struggle Between Madrid, Cádiz and Havana Interests', in Nils Jacobsen and Hans-Jürgen Puhle, eds, *The Economies of Mexico and Peru During the Late Colonial Period, 1760–1810* (Berlin, 1986), 247.
164. AGI Santo Domingo 2585, Ulloa to Grimaldi, 8 March 1766; on more general features of Spanish rule in Louisiana, see Gilbert C. Din, ed., *The Spanish Presence in Louisiana, 1763–1803* (Lafayette, LA, 1996).

165. AGI Santo Domingo 2585, Ulloa to Grimaldi, 19 June 1766.
166. PRO CO 5/574, Johnstone, 9 November 1764, fo. 66; AGI Cuba 109, Johnstone to Ulloa, 19 June 1766, fo. 1344; on Johnstone's tenure in West Florida, see Robin F.A. Fabel, *Bombast and Broadsides: the Lives of George Johnstone* (Tuscaloosa, 1987), esp. 36–56; on Johnstone's political attitudes, see Gabriel Paquette, 'The Image of Imperial Spain in British Political Thought, 1750–1800', *Bulletin of Spanish Studies*, 81:2 (2004): esp. 207–13.
167. AGI Santo Domingo 2585, Ulloa to Grimaldi, 18 September 1766.
168. AGI Santo Domingo 2585, Grimaldi to Ulloa, 23 July 1766; Ulloa issued tighter regulations for foreign trade and the sale of imports which, though intended to protect ordinary citizens from monopolistic prices, was primarily aimed to eliminate smuggling by requiring presentation of authenticated licenses. See J.P. Moore, *Revolt in Louisiana: the Spanish Occupation, 1766–1770.* (Baton Rouge and London, 1976), 105; Bibiano Torres Ramirez, *Alejandro O'Reilly en las Indias* (Seville, 1969), 116–17; Light Townsend Cummins, *Spanish Observers and the American Revolution, 1775–1783* (Baton Rouge, 1991), 13.
169. BPR II/2829, 'Dictamenes de los Señores Duque de Alba, Jayme Masones de Lima, Juan Gregorio Muniain, Miguel de Muzquiz, el Conde de Aranda, Julian de Arriaga ... de Resultas de la Junta Formada en el Secretario de Estado, con la Motivación de la Sublevación Acaecida en Luisiana Contra su Gobernador D. Antonio de Ulloa' (March 1769), fos. 89–96 passim.
170. AGI Santo Domingo 2666, Manuel de la Heras to Floridablanca, 9 January 1779.
171. AGI Santo Domingo 2666, O'Reilly to Grimaldi, 17 October 1769.
172. AGI Cuba 175A, Gálvez to Governor of Louisiana, 11 July 1780, fo. 166.
173. Raynal, *A Political and Philosophical History of the Settlements and Trade of the Europeans in the East and West Indies.* Trans. J.O. Justamond, 3rd edn, 4 vols (Dublin, 1779), vol. 4, book 15, 4; Anon., *Reflections on the Terms of the Peace* (London, 1763), 7; Whately, *Regulations Lately Made Concerning the Colonies*, 16.
174. AGI Santo Domingo 2565, Martin Navarro to Antonio Valdés, 15 January 1789, fo. 315.
175. BL Add Mss. 36806, 28 October 1782, fo. 141.
176. AGI Cuba 150, letter from Francisco Felipe Fatio, quoted in Vincente Manuel y Velasco Zespedes to José de Gálvez, 18 March 1785.
177. AGI Cuba 150, Zespedes to Gálvez, 10 October 1785.
178. AGI Indiferente 2436, 'Informe de la Extensión que ha tenido el Comercio de Indias por un Efecto de la Libertad', 26 January 1788.
179. AGI Santo Domingo 2665, Dictamen de Diego de Gardoqui, 12 October 1791; on contraband in the region, see Héctor R. Feliciano Ramos, *El Contrabando Inglés en el Caribe y el Golfo de Mexico (1748–1778)*, esp. 337.
180. For a perspective that disputes the view that these North American provinces functioned as a 'laboratory in which the Spanish government conducted experiments in colonial policy ... designed as *experimentum in anima vili*, to be extended if successful to the rest of the Spanish empire, see A.P. Whitaker's ancient but stimulating essay, 'The Commerce of Louisiana and the Floridas at the End of the Eighteenth Century', 203, 195.
181. J.A. Barbier, *Reform and Politics in Bourbon Chile*, 7, 190.
182. AGI Indiferente 2436, Ambrosio O'Higgins to Antonio Valdés, 21 September 1789.
183. AGI Santo Domingo 2665, Dictamen de Diego de Gardoqui, 12 October 1791.

4 Colonial Elites and Imperial Governance

1. On the formation of separate, Creole identity as a prelude to independence, see Anthony Pagden, 'Identity Formation in Spanish America', in Pagden and Canny, eds, *Colonial Identity in the Atlantic World 1500–1800*, (Princeton, 1987), 92.
2. Antonio de Ulloa and Jorge Juan, *A Voyage to South America* (London, 1760), book 1, chapter 1, 47.
3. Among the most outstanding works on this theme, see Antonello Gerbi, *The Dispute of the New World: The History of a Polemic, 1750–1900* (Pittsburgh, 1973); D.A. Brading, *The First America: the Spanish Monarchy, Creole Patriots and the Liberal State, 1492–1867* (Cambridge, 1991); and Cañizares-Esguerra, *How to Write the History of the New World: Histories, Epistemologies and Identities in the Eighteenth-Century Atlantic World* (Stanford, 2001).
4. Brian Hamnett, 'Process and Pattern: A Re-Examination of the Ibero-American Independence Movements, 1808–1826', *JLAS*, 29 (1997): 283–4.
5. M.A. Burkholder and D.S. Chandler, *From Impotence to Authority: The Spanish Crown and the American Audiencias, 1687–1808* (London, 1977); Jaime E. Rodríguez O., *The Independence of Spanish America* (Cambridge, 1998).
6. One must, of course, distinguish between intentions and results. As John Fisher pointed out, though Cádiz lost its legal monopoly in 1778, it continued to handle the overwhelming proportion of transatlantic trade: 76 per cent of imports from Spanish America in terms of value in 1782–96 and 84 per cent of the return traffic in the same period. See Fisher, 'Commerce and Imperial Decline: Spanish Trade with Spanish America, 1797–1820', *JLAS*, 30 (1998): 462; in a similar vein, the Bourbon focus on trade policy on the imperial periphery should not obscure the Crown's reliance on bullion, mainly from Peru and Mexico, which accounted for 77 per cent of the cargo value of imports into Spain until at least 1778. See David Brading, 'Bourbon Spain and its American Empire', *Historical Journal*, 39 (1981): 961–9.
7. There is an abundant and excellent literature on resistance and revolt in the late eighteenth century: Kenneth J. Andrien, 'Economic Crisis, Taxes and the Quito Insurrection of 1765', *Past and Present*, 129 (1990): 104–31; Anthony McFarlane, 'Rebellions in Late Colonial Spanish America: A Comparative Perspective', *Bulletin of Latin American Research* 14:3 (1995): 313–38; John Leddy Phelan, *The People and the King: The Comunero Revolution in Colombia, 1781* (Madison, 1978); Sergio Serulnikov, *Subverting Colonial Authority: Challenges to Spanish Rule in the Eighteenth-century Southern Andes* (Durham and London, 2003); and David T. Garrett, '"His Majesty's Most Loyal Vassals": The Indian Nobility and Túpac Amaru', *HAHR*, 84:4 (2004): 575–617.
8. J.H. Elliott, *Empires of the Atlantic World: Britain and Spain in America, 1492–1830* (New Haven and London, 2006), 319; Anthony Pagden and Nicholas Canny, 'Afterword: From Identity to Independence', in *Colonial Identity in the Atlantic World 1500–1800* (Princeton, 1987), 275.
9. It must be noted, as Anthony McFarlane argued, that these rebellions and conspiracies 'did not generally indicate desire for independence from Spain ... it was aimed at perpetuating past practices not with overthrowing them ... enmity toward metropolitan Spaniards was insufficiently strong or widespread to underpin nationalistic sentiment or to provide a focus for rebellion against Spain'. See McFarlane, 'Identity, Enlightenment and Political Dissent in Late Colonial Spanish America', *Transactions of the Royal Historical Society*, 6th series 8 (1998):

322; other historians argue that it was not resistance, but rather the death of José de Gálvez, Minister of the Indies, in 1787 that led 'not to the completion of the process of administrative re-organisation, but an abrupt halt and repeal of some of the key measures already enforced'. See John Fisher, *Government and Society in Colonial Peru: The Intendant System, 1784–1814* (London, 1970): 60.

10. Elliott, *Empires of the Atlantic World*, 324, 365.

11. Victorián de Villava, 'Apuntes para una Reforma de España' (1797) in Ricardo Levene, ed., *Vida y Escritos de Victorián de Villava* (Buenos Aires, 1946), appendix, cxvi.

12. Francisco Silvestre, Governor and *Visitor* of Antioquía (New Granada), quoted in Margarita Garrido de Payan, 'The Political Culture of New Granada, 1770–1815' (PhD dissertation, University of Oxford, 1990), 35.

13. BPR II/2866, Josef Fuertes, 'Pensamientos, o Proyecto Sobre Volver a Reconciliar con la Madre Patria las Provincias Discolas de la América Meridional' (1781), fo. 261v.; such a scheme was not peculiar to Spain: John Fothergill's *Considerations Relative to the North American Colonies* (1765) had made the identical point. See Van Alstyne, *Empire and Independence: The International History of the American Revolution* (New York, 1965), 28.

14. Valentín de Foronda, 'Carta Sobre Lo Que Debe Hacer un Príncipe que Tenga Colonias a Gran Distancia' (1800) in *Escritos Políticos y Constitucionales* (Vitoria, 2002), 249.

15. AGI Santo Domingo 2665, Navarro to Valdés, 16 April 1789, fos. 327–8.

16. For the purposes of this chapter, borrowing John Keane's formulation, civil society is defined as a 'complex and dynamic ensemble of legally protected non-government institutions that tend to be non-violent, self-governing, self-reflexive and permanently in tension with each other and with the state institutions that "frame", construct and enable their activities' in Keane, *Civil Society: Old Images, New Visions* (Cambridge, 1998), 6; this chapter de-emphasizes conflict and stresses cooperation between the Bourbon state and Spanish American civil society institutions.

17. As Carlos Marichal demonstrated, the American contribution to the ordinary income of the Spanish Crown increased in both absolute and relative terms between 1790 and 1810, rising from 25 per cent in 1790 to 40 per cent in the 1802–4 period, before increasing again to 50 per cent between 1808 and 1811. See Marichal, 'Beneficios y Costes Fiscales del Colonialismo: Las Remesas Americanas a España, 1760–1814', *Revista de Historia Económica*, 15:3 (1997): 478.

18. Though this chapter focuses on the mercantile privileges extended by the Crown, it must be remembered that other concessions were extended as well in precisely the same period. The *fuero militar*, for example, which granted immunity in criminal and civil cases to military personnel, was extended to officers in New Spain in 1766. See Elliott, *Empires of the Atlantic World*, 300.

19. As McFarlane pointed out, 'so long as Spain remained politically stable, creoles' defence of their character as Americans, their exaltation of the American environment, and criticism of Spanish government were all comfortably contained within the existing political structure'. See McFarlane, 'Identity, Enlightenment and Political Dissent', 327.

20. This concept is developed by Peter Evans, 'Introduction', in Evans, ed., *State-Society Synergy: Government and Social Capital in Development* (Berkeley, 1991), 2.

21. For a contrasting view, which construes the creation of *Consulados* as an 'explicit manifestation of [the Crown's] impotence', see Manuel Lucena-Giraldo,

'¿Filántropos u Oportunistas? Ciencia y Política en los Proyectos de Obras Públicas del Consulado de Cartegena de Indias, 1795–1810', *RI*, 52 (1992): 627–46.

22. Francisco de Saavedra, quoted in Peggy K. Liss, *Atlantic Empires: The Network of Trade and Revolution, 1713–1826* (Baltimore and London, 1983), 128.

23. On the emergence of a public sphere in the late colonial period, see Victor Uribe-Uran, 'The Birth of the Public Sphere in Latin America during the Age of Revolution', *Comparative Studies in Society and History*, 42:2 (2000): 425–57.

24. For an overview of the connection between enlightened reform and science, see Antonio Lafuente et al., *Carlos III y la Ciencia de la Ilustración* (Madrid, 1987); Alexander von Humboldt, quoted in Iris Engstrand, *Spanish Scientists in the New World: The Eighteenth-Century Expeditions* (Seattle and London, 1981), 11.

25. Describing the coalescence of an intelligentsia in New Granada, Renán Silva convincingly argued that the '*Ilustrados*' were a cultural group, of varying social origins, who, on the common basis of reading, conversation, as well as theoretical and practical projects, especially related to the natural sciences, encountered a constellation of references which constituted the building blocks of their common identity'. See Silva, *Los Ilustrados de Nueva Granada, 1760–1808: Genealogía de una Comunidad de Interpretación* (Medellín, 2002), 583.

26. The major work, in both English and Spanish, on the Economic Societies remains Robert Jones Shafer's *The Economic Societies of the Spanish World, 1763–1821* (Syracuse, 1958); on the discourse of 'improvement' in the contemporary British empire with significant application to other European empires, see the pioneering study by Drayton, *Nature's Government: Science, Imperial Britain and the 'Improvement' of the World* (New Haven and London, 2000); John Lynch recently pointed out that 'the Enlightenment remains one of the understudied subjects of Latin American History ... the ideological origins of the Spanish American revolutions is still waiting to be written'. See Lynch, 'Spanish American Independence in Recent Historiography', in Anthony McFarlane and Eduardo Posada-Carbó, eds, *Independence and Revolution in Spanish America: Perspectives and Problems* (London, 1999), 35–6. The present chapter hopes to make a small contribution towards this larger project.

27. José Ignacio de Pombo, 18 April 1807, reprinted in *Escritos de Dos Economistas Coloniales: Don Antonio de Narváez y la Torre y Don José Ignacio de Pombo* (Bogotá, 1965); for the intellectual context of the *Consulado's* activities, see J.F. Wilhite, 'The Enlightenment and Education in New Granada, 1760–1830' (PhD dissertation, University of Tennessee, 1976), esp. 248–315 passim.

28. Robert Sidney Smith, *The Spanish Merchant Guild: A History of the Consulado, 1250–1700* (Durham, 1940), 3–15 passim.

29. C.H. Haring, *The Spanish Empire in America* (New York, 1947), 256, 300.

30. Some petitions to establish *Consulados* were rejected, including those from merchants in Badajoz, Gijón, and Pamplona; the *Consulado* of Santander recognized that it existed at the pleasure of the King and therefore spent some of its meagre funds to erect an equestrian statue of Charles III in the city centre, acknowledging the 'benefits which [Charles III] brought to this port and its commerce'; see AGI Indiferente General 2405A, *Consulado* of Santander, 'Obras de que esta hecho cargo y otras premeditadas', 3 June 1788.

31. There had been an earlier attempt to establish a *Consulado* in New Granada in 1694, but it was dissolved in 1713; in 1784, a *Consulado* for Mompox was formed,

but soon became defunct. See Garrido de Payan, 'The Political Culture of New Granada', 50.

32. Brian Hamnett made a related point in relation to the *Consulados* of New Spain in his important article 'Mercantile Rivalry and Peninsular Division: The *Consulados* of New Spain and the Impact of the Bourbon Reforms, 1789–1824', *Ibero-Amerikanisches Archiv*, 2 (1976): 276.

33. On the *Consulado* of Lima in the period, see Patricia H. Marks, 'Confronting a Mercantile Elite: Bourbon Reformers and the Merchants of Lima, 1765–1796', *The Americas*, 60:4 (2004): 519–58.

34. Burkholder and Chandler, *From Impotence to Authority*.

35. Hamnett, 'Mercantile Rivalry and Peninsular Division', 274, 278.

36. The new measures were an assault on the corporate power and privileges, not the profits, of Mexico and Peru. As Fisher suggested: 'agricultural economies in regions hitherto marginalized from the official routes of transatlantic trade—notably in the Río de la Plata, Venezuela, Central America and Cuba—experienced upsurges in export-led production, but not at the expense of traditional centers of Spanish authority, Mexico and Peru, which maintained their majority shares of commercial activity in their respective regions, particularly because of the continuing predominance of silver in exports to Spain'. See Fisher, 'Commerce and Imperial Decline', 461.

37. Linda Salvucci noted that in Mexico royal bureaucrats, especially at the local level, became embedded in family and commercial networks and more often acted out of motives of greed than good governance. See her 'Costumbres Viejas, "Hombres Nuevos": José de Gálvez y la Burocracia Fiscal Novohispana (1754–1800)', *Historia Mexicana*, 33:2 (1983): 224–64 passim.

38. AGI Caracas 908, Francisco de Saavedra to Gálvez, 2 May 1785; the Peruvian viceroy, Gil de Taboada, diagnosed the same condition, but put less emphasis on public happiness: 'on the day when [Americans] can supply themselves with all that is necessary, their dependence will be voluntary, and neither the military forces that we have there nor the gentleness of government nor the best-administered justice will be sufficient to secure our possession'; quoted in Marks, 'Confronting a Mercantile Elite', 525.

39. AGI Santa Fe 957, Juan Francisco Gil y Lemos to Antonio Valdés, 15 March 1789; ibid., 30 Oct. 1790.

40. Viceroy Pedro Mendinueta to his successor Antonio Amar y Borbón (1803), in José García y García, ed., *Relaciones de los Virreyes del Nuevo Reino de Granada* (New York, 1869), 508; many officials, it must be conceded, held Creoles in contempt. New Granada's viceroy in the 1780s, for example, complained that his subjects were 'incapable of understanding the justification for royal taxes. All they aspire to is their own self-interest, which is absolute and unlimited libertinism (...) the goal of government must be to force the plebeians to respect public authority so that their subordination and obedience is preserved'. F. Gutiérrez de Piñeres to Gálvez, quoted in Phelan, *The People and the King*, 33.

41. AGI Caracas 152, José María Chacón to Antonio Valdés, 25 Jan. 1788.

42. AGI Caracas 908, Francisco de Saavedra to José de Gálvez, 2 May 1785.

43. Ibid.

44. AGI Caracas 908, *Cabildo* to the Council of the Indies, 16 July 1788.

45. AGI Estado 54, no. 3, Lázaro Maria de Herrera and José Ignacio de Pombo to Viceroy Caballero y Góngora, March 1789; notwithstanding these pledges, the rise of the colonial *Consulado* was a gradual process. In Buenos Aires, for example,

it was preceded by the emergence of informal merchant associations (*Juntas de Comerciantes y Mercaderes*). There often was a sizable lag between the initial petition—the majority of which were presented in the early 1780s—and the grant of a royal charter, the majority of which were approved in the mid-1790s. Susan Migden Socolow argued that this lengthy petition process is evidence that the merchants possessed 'virtually no power vis-à-vis the entire colonial empire and in metropolitan Spain'. See Socolow, *The Merchants of Buenos Aires, 1778–1810: Family and Commerce* (Cambridge, 1978), 173.

46. R.L. Woodward, *Class Privilege and Economic Development: The Consulado de Comercio of Guatemala, 1793–1871* (Chapel Hill, 1966), 25–6.

47. *Real Cédula de Erección del Consulado de Chile* (Madrid, 1795), 20; the *cédula* for the creation of the *Consulado* of Buenos Aires employed identical language; see AGI Buenos Aires 583.

48. Pedro Navarro Floria, *Manuel Belgrano y el Consulado de Buenos Aires, Cuna de la Revolución (1790–1806)* (Buenos Aires, 1999), 48; on this *Consulado's* activities and for an appraisal of its accomplishments, see German O.E. Tjarks, *El Consulado de Buenos Aires y sus Proyecciones en la Historia del Río de la Plata* (Buenos Aires, 1962), vol. I, 103; vol. II, 874; on colonial *Consulados* more generally, see Manuel Nuncs Dias, *El Real Consulado de Caracas (1793–1810)* (Caracas, 1971), esp. 232, 574.

49. P.J. Lampros, 'Merchant-Planter Cooperation and Conflict: the Havana *Consulado*, 1794–1832', (PhD dissertation, Tulane University, 1980), 14–28 passim.

50. As Carlos Díaz Rementería wrote, the *avería* began as a 'special tax by which interested parties collaborated to finance the costs of *armadas* to protect the *flota*', in Sánchez Bella et al., *Historia del Derecho Indiano* (Madrid, 1992), 381; R.S. Smith, 'Origins of the *Consulado* in Guatemala', *HAHR*, 26:2 (1946), 159; some *Consulados* also were empowered to take the *peage*, a toll collected on vehicles and pack animals using the roads.

51. AGI Chile 445, *Consulado* to Gardoqui, 16 June 1797; the figures are extrapolated from a chart entitled: 'Estado que Manifiesta lo que ha producido el ½ percent de avería concedido por SM a este Real Consulado en 1796'; AGI Buenos Aires 586; the figures are extrapolated from a chart entitled: 'Productos correspondientes al Tribunal de Consulado por el medio por ciento de avería cobrado ... en 1796'.

52. Pierre Samuel Dupont de Nemours (1739–1817), quoted in Terence Hutchinson, *Before Adam Smith: the Emergence of Political Economy, 1662–1776* (Oxford, 1988), 290.

53. Stanley Stein and Barbara Stein, *Silver, Trade and War: Spain and America in the Making of Early Modern Europe* (Baltimore and London, 2000), 164–72 passim.

54. Aline Helg, *Liberty and Equality in Caribbean Colombia, 1770–1835* (Chapel Hill and London, 2004), 48.

55. AGI Caracas 908, Francisco de Saavedra to José de Gálvez, 2 May 1785; the Viceroy of Santa Fe also cited road construction as a principal rational for the *Consulados*, see AGI Santa Fe 957, Juan Francisco Gil y Lemos to Antonio Valdés, 15 March 1789.

56. Kenneth J. Andrien, *The Kingdom of Quito, 1690–1830: The State and Regional Economic Development* (Cambridge, 1995), 214–5.

57. Nicolas Calvo y O'Farrill, 'Sobre la Necesidad de Construir Caminos en esta Isla, Medios de Hacerlos y Dirección que Deben Tener', in *Memorias de la Sociedad Patriótica de la Habana* (Havana, 1795), vol. III, appendix, doc. 2; before the establishment of the *Consulado* in 1794, there had been strenuous efforts in 1791–2 by the Governor-General, Luís de Las Casas, in collaboration with the sugar magnates,

to compel inhabitants to volunteer personal labour in order to maintain bridges and roads. On this effort, see Sherry Johnson, *Social Transformation of Eighteenth-Century Cuba* (Gainesville, 2001), 129–35 passim.

58. AGI Buenos Aires 585, unsigned, first (top) document in *legajo*.
59. AGI Caracas 152, José María Chacón to Antonio Valdés, 25 Jan. 1788.
60. AGI Estado 25, no. 41/1, Marqués de Branciforte to Godoy, n.d., fos. 1, 4.
61. Vicente Basadre, 'Memoria sobre la Construcción de Sumideros para Purificar la Atmosfera' (1797), in Javier Ortíz de la Tabla DuCasse, ed., *Memorias Políticas y Económicas del Consulado de VeraCruz, 1796–1822* (Seville, 1985), 15.
62. José Donato de Austria, 'Memoria Sobre la Construcción de un Camino Carretero desde VeraCruza México' (1800), in Ortíz de la Tabla DuCasse, ed., *Memorias Políticas y Económicas del Consulado de VeraCruz*, 27.
63. BPR II/2896, 'Relación del Gobierno del Exmo. Sr. D. Josef de Ezpeleta (...) a su Succesor el Exmo. D. Pedro Mendinueta' (1796), fo. 274v.
64. AGI Chile 445, *Consulado* to Miguel Cayetano Soler, 13 June 1800; there is some evidence of sporadic collaboration between the colonial and peninsular *Consulados*. Santiago and La Coruña, for example, compared their independent efforts to improve the quality of linen production. See Maria del Carmen Sánchez Rodríguez de Castro, *El Real Consulado de La Coruña: Impulsar de la Ilustración (1785–1833)* (La Coruña, 1992), 83.
65. AGI Santa Fe 957, Joachim de Cañavernal to Diego de Gardoqui, 3 Nov. 1795.
66. Viceroy Amar y Borbón, quoted in Silva, *Los Ilustrados de Nueva Granada*, 629–30.
67. AGI Chile 445, *Consulado* to Cayetano Soler, 15 July 1800.
68. McFarlane, *Colombia Before Independence: Economy, Society and Politics under Bourbon Rule* (Cambridge, 1993), 316; Hamnett, 'Mercantile Rivalry and Peninsular Division', passim; Lampros, 'Merchant-Planter Cooperation and Conflict', passim.
69. David McNally, *Political Economy and the Rise of Capitalism: A Reinterpretation* (Berkeley, 1988), especially Chapter 3, 'Paradox of the Physiocrats: State Building and Agrarian Capitalism in Eighteenth-century France', 124–5.
70. This analysis draws on Albert Hirschman's observation that 'the by-product of individuals acting predictably in accordance with their economic interests was therefore not an easy *balance*, but a strong *web* of interdependent relationships (...) ambition, the lust for power and the desire for respect can all be satisfied by economic improvement'. See Hirschman, *The Passions and the Interests: Political Arguments for Capitalism before its Triumph* (Princeton, 1997), 51, 110.
71. McFarlane, *Colombia*, 316.
72. Manuel Belgrano, 'Medios Generales de Fomentar la Agricultura, Animar la Industria, y Proteger el Comercio en un País Agricultor' (1796), in *Documentos del Archivo Belgrano* (Buenos Aires, 1913), vol. I, 59; on the impact of physiocracy in the Spanish empire, see Ernest Lluch and Lluís Argemí i d'Abadal, 'La Fisiocracia en España', in *Agronomía y Fisiocracia en España (1750–1820)* (Valencia, 1985); on the translation of works of European political economy into Spanish, see Llombart, 'Traducciones Españolas de Economia Política (1700–1812)' Catálogo Bibliografico y una Nueva Perspectiva', *Cromohs*, 9 (2004): 1–14.
73. AGI Buenos Aires 585; such an embrace of physiocracy would have not been construed as politically radical. As McNally suggested in his discussion of Quesnay, 'the unity and stability of the social order presuppose a centralised political authority which can establish the framework by which private interests unintentionally further the general welfare'; see McNally, *Political Economy*, 124. For an alternate view, which argues that physiocracy 'implicitly attacked the traditional

notion of monarchy', see Elizabeth Fox-Genovese, *The Origins of Physiocracy: Economic Revolution and Social Order in Eighteenth-Century France* (Ithaca, and London, 1976), 65.

74. Jeremy Adelman, *Republic of Capital: Buenos Aires and the Legal Transformation of the Atlantic World* (Stanford, 1999), 58, 63; for additional treatment of Belgrano's economic ideas, see Oreste Popescu, 'The Economic Development of Argentina in the Thinking of Manuel Belgrano', in *Studies in the History of Latin American Economic Thought* (London and New York, 1997), 156–171; and Navarro Floria, 'Notas para un Estudio del Ideario Económico y Político de Manuel Belgrano', *Quinto Centenario*, 13 (1987): 183; on the importance of Campomanes in Belgrano's thought, see Jorge I. Segura, *El Pensamiento Económico de Manuel Belgrano* (Mendoza, 1953), 7.

75. On this idea, see John Robertson's important *The Case for the Enlightenment: Scotland and Naples, 1680–1760* (Cambridge, 2005), 38; in relation to the Spanish Atlantic World, Jorge Cañizares-Esguerra described political economy as part of a 'patriotic epistemological discourse at the core of the Spanish enlightenment (...) of a "cosmopolitan" kind'. See his 'Eighteenth-Century Spanish Political Economy: Epistemology of Decline', *Eighteenth-Century Thought*, 1 (2003): 301, 314.

76. AGI Indiferente General 2467, Real Consulado de Caracas to Madrid, 18 April 1801.

77. Manuel de Salas to Diego Gardoqui (1796), in *Escritos de Manuel de Salas* (Santiago, 1910), vol. I, 161; for an older but very thorough treatment of the organization and activities of Santiago's *Consulado*, see Elsa Urbina Reyes, 'El Tribunal del Consulado de Chile: Sus Origenes y Primeros Años', *Boletín de la Academia Chilena de la Historia*, 29 (1962): 104–43.

78. AN (Chile) Tribunal del Consulado, vol. 34, 'Representación al Ministerio de Hacienda sobre "El Estado de la Agricultura, Industria y Comercio en Chile"', Jan. 1798.

79. AGI Chile 443, 'Memoria de Consulado de Chile', 29 February 1797.

80. AN (Chile) Tribunal del Consulado, vol. 34, 'Representación al Ministerio de Hacienda sobre "El Estado de la Agricultura, Industria y Comercio en Chile"', Jan. 1796.

81. Belgrano, 'Medios Generales de Fomentar la Agricultura', in Roque Gondra, *Las Ideas Económicas de Manuel Belgrano*, 2nd edn, (Buenos Aires, 1927), 156.

82. AN (Chile) Tribunal del Consulado, vol. 34, Memoria, Jan. 1799.

83. AN (Chile) Tribunal del Consulado, vol. 34, 'Memorial Sobre Educación Popular', 1808.

84. William Callahan, *Honor, Commerce, and Industry in Eighteenth-Century Spain* (Boston, 1972).

85. Belgrano, 'Memoria' of 14 June 1798, reprinted in Roque Gondra, *Las Ideas Económicas*, 194.

86. AN (Chile) Tribunal del Consulado, vol. 34, 'Representación al Ministerio de Hacienda sobre "El Estado de la Agricultura, Industria y Comercio en Chile"', Jan. 1796; Luís Celis Muñoz, *El Pensamiento Político de Manuel de Salas* (Santiago, 1954), 50; Valle, quoted in Woodward, *Class Privilege*, 107.

87. AN (Chile) Tribunal del Consulado, vol. 34, *Memoria* of Anselmo de la Cruz, Jan. 1807.

88. Juan Egaña, 'Oración Inaugural para la Apertura de los Estudios de la Real Universidad de San Felipe en el Año 1804', in *Escritos Inéditos y Dispersos* (Santiago, 1949), 14–17 passim.

89. Pombo (1810), quoted in Silva, *Los Ilustrados de Nueva Granada*, 399; on the translation and dissemination of Adam Smith in the Spanish Atlantic World, see R.S. Smith, '*The Wealth of Nations* in Spain and Hispanic America, 1780–1830', *Journal of Political Economy*, 65:1 (1957): 104–25.

90. AN (Cuba) Real Consulado, leg. 101, doc. 4990, José Ignacio Echegoyen, 20 Feb. 1798; on collaboration between planters and Crown officials in Cuba, see Johnson, *Social Transformation*, 128–66 passim.

91. A.J. Kuethe, *Cuba, 1753–1815: Crown, Military and Society* (Knoxville, 1986), 74.

92. For an overview of the *Consulado*'s activities, see Salvador Arregui Martínez-Moya, 'El Real Consulado de la Habana, 1794–1834' (PhD dissertation, University of Murcia, 1992); and Lampros, 'Merchant-Planter Cooperation and Conflict'.

93. Francisco Arango y Parreño, 'Discurso Sobre la Agricultura de la Habana y Medios de Fomentarla', in *Obras* (Havana, 1952), vol. I, 117–18; W. Pierson, 'Francisco Arango y Parreño', *HAHR*, 16:4 (1936): 467–8; Francisco J. Ponte Domínguez, *Arango Parreño: Estadista Colonial Cubano* (Havana, 1937), esp. 6–77; Dale Tomich, 'The Wealth of Empire: Francisco Arango y Parreño, Political Economy and the Second Slavery in Cuba', *Comparative Studies in History and Society*, 45:1 (2003): 5–7; for a negative view of Arango's activities, see Johnson, *Social Transformation*.

94. *Memorias de la Sociedad Patriótica de la Habana* (Havana, 1794), vol. II, 133–4.

95. Arango and his fellow champions of less-regulated trade conveniently failed to mention the major injections of capital which Cuba regularly received from the mid-1760s. As Stein and Stein indicated, 'an impressive proportion of [New Spain's] surplus funds was earmarked for financing Cuba's defences' in *Apogee of Empire: Spain and New Spain in the Age of Charles III, 1759–1789* (Baltimore and London, 2003), 353; Marichal and Souto Mantecón estimated that 'remittances sent by the Royal Treasury of New Spain during the eighteenth century to the Caribbean military posts tended to surpass the value of the royal silver transferred annually to the metropolis' in 'Silver and *Situados*: New Spain and the Financing of the Spanish Empire in the Caribbean in the Eighteenth Century', *HAHR*, 74:4 (1994): 587–613, 588–9.

96. Arango y Parreño, 'Reflexiones Sobre la Mejor Organización del Consulado de la Habana, Considerado como Tribunal', in *Obras*, vol. I, 209.

97. Arango y Parreño, 'Discurso Sobre la Agricultura de la Habana y Medios de Fomentarla', in *Obras*, vol. I, 153.

98. AGI Estado 5B, no. 4, 'Puntos que ha tratado en la Junta de Gobierno del Real Consulado de la Isla de Cuba ... Arango en la Relación que de su viaje ha hecho' (1796 ?), fos. 1–5 passim.

99. AGI Estado 3, no. 7/6, Arango y Parreño, 22 April 1796, fo. 2.

100. *Memorias de la Sociedad Patriótica de la Habana*, vol. I, 35.

101. Also called the *Sociedad Patriótica* in America and, of course, the *Sociedad Ecónomica de Amigos del País* in peninsular Spain.

102. Shafer, *Economic Societies of the Spanish World*, 48–9; these essay prizes usually related to a specific aspect of agriculture. For example, AN (Cuba) Real Consulado, leg. 92, doc. 3926, 'Expediente Relativo a los Premios Ofrecidos por la Real Sociedad Patriotica a los Mejores Escritos Sobre Ciertos Ramos de Agricultura, especialmente Café, Añil y Algodon', 15 Jan. 1796; AN (Cuba) Real Consulado, leg, 99, doc. 3841, 'Expediente Relativo al Premio ... al que componga el Mejor Tratado para el Gobierno Económico de los Ingenios de Fabricar Azúcar en esta Isla', 17 Jan. 1799.

103. Francisco José Caldas (1811), quoted in Antonio LaFuente, 'Enlightenment in an Imperial Context: Local Science in the late Eighteenth-Century Hispanic World', *Osiris*, 15 (2000), 170.

104. Rocío Sánchez Lissén, 'Aportaciones de las Reales Sociedades Económicas de Amigos del País al Pensamiento Económico Español', in Maria Consolación España, ed., *Las Reales Sociedades Económicas de Amigos del País y el Espíritu Ilustrado: Análisis de sus Realizaciones* (Seville, 2001), 125, 127; though largely modelled on foreign precedent, foreign visitors to Spain offered little praise for the Amigos del País societies. Henry Swinburne noted that they had 'gone on but slowly in their improvements in literature and agriculture. I doubt that they have yet got into a proper method; for they undertake many things and finish none'. See his *Travels through Spain in the Years 1775 and 1776* (London, 1787), vol. II, 203; on British views of the Bourbon reforms, see Paquette 'The Image of Imperial Spain in British Political Thought, 1750–1800', *Bulletin of Spanish Studies*, 81:2 (2004): 187–214.

105. *Memorias de la Sociedad Patriótica de la Habana*, vol. I, 2; on this subject, see Izaskun Álvarez Cuartero, 'Las Sociedades Económicas de Amigos del País en Cuba (1787–1832): Una Aportación al Pensamiento Ilustrado', in Consuelo Naranjo Orovio and Tomás Mallo Gutiérrez, eds, *Cuba: Perla de las Antillas* (Madrid, 1994), esp. 37–8.

106. AGI Estado, no. 7/3, 'Discurso Sobre las Utilidades que Puede Producir Una *Sociedad Económica* de Guatemala' (1795), fo. 6; Shafer, *Economic Societies*, 259; ironically, though the societies evinced a cosmopolitan commitment to the diffusion of useful knowledge, the American societies corresponded neither with one another nor with their peninsular counterparts.

107. AHN Estado 2927, no. 301, 'Ordenanzas para el Reglamento de una Academia de Jovenes Comerciantes [en Barcelona]' (1787); AHN Estado 3188, no. 377, Eugenio de Santiago Palomares, 'Establecimientos de una Escuela de Comercio en Madrid o Valencia' (July 1786).

108. AN (Cuba) Real Consulado, leg. 179, doc. 8213, Patriotic Society to Godoy, 21 March 1797; AGI Estado 1, no. 32/1, Count of Santa Clara to Godoy, 22 March 1797, fo. 1.

109. *Memorias de la Sociedad Patriótica de la Habana*, vol. I, 18–19.

110. *Memorias de la Sociedad Patriótica de la Habana*, vol. III, 11.

111. AGI Buenos Aires 587, Consulado to Secretary of State, 24 April 1802 [includes description of the Santander school]; AN (Cuba) Real Consulado, leg. 179, doc. 8213, 'Expediente Sobre Establecer en Esta Ciudad un Instituto de Ciencias Naturales y Proyecto de una Escuela de Nautica', 2 Dec. 1796.

112. *Memorias de la Sociedad Patriótica de la Habana*, vol. III, 19.

113. María Dolores González-Ripoll Navarro, *Cuba, La Isla de los Ensayos: Cultura y Sociedad (1790–1815)* (Madrid, 1999), 198–200; AN (Cuba) Real Consulado, leg. 92, doc. 3925, 'Expediente Traducir al Castellano las Obras Francesas de Du Trône de la Couture y de Corbeaux, acerca del Cultivo de la Caña', 15 January 1796. Their works were, respectively, *Précis Sur la Canne et Sur les Moyens d'en Extraire le Sel Essentiel & c* and *Essai sur l'Arte de Cultiver la Canne et d'en Extraire le Sucre*; *Memorias de la Sociedad Patriótica de la Habana*, vol. I, 13.

114. *Memorias de la Sociedad Patriótica de la Habana*, vol. I, 14–15; on the sugar planters' embrace of new technology, see Maria M. Portuondo, 'Plantation Factories: Science and Technology in late Eighteenth-Century Cuba', *Technology and Culture*, 44 (2003): 231–57.

115. AN (Cuba) Real Consulado, leg. 101, doc. 4990, José Ignacio Echegoyen, 20 Feb. 1798.
116. AN (Cuba) Real Consulado, leg. 22, doc. 1295, 'List of books in a box shipped by the American Brig *Boston* for Havana, to the care of Antonio de Frias for, and on the account of, the President of the *Consulado*', 11 Nov. 1811.
117. Irving A. Leonard and Robert Sidney Smith, 'Documents: A Proposed Library for the Merchant Guild of VeraCruz, 1801', *HAHR*, 24:1 (1944): 84–102; Harry Bernstein, 'Documents: A Provincial Library in Colonial Mexico, 1802', *HAHR*, 26:2 (1946): 162–83; the catalogue of La Coruña's *Consulado's* library reflects similar tastes, but with a very high percentage (76 per cent) of eighteenth-century books. See Sánchez Rodríguez de Castro, *El Real Consulado*, 259.
118. *Memorias de la Sociedad Patriótica de la Habana*, vol. II, 16.
119. *Memorias de la Sociedad Patriótica de la Habana*, vol. III, 107–8.
120. Fernando Ortíz, 'La Hija Cubana del Iluminismo', in *Recopilación Para la Historia de la Sociedad Económica Habanera: Tomo V* (Havana, 1943), 14.
121. As McFarlane pointed out, 'creole ideas about cultural identity and political rights were still expressed in the political language of the *ancien régime*, and, if creoles accorded themselves distinct identities within the Spanish monarchy, they did not imagine themselves outside of it'. See his 'Identity, Enlightenment and Political Dissent', 322.
122. In pursuing this argument, the present author does not disagree with Fisher, 'Commerce and Imperial Decline', which argued that the 'quest for free trade cannot be seen as a dominant factor in determining the political attitudes of Spanish Americans toward the crisis of the Spanish monarchy in 1808–1810'. Rather, this chapter has suggested how traditionally cooperative elites justified, employing certain political and economic ideas, their incremental divergence from official policy *within* the boundaries of the empire's territorial integrity and political unity.
123. Fisher, 'Commerce and Imperial Decline', 462; for a nuanced view of Anglo-Spanish commercial relations in this period, see Adrian Pearce, '*Rescates* and Anglo-Spanish Trade during the French Revolutionary Wars, ca. 1797–1804', *JLAS*, 38 (2006): 607–24.
124. Jerry Cooney, 'Oceanic Commerce and Platine Merchants, 1796–1806: The Challenges of War', *The Americas*, 45 (1989): 509–10.
125. For another perspective on *comercio neutral*, which stresses the Crown's dire position, see Jacques Barbier, 'Peninsular Finance and Colonial Trade: The Dilemma of Charles IV's Spain', *JLAS*, 12 (1980): 21–37.
126. Jeremy Adelman, *Sovereignty and Revolution in the Iberian Atlantic* (Princeton, 2006), 140.
127. AGN IX 4–6-3, *Consulado* to Madrid (1798), fo. 134.
128. AGI Indiferente General 2467.
129. AGN IX 4–7-9, Vicente Antonio del Murriela, 29 Oct. 1798; Socolow, *The Merchants of Buenos Aires*, 125–9 passim.
130. AN (Cuba) Real Consulado, leg. 112, doc. 4702, Letter 'Sobre Cumplimiento de la Real Orden de 26 de Agosto de 1802, Relativa a la Situación de la Agricultura y Comercio de esta Colonia y especialmente del Contrabando', 25 May 1803.
131. AN (Cuba) Intendencia, leg. 876, doc. 22, Anon., Oct. 1798.
132. AN (Cuba) Real Consulado, leg. 112, doc. 4702.
133. McFarlane, *Colombia*, 307; Fisher, 'Commerce and Imperial Decline', 459.
134. Brading, 'Bourbon Spain and its American Empire', 961–9.

135. P. Michael McKinley, *Pre-Revolutionary Caracas: Politics, Economy and Society, 1777–1811* (Cambridge, 1985), 37.

136. AGI Buenos Aires 586, *Consulado* to Secretary of State, 23 Aug. 1798; the benefits of neutral trade did not counterbalance the negative effects of disrupted commerce. As J.C. Brown noted, 'wartime and neutral shipping did not compensate Buenos Aires and Montevideo for the peacetime European trade to which they had become accustomed', in *A Socioeconomic History of Argentina, 1776–1860* (Cambridge, 1979), 47.

137. Cooney, 'Oceanic Commerce and Platine Merchants', 516.

138. AGI Indiferente General 2467, *Consulado* of Cartagena to Secretary of State, 31 Jan. 1799.

139. AGI Indiferente General 2467, Juan Bautista Echezuria [of the *Consulado* of Caracas] to Madrid, 18 April 1801.

140. AGI Indiferente General 2467, Pedro Mendinueta [Viceroy of New Granada] to Madrid, 19 Sept. 1799; McFarlane, *Colombia*, 300.

141. AGI Indiferente General 2467, Vicente Emparam [*Superintendante General* of Cumaná], 21 August 1799; on Venezuelan debates concerning *comercio neutral*, see Antonio García-Baquero González, 'El Comercio de Neutrales en Venezuela (1796–1802)' in his *El Comercio Colonial en la Época del Absolutismo Ilustrado: Problemas y Debates* (Granada, 2003).

142. Hernán Asdrúbal Silva, 'La Estructuración del Comercio y la Navegación desde el Río de la Plata a Cuba', *AEA*, 51:2 (1994): 61–7 passim.

143. McFarlane, *Colombia*, table #9, 374, 302.

144. AN (Cuba) Real Consulado, leg. 74, doc. 2845, 'Expediente Sobre Comercio Reciprico de esta Plaza con la de Montevideo', 18 Aug. 1812; reply 12 December 1812; AN (Cuba) Real Consulado, leg. 73, doc. 2804, 'Expediente (...) para Cimentar el Comercio Reciprico de Frutos, entre Buenos Aires y esta Colonia', 23 Aug. 1803.

145. Liss, *Atlantic Empires*, 174.

146. AN (Cuba) Real Consulado, leg. 72, doc. 2788, 12 Feb. 1799.

147. AN (Cuba) Real Consulado, leg. 73, doc. 2804, 'Expediente (...) para Cimentar el Comercio Reciprico de Frutos, entre Buenos Aires y esta Colonia', 23 Aug. 1803.

148. Letter found in AN (Cuba) Real Consulado, leg. 72.

149. [Anon.], *War in Disguise; or, the Frauds of the Neutral Flags* (London, 1805), 72; North American commerce with Cuba exploded in this period: in 1798, 58 North American ships called at Havana; in 1801, 98 arrived; and in 1807, 138 traded there. See J.H. Coatsworth, 'American Trade with European Colonies in the Caribbean and South America, 1790–1812', *William and Mary Quarterly*, 24:2 (1967): 248.

150. Lampros, 'Merchant-Planter Cooperation and Conflict', 189.

151. Brading, *The First America*, 5.

152. Adelman, *Republic of Capital*, 68.

153. Adapted from T.C.W. Blanning, *Reform in Revolution in Mainz, 1743–1803* (Cambridge, 1974), 34–7.

154. This analysis draws on the insights from T.C.W. Blanning, *The Culture of Power and the Power of Culture: Old Regime Europe, 1660–1789* (Oxford and New York, 2002), 13.

155. It is necessary to acknowledge, however, Anthony Pagden's keen observation that less regulated trade 'meant creating a polity which was potentially open to foreign political influence'. See Pagden, 'Heeding Heraclides: Empire and its

Discontents, 1619–1812′, in Richard L. Kagan and Geoffrey Parker, eds, *Spain, Europe and the Atlantic World: Essays in Honour of John H. Elliott* (Cambridge, 1995), 328.

156. Elliott, *Empires of the Atlantic World*, 374; Adelman, in *Sovereignty and Revolution*, cogently argued that 'American secession was a reaction to the metropolitan effects of Atlantic warfare, and not the expression of accumulated colonial grievances that spawned a separate political identity', 219.

157. McFarlane recently made a similar point, with relation to New Granada's intelligentsia: 'They sought emancipation from the intellectual burdens of the Spanish past, not from the Spanish government. However, this did not make their ideas and attitudes entirely devoid of political significance: they introduced new ways of seeing and understanding their society, and favoured innovation over tradition ... they formed networks ... that transcended local boundaries and which, in times of political turmoil, could be turned to other purposes' in Anthony McFarlane, 'Science and Sedition in Spanish America: New Granada in the Age of Revolution, 1776–1810', in Manning and France, eds, *Enlightenment and Emancipation* (Bucknell, 2006), 113.

Conclusion: Enlightenment, Governance, and Reform in Spain and its Empire: A Reconsideration

1. Gerónimo de Uztáriz, *Theory and Practice of Commerce and Maritime Affairs*. Trans. John Kippax (London, 1751), vol. I, 186.
2. William Robertson, *History of America* (London, 1777), vol. III, book 8, 337.
3. Stanley Stein and Barbara Stein, *Apogee of Empire: Spain and New Spain in the Age of Charles III, 1759–1789* (Baltimore and London, 2003), 23; Stein and Stein, *The Colonial Heritage of Latin America: Essays on Economic Independence in Perspective* (New York, 1970), 92–93, 103–104.
4. John Elliott made this point in 'Afterword: Atlantic History: A Circumnavigation' in Armitage and Braddick, eds, *The British Atlantic World, 1500–1800* (London, 2002), 239.
5. Pedro Rodríguez de Campomanes, *Discurso Sobre la Educación Popular de los Artesanos y su Fomento* (Madrid, 1775), vol. VI, cxciii.

Glossary

Alcabala:	a sales tax.
Alcalde Mayor:	the chief Spanish magistrate of a district; also known as a *corregidor*.
Audiencia:	the highest court of justice within a kingdom, with administrative, legislative, and consultative authority.
Cabildo:	a municipal council; sometimes called the *ayuntamiento*.
Cédula:	a royal order issued through the Council of the Indies.
Concordat:	a negotiated treaty between Papacy and lay state establishing and apportioning mutual rights and powers over a (National) Catholic Church.
Consulta:	a written opinion of the royal councils or colonial *audiencias*.
Contador:	an accountant or comptroller.
Corregidor:	a magistrate and chief administrative officer for a provincial jurisdiction.
Curia:	the Papal court and government.
Diocese:	the sphere of jurisdiction of a bishop.
Encomienda:	a grant of Indian tribute with effective control of labour.
Espolios:	revenues from vacant benefices and the property of deceased prelates.
Estanco:	monopoly and its administration (usually used for tobacco).
Fiscal:	a Crown attorney usually prosecuting in an *audiencia*.
Fuero:	a special judicial privileges enjoyed by a particular group.
Gracia:	a royal exemption.
Gravámenes:	mortgage, debts, charges.
Hacendados:	plantation owners.
Informe:	a report.
Junta de Diezmo:	the body established to oversee the collection of tithes.
Mayorazgo:	the feudal device of entail which prevented heirs from selling or distributing property so that it was passed intact from generation to generation.
Mesta:	the privilege enjoyed by a small group of peninsular nobles to herd annually thousands of seasonally migrant sheep across communal and private lands.
Mita:	the colonial forced labour draft that provided Indian workers on a rotational basis; it required 1/7 of the male population to work in the mines of Potosí for one year out of seven. In New Spain, it was called the *repartimiento*.
Mortmain:	lands held inalienably by Church (amortized) and, as such, not subject to taxation.
Oidor:	a judge of the *audiencia*.
Pleito:	a lawsuit.
Synod:	a smaller regional assembly of clergy and leading laymen which made doctrinal pronouncements and sometimes functioned as a court.
Temporalidades:	the branch of the Treasury dealing with ecclesiastical properties.
Visita General:	a general inspection of a kingdom or province on behalf of the Crown.

Bibliography

Manuscripts

Archives:

Archivo del Conde de Campomanes [Fundación Universitaria Española] (Madrid, Spain):
1–9, 4–6, 17–2, 22–4, 25–17, 30–20, 30–26, 38–2, 48–118, 57–9, 60–2, 60–7, 60–21, 71–6.

Archivo General de Indias (Seville, Spain):
Buenos Aires 41, 583, 585, 586, 587; *Caracas* 152, 443, 444, 473, 478, 908; *Charcas* 445; *Chile* 187, 197, 219, 221, 316, 443, 444, 445; *Cuba* 1, 3a, 5a, 44, 70a, 82, 109, 126, 128, 149a, 150, 174a, 175a, 177a, 186a, 186b, 187a, 193a, 193b, 471,1054, 1055, 1109, 1211, 1224, 1257 1289, 2357; *Estado* 1, 3, 5B, 25, 48, 54, 57, 59, 61, 62, 86A; *Guatemala* 665, 666, 887; *Lima* 1508; *Mexico* 1242; *Panama* 256, 257, 306, 307; *Santo Domingo* 846, 1509, 2116, 2530, 2532, 2542a, 2543, 2565, 2581, 2585, 2587, 2588, 2589, 2595, 2596, 2665, 2666, 2667, 2668, 2669, 2670; *Santa Fe* 578, 585, 606, 638, 660, 956, 957, 958, 659, 758b; *Indiferente* 1629, 1652, 1656, 2405A, 2410, 2411, 2427, 2435, 2436, 2437, 2467, 2823.

Archivo General de la Nación (Buenos Aires, Argentina):
Legajos: IX-4–3-6; IX 4–7-3; IX-4–6-3; IX-8–10-3; IX 4–7-9.

Archivo General de Simancas (Simancas, Spain):
Colección Estado 5180–5183, 5187, 5220, 6095–6097, 6099, 6946, 6947, 6952, 7002, 7003, 7005, 7286, 7289, 7290, 7433, 8138.

Archivo Histórico Nacional (Madrid, Spain):
Consejos 5530; *Estado* 2831–1, 2927, 2931, 2938, 3188.

Arquivo Histórico Ultramarino (Lisbon, Portugal):
São Tomé, Caixa 16.

Archivo Nacional (Santiago, Chile):
Fondos: Capitanía General, Claudio Gay, Tribunal del Consulado, Vicuña MacKenna, Varios.

Archivo Nacional de Cuba (Havana, Cuba):
Fondos: Asuntos Políticos, Capitanía General, Floridas, Hacienda, Real Consulado.

Biblioteca Nacional José Martí (Havana, Cuba):
Memorias de la Sociedad Patriótica de la Habana (1793–1817).

Biblioteca del Palacio Real (Madrid, Spain):
II/ 967, 1241, 1389, 1819, 2639, 2656, 2666, 2757, 2760, 2762, 2817, 2818, 2819, 2827, 2828, 2829, 2840, 2843, 2845, 2847, 2851, 2853, 2866, 2867, 2873, 2875, 2879, 2880, 2895, 2896, 2898, 3084; III/471; VIII/ 14796; Map. 391, 392.

Biblioteca de la Real Academia de la Historia (Madrid, Spain):
9–25-8–4724; 11–3-1–8234, 8235.

Biblioteca Nacional (Madrid, Spain):
Mss 7227; 18,182; Caja Foll. 320 (16).

British Library (London, England):
Mss 36806.

Public Records Office (London, England):
CO 5, FO 72, 117/1.

Periodicals:
Correo de los Ciegos de Madrid (1786–7).
Correo Literario de la Europa (1781).
Diario Curioso (1783–7).
El Censor (1781).
El Hablador Juicioso, y Critico Imparcial (1763).
El Mercurio Histórico y Político (1759–63).
El Pensador (various years).
Espíritu de los Mejores Diarios Literarios que Se Publican en Europa (1788).
Nuevas Efemérides de España Históricas y Literarias (1785).
Papel Periódico de la Havana (1792–1805).
Seminario Económico (1767).
Telégrafo Mercantil Rural Político, Económico o Historiógrafo del Río de la Plata (1801–02).

Spain and the Spanish empire

Primary printed sources:
[Almodóvar, Duque de]. *Década Epistolar Sobre el Estado de Las Letras en Francia.* Madrid, 1781.
[Malo de Luque, Eduardo (Almodóvar)]. *Historia Política de los Establecimientos Ultramarinos de las Naciones Europeas.* 5 vols. Madrid: D. Antonio de Sancha, 1784–90 [1795].
Álvarez, Francisco. *Noticia del Establecimiento y Población de las Colonias Inglesas en la América Septentrional* [1778]. Ed. Patricio Hidalgo Nuchera. Madrid: Ediciones Doce Calles, 2000.
Arango y Parreño, Francisco de. *Obras.* 2 vols. Havana: Dirección de Cultura, 1952.
Arriquibar, Nicolás de. *Recreación Política: Reflexiones Sobre el Amigo de los Hombres en su Tratado de Población, Considerado Con Respecto a Nuestros Intereses.* 2 vols. Madrid, 1779.
Ayala, Manuel Josef de. *Notas a la Recopilación de Indias: Origen e Historia Ilustrada de las Leyes de Indias* [1787]. Ed. Juan Manzano Manzano. Madrid: Ediciones Cultura Hispanica, 1945.

[Azara, José Nicolás de]. *Profecía Política, Verificada en Lo Que Está Suciendo a Los Portugueses Por Su Ciega Afacion a Los Ingleses.* Sevilla, 1762.

———. *El Espíritu de D. José Nicolás de Azara Descubierto en su Correspondencia Epistolar con Don Manuel de Roda.* 3 vols. Madrid, 1846.

Bajamar, Marqués de [Antonio Porlier y Sopranis]. *Discursos al Consejo de Indias.* Ed. Maria Soledad Campos Díez. Madrid: Centro de Estudios Políticos y Constitucionales, 2002.

Beccatini, Francisco. *Vida de Carlos III.* Trans. from Italian. 2 vols. Madrid, 1790.

Belgrano, Mariano. *Documentos del Archivo del Belgrano.* 7 vols. Buenos Aires: Museo Mitre/Coni Hermanos, 1913.

Cabarrús, Francisco de. *Cartas Sobre los Obstáculos que la Naturaleza, la Opinion y las Leyes Oponen a la Felicidad Pública. Escritas por Conde de Cabarrús al Señor D. Gaspar de Jovellanos.* Madrid: Don Pedro Real, 1808.

Cabra, Geronimo Josef de. *Pruebas del Espíritu del Sr. Melon y las Proposiciones de Economía Civil y Comercio del Sr. Normante. Examen Escripturistico-Theologico-Dogmatico de Ambas Obras.* Madrid, 1787.

Cadalso, José de. *Defensa de la Nación Española Contra la Carta Persiana de Montesquieu* [1764]. Ed. G. Mercadier. Toulouse: University of Toulouse, 1970.

Campillo y Cossío, José del. *Nuevo Sistema de Gobierno Económico Para América.* Ed. M. Ballesteros Gaibrois. Oviedo: GEA, 1993.

Carlos III. *Cartas a Tanucci (1759–1763).* Ed. Maximiliano Barrio. Madrid: Banco Bilbao Vizcaya, 1988.

———. *Real Cédula ... que Contiene la Instrucción y Fuero de Población, y que se Debe Observar en las que se Formen de Nuevo en la Sierra Morena con Naturales y Estrangeros Católicos.* Madrid, 1767.

———. *Reglamento y Aranceles Reales para el Comercio Libre en España a Indias: 12 Octubre 1778.* Seville: CSIC, 1978.

Carlos IV. *Real Cédula de Erección del Consulado de Chile.* Madrid, 1795.

Castillo de Bobadilla, Geronimo. *Política Para Corregidores y Señores de Vassallos.* 2 vols. Madrid, 1978 [1704].

Castro, Juan de. *Medio Para Sanar la Monarquía de España.* Madrid, 1668.

Castro, Juan Francisco de. *Discursos Críticos Sobre las Leyes y Sus Intérpretes.* 2 vols. Madrid, 1765.

Danvila y Villarrasa, Bernardo Joaquin. *Lecciones de Economía Civil, o de el Comercio Escrito para el Uso de los Caballeros del Real Seminario de Nobles.* Madrid, 1779.

Díaz de Espada Juan José (Obispo de Espada). *Papeles.* Ed. Eduardo Torres-Cuevas. Havana: Ediciones-Imagen Contemporanea, 2002.

Egaña, Juan. *Proyecto de una Constitución para el Estado de Chile.* Santiago, 1813.

———. *El Chileno Consolado en los Presidios o, Filosofía de la Religión.* London, 1826.

———. *Escritos Inéditos y Dispersos.* Ed. Raúl Silva Castro. Santiago: Imprenta Universitaria, 1949.

———. *Antología.* Ed. Raúl Silva Castro. Santiago: Andres Bello, 1969.

———. *Minería y Metalurgia Colonial en el Reyno de Chile* [1803]. Ed. Gaston Fernandez Montero. Santiago: AGD Impresores, 2000.

[Egaña, Mariano]. *Cartas de Don Mariano Egaña a Su Padre, 1824–1829.* Santiago: Editorial Nascimiento, 1948.

Escritos de Dos Economistas Coloniales: Don Antonio de Narváez y la Torre y Don Jose Ignacio de Pombo. Ed. Sergio Ortíz. Bogotá: Banco de la Republica, 1965.

Forner, Juan Pablo. *Oración Apologética por la España y Su Mérito Literario.* Ed. A. Zamora Vicente. Badajoz: Diputatión Provincial, 1945.

Foronda, Valentín de. *Miscelánea, o Colección de Varios Discursos.* Madrid, 1787.

——. *Cartas sobre los Asuntos Más Exquisitos de la Económia-Política*. 3 vols. Madrid, 1789.

——. *Escritos Políticos y Constitucionales*. Ed. Ignacio Fernández Sarasola. Vitoria: University of País Vasco, 2002.

López Madera, Gregorio. *Excelencias de la Monarquía y Reyno de España*. Madrid, 1625.

Memorias de la Sociedad Económica. 5 vols. Madrid: Anton de Sancha, 1780–1805.

Memorias Políticas y Económicas del Consulado de VeraCruz, 1796–1822. Ed. Javier Ortiz de la Tabla DuCasse. Seville: C.S.I.C, 1985.

Muñoz, Antonio. *Discurso Sobre Economía Política*. Madrid: Joachim de Ibarra, 1769.

Muñoz, Juan Bautista. *Historia del Nuevo Mundo*. Valencia: Generalitat Valenciana, 1990.

Muratori, Luís Antonio. *La Pública Felicidad: Objeto de los Buenos Príncipes*. Trans. Pascual Arbuxach. Madrid: Imprenta Real, 1790.

Normante y Carcavilla, Lorenzo. *Proposiciones de Economía Civil y Comercio*. Zaragoza, 1785.

——. *Discurso Sobre la Utilidad de los Conocimientos de Economía Civil*. Zaragoza, 1786.

Olavide, Pablo de. 'Informe Sobre la Ley Agraria'. In *Obras Selectas*. Ed. Estuardo Núñez. Lima: Banco de Crédito del Peru, 1987.

——. *Plan de Estudios Para la Universidad de Sevilla* [1768]. Ed. Francisco Aguilar Piñal. Seville: University of Seville Press, 1989.

Real Academia de la Historia. *Catálogo de la Colección de D. Juan Bautista Muñoz Interesantes para la Historia de América*. 3 vols. Madrid: RAH, 1956.

Relaciones de los Virreyes del Nuevo Reino de Granada. Ed. José Antonio Garcia y Garcia. New York, 1869.

Rodríguez de Campomanes, Pedro. *Itinerario de las Carreras de Posta de Dentro, y Fuera del Reyno* [1761]. Madrid: Ministerio de Fomento, 2002.

——. *Noticia Geografica del Reyno y Caminos de Portugal*. Madrid, 1762.

——. *Bosquejo de la Política-Económica Española Delineado Sobre el Estado Presente de Sus Intereses* [1750]. Ed. Jorge Cejudo. Madrid: Editorial Nacional, 1984.

——. *Reflexiones sobre el Comercio Exterior a Indias* [1762]. Ed. V. Llombart Rosa. Madrid: Instituto de Estudios Fiscales, 1988.

——. *Discurso sobre el Fomento de la Industria Popular*. Madrid, 1774.

——. *Discurso Sobre la Educación Popular de los Artesanos y su Fomento*. Madrid, 1775.

——. *Inéditos Políticos*. Ed. Santos M. Coronas González. Oviedo: Principado de Asturias, 1998.

Salas, Manuel de. *Escritos de Manuel de Salas*. 3 vols. Santiago, 1910.

Sempere y Guarinos, Juan. *Historia del Luxo y de las Leyes Suntuarias de España*. 2 vols. Madrid, 1788.

——. *Biblioteca Española Economía-Política*. Madrid, 1801–20.

——. *Historia de los Vínculos y Mayorazgos [1805]*. Alicante: Instituto de Cultura Juan-Gil Alberti, 1990.

Ulloa, Antonio de. *La Marina: Fuerzas Navales de la Europa y Costas de Berberia*. Ed. Juan Jelguera Quijada. Cádiz: University of Cádiz, 1995.

Ulloa, Antonio de. *Conversaciones de Ulloa con sus tres Hijos en Servicio de la Marina Instructiva*. Madrid, 1795.

Ulloa, Antonio de and Jorge Juan. *A Voyage to South America*. London, 1760.

Ulloa, Antonio de and Jorge Juan. *Noticias Secretas de América*. Ed. Luis J. Ramos Gómez. Madrid, 1990.

Ulloa, Bernardo de. *Restablecimiento de las Fábricas, Tráfico y Comercio Español*. Madrid, 1740.

Uztáriz, Gerónimo de. *The Theory and Practice of Commerce and Maritime Affairs*. Trans. John Kippax. 2 vols. London, 1751.

Villava, Victorián de. *Apuntes Para Una Reforma de España sin Trastorno del Gobierno Monarquico ni la Religión*. Buenos Aires, 1822.

Ward, Bernardo. *Obra Pía: y Eficaz Modo para Remediar la Miseria de la Gente de España*. 2nd edn. Madrid, 1767.

——. *Proyecto Económico, en que se Proponen Varias Providencias Dirigidas à Promover los Intereses de España, con los Medios y Fondos Necesarios para Plantificación*. Madrid, 1779.

Secondary sources

[Trevor-Roper, Hugh]. 'The Spanish Enlightenment'. *Times Literary Supplement*. 15 March 1957: 153–5.

Addy, George M. *The Enlightenment in the University of Salamanca*. Durham: Duke UP, 1966.

Adelman, Jeremy. *Republic of Capital: Buenos Aires and the Legal Transformation of the Atlantic World*. Stanford: Stanford UP, 1999.

——. *Sovereignty and Revolution in the Iberian Atlantic*. Princeton: Princeton UP, 2006.

Aiton, A.S. 'Spanish Colonial Reorganization Under the Family Compact'. *HAHR* 12 (1932): 269–77.

Alcázar Molina, Cayetano. *Los Hombres del Reinado de Carlos III: D. Pablo de Olavide (El Colonizador de Sierra Morena)*. Madrid: Editorial Voluntad, 1927.

——. *El Conde de Floridablanca: Siglo XVIII*. Madrid: M. Aguilar, 1936.

Aldridge, A. Owen, ed. *The Ibero-American Enlightenment*. Urbana and London: University of Illinois Press, 1971.

Álvarez de Morales, Antonio. *Inquisición e Ilustración, 1700–1834*. Madrid: Fundación Universitaria Española, 1982.

——. 'El Jansenismo en España y Su Caracter de Ideología Revolucionaria'. *Revista de Historia das Ideias* [Coimbra] 10 (1988): 347–57.

——. *El Pensamiento Político y Jurídico de Campomanes*. Madrid: Instituto Nacional de Administración Pública, 1989.

——. 'Genovesi y el Derecho Natural y de Gentes en España'. *AHDE*, 67 (1997): 413–31.

Álvarez de Toledo, Cayetana. *Politics and Reform in Spain and Viceregal Mexico: The Life and Thought of Juan de Palafox, 1600–1659*. Oxford: Oxford UP, 2004.

Amores, Juan B. *Cuba en la Época de Ezpeleta (1785–1790)*. Pamplona: University of Navarra, 2000.

Amunátegui, Miguel Luis. *Los Precursores de la Independencia Chilena*. 2 vols. Santiago: Imprenta, Litografia, Encuadernación 'Barcelona', 1909.

Andreo García, Juan. 'Del "Libre Comercio" a la Quiebra del Sistema Colonial (1789–1796): El Comercio de Venezuela'. *AEA*, 51:2 (1994): 25–60.

Andrien, Kenneth J. 'Economic Crisis, Taxes and the Quito Insurrection of 1765'. *Past and Present*, 129 (1990): 104–31.

——. *The Kingdom of Quito, 1690–1830: The State and Regional Economic Development*. Cambridge: Cambridge UP, 1995

——. 'The *Noticias Secretas de América* and the Construction of a Governing Ideology for the Spanish American Empire'. *Colonial Latin American Review*, 7:2 (1998): 175–92.

Anes, Gonzalo. *La Ley Agraria*. Madrid: Alianza Editorial, 1995.

Archer, Christon I., ed. 'Spain and the Defence of the Pacific Ocean Empire, 1750–1810' *Canadian Journal of Latin American and Caribbean Studies*, 11 (1986): 15–41.

——. *The Birth of Modern Mexico, 1780–1824*. Wilmington: Scholarly Resources Press, 2003.

Arcila Farías, Eduardo. *El Siglo Ilustrado en América: Reformas Económicas del Siglo XVIII en Nueva España*. Caracas: Ministerio de Educación, 1955.

——. *Fundamentos Económicos del Imperio Español en América*. Caracas: Universidad Central de Venezuela, 1985.

Argemí d'Abadal, Lluís, ed. *Agricultura e Ilustración: Antología del Pensamiento Agrario Ilustrado*. Madrid: Ministerio de Agricultura, 1988.

Artola, Miguel. 'Campillo y las Reformas de Carlos III'. *Revista de Indias*, 12 (1952): 685–714.

——. 'América en el Pensamiento Español de Siglo XVIII'. *Revista de Indias*, 29 (1969): 51–77.

Aruca Alonso, Lohania S., eds. *La Real Comisión de Guantánamo en la Isla de Cuba, 1797–1802*. Havana. Edición Unión, 2003.

Asdrúbal Silva, Hernán. 'La Estructuración del Comercio y la Navegación desde el Río de la Plata a Cuba'. *AEA*, 51:2 (1994): 61 73.

Astigarraga, Jesús. 'Victorián de Villava, Traductor de Gaetano Filangieri'. *Cuadernos Aragoneses de Economía*, 7:1 (1997): 171–86.

——. 'The Light and Shade of Italian Economic Thought in Spain (1750–1850)'. In *From Economistas to Economists: The International Spread of Italian Economic Thought*. Florence: PoliStampa, 2000.

——. *Los Ilustrados Vascos: Ideas, Instituciones y Reformas Económicas en España*. Barcelona: Crítica, 2003.

Aymes, Jean-René. *Ilustración y Revolución Francesa en España*. Lleida: Editorial Milenio, 2005.

Bakewell, Peter. *A History of Latin America*. Oxford: Blackwell Publishers, 1997.

Bello, Eduardo and Antonio Rivera, eds. *La Actitud Ilustrada*. Valencia: Biblioteca Valenciana, 2002.

Bannon, John F. *The Spanish Borderlands Frontier, 1513–1821*. New York and London, 1970.

Baras Escolá, Fernando. 'Política e Historia en la España del Siglo XVIII: Concepciones Historiográficas de Jovellanos'. *BRAH*, 191:2 (1994): 295–385.

Barbier, Jacques. 'The Culmination of the Bourbon Reforms, 1787–1792'. *HAHR*, 57 (1977): 51–68.

——. *Reform and Politics in Bourbon Chile, 1755–1796*. Ottowa: University of Ottowa Press, 1980.

——. 'Imperial Policy Toward the Port of Vera Cruz, 1788–1808: The Struggle Between Madrid, Cádiz and Havana Interests'. In Nils Jacobsen and Hans-Jürgen Puhle, eds. *The Economies of Mexico and Peru During the Late Colonial Period, 1760–1810*. Berlin: Colloquium Verlag, 1986.

Bauer, Arnold. 'The Church and Spanish Agrarian Structure: 1765–1865'. *The Americas*, 28:1 (1971): 78–98.

Belaunde, Victor Andres. *Bolívar and the Political Thought of the Spanish American Revolution*. New York: Octagon Books, 1930.

Bernstein, Harry. 'Documents: A Provincial Library in Colonial Mexico, 1802'. *HAHR*, 26:2 (1946): 162–83.

Bianchi, Diana. *La Ilustración y la Pobreza: Debates Metropolitanos y Realidades Coloniales*. Montevideo: Facultad de Humanidades, 2001.

Bitar Letayf, Marcelo. *Economistas Españoles del Siglo XVIII: Sus Ideas sobre la Libertad del Comercio con Indias*. Madrid: Ediciones Cultura Hispanica, 1968.

Blanco Martínez, Rogelio. *La Ilustración en Europa y en España*. Madrid: Ediciones Endymion, 1999.

Bobb, Bernard E. *The Viceregency of Antonio María Bucareli in New Spain, 1771–1779.* Austin: University of Texas Press, 1962.

Brading, D.A. *Miners and Merchants in Bourbon Mexico, 1763–1810.* Cambridge: Cambridge UP, 1971.

———. 'Government and Elite in Late Colonial Mexico'. *HAHR*, 53:3 (1973): 389–414.

———. 'Bourbon Spain and its American Empire'. *Historical Journal*, 39:4 (1981): 961–9.

———. 'Tridentine Catholicism and Enlightened Despotism in Bourbon Mexico'. *JLAS*, 15:1 (1983): 1–22.

———. 'Bourbon Spain and its American Empire'. In *The Cambridge History of Latin America*. Ed. Leslie Bethell. Vol. I. Cambridge: Cambridge UP, 1984.

———. *The First America: The Spanish Monarchy, Creole Patriots and the Liberal State, 1492–1867.* Cambridge: Cambridge UP, 1991.

Bradley, James E. and D.K. Kley, eds. *Religion and Politics in Enlightenment Europe.* South Bend: University of Notre Dame Press, 2002.

Bravo Lira, Bernardino. 'El Absolutismo Ilustrado en España e Indias Bajo Carlos III (1759–1788)'. *Revista Chilena de Historia del Derecho* [Chile] 14 (1991): 11–34.

Brown, Jonathan C. *A Socioeconomic History of Argentina, 1776–1860.* Cambridge Latin American Studies 35. Cambridge: Cambridge UP, 1979.

Brown, Vera Lee. 'Studies in the History of Spain in the Second Half of the Eighteenth Century'. *Smith College Studies in History*, 15: 1 (1929–30).

Burkholder, M.A. 'The Council of the Indies in the Late Eighteenth Century: A New Perspective'. *HAHR*, 56:3 (1976): 404–23.

Burkholder, M.A. and D.S. Chandler. *From Impotence to Authority: The Spanish Crown and the American Audiencias, 1687–1808.* Columbia and London: University of Missouri Press, 1976.

Burkholder, M.A. and Lyman Johnson. *Colonial Latin America.* 5th edn. New York and Oxford: Oxford UP, 2002.

Bustamante, Jesus and Mónica Ovijada, eds. *Élites, Intelectuales y Modelos Colectivos: Mundo Ibérico (Siglos XVI–XIX).* Madrid: CSIC, 2002.

Bustelo García del Real, Francisco. 'La Población Española en la Segunda Mitad del Siglo XVIII'. *Moneda y Crédito*, 123 (1972): 53–104.

Bustos Rodríguez, D. Manuel. *El Pensamiento Socio-Económico de Campomanes.* Oviedo: Instituto de Estudios Asturianos, 1982.

Calderón España, María Consolación, coord. *Las Reales Sociedades Económicas de Amigos del País y el Espíritu Ilustrado: Análisis de sus Realizaciones.* Seville: Real Sociedad Económica Sevillana de Amigos del País, 2001.

Callahan, William J. *Honor, Commerce, and Industry in Eighteenth-Century Spain.* Boston: Harvard Business School 1972.

———. *Church, Politics and Society in Spain, 1750–1874.* Cambridge, MA: Harvard UP, 1984.

Cañizares-Esguerra, Jorge. *How to Write the History of the New World: Histories, Epistemologies and Identities in the Eighteenth-Century Atlantic World.* Stanford: Stanford UP, 2001.

———. 'Eighteenth-Century Spanish Political Economy: Epistemology of Decline'. *Eighteenth-Century Thought*, 1 (2003): 295–314.

Capel, Manuel. *La Carolina, Capital de las Nuevas Poblaciones: Un Ensayo de Reforma Socio-Económica de España en el Siglo XVIII.* Jaén: CSIC, 1970.

Castellano, Juan Luis, ed. *Sociedad, Administración y Poder en la España del Antiguo Régimen.* Granada: University of Granada, 1996.

Castellano de Losad, Basilio Sebastian. *Historia de la Vida Civil y Política ... Don José Nicolás de Azara.* 2 vols. Madrid, 1849.

Castells, Irene. *Crisis del Antiguo Régimen y Revolución Liberal en España (1789–1845)*. Barcelona: Editorial Ariel, SA, 2000.

Castro, Concepción de. *Campomanes: Estado y Reformismo Ilustrado*. Madrid: Alianza Editorial, 1996.

Caughey, John. 'Bernardo de Gálvez and the English Smugglers on the Mississippi, 1777'. *HAHR*, 12 (1932): 46–58.

Celis Muñoz, Luís. *El Pensamiento Política de Manuel de Salas*. Santiago: Editorial Universitaria, 1954.

Chastagnaret, Gérard and Gérard Dufour, eds. *Le Règne de Charles III: Le Despotisme Éclairé en Espagne*. Paris: CNRS, 1994.

Chiaramonte, Jose Carlos. *La Critica Ilustrada de la Realidad: Económia y Sociedad en el Pensamiento Argentino e Iberoamericano del Siglo XVIII*. Buenos Aires: CEAL, 1982.

——. *La Ilustración en el Rio de la Plata: Cultura Eclesiastica y Cultura Laica Durante el Veirreinato*. Buenos Aires: Puntosur, 1989.

Chiareno, Osvaldo. *Noticias Bio-Bibliograficas Sobre Economistas Españoles del Siglo XVIII*. Genoa: Tolozzi YC, 1962.

Christelow, Allan. 'French Interest in the Spanish Empire during the Ministry of the Duc de Choiseul, 1759 1771'. *HAHR*, 21 (1941): 515 37.

Cid Celis, Gustavo. *Juan Egaña, Constitucionalista y Procer Americano*. Santiago: Universidad de Chile, 1941.

Coatsworth, John H. 'American Trade with European Colonies in the Caribbean and South America, 1790–1812'. *William and Mary Quarterly*, 24:2 (1967): 243–66.

Colección Ensayo. *La América Española en la Época de las Luces: Tradición, Innovación, Representación*. Madrid: Ediciones de Cultura Hispánica, 1988.

Coletes Blanco, Agustín. 'Notas Sobre la Influencia de Feijoo en Inglaterra: Algunas Traducciones y Menciones'. *Boletín del Centro de Estudios del Siglo XVIII* [Oviedo] 3 (1979): 19–51.

Collier, Simon. *The Ideas and Politics of Chilean Independence, 1808–1833*. Cambridge: Cambridge UP, 1967.

Collins, Roger. *Early Medieval Spain: Unity in Diversity, 400–1000*. London and Basingstoke: Macmillan Press, 1983.

Cook, W.L. *Flood Tide of Empire: Spain and the Pacific Northwest, 1542–1819*. New Haven: Yale UP, 1973.

Cooney, Jerry W. 'Oceanic Commerce and Platine Merchants, 1796–1806: The Challenge of War'. *The Americas*, 45 (1989): 509–24.

Coronas González, S.M. *Ilustración y Derecho. Los Fiscales del Consejo de Castilla en el Siglo XVIII*. Madrid: Ministerio de Administración Pública, 1992.

——, ed. *In Memoriam: Pedro Rodríguez de Campomanes*. Oviedo: Real Instituto de Estudios Asturianos, 2002.

Cortes Peña, Antonio Luis. *La Política Religiosa de Carlos III: Las Ordenes Mendicantes*. Granada: University of Granada Press, 1989.

Coxe, William. *Memoirs of the Kings of Spain of the House of Bourbon*. 5 vols. London: Longman, Hurst and Rees, 1815.

Cruz, Jesús. *Gentlemen, Bourgeois and Revolutionaries: Political Change and Cultural Persistence among the Spanish Dominant Groups, 1750–1850*. Cambridge: Cambridge UP, 1996.

Cunningham, C.H. *The Audiencia in the Spanish Colonies as Illustrated by the Audiencia of Manila 1583–1800*. Berkeley: University of California Press, 1919.

Derozier, Alberto. *Escritores Políticos Españoles (1789–1854)*. Madrid: Ediciones Turner, 1994.

Din, Gilbert C., ed. *The Spanish Presence in Louisiana, 1763–1803*. Lafayette, LA: University of Southwest Louisiana, 1996.

Din, Gilbert. *Spaniards, Planters and Slaves: The Spanish Regulation of Slavery in Louisiana, 1763–1803*. College Station: Texas A & M UP, 1999.

Diz, Alejandro. *La Idea de Europa en la España del Siglo XVIII*. Madrid: Centro de Estudios Políticos y Constitucionales, 2000.

Domínguez, Jorge I. *Insurrection or Loyalty: The Breakdown of the Spanish American Empire*. London and Cambridge, MA: Harvard UP, 1980.

Domínguez Ortiz, Antonio. *Sociedad y Estado en el Siglo XVIII Español*. Barcelona: Editorial Ariel, SA, 1976.

———. *Carlos III y la España de la Ilustración*. Madrid: Alianza Editorial, 1988.

Donoso, Ricardo. *Las Ideas Políticas en Chile*. Mexico City: Fondo de Cultura Económica, 1946.

Dym, Jordana. '"Our Pueblos, Fractions with No Central Unity": Municipal Sovereignty in Central America, 1808–1821'. *HAHR*, 86:3 (2006): 431–66.

Egido, Teófanes and Isidoro Pinedo. *Las Causas 'Gravisimas' y Secretas de la Expulsion de los Jesuitas por Carlos III*. Madrid: Fundación Universitaria Española, 1994.

———. *Carlos IV*. Madrid: Arlanza Ediciones, 2001.

El Mundo Hispánico en el Siglo de Las Luces. 2 Vols. Madrid: Editorial Complutense, 1996.

Elliott, J.H. *Imperial Spain, 1469–1716*. London: Edward Arnold, 1963.

———. *The Old World and the New, 1492–1650*. Cambridge: Cambridge UP, 1970.

———. *Spain and its World, 1500–1700: Selected Essays*. New Haven and London: Yale UP, 1989.

———. 'A Europe of Composite Monarchies'. *Past and Present*, 137 (1992): 48–71.

———. 'Britain and Spain in America: Colonists and Colonised'. The Stenton Lectures at the University of Reading, 1994.

———. 'Rey y Patria en el Mundo Hispánico'. In Victor Mínguez and Manuel Chust, eds. *El Imperio Sublevado: Monarquía y Naciones en España e Hispanoamérica*. Madrid: CSIC, 2004.

———. *Empires of the Atlantic World: Britain and Spain in America, 1492–1830*. New Haven and London: Yale UP, 2006.

Elorza, Antonio. *La Ideología Liberal en la Ilustración Española*. Madrid: Editorial Tecnos, 1970.

Elósegui, Maria and Maria Dolores Bosch. 'El Ensayo de Hume sobre el Refinamento en las Artes y su Influencia en la Ilustración Española'. *Dieciocho*, 19:1 (1996): 101–27.

Engstrand, Iris. *Spanish Scientists in the New World: The Eighteenth-Century Expeditions*. London and Seattle: University of Washington Press, 1981.

Escudero, José Antonio. *Administración y Estado en España Moderna*. Madrid: Junata de Castilla y León, 1999.

Esdaile, Charles. *Spain in the Liberal Age: From Constitution to Civil War, 1808–1939*. Oxford: Blackwells, 2000.

Esponera Cerdán, Alfonso. 'El Alicantino de los Reyes OFM y su Dictamen Sobre la *Historia* de W. Robertson (1778)'. *Estudis: Revista de Historia Moderna*, [Valencia] 23 (1997): 297–320.

Eyzaguirre, Jaime. *Ideario y Ruta de la Emancipación Chilena*. Santiago: Editorial Universitaria, 1991.

Feliciano Ramos, Hector R. *El Contrabando Ingles en el Caribe y el Golfo de Mexico (1748–1778)*. Seville: Diputación Provincial de Sevilla, 1990.

Feliu Cruz, Guillermo. *El Pensamiento de O'Higgins: Estudio Histórico*. Santiago: Imprenta Universitaria, 1954.

Fernández, Roberto. *Carlos III*. Madrid: Arlanza Ediciones, 2001.

Fernández Durán, Reyes. *Gerónimo de Uztáriz (1670–1732): Una Política Económica para Felipe V.* Madrid: Minerva Ediciones, 1999.

Fernández Murga, Félix. *Carlos III y el Descubrimiento de Herculano.* Salamanca: University of Salamanca, 1989.

Ferns, H.S. *Britain and Argentina in the Nineteenth Century.* Oxford: Clarendon Press, 1960.

Ferrer Benimeli, José A, ed. *El Conde Aranda y Su Tiempo.* 2 vols. Zaragoza: Institución 'Fernando el Católico'/CSIC, 2000.

Ferrer del Río, Antonio. *Historia del Reinado de Carlos III en España.* 4 vols. Madrid, 1856.

Fisher, Lillian Estelle. *Viceregal Administration in the Spanish American Colonies.* Berkeley: University of California Press, 1926.

Fisher, John R. *Government and Society in Colonial Peru: The Intendant System, 1784–1814.* London: Athlone Press, 1970.

———. *The Economic Aspects of Spanish Imperialism in America, 1492–1810.* Liverpool: Liverpool UP, 1997.

———. 'Commerce and Imperial Decline: Spanish Trade with Spanish America, 1797–1820'. *JLAS*, 30 (1998): 459–79.

Fisher, J.R., A.J. Kuethe and A. McFarlane, eds. *Reform and Insurrection in Bourbon New Granada and Peru.* Baton Rouge: LSU Press, 1990.

Floyd, Troy S. 'The Guatemalan Merchants, the Government and the *Provincianos,* 1750–1800'. *HAHR,* 41:1 (1961): 91–110.

Fontana, Josep, ed. *El Comercio Libre entre España y América (1765–1824).* Madrid: Fundación Banco Exterior, 1987.

Franco Rubio, Gloria A. *La Vida Cotidiana en Tiempos de Carlos III.* Madrid: Ediciones Libertarias, 2001.

Fuentes Quintana, Enrique, ed. *Economía y Economistas Españoles. Volume 3: La Ilustración.* Barcelona: Galaxia Gutenberg, 2000.

Galera Gómez, Andres. *La Ilustración Espanola y el Conocimiento del Nuevo Mundo.* Madrid: CSIC, 1988.

Garate Ojanguren, Montserrat. *Comercio Ultramarino e Ilustración: La Real Compañía de la Habana.* San Sebastián: Gobierno Vasco, 1993.

García del Pino, César. *Toma de la Habana por los Ingleses y Sus Antecedentes.* La Habana: Editorial de Ciencias Sociales, 2003.

García-Baquero González, Antonio. *Cádiz y el Atlántico (1717–1778): El Comercio Español Bajo el Monopolio Gaditano.* 2 vols. 2nd edn. Cádiz: CSIC, 1988.

———. *El Comercio Colonial en la Época del Absolutismo Ilustrado: Problemas y Debates.* Granada: Universidad de Granada, 2002.

Garcia Bernal, M.C. 'Politica Indigenista del Reformismo de Carlos III y Carlos IV'. *Temas Americanistas,* 13 (1997): 8–16.

García Cárcel, Ricardo. *La Leyenda Negra: Historia y Opinión.* Madrid: Alianza Editorial, 1992.

———. *La Construcción de las Historias de España.* Madrid: Marcial Pons, 2004.

———, ed. *Historia de España Siglo XVIII: La España de los Borbones.* Madrid: Cátedra, 2002.

García Pérez, Rafael D. *El Consejos de Indias Durante los Reinados de Carlos III y Carlos IV.* Pamplona: Ediciones de la Universidad de Navarra, 1998.

García Regueiro, Ovidio. 'Intereses Estamentales y Pensamiento Económico: La Versión Española de la *Historia* de Raynal'. *Moneda y Crédito,* 149 (1979): 85–118.

———. *'Ilustración' e Intereses Estamentales: Antagonismo entre Sociedad Tradicional y Corrientes Innovadoras en la Versión Española de la 'Historia' de Raynal.* Madrid: Editorial Complutense, 1982.

——. 'América en la Política de Estado de Carlos III'. *Cuadernos Hispanoamericanos,* Comp. 2 (1988): 25–52.

García Ruiperez, Mariano. 'El Pensamiento Económico Ilustrado y las Compañías de Comercio'. *Revista de Historia Económica,* 4:3 (1986): 521–48.

Garrett, David T. '"His Majesty's Most Loyal Vassals": The Indian Nobility and Túpac Amaru'. *HAHR,* 84:4 (2004): 575–617.

Giménez López, Enrique, ed. *Expulsíon y Exilio de los Jesuitas Españoles.* Alicante: University of Alicante Press, 1997.

Glendinning, Nigel. *A Literary History of Spain: The Eighteenth Century.* New York: Barnes and Noble, 1972.

Glick, Thomas F. 'Science and Independence in Latin America (with Special Reference to New Granada)'. *HAHR,* 71:2 (1991): 307–34.

Goebel, Julius. *The Struggle for the Falkland Islands: A Study in Legal and Diplomatic History.* New Haven and London: Yale UP, 1970.

Gomariz, José. 'Francisco de Arango y Parreño: El Discurso Esclavista de la Ilustración Cubana'. *Cuban Studies,* 35 (2004): 45–61.

Góngora, Mario. *Studies in the Colonial History of Latin America.* Trans. Richard Southern. Cambridge: Cambridge UP, 1975.

González, Juan Batista. *La Estrategia Española en América Durante el Siglo de las Luces.* Madrid: Editorial Mapfre, 1992.

González-Ripoll Navarro, Maria Dolores. *Cuba: La Isla de los Ensayos: Cultura y Sociedad (1790–1815).* Madrid: CSIC, 1999.

Grice-Hutchinson, Marjorie. *Economic Thought in Spain: Selected Essays of Marjorie Grice-Hutchinson.* Eds. L.S. Moss and C.K. Ryan. Aldershot: Edward Elgar, 1993.

Guerra, François-Xavier, ed. *Revoluciones Hispánicas: Independencias Americanas y Liberalismo Español.* Madrid: Editorial Complutense, 1995.

Guerrero, Ana Clara. *Viajeros Británicos en la España de Siglo XVIII.* Madrid: Aguilar, 1990.

Guillamon Álvarez, Francisco Javier. 'Institutional Reform and Municipal Government in the Spanish Empire in the Eighteenth Century'. *Itinerario* [Netherlands] 20:3 (1996): 109–23.

Guimerá, Agustín, ed. *El Reformismo Borbónico: Una Visión Interdisciplinar.* Madrid: Alianza Editorial, 1996.

Guiteras, Pedro J. *Historia de la Conquista de la Habana por los Ingleses.* Havana: Oficina del Historiador, 1962.

Halperín Donghi, Tulio. *The Contemporary History of Latin America.* Ed. and Trans. J.C. Chasteen. London: Macmillan, 1993.

Hamilton, Bernice. *Political Thought in Sixteenth-Century Spain: a Study in the Political Ideas of Vitoria, de Soto, Suárez and Molina.* Oxford: Clarendon Press, 1963.

Hamilton, Earl J. 'Monetary Problems in Spain and Spanish America, 1751–1800'. *Journal of Economic History,* 4 (1944): 21–48.

Hamnett, Brian R. *Politics and Trade in Southern Mexico, 1750–1821.* Cambridge UP, 1971.

——. 'Mercantile Rivalry and Peninsular Division: The Consulados of New Spain and the Impact of the Bourbon Reforms, 1789–1824'. *Ibero-Amerikanisches Archiv,* 2 (1976): 273–305.

——. 'Process and Pattern: A Re-Examination of the Ibero-American Independence Movements, 1808–1826'. *JLAS,* 29:2 (1997): 279–328.

Hanisch Epindola, S.I. *La Filosofía de Don Juan Egaña.* Santiago: Universidad Católica de Chile, 1964.

Hargreaves-Mawdsley, W.N. *Eighteenth-Century Spain, 1700–1788: A Political, Diplomatic and Institutional History.* London: Macmillan, 1979.

Haring, C.H. *The Spanish Empire in America*. New York: Oxford UP, 1947.

Hauben, P.J. 'White Legend Against Black: Nationalism and Enlightenment in a Spanish Context'. *The Americas*, 34 (1977): 1–19.

Helg, Aline. *Liberty and Equality in Caribbean Colombia, 1770–1835*. Chapel Hill and London: University of North Carolina Press, 2004.

Hernández Benítez, Mauro. 'Carlos III: un Mito Progresista', in Equipo Madrid, *Carlos III, Madrid y la Ilustración: Contradicciones de un Proyecto Reformista*. Madrid: Siglo XXI, 1988.

Hernández Franco, Juan. 'Del Tercer Pacto de Familia al Tratado de Aranjuez: Afirmación de la Seperación Exterior Respecto a Francia'. In Carmen Maria Cremades Griñan, ed. *Estado y Fiscalidad en el Antiguo Régimen*. Murcia: University of Murcia, 1989.

Herr, Richard. *The Eighteenth-Century Revolution in Spain*. Princeton: Princeton UP, 1958.

——. 'The Twentieth-century Spaniard Views the Spanish Enlightenment'. *Hispania*, 45:2 (1962): 183–93.

——. *Rural Change and Royal Finances in Spain at the End of the Old Regime*. Berkeley: University of California Press, 1989.

Herrero, Javier. *Las Orígenes del Pensamiento Reaccionario Español*. Madrid· Alianza Editorial, 1988.

Herzog, Tamar. *Defining Nations: Immigrants and Citizens in Early Modern Spain and Spanish America*. New Haven and London: Yale UP, 2003.

Hoberman, Louisia Schell and Susan Midgen Socolow, eds. *Cities and Society in Colonial Latin America*. Albuquerque: University of New Mexico Press, 1986.

Hopkins, A.G. 'Informal Empire in Argentina: An Alternative View'. *JLAS*, 26 (1994): 469–84.

Hull, Anthony H. *Charles III and the Revival of Spain*. Washington: UP of America, 1980.

Hussey, R.D. *The Caracas Company, 1728–1784: A Study in the History of Spanish Monopolistic Trade*. Cambridge, MA: Harvard UP, 1934.

Ingenieros, José. *La Evolución de las Ideas Argentinas*. 2 vols. Buenos Aires: Talleres Graficos Argentinos, 1918.

Jago, Charles. 'The Eighteenth-Century Economic Analysis of the Decline of Spain'. In Paul Fritz and David Williams, eds. *The Triumph of Culture: Eighteenth-Century Perspectives*. Toronto: A.M. Hakkert Ltd., 1972.

Johnson, Lyman and Kenneth Andrien, eds. *The Political Economy of Spanish America in the Age of Revolution, 1750–1850*. Albuquerque: University of New Mexico Press, 1994.

Johnson, Sherry. *The Social Transformation of Eighteenth-Century Cuba*. Gainseville: University of Florida Press, 2001.

Juan Vidal, Josep and Enrique Martínez Ruiz. *Política Interior y Exterior de los Borbones*. Madrid: Ediciones ISTMO, 2001.

Juárez Medina, Antonio. *Las Reediciones de Obras en Erudición de los Siglos XVI and XVII Durante el Siglo XVIII Español*. Bern: Peter Lang, 1988.

Kamen, Henry. *The Duke of Alba*. New Haven and London: Yale UP, 2004.

King, James Ferguson. 'Evolution of the Free Slave Trade Principle in Spanish Colonial Administration'. *HAHR*, 22:1 (1942): 34–56.

King, P.D. *Law and Society in Visigothic Spain*. Cambridge: Cambridge UP, 1972.

Kinnaird, Lawrence, ed. *Spain in the Mississippi Valley, 1765–94: Translations of Materials from the Spanish Archives of the Bancroft Library. Part I: The Revolutionary Period, 1765–1781*. Washington: US Government Printing Office, 1949.

Kinsbruner, Jay. 'The Political Status of Chilean Merchants at the End of the Colonial Period: The Concepción Example, 1790–1810'. *The Americas*, 29:1 (1972): 30–56.

Klein, Herbert S. 'Structure and Profitability of Royal Finance in the Viceroyalty of the Río de la Plata in 1790'. *HAHR*, 53:3 (1973): 440–69.

Knight, Franklin W. 'Origins of Wealth and the Sugar Revolution in Cuba, 1750–1850'. *HAHR*, 57:2 (1977): 231–53.

Knight, Franklin W. and Peggy K. Liss, eds. *Atlantic Port Cities: Economy, Culture and Society in the Atlantic World, 1650–1850*. Knoxville: University of Tennessee Press, 1991.

Krebs Wilckens. Ricardo. *El Pensamiento Histórico, Político, y Económico del Conde de Campomanes*. Santiago: Universidad de Chile, 1960.

Kuethe, Allan J. *Cuba, 1753–1815: Crown, Military and Society*. Knoxville: University of Tennessee Press, 1986.

Kuethe, Allan J. and G. Douglas Inglis. 'Absolutism and Enlightened Reform: Charles III, the Establishment of the *Alcabala*, and Commercial Reorganization in Cuba'. *Past & Present*, 109 (1985): 118–43.

Kuethe, Allan J. and Lowell Blaisdel. 'French Influence and the Origins of Bourbon Colonial Reorganization'. *HAHR*, 71 (1991): 579–607.

Kuethe, Allan J. and E. Vila Vilar, eds. *Relaciones de Poder y Comercio Colonial: Nuevas Perspectivas*. Seville: CSIC, 1999.

Lafarga, Francisco. 'La Traducción en La España del Siglo XVIII'. In S.M. Santamaría, ed. *Traveses Culturales: Literatura, Cine, Traducción*. Vitoria: University of the Pais Vasco, 1997.

LaForce, James Clayburn. *The Development of the Spanish Textile Industry, 1750–1800*. Berkeley: University of California Press, 1965.

Lafuente, Antonio, José Luis Peset and Manuel Sellés, eds. *Carlos III y la Ciencia de la Ilustración*. Madrid: Alianza Editorial, 1987.

Lafuente, Antonio. 'Enlightenment in an Imperial Context: Local Science in the Late Eighteenth-Century Hispanic World'. *Osiris*, 15 (2000): 155–73.

Lafuente, Modesto. *Historia General de España*. Part III, Vol. 20. Madrid, 1853.

Latasa, Pilar, ed. *Reformismo y Sociedad en la América Borbónica*. Pamplona: Ediciones Universidad de Navarra, 2003.

Leonard, Irving A. and Robert S. Smith. 'Documents: A Proposed Library for the Merchant Guild of VeraCruz, 1801'. *HAHR*, 24:1 (1944): 84–102.

Lesser, Ricardo, *Los Orígenes de la Argentina: Historia del Reino del Río de la Plata*. Buenos Aires: Biblos, 2003.

Levene, Ricardo. *Vida y Escritos de Victorián de Villava*. Buenos Aires: Facultad de Filosofia y Letras, 1946.

——. *El Mundo de las Ideas y la Revolución Hispanoamericana de 1810*. Santiago: Editorial Juridica de Chile, 1956.

Liss, Peggy K. *Atlantic Empires: The Network of Trade and Revolution, 1713–1826*. Baltimore and London: The Johns Hopkins UP, 1983.

Llombart, Vicent. *Campomanes, Economista y Político de Carlos III*. Madrid: Alianza Editorial, 1992.

——. 'Traducciones Españolas de Economia Política (1700–1812): Catálogo Bibliografico y una Nueva Perspectiva'. *Cromohs*, 9 (2004): 1–14.

Lluch, Ernest and Lluís Argemí d'Abadal. *Agronomía y Fisiocracia en España, 1750–1820*. Valencia: IAM, 1985.

——. 'Physiocracy in Spain'. *History of Political Economy*, 26:4 (1994): 613–27.

Lockhart, James. 'The Social History of Colonial Spanish America: Evolution and Potential'. *Latin American Research Review*, 7:1 (1972): 6–45.

López, François. 'La Historia de las Ideas en el Siglo XVIII: Concepciones Antiguas y Revisiones Necesarias'. *Boletín del Centro de Estudios del Siglo XVIII* [Oviedo] 3 (1975): 3–18.

——. 'Rasgos Peculiares de la Ilustración en España'. In *Mayans y la Ilustración*. Oliva: Ayuntamiento de Oliva, 1982.

López Cantos, Angel. *Don Francisco de Saavedra, Segundo Intendante de Caracas*. Seville: EEHA, 1973.

Los Reyes Gómez, Fermín de. *El Libro en España y América. Legislación y Censura (Siglos XV-XVIII)*. 2 vols. Madrid: Editorial AND, 2000.

Lucena-Giraldo, Manuel. '¿Filántropos u Oportunistas? Ciencia y Política en los Proyectos de Obras Públicas del Consulado de Cartegena de Indias, 1795–1810'. *Revista de Indias*, 52 (1992): 627–46.

Lynch, John. *Spanish Colonial Administration, 1782–1810: The Intendant System in the Viceroyalty of the Río de la Plata*. London: Athlone Press, 1958.

——. *Bourbon Spain, 1700–1808*. Oxford: Basil Blackwell, 1989.

——. 'The Institutional Framework of Colonial Spanish America'. *JLAS*, Supplement 24 (1992): 69–77.

——. 'Spanish American Independence in Recent Historiography'. In Anthony McFarlane and Eduardo Posada-Carbó, eds. *Independence and Revolution in Spanish America: Perspectives and Problems*. London: Institute of Latin American Studies, 1999.

Mackay, Ruth. *The Limits of Royal Authority: Resistence and Obedience in Seventeenth-Century Castile*. Cambridge: Cambridge UP, 1999.

MacLachlan, Colin M. *Spain's Empire in the New World: The Role of Ideas in Institutional and Social Change*. Berkeley: University of California Press, 1988.

Maltby, William S. *The Black Legend in England: The Development of Anti-Spanish Sentiment, 1558–1660*. Durham: Duke UP, 1971.

Marañón, Gregorio. *Vida e Historia*. 8th edn. Madrid: Espasa-Calpe, 1962.

Maravall, José Antonio. 'La Idea de Felicidad en el Programa de la Ilustración'. In Haïm Vidal Sephiha, ed. *Mélanges Offerts à Charles Vincent Aubrun*. Paris: Éditions Hispaniques, 1975.

——. *Culture of the Baroque: Analysis of a Historical Structure*. Trans. Terry Cochrane. Minneapolis: University of Minnesota Press, 1986.

Marías, Julián. *La España Posible en Tiempo de Carlos III*. Madrid: Sociedad de Estudios y Publicaciones, 1963.

Marichal, Carlos. 'Beneficios y Costes Fiscales del Colonialismo: Las Remesas Americanas a España, 1760–1814'. *Revista de Historia Económica*, 15:3 (1997): 475–505.

Marichal, Carlos and Matilda Souto Mantecón. 'Silver and *Situados*: New Spain and the Financing of the Spanish Empire in the Caribbean in the Eighteenth Century'. *HAHR*, 74:4 (1994): 587–613.

Mariluz Urquijo, José M. *Bilbao y Buenos Aires: Proyectos Dieciochescos de Compañías de Comercio*. Buenos Aires: University of Buenos Aires, 1981.

Marks, Patricia H. 'Confronting a Mercantile Elite: Bourbon Reformers and the Merchants of Lima, 1765–1796'. *The Americas*, 60:4 (2004): 519–58.

Marrero, Levi. *Cuba: Económia y Sociedad. Vol. 7: Del Monopolio hacia la Libertad Comercial: 1700–1763*. Madrid: Editorial Playor, SA, 1986.

Martínez Albiach, Alfredo. 'Campomanes "Regalista"'. *Burgense*, 35:2 (1994): 423–68.

Martínez Dalmau, Eduardo. *La Política Colonial y Extranjera de los Reyes Españoles de la Casa de Austria y Borbón*. Havana: Academia de la Historia de Cuba, 1943.

Martiré, Eduardo. 'Guión Sobre el Proceso Recopilador de las Leyes de Indias'. In Francisco de Icaza DuFour, coord., *Recopilación de Leyes de los Reynos de las Indias. Estudios Histórico-Jurídicos*. Mexico City: Miguel Angel Porrúa, 1987.

Matilla Quizá, María Jesús. 'Las Compañías Privilegiadas en la España del Antiguo Régimen'. In Miguel Artola, ed. *La Economía Española al Final del Antiguo Régimen. IV: Instituciones*. Madrid: Alianza/Banco de España, 1982.

Maxwell, Kenneth R. 'Hegemonies Old and New: The Ibero-Atlantic in the Long Eighteenth Century'. In Jeremy Adelman, ed. *Colonial Legacies: The Problem of Persistence in Latin American History*. New York and London: Routledge, 1999.

McFarlane, Anthony. *Colombia Before Independence: Economy, Society and Politics under Bourbon Rule*. Cambridge: Cambridge UP, 1993.

——. 'Political Corruption and Reform in Bourbon Spanish America'. In Walter Little and Eduardo Posada-Carbó, eds. *Political Corruption in Europe and Latin America*. London: Palgrave Macmillan, 1996.

——. 'Identity, Enlightenment and Political Dissent in Late Colonial Spanish America'. *Transactions of the Royal Historical Society*, 6th Series. 8 (1998): 309–36.

——. 'Science and Sedition in Spanish America: New Granada in the Age of Revolution, 1776–1810'. In Susan Manning and Peter France, eds. *Enlightenment and Emancipation*. Bucknell: Bucknell UP, 2006.

McKinley, P. Michael. *Pre-Revolutionary Caracas: Politics, Economy and Society, 1777–1811*. Cambridge: Cambridge UP, 1985.

Menéndez Pelayo, Marcelino. *Historia de los Heterodoxos Españoles*. Vol. II. Madrid: CSIC, 1992.

Merino, Luis. 'The Relation between the "Noticias Secretas" and the "Viaje"'. *The Americas*, 13:2 (1956): 111–25.

Molina Martínez, Miguel. *Antonio de Ulloa en Huancavelica, 1758–1764*. Granada: Universidad de Granada, 1995

Moore, John Preston. *Revolt in Louisiana: The Spanish Occupation, 1766–1770*. Baton Rouge and London: Louisiana State UP, 1976.

Morales Moya, A. 'La Ideología de la Ilustración Española'. *Revista de Estudios Políticos*, 59 (1988): 65–106.

Moreno Fraginals, Manuel. *El Ingenio: Complejo Económico Social Cubano del Azúcar*. 3 vols. Havana: Editorial de Ciencias Sociales, 1978.

Morse, Richard M. 'Toward a Theory of Spanish American Government'. *Journal of the History of Ideas*, 15:1 (1954): 71–93

Muñoz Pérez, José. 'La Idea de América en Campomanes'. *AEA*, 10 (1953): 209–64.

——. 'Los Proyectos Sobre España e Indias en el Siglo XVIII: el Proyectismo como Genero'. *Revista de Estudios Políticos*, 81 (1955): 169–96.

Muriel, Andrés. *Gobierno del Señor Rey Don Carlos III, o Instrucción Reservada Para Direccion de la Junta de Estado*. Madrid, 1839.

Muro Orejón, Antonio. 'El Nuevo Código de las Leyes Indianas. Proyectos de Recopilación Legislativa Posteriores a 1680'. *Revista de Ciencias Jurídicas y Sociales*, 12 (1929): 287–339.

Narancio, E.M. 'Las Ideas Políticas en el Río de la Plata a Comienzos de Siglo XIX'. *Revista de la Facultad de Humanidades y Ciencias* [Montevideo] 14 (1955): 97–183.

Naranjo Orovio, Consuelo and Tomás Mallo Gutierréz, eds. *Cuba, La Perla de las Antillas*. Madrid: Ediciones Doce Calles, 1994.

Nava Rodríguez, María Teresa. 'La Real Academia de la Historia Como Modelo de Unión Entre el Estado y la Cultura'. *Cuadernos de Historia Moderna y Contemporánea*, 8 (1987): 127–55.

——. 'Robertson, Juan Bautista Muñoz, y la Academia de la Historia'. *Boletín de la Real Academia de la Historia* [Spain] 187 (1990): 435–56.
Navarro Floria, Pedro. 'Notas Para un Estudio del Ideario Económico y Político de Manuel Belgrano'. *Quinto Centenario*, 13 (1987): 173–96.
——. 'Las Ideas Económicas en la Formación de Una Mentalidad Rioplatense (1790–1806)'. *AEA*, 46 (1989): 321–81.
——. *Manuel Belgrano y el Consulado de Buenos Aires, Cuna de la Revolución (1790–1806)*. Buenos Aires: Instituto Nacional Belgraniano, 1999.
Navarro García, Luis. *Intendencias en Indias*. Seville: Escuela de Estudios Hispanoamericanos, 1959.
Nieto-Phillips, John and Christopher Schmidt-Nowara, eds. *Interpreting Spanish Colonialism: Empires, Nations and Legends*. Albuquerque: University of New Mexico Press, 2005.
Novales, Alberto Gil. *Del Antiguo al Nuevo Régimen en España*. Caracas: Academia Nacional de la Historia, 1986.
Nunes Dias, Manuel. *El Real Consulado de Caracas (1793–1810)*. Caracas: Academia Nacional de la Historia, 1971.
O'Callaghan, Joseph F. *A History of Medieval Spain*. Ithaca and London: Cornell UP, 1975.
Olaechea, Rafael. 'Contribución al Estudio del "Motín Contra Esquilache"'. In *Homenaje al Dr. Eugenio Frutos Cortes*. Zaragoza: University of Zaragoza, 1977.
Oliveras Samitier, Jordi. *Nuevas Poblaciones en la España de la Ilustración*. Barcelona: Fundación de Arquitectos, 1998.
Ortiz, Fernando. 'La Hija Cubana del Iluminismo'. Excerpted from *Recopilación para la Historia de la Sociedad Económica Habanera: Tomo V*. Havana: Molina y Compañía, 1943.
Pagden, Anthony. 'Identity Formation in Spanish America'. In Pagden and Nicholas Canny, eds. *Colonial Identity in the Atlantic World 1500–1800*. Princeton: Princeton UP, 1987.
——. *Spanish Imperialism and the Political Imagination: Studies in European and Spanish American Social and Political Theory, 1513–1830*. New Haven and London: Yale UP, 1990.
——. 'Liberty, Honour and *Comercio Libre*: The Structure of the Debates over the State of the Spanish Empire in the Eighteenth Century'. In Pagden, *The Uncertainties of Empire: Essays in Iberian and Ibero-Atlantic History*. Aldershot: Varorium, 1994.
——. 'Heeding Heraclides: Empire and its Discontents, 1619–1812'. In Richard Kagan and Geoffrey Parker, eds. *Spain, Europe and the Atlantic World: Essays in Honour of John H. Elliott*. Cambridge: Cambridge UP, 1995.
——. *Lords of All the World: Ideologies of Empire in Spain, Britain and France, c. 1500–1800*. New Haven and London: Yale UP, 1995.
Pajares, Eterio. 'Traducción Inglés-Español en el Siglo XVIII'. In *El Mundo Hispánico en el Siglo de las Luces*. Madrid: Editorial Complutense, 1996.
Palacio Atard, Vicente. *Los Españoles de la Ilustración*. Madrid: Ediciones Guadarrama, 1964.
——. *La España del Siglo XVIII: el Siglo de las Reformas*. Madrid: UNED, 1978.
Paquette, Gabriel B. 'Enlightenment, Empire and Regalism: New Directions in Eighteenth-century Spanish History'. *European History Quarterly*, 35:1 (2005): 107–17.
Parcero Torre, Celia María. *La Pérdida de la Habana y Las Reformas Borbónicas en Cuba (1760–1773)*. Madrid: Junta de Castilla y León, 1998.
Parry, J.H. *The Spanish Theory of Empire in the Sixteenth Century*. Cambridge, MA: Harvard UP, 1946.

Pastore, Rodolfo E. 'Formación Económica de la Elite Intelectual Rioplatense en el Marco de la España Ilustrado: El Caso de Manuel Belgrano'. *Spagna Contemporanea*, 18 (2000): 33–47.

Pearce, Adrian. 'Rescates and Anglo-Spanish Trade during the French Revolutionary Wars, ca. 1797–1804'. *JLAS*, 38 (2006): 607–24.

Perdices Blas, Luís. *Pablo de Olavide (1725–1803): El Ilustrado*. Madrid: Editorial Complutense, 1993.

——. *La Economía Política de la Decadencia de Castilla en el Siglo XVII: Investigaciones de los Arbitristas sobre la Naturaleza y Causas de la Riqueza de las Naciones*. Madrid: Editorial Síntesis, 1996.

Pérez Paricio, Josefina. 'La Aperdida de la Isla de Trinidad'. *AEA*, 22 (1965): 1–229.

Petrie, Charles. *King Charles III of Spain: An Enlightened Despot*. London: Constable & Co. Ltd., 1971.

Pezuela, Jacobo de la. *Ensayo Histórico de la Isla de Cuba*. New York: Imprenta Española 'R. Rafael', 1842.

Phelan, John Leddy. *The People and the King: The Comunero Revolution in Colombia, 1781*. Madison: University of Wisconsin Press, 1978.

Pimentel, Juan. *La Física de la Monarquía: Ciencia y Política en el Pensamiento Colonial de Alejandro Malaspina (1754–1810)*. Madrid: Doce Calles, 1998.

Polt, John H.R. 'Jovellanos and his English Sources: Economic, Philosophical and Political Writings'. *Transactions of the American Philosophical Society*, n.s. 54, part 7 (1964): 5–68.

Ponte Domínguez, Francisco J. *Arango y Parreño: Estadista Colonial Cubano*. Havana: Molina y Cia, 1937.

Popescu, Oreste. *Studies in the History of Latin American Economic Thought*. London and New York: Routledge, 1997.

Portillo Valdés, José María. *Revolución de Nación: Orígenes de la Cultura Constitucional en España, 1780–1812*. Madrid: Centro de Estudios Políticos y Constitucionales, 2000.

Portuondo, Maria M. 'Plantation Factories: Science and Technology in Late Eighteenth-Century Cuba'. *Technology and Culture*, 44 (2003): 231–57.

Priestley, Herbert Ingram. *José de Gálvez: Visitor-General of New Spain (1765–1771)*. Berkeley: University of California Press, 1916.

Puerto Sarmiento, Francisco Javier. *La Ilusión Quebrada. Botánica, Sanidad y Política Científica en la España Ilustrada*. Madrid: CSIC, 1988.

Quiroz, Alfonso W. 'Implicit Costs of Empire: Bureaucratic Corruption in Nineteenth-Century Cuba'. *JLAS*, 35 (2003): 473–511.

Ramos Gómez, Luis J. *El Centenario de Don Antonio de Ulloa*. Seville: CSIC, 1995.

Rao, Anna María. 'Carlos de Borbón en Nápoles'. *Trienio*, 24 (1994): 5–41.

Rawlings, Helen. *Church, Religion and Society in Early Modern Spain*. New York: Palgrave Macmillan, 2002.

Razuváev, V. *Bernardo O'Higgins: Conspirador, General, Estadista*. Moscow: Editorial Progreso, 1989.

Reder Gadow, Marion. 'Teoria y Realidad en la Aplicación del Fuero de las Nuevas Poblaciones'. In *Actas VI Congreso Histórico Sobre Nuevas Poblaciones*. La Carlota: Ayuntamiento de La Carlota, 1994.

Rico Giménez, Juan. *De La Ilustración al Liberalismo: El Pensamiento de Sempere y Guarinos*. Alicante: University of Alicante, 1997.

Ringrose, David R. *Spain, Europe and the 'Spanish Miracle', 1700–1900*. Cambridge: Cambridge UP, 1996.

Rípodas Ardanaz, Daisy. *Refracción de Ideas en Hispanoamerica Colonial*. Buenos Aires: Ediciones Culturales Argentinas, 1983.

Risco, Antonio. 'Sobre la Nocion de "Academia" en el Siglo XVIII Español'. *Boletín del Centro Estudios de Siglo XVIII*, 10 (1983): 35–57.

Rodríguez Casado, Vicente. *La Política y Los Políticos en el Reinado de Carlos III*. Madrid: Ediciones Rialp, 1962.

Rodríguez Díaz, Laura. *Reforma e Ilustración en la España del Siglo XVIII*. Madrid: Fundación Universitaria Española, 1975.

Rodríguez O., Jaime E. *The Independence of Spanish America*. Cambridge: Cambridge UP, 1998.

Rodríguez Sánchez de León, María José. 'La Institución Académica en el Siglo XVIII: Sociabilidad y Quehacer Literaria'. *Cuadernos de la Ilustración y Romanticismo* [Cádiz] 8 (2000): 3–19.

Roma Ribes, Isabel. 'Libros de Muratori Traducidos al Castellano'. *Revista de Historia Moderna* [Alicante] 4 (1984): 113–48.

Romero, José Luís. *A History of Argentine Political Thought*. Trans. T.F. McGann. Stanford: Stanford University Press, 1963.

Roque Gondra, Luis. *Las Ideas Económicas de Manuel Belgrano*. 2nd edn. Buenos Aires: Universidad de Buenos Aires, 1927.

Rubio, Antonio. *La Crítica del Galicismo en España (1726–1832)*. Mexico City: Universidad Nacional Autónoma de México, 1937.

Saavedra Alías, Imaculada Arias de. 'Irlandeses en la Alta Administración Española del Siglo XVIII'. In Maria Bergoña Villar García, ed. *La Emigración Irlandesa en el Siglo XVIII*. Malaga: University of Malaga, 2000.

Salvatore, Ricardo D. 'The Strength of Markets in Latin America's Sociopolitical Discourse, 1750–1850'. *Latin American Perspectives*, 26 (1999): 22–43.

Salvucci, Linda K. 'Costumbres Viejas, "Hombres Nuevos": José de Gálvez y la Burocracia Fiscal Novohispana (1754–1800)'. *Historia Mexicana*, 33:2 (1983): 224–64.

Sánchez Agesta, Luis. *El Pensamiento Político del Despotismo Ilustrado*. Madrid: Instituto de Estudios Políticos, 1953.

Sánchez-Blanco, Francisco. *La Mentalidad Ilustrada*. Madrid: Taurus, 1999.

——. *El Absolutismo y las Luces en el Reinado de Carlos III*. Madrid: Marcial Pons, 2002.

Sánchez Bella, Ismael et al. *Historia del Derecho Indiano*. Madrid: Mapfre, 1992.

Sánchez Espinosa, Gabriel. *Las Memorias de José Nicolás de Azara. Estudio y Edición del Texto*. Berlin: Peter Lang, 1994.

——. *La Biblioteca de José Nicolás Azara*. Madrid: Real Academia de Bellas Artes de San Fernando, 1997.

Sánchez Hormigo, Alfonso. *La Cátedra de Economía Civil y Comercio de la Real Sociedad Económica Aragonesa de Amigos de País (1784–1846)*. Zaragoza: Real Sociedad Aragonesa de Amigos del País, 2003.

Sánchez Pedrote, Enrique. 'El Coronel Hodgson y la Expedición a la Costa de los Mosquitos'. *AEA*, 24 (1967): 1205–35.

Sánchez Rodríguez de Castro, Maria del Carmen. *El Real Consulado de La Coruña: Impulsar de la Ilustración (1785–1833)*. La Coruña: Ediciós do Castro, 1992.

Sarabia Viejo, Maria Justina, ed. *Europa e Iberoamérica: Cinco Siglos de Intercambios*. 3 vols. Seville: Junta de Andalucia, 1992.

Sarrailh, Jean. *La España Ilustrada de la Segunda Mitad del Siglo XVIII*. Mexico City: Fondo de Cultura Económica, 1957.

Schröter, Bernd and Karin Schülle, eds. *Tordesillas y sus Consecuencias: la Politica de las Grandes Potencias Europeas Respecto a América Latina, 1494–1898*. Madrid: IberoAmerica, 1995.

Schurz, W.L. 'The Royal Philippine Company'. *HAHR*, 3:4 (1920): 491–508.

Segura, Jorge I. *El Pensamiento Económico de Manuel Belgrano*. Mendoza: Junta de Estudios Históricos, 1953.

Shafer, Robert Jones. *The Economic Societies of the Spanish World (1763–1821)*. Syracuse: Syracuse UP, 1958.

Silva, Renán. *Los Ilustrados de Nueva Granada, 1760–1808: Genealogía de una Comunidad de Intrepretación*. Medellín: Banco de la República y Fondo Editorial Universidad EAFIT, 2002.

Smith, Robert Sidney. *The Spanish Merchant Guild: A History of the Consulado, 1250–1700*. Durham: Duke UP, 1940.

——. 'Spanish Antimercantilism of the Seventeenth Century: Alberto Struzzi and Diego José Dormer'. *Journal of Political Economy*, 48 (1940): 401–11.

——. 'The Institution of the *Consulado* in New Spain'. *HAHR*, 34:1 (1944): 61–83.

——. 'Origins of the *Consulado* of Guatemala'. *HAHR*, 26:2 (1946): 150–61.

——. 'Economists and the Enlightenment in Spain, 1750–1800'. *Journal of Political Economy*, 63 (1955): 345–8.

——. 'The *Wealth of Nations* in Spain and Hispanic America, 1780–1830'. *Journal of Political Economy*, 65:1 (1957): 104–25.

——. 'A Research Report on *Consulado* History'. *Journal of Inter-American Studies*, 3:1 (1961): 41–52.

Socolow, Susan Migden. *The Merchants of Buenos Aires, 1778–1810: Family and Commerce*. Cambridge: Cambridge UP, 1978.

——. 'Recent Historiography of the Río de la Plata: Colonial and Early National Periods'. *HAHR*, 64:1 (1984): 105–20.

——. *The Bureaucrats of Buenos Aires, 1769–1810: Amor al Real Servicio*. Durham and London: Duke UP, 1987.

Solano, Francisco de. *Antonio de Ulloa y La Nueva España*. Mexico: Universidad Nacional Autónoma de México, 1979.

Soto Arango, Diana et al, eds. *Recepción y Difusión de Textos Ilustrados: Intercambio Científico entre Europa y América en la Ilustración*. León: University of León, 2003.

Spalding, Karen, ed. *Essays in the Political, Economic and Social History of Colonial Latin America*. Newark: University of Delaware Press, 1982.

Spell, Jefferson Rea. *Rousseau in the Spanish World Before 1833: A Study in Franco-Spanish Literary Relations*. 2nd edn. New York: Gordian Press, 1969.

Stein, Stanley J. 'Bureaucracy and Business in the Spanish Empire, 1759–1804: The Failure of a Bourbon Reform in Mexico and Peru'. *HAHR*, 61 (1981): 2–28.

Stein, Stanley J. and Barbara H. *The Colonial Heritage of Latin America: Essays on Economic Independence in Perspective*. New York: Oxford UP, 1970.

——. *Silver, Trade and War: Spain and America in the Making of Early Modern Europe*. Baltimore and London: The Johns Hopkins UP, 2000.

——. *Apogee of Empire: Spain and New Spain in the Age of Charles III, 1759–1789*. Baltimore and London: The Johns Hopkins UP, 2003.

Stoetzer, O. Carlos. *The Scholastic Roots of the Spanish American Revolution*. New York: Fordham UP, 1979.

Swinburne, Henry. *Travels Through Spain in the Years 1775 and 1776*. 2nd edition. 2 vols. London, 1787.

Thomas, Hugh. *Rivers of Gold: The Rise of the the Spanish Empire, from Columbus to Magellan.* New York: Random House, 2004.

Thompson, E.A. *The Goths in Spain.* Oxford: Clarendon Press, 1969.

Tiryakian, Josefina Cintron. 'Campillo's Pragmatic New System: A Mercantile and Utilitarian Approach to Indian Reform in Spanish Colonies of the Eighteenth Century'. *History of Political Economy*, 10:2 (1978): 233–57.

Tjarks, Germán O.E. *El Consulado de Buenos Aires y sus Proyecciones en la Historia del Río de la Plata.* 2 vols. Buenos Aires: Universidad de Buenos Aires, 1962.

Tomich, Dale. 'The Wealth of Empire: Francisco Arango y Parreño, Political Economy and the Second Slavery in Cuba'. *Comparative Studies in History and Society*, 45:1 (2003): 4–28.

Tornero, Pablo. 'Emigración, Población y Esclavitud en Cuba (1765–1817)'. *AEA*, 44 (1987): 229–80.

Torres Ramirez, Bibiano. *Alejandro O'Reilly en las Indias.* Seville: CSIC, 1969.

Townsend Cummins, Light. *Spanish Observers and the American Revolution, 1775–1783.* Baton Rouge and London: Louisiana State UP, 1991.

Tudisco, Anthony. 'America in Some Travelers, Historians and Political Economists of the Spanish Eighteenth-Century'. *The Americas*, 15:1 (1958): 1–22.

Urbina Reyes, Elsa. 'El Tribunal del Consulado de Chile: Sus Origenes y Primeros Años'. *Boletín de la Academia Chilena de la Historia*, 29 (1962): 104–43.

Uribe-Uran, Victor M. 'The Birth of a Public Sphere in Latin America during the Age of Revolution'. *Comparative Studies in Society and History*, 42:2 (2000): 425–57.

Urzainqui, Inmaculada et al, eds. *La República de las Letras en la España del Siglo XVIII.* Madrid: CSIC, 1995.

Vallejo, Jesús. 'Estudio Preliminar'. In Duque de Almodóvar. *Constitución de Inglaterra.* Madrid: Centro de Estudios Políticos y Constitucionales, 2000.

Velasco Moreno, Eva. 'Las Academias de la Historia en el Siglo XVIII: Una Comparación entre Francia y España'. In *El Mundo Hispánico en el Siglo de las Luces.* Madrid: Editorial Complutense, 1996.

Venturi, Franco. 'Spanish and Italian Economists and Reformers in the Eighteenth Century'. In *Italy and the Enlightenment: Studies in a Cosmopolitan Century.* Ed. Stuart Woolf and trans. Susan Corsi. New York UP, 1972.

Villalobos R., Sergio. *Tradición y Reforma en, 1810.* Santiago: Universidad de Chile, 1961.

University of Chile. *Estudios Sobre la Época de Carlos III en el Reino de Chile.* Santiago: University of Chile, 1989.

Walker, G.J. *Spanish Politics and Imperial Trade, 1700–1789.* London and Basingstoke: Macmillan, 1979.

Weber, David J. *Bárbaros: Spaniards and their Savages in the Age of Enlightenment.* New Haven and London: Yale UP, 2005.

Whitaker, A.P. 'The Commerce of Louisiana and the Floridas at the End of the Eighteenth Century'. *HAHR*, 8:2 (1928): 190–203.

——. 'Antonio de Ulloa'. *HAHR*, 15:2 (1935): 155–94.

——. *Latin America and the Enlightenment.* Ithaca: Cornell UP, 1961.

——. 'Changing and Unchanging Interpretations of the Enlightenment in Spanish America'. *Proceedings of the American Philosophical Society*, 114:4 (1970): 256–71.

Wilhite, John F. 'The Disciples of Mutis and the Enlightenment in New Granada: Education, History and Literature'. *The Americas*, 37:2 (1980): 179–92.

Wilson, Charles. 'Geronymo de Ustariz [sic], Un Fundamento Intelectual Para el Renacimiento Económica Español del Siglo XVIII'. In Alfonso Otazu, ed. *Dinero y Crédito (Siglos XVI al XIX).* Madrid: Artes Gráficas Benzal, 1978.

Woodward Jr., Ralph Lee. *Class Privilege and Economic Development: The Consulado de Comercio of Guatemala, 1793–1871*. Chapel Hill: University of North Carolina Press, 1966.

Wortman, Miles. *Government and Society in Central America, 1680–1840*. New York: Columbia UP, 1982.

Yagüe Bosch, Javier. 'Defensa de España y Conquista de América en el Siglo XVIII: Cadalso y Forner'. *Dieciocho*, 28 (2005): 121–40.

Yun-Casalilla, Bartolomé. 'The American Empire and the Spanish Economy: An Institutional and Regional Perspective'. *Revista de Historia Económica*, 16 (1998): 123–56.

Zamora, Germán. 'La Reforma de los Estudios Filosóficos en España Bajo Carlos III: Modelos Extranjeros'. *Laurentianum* [Rome] 3 (1980): 347–75.

Mengs, Tiepolo, and Aesthetics in Spain

Barcham, William L. *Giambattista Tiepolo*. London: Thames & Hudson Ltd., 1992.

Carrete y Parrando, Juan. 'Pedro Rodríguez Campomanes: Informes Sobre la Real Academia de Bellas Artes de San Fernando'. *Revista de Ideas Estéticas*, 137 (1977): 75–90.

Crivellato, Valentino. *Tiepolo*. Trans. Anthony Rhodes. London: Weidenfeld and Nicolson, 1962.

De Ceballos, Alfonso Rodríguez G. *El Siglo XVIII: Entre Tradición y Academia*. Madrid: Silax, 1992.

Fabre, Francisco José. *Descripción de las Alegorías Pintadas en las Bóvedas del Real Palacio de Madrid*. Madrid, 1829.

Jones, Leslie. 'Peace, Prosperity and Politics in Tiepolo's *Glory of the Spanish Monarchy*'. *Apollo*, 114 (1981): 220–7.

Levey, Michael. *Rococo to Revolution: Major Trends in Eighteenth-Century Painting*. London: Thames and Hudson, 1967.

Mengs, Anthony Raphael. *The Works of Anthony Raphael Mengs*. Trans. from the Italian *Published by Don Joseph Nicolás D'Azara*. 2 vols. London, 1796.

Mulvey, Jeremy. 'Palace Decoration at the Spanish Bourbon Court during the Eighteenth Century'. *Apollo*, (1981): 228–35.

Pelzel, Thomas. A.R. *Anton Raphael Mengs and Neoclassicism*. New York: Taylor and Francis, 1979.

Polt, J.H.R. 'Anton Raphael Mengs in Spanish Literature'. In Jordi Aladro-Font, ed. *Homenaje a Don Luis Monguío*. Newark: Juan de la Cuesta, 1997.

Potts, Alex. *Flesh and the Ideal: Winckelmann and the Origins of Art History*. New York and London: Yale UP, 1994.

Sánchez Canton, F.J. *J.B. Tiepolo en España*. Madrid: Instituto Diego Velázquez del CSIC, 1953.

Urrea Fernández, Jesús. *La Pintura Italiana del Siglo XVIII España*. Valladolid: University of Valladolid, 1977.

Whistler, Catherine. 'G.B. Tiepolo and Charles III: The Church of S. Pascual Baylon at Aranjuez'. *Apollo*, 121 (1985): 321–7.

——. 'G.B. Tiepolo at the Court of Charles III'. *Burlington Magazine*, 128 (1986): 199–203.

Winckelmann, Johann Joachim. *Reflections on the Painting and Sculpture of the Greeks*. Trans. Henry Fuseli. London: Routledge, 1999.

Wittkower, R. 'Imitation, Eclecticism and Genius'. In E.R. Wasserman, ed. *Aspects of the Eighteenth Century*. London: Oxford UP, 1965.

Enlightened Absolutism and State-Building in Early Modern Europe

Alcázar Molina, Cayetano. 'El Despotismo Ilustrado en España'. *Bulletin of the International Committee of the Historical Sciences*, 5 (1933): 727–51.

Anderson, Perry. *Lineages of the Absolutist State*. London: Verso, 1974.

Anderson, M.S. *Historians and Eighteenth-Century Europe, 1715–1789*. Oxford: Clarendon Press, 1979.

Beales, Derek. *Enlightenment and Reform in Eighteenth-century Europe*. London and New York: I.B. Tauris, 2005.

Blanning, T.C.W. *Joseph II and Enlightened Despotism*. London: Longman, 1970.

——. *Reform and Revolution in Mainz, 1743–1803*. Cambridge: Cambridge UP, 1974.

Bodin, Jean. *On Sovereignty*. Ed. and trans. Julian H. Franklin. Cambridge: Cambridge UP, 1992.

Bonney, Richard. 'Absolutism: What's in a Name?'. *French History*, 1:1 (1987): 93–117.

——. *The Limits of Absolutism in Ancien Regime France*. Brookfield: Ashgate, 1995.

Brewer, John and Ekhart Hellmuth, eds. *Rethinking Leviathan: The Eighteenth-Century State in Britain and Germany*. Oxford: Oxford UP, 1999.

Bruun, Geoffrey. *The Enlightened Despots*. New York: Henry Holt and Co., 1929.

Burke, Peter. *The Fabrication of Louis XIV*. New Haven and London: Yale UP, 1992.

Clark, Samuel. *State and Status: The Rise of the State and Aristocratic Power in Western Europe*. London and Montreal: McGill-Queen's UP, 1995.

Downing, Brian M. *The Military Revolution and Political Change: The Origins of Democracy and Autocracy in Early Modern Europe*. Princeton: Princeton UP, 1992.

Ertman, Thomas. *Birth of the Leviathan: Building States and Regimes in Medieval and Early Modern Europe*. Cambridge: Cambridge UP, 1997.

Franklin, Julian H. *Jean Bodin and the Rise of Absolutist Theory*. Cambridge: Cambridge UP, 1973.

Gagliardo, John G. *Enlightened Despotism*. New York: Harlan Davidson, 1967.

Hartüng, Fritz. *Enlightened Despotism*. Trans. H. Otto and G. Barraclough. London: Routledge and Kegan Paul, 1957.

Henshall, Nicholas. *The Myth of Absolutism: Change and Continuity in Early Modern European Monarchy*. New York and London: Longman, 1992.

Keohane, Nanner L.O. *Philosophy and the State in France: The Renaissance to the Enlightenment*. Princeton: Princeton UP, 1980.

Kimmel, Michael S. *Absolutism and its Discontents: State and Society in Seventeenth-century France and England*. New Brunswick: Transaction Books, 1988.

Koebner, R. 'Despot and Despotism: Vicissitudes of a Political Term'. *Journal of the Warburg and Courtauld Institutes*, 14 (1951): 275–302.

Lhéritier, Michel. 'Le Rôle Historique de Despotisme Éclairé, Particulièrement au XVIIIe Siècle'. *Bulletin of the International Committee of the Historical Sciences*, 1 (1928): 601–12.

Miller, John, ed. *Absolutism in Seventeenth Century Europe*. New York: St. Martin's Press, 1990.

Parker, David. *The Making of French Absolutism*. London: Edward Arnold, 1983.

Parker, Geoffrey. *Empire, War and Faith in Early Modern Europe*. London: Allen Lane, 2002.

Phelan. 'Authority and Flexibility in the Spanish Imperial Bureaucracy'. *Administrative Science Quarterly*, 5 (1960): 47–65.

Raeff, Marc. *The Well-Ordered Police State: Social and Institutional Change through Law in the Germanies and Russia*. New Haven and London: Yale UP, 1983.

Rees Jones, Ricardo. *El Despotismo Ilustrado y Los Intendantes de la Nueva España*. Mexico City: Universidad Nacional Autónoma de México, 1983.

Scott, H.M., ed. *Enlightened Absolutism: Reform and Reformers in Late Eighteenth-Century Europe*. Basingstoke: Macmillan, 1990.

Shennan, J.H. *The Origins of the Modern European State, 1450–1725*. London: Hutchinson Library, 1974.

——. *Liberty and Order in Early Modern Europe: The Subject and the State, 1650–1800*. London: Longman, 1986.

Thomson, Janice E. *Mercenaries, Pirates and Sovereigns: State-Building and Extra-territorial Violence in Early Modern Europe*. Princeton: Princeton UP, 1994.

Tocqueville, Alexis de. *The Old Régime and the French Revolution*. Trans. Stuart Gilbert. Garden City: Doubleday Anchor Books, 1955.

Tuck, Richard. *Natural Rights Theories*. Cambridge: Cambridge UP, 1979.

Wines, Roger, ed. *Enlightened Despotism: Reform or Reaction?* Boston: D.C. Heath and Co., 1967.

Regalism, Religion, and Law

Primary printed sources:

Azara, José Nicolás de. *El Espíritu de Don José Nicolás de Azara, Descubierto en su Correspondencia Epistolary con Don Manuel de Roda*. 3 vols. Madrid 1846.

León Tello, Francisco José. 'Retrato Histórico y Elogio Fúnebre de Cavallero Don Josef Nicolás de Azara'. In *Tratadistas Españoles de Arte en Italia en el Siglo XVIII*. Madrid: University Complutense, 1981.

Bossuet, Jacques-Benigne. *Politics Drawn from the Very Words of Holy Scripture*. Trans. and ed. Patrick Riley. Cambridge: Cambridge UP, 1999.

Dante. *Monarchy*. Trans. and ed. Prue Shaw. Cambridge: Cambridge UP, 1996.

Giannone, Pietro. *Dell'istoria Civile del Regno di Napoli* (On the Civil History of the Kingdom of Naples). Trans. James Ogilvie. London, 1729–30.

Marsiglio of Padua. *Writings on Empire: Defensor Minor*. Ed. Cary J. Nederman. Cambridge: Cambridge UP, 1993.

Rodríguez Campomanes, Pedro. *Tratado de la Regalía de Amortización*. Madrid, 1765.

——. *Dictamen Fiscal de Expulsión de los Jesuitas de Espana (1766–67)*. Ed. Jorge Cejuda and Teofanes Egido. Madrid: Fundación Universitaria Española, 1977.

——. *Juicio Imparcial Sobre Las Letras En Forma de Breve, que Ha Publicado La Curia Romana, en que se Intentan Derogar Ciertos Edictos del Serenisimo Señor Infante Duque de Parma y Disputarla la Soberanía Temporal con este Pretexto*. Madrid, 1768.

Secondary sources:

Aston, Nigel. *Christianity and Revolutionary Europe, 1750–1830*. Cambridge: Cambridge UP, 2002.

Batllori, Miguel. 'La Expulsión de los Jesuitas y el Jurisdiccionalismo Antirromano: Raíces Napolitanas y Austracistas'. In *Carlos III y la Ilustración*. Ed. Ministerio de Cultura. 2 vols. Madrid: Ministerio de Cultura, 1988.

Benlloch Poveda, Antonio. 'Antecedentes Doctrinales del Regalismo Borbónico: Juristas Españoles en las Lecturas de los Regalistas Europeos Modernos'. *Revista de Historia Moderna* [Alicante] 4 (1984): 293–322.

Berman, H.J. *Law and Revolution: The Formation of the Western Legal Tradition*. London and Cambridge, MA: Harvard UP, 1983.

Brading D.A. *Church and State in Bourbon Mexico. The Diocese of Michocán, 1749–1810*. Cambridge: Cambridge UP, 1994.

——. 'The Catholic Monarchy'. In Serge Gruzinski and Nathan Wachtel, eds. *Le Nouveau Monde: Mondes Nouveaux. L'Experience Americaine*. Paris: EHESS, 1996.

Brundage, James A. *Medieval Canon Law*. London and New York: Longman, 1995.

Cañeque, Alejandro. *The King's Living Image: The Culture and Politics of Viceregal Power in Colonial Mexico*. New York and London: Routledge, 2004.

Corona Baratech, Carlos E. *José Nicolás de Azara: Un Embajador Español en Roma*. Zaragoza: Institucion 'Fernando el Católico', 1948.

Coronas González, Santos M. *Ilustración y Derecho: Los Fiscales del Consejo de Castilla en el Siglo XVIII*. Madrid: Ministerio para las Administraciones Publicas, 1992.

De Egaña, Antonio. *La Teoría del Regio Vicariato Español en Indias*. Rome: Gregorian University, 1958.

De la Hera, Alberto. *El Regalismo Borbónico en su Proyección Indiana*. Madrid: Ediciones Rialp, S.A., 1963.

——. 'Notas Para el Estudio del Regalismo Español en el Siglo XVIII'. *AEA*, 31 (1974): 409–40.

Díaz de Cerio, Franco. 'Jansenismo Histórico y Regalismo Borbónico Español a Finales de Siglo XVIII'. *Hispania Sacra*, 33 (1981): 93–116.

Farriss, Nancy. *Crown and Clergy in Colonial Mexico, 1759–1821: The Crisis of Ecclesiastical Privilege*. London: Athlone Press, 1968.

Harding, Alan. *Medieval Law and the Foundations of the State*. Oxford: Oxford UP, 2002.

Hsia, R. Po-Chia. *The World of Catholic Renewal, 1540–1770*. Cambridge: Cambridge UP, 1998.

Marti Gilabert, Francisco. *Iglesia y Estado en el Reinado de Fernando VII*. Pamplona: University of Navarra, 1994.

Martín, Isidoro. 'Panorama del Regalismo Español hasta la Vigente Concordato de 1953'. *Revista de la Facultad de Derecho de la Universidad de Madrid*, 5 (1961): 279–303.

Martiré, Eduardo. 'Guión Sobre el Proceso Recopilador de las Leyes de Indias'. In Francisco de Icaza DuFour, ed. *Recopilación de Leyes de los Reynos de las Indias: Estudios Historicos-Juridicos*. Mexico City: Miguel Angel Porrúa, 1987.

Mecham, J. Lloyd. *Church and State in Latin America: A History of Politico-Ecclesiastical Relations*. Revised edition. Chapel Hill: University of North Carolina Press, 1966.

Mestre Sanchis, Antonio. *Despotismo y Ilustración en España*. Barcelona: Editorial Ariel, 1976.

Miguélez, Manuel. *Jansenismo y Regalismo en España*. Valladolid, 1895.

Miller, Samuel J. *Portugal and Rome, c. 1748–1830: An Aspect of the Catholic Enlightenment*. Rome: Gregorian University, 1978

Moxó, Salvador de. 'Un Medievalista en el Consejo de Hacienda: Don Francisco Carrasco, Marques de la Corona (1715–1791)'. *AHDE*, 29 (1959): 609–68.

Muldoon, James. *Canon Law, the Expansion of Europe, and World Order*. Aldershot: Ashgate Variorum, 1998.

Noel, Charles C. 'Opposition to Enlightened Reform in Spain: Campomanes and the Clergy, 1765–1775'. *Societas*, (1973): 21–43.

——. 'The Clerical Confrontation with the Enlightenment in Spain'. *European Studies Review*, 5:2 (1975): 103–22.

——. 'The Crisis of 1758–1759 in Spain: Sovereignty and Power during a "Species of Interregnum"'. In Robert Oresko, G.C. Gibbs and H.M. Scott, eds. *Royal and Republican Sovereignty in Early Modern Europe: Essays in Memory of Ragnhild Hatton*. Cambridge: Cambridge UP, 1997.

Olaechea, Rafael. *Las Relaciones Hispano-Romanas en la Segunda Mitad del Siglo XVIII: La Agencia de Preces*. 2 vols. Zaragoza: El Noticiero, 1965.

——. 'Relaciones entre Iglesia y Estado en el Siglo de las Luces'. In José Antonio Ferrer Benimeli, ed. *Relaciones Iglesia-Estado en Campomanes*. Madrid: Fundación Universitaria Española, 2002.

Pinedo, Isidoro. *Manuel de Roda. Su Pensamiento Regalista*. Zaragoza: Institución 'Fernando el Católico', 1981.

Pruna Goodgall, Pedro M. *Los Jesuitas en Cuba hasta 1767*. Havana: Editorial de Ciencias Sociales, 1991.

Rodríguez Casado, Vincente. 'Iglesia y Estado en el Reinado de Carlos III'. *Estudios Americanos*, 1 (1948): 5–57.

Sanchez Bella, Ismael. *Iglesia y Estado en la América Española*. Pamplona: Universidad de Navarra, SA, 1991.

Scott, H.M. 'Religion and *Realpolitik*: The Duc de Choiseul, the Bourbon Family Compact and the Attack on the Society of Jesus, 1758–1775'. *International History Review*, 25:1 (2003): 37–62.

Sheehan, Jonathan. 'Enlightenment, Religion and the Enigma of Secularization: A Review Essay'. *American Historical Review*, 108:4 (2003): 1061–80.

Shiels, W. Eugene. *King and Church: The Rise and Fall of Patronato Real*. Chicago: Loyola UP, 1961.

Téllez Alarcia, Diego. 'Guerra y Regalismo a Comienzos del Reinado de Carlos III: El Final del Ministerio Wall'. *Hispania*, 61:3 (2001): 1051–90.

Teófanes Egido. 'El Regalismo y las Relaciones Iglesia-Estado en el Siglo XVIII'. In *Historia de la Iglesia en España. Volume 4: Siglos XVII-XVIII*. Ed. Antonio Mestre Sanchis. Madrid: Biblioteca de Autores Cristianos, 1979.

Tomas y Valiente, Francisco. *Manual de Historia del Derecho Español*. 4th edn. Madrid: Tecnos, 2002.

Ullmann, Walter. *The Growth of Papal Government in the Middle Ages: A Study of the Ideological Relation of Clerical to Lay Power*. London: Methuen, 1962.

Van Kley, Dale. *The Jansenists and the Expulsion of the Jesuits from France, 1757–1765*. London and New Haven: Yale UP, 1975.

Ward, W.R. *Christianity Under the Ancien Régime, 1648–1789*. Cambridge: Cambridge UP, 1999.

Naples

Acton, Harold. *The Bourbons of Naples, 1734–1825*. London: Methuen and Co Ltd, 1974.

Chorley, Patrick. *Oil Silk and Enlightenment: Economic Problems in XVIII century Naples*. Naples: Instituto Italiano per gli Studi Storici, 1965.

Croce, Benedetto. *History of the Kingdom of Naples*. Ed. H. Stuart Hughes. Trans. Francis Frenaye. Chicago and London: University of Chicago Press, 1970.

Di Pinto, Mario, ed. *I Borbone di Napoli e I Borbone de Spagna*. Napoli: Guida Editori, 1985.

Ferrone, Vincenzo. *The Intellectual Roots of the Italian Enlightenment: Newtonian Science, Religion and Politics in the Early Eighteenth Century*. Trans. Sue Brothertone. Atlantic Highlands: Humanities Press, 1995.

Imbruglia, Girolamo, ed. *Naples in the Eighteenth Century: The Birth and Death of a Nation State*. Cambridge: Cambridge UP, 2000.

Reinert, Sophus A. 'Blaming the Medici: Footnotes, Falsification and the Fate of the "English Model" in Eighteenth-Century Italy'. *History of European Ideas*, 32 (2006): 430–55.

Richard Bellamy, '"Da metafisico a mercatante"—Antonio Genovesi and the Development of a New Language of Commerce in Eighteenth-Century Naples'. In

Anthony Pagden, ed. *The Languages of Political Theory in Early-Modern Europe.* Cambridge: Cambridge UP, 1987.

Robertson, John. 'Antonio Genovesi: The Neapolitan Enlightenment and Political Economy'. *History of Political Thought*, 8 (1987): 335–44.

——. 'The Enlightenment Above National Context: Political Economy in Eighteenth-Century Scotland and Naples'. *Historical Journal*, 40 (1997): 667–97.

Rosa, Luigi de. 'Immobility and Change in Public Finance in the Kingdom of Naples, 1699–1806'. *Journal of European Economic History*, 27 (1998): 9–28.

Stone, Harold Samuel. *Vico's Cultural History: The Production and Transmission of Ideas in Naples, 1685–1750.* Leiden and New York: E.J. Brill, 1997.

Venturi, Franco. 'History and Reform in the Middle of the Eighteenth Century'. In J.H. Elliott and H.G. Koenigsberger, eds. *The Diversity of History: Essays in Honour of Sir Herbert Butterfield.* London: Routledge and Kegan Paul, 1970.

——. *Italy and the Enlightenment: Studies in a Cosmopolitan Century.* Ed. Stuart Woolf. Trans. Susan Corsi. New York: NYU Press, 1972.

——. 'Church and Reform in Enlightenment Italy: The Sixties of the Eighteenth Century'. *Journal of Modern History*, 48 (1976): 215–32.

Britain and its empire

Primary sources:

Blaquiere, Edward. *Anecdotes of the Spanish and Portuguese Revolutions.* London, 1822.

Burke, William. *South American Independence: Or, the Emancipation of South America, the Glory and Interest of England.* London, 1807.

Burke, William. *Additional Reasons, for Our Immediate Emancipation of Spanish America.* London, 1808.

Cary, John. *An Essay on the State of England, in Relation to Trade, its Poor and Its Taxes for Carrying on the Present War Against France.* Bristol, 1695.

[Child, Sir Josiah]. *A Discourse about Trade.* London, 1668, 1690.

Clarke, Edward. *Letters Concerning the Spanish Nation.* London, 1763.

Coke, Roger. *A Discourse of Trade.* London, 1670.

Davenant, Charles. *An Essay Upon the Ways and Means of Supplying the War.* London, 1695.

——. *Discourse on the Public Revenues and on the Trade of England.* 2 parts. London, 1698.

——. *Essays Upon Peace at Home and War Abroad.* 2 parts. London, 1704.

[Gee, Joshua]. *The Trade and Navigation of Great Britain Considered.* London, 1729.

King, Charles. *The British Merchant; or, Commerce Preserv'd.* London, 1721.

Mun, Thomas. *A Discourse on Trade Unto the East Indies.* London, 1621.

——. *England's Treasure by Forraign Trade or, the Balance of our Forraign Trade is the Rule of our Treasure.* London, 1664.

Petty, William. *Political Arithmetick, or a Discourse.* London, 1691.

Robertson, William. *The History of America,* [1777]. 6th edn, 3 vols. London: A. Strahan, 1792.

——. *The History of America* [Books 9 &10]. London: Thoemmes Press, 1996.

Smith, Adam. *Investigación de la Naturaleza y Causas de la Riqueza de las Naciones.* Trans. Josef Alonso Ortiz. Valladolid, 1794.

Townsend, Joseph. *A Journey Through Spain in the Years 1786 and 1787.* 2nd edn, 3 vols. London, 1792.

Trevers, Joseph. *An Essay to Restoring Our Decayed Trade.* London, 1675.

Walton, William. *An Exposé on the Dissentions of Spanish America.* London, 1814.

Wood, William. *A Survey of Trade in Four Parts.* London, 1718.

Secondary sources:

Anderson, Gary and R.D. Tollison. 'Apologiae for Chartered Monopolies in Foreign Trade, 1600–1800'. *History of Political Economy*, 15:4 (1983): 549–65.

Armitage, David. *The Ideological Origins of the British Empire*. Cambridge: Cambridge UP, 2000.

Armytage, Frances. *The Free Port System in the British West Indies: A Study in Commercial Policy, 1766–1822*. London and New York: Longman, Green and Co., 1953.

Bayly, C.A. *Imperial Meridian: The British Empire and the World, 1780–1830*. London: Longman, 1989.

Bowen, H.V. *Revenue and Reform: The Indian Problem in British Politics, 1757–1773*. Cambridge: Cambridge UP, 1991.

Brown, Stewart J., ed. *William Robertson and the Expansion of Empire*. Cambridge: Cambridge UP, 1997.

Brown, V.L. 'Anglo-Spanish Relations in America in the Closing Years of the Colonial Era'. *HAHR*, 5:3 (1922): 329–482.

Christelow, Allan. 'The Economic Background of the Anglo-Spanish War of 1762'. *Journal of Modern History*, 18 (1946): 22–36.

——. 'Great Britain and the Trade from Cádiz and Lisbon to Spanish America and Brazil, 1759–1783'. *HAHR*, 29:1 (1947): 2–29.

Conn, Stetson. *Gibraltar in British Diplomacy in the Eighteenth Century*. New Haven: Yale UP, 1942.

Dickinson, H.T., ed. *Britain and the American Revolution*. London and New York: Longman, 1990.

Drayton, Richard. *Nature's Government: Science, Imperial Britain and the 'Improvement' of the World*. New Haven and London: Yale UP, 2000.

Ehrman, J. *The British Government and Commercial Negotiations in Europe, 1783–1793*. Cambridge: Cambridge UP, 1962.

Fabel, Robin F.A. *Bombast and Broadsides: The Lives of George Johnstone*. Tuscaloosa and London: University of Alabama Press, 1987.

——. *The Economy of British West Florida, 1763–1783*. Tuscaloosa and London: University of Alabama Press, 1988.

Goebel, Julius. *The Struggle for the Falkland Islands: A Study in Legal and Diplomatic History*. New Haven: Yale UP, 1982.

Gold, Robert L. *Borderland Empires in Transition: The Triple-Nation Transfer of Florida*. London and Amsterdam: Feffer and Simons, 1969.

Harlow, Vincent T. *The Founding of the Second British Empire, 1763–1793*. 2 vols. London: Longman, Green and Co., 1952.

Hont, Istvan. 'Free Trade and the Economic Limits to National Politics: Neo-Machiavellian Political Economy Reconsidered'. In John Dunn, ed. *The Economic Limits to Modern Politics*. Cambridge: Cambridge UP, 1990.

Humphreys, R.A. 'William Robertson and his *History of America*'. In *Tradition and Revolt in Latin America and Other Essays*. London: Athlone Press, 1969.

Köntler, Lazlo. 'William Robertson and his German Audience on European and Non-European Civilisation'. *Scottish Historical Review*, 80:1 (2001): 63–89.

Marshall, P.J. and Glyndwr Williams. *The Great Map of Mankind: British Perceptions of the World in the Age of Enlightenment*. London: J.M. Dent and Sons, 1982.

Miller, Rory. *Britain and Latin America in the Nineteenth and Twentieth Centuries*. London and New York: Longman Books, 1993.

O'Brien, Karen. 'Between Enlightenment and Stadial History: William Robertson and the History of Europe'. *British Journal for Eighteenth Century Studies*, 16 (1993): 53–63.

———. *Narratives of Enlightenment: Cosmopolitan History from Voltaire to Gibbon.* Cambridge: Cambridge UP, 1997.

Oz-Salzberger, Fania. *Translating the Enlightenment: Scottish Civic Discourse in Eighteenth-Century Germany.* Clarendon: Oxford UP, 1995.

Paquette, Gabriel. 'The Image of Imperial Spain in British Political Thought, 1750–1800'. *Bulletin of Spanish Studies,* 81:2 (2004): 187–214.

———. 'The Intellectual Context of British Diplomatic Recognition of the South American Republics, c. 1800–1830'. *Journal of Transatlantic Studies,* 2:1 (2004): 75–95.

Stokes, Eric. *The English Utilitarians and India.* Oxford: Clarendon Press, 1959.

Taft Manning, Helen. *British Colonial Government after the American Revolution, 1782–1820.* New Haven: Yale UP, 1933.

Van Alstyne, Richard. *Empire and Independence: The International History of the American Revolution.* New York: Wiley & Sons, 1965.

Winn, Peter. 'British Informal Empire in Uruguay in the Nineteenth Century'. *Past & Present,* 73 (1976): 100–26.

General Enlightenment and Eighteenth-Century Sources

Armitage, David and M.J. Braddick, eds. *The British Atlantic World, 1500–1800.* London: Palgrave Macmillan, 2002.

Bailyn, Bernard. 'The Idea of Atlantic History'. *Itinerario,* 20:1 (1996): 19–44.

Black, Jeremy. *Eighteenth Century Europe, 1700–1784.* London: Macmillan, 1990.

Blanning, T.C.W. *The Culture of Power and the Power of Culture: Old Regime Europe, 1660–1789.* New York: Oxford UP, 2002.

Blussé, Leonard and Femme Gaastra, eds. *Companies and Trade: Essays in Overseas Trading Companies During the Ancien Régime.* Leiden: Martinus Nijhoff/ Leiden UP, 1981.

Brewer, Anthony. 'The Concept of Growth in Eighteenth-Century Economics'. *History of Political Economy,* 27:4 (1995): 609–38.

Burns, J.H., ed. *The Cambridge History of Medieval Political Thought, c. 350–c. 1450.* Cambridge. Cambridge UP, 1988.

Carvalho e Melo, Sebastião de. *Escritos Económicos de Londres (1741–1742).* Ed. José Bareto. Lisbon: Biblioteca Nacional, 1986.

Cassirer, Ernst. *The Philosophy of Enlightenment.* Trans. Fritz C.A. Koelln and J.P. Pettegrove. Boston: Beacon Press, 1962.

Cheney, Paul. 'Finances, Philosophical History and the "Empire of Climate": Enlightenment Historiography and Political Economy'. *Historical Reflections,* 31 (2005): 141–67.

Crocker, Lester G. 'Interpreting the Enlightenment: A Political Approach'. *Journal of the History of Ideas,* 46:2 (1985): 211–30.

Evans, R.J.W. *The Making of the Habsburg Monarchy, 1550–1700: An Interpretation.* Oxford: Clarendon Press, 1979.

Fox-Genovese, Elizabeth. *The Origins of Physiocracy: Economic Revolution and Social Order in Eighteenth-Century France.* Ithaca and London: Cornell UP, 1976.

Gaspar, D.B. and David Geggus, eds. *A Turbulent Time: The French Revolution and the Greater Caribbean.* Bloomington: Indiana UP, 1997.

Gay, Peter. *The Enlightenment: An Interpretation. Vol. I: The Rise of Modern Paganism.* London: Weidenfeld and Nicolson, 1967.

———. *The Enlightenment: An Interpretation. Vol. II: The Science of Freedom.* London: Weidenfeld and Nicolson, 1970.

Grieder, Josephine. *Anglomania in France, 1740–1789: Fact, Fiction and Political Discourse.* Geneva and Paris: Librairie Droz, 1985.

Hampson, Norman. *The Enlightenment.* The Pelican History of European Thought, Vol. IV. Harmondsworth: Penguin, 1968.

Himmelfarb, Gertrude. *The Roads to Modernity: The British, French and American Enlightenments.* New York: Alfred Knopf, 2004.

Hof, Ulrich Im. *The Enlightenment.* Trans. W.G. Tuill. Oxford and Cambridge, MA: Blackwell, 1994.

Hont, Istvan. *Jealousy of Trade: International Competition and the Nation-State in Historical Perspective.* Cambridge, MA: Harvard UP, 2005.

Hutchinson, Terence. *Before Adam Smith: The Emergence of Political Economy, 1662–1776.* Oxford and New York: Basil Blackwell, 1988.

Irving, Dallas D. 'The Abbé Raynal and British Humanitarianism'. *Journal of Modern History,* 3 (1931): 564–77.

Iverson, John. 'Introduction to "Forum: Emulation in France, 1750–1800"'. *Eighteenth-Century Studies,* 36:2 (2003): 217–22.

Jordanova, Ludmilla. 'The Authoritarian Response'. In Jordanova and Peter Hulme, eds. *The Enlightenment and its Shadows.* London and New York: Routledge, 1990.

Keane, John. *Civil Society: Old Images, New Visions.* Cambridge: Polity Press, 1998.

Lowenthal, David. 'Colonial Experiments in French Guiana, 1760–1800'. *HAHR,* 32:1 (1952): 22–43.

Lüsebrink, Hans-Jürgen and Manfred Tietz. *Lectures de Raynal: l'Histoire des Deux Indes en Europe et en Amérique au XVIII Siècle.* Studies in Voltaire and the Eighteenth Century 286. Oxford: The Voltaire Foundation and the Taylor Institution, 1991.

Manuel, Frank. *The Age of Reason.* Ithaca: Cornell UP, 1951.

Maxwell, Kenneth. "The Atlantic in the Eighteenth Century: A Southern Perspective on the Need to Return to the "Big Picture"', *Transactions of the Royal Historical Society,* 6th series (1993), Cambridge: Cambridge UP.

——. *Pombal: Paradox of the Enlightenment.* Cambridge: Cambridge UP, 1995.

McNally, David. *Political Economy and the Rise of Capitalism: A Reinterpretation.* Berkeley and London: University of California Press, 1988.

Meek, R.L. *The Economics of Physiocracy: Essays and Translations.* London: George Allen and Unwin Ltd., 1962.

——. *Precursors of Adam Smith.* London: Dent, 1973.

Montesquieu, Charles de Secondat (Baron de). *Persian Letters.* Trans. C.J. Betts. London: Penguin Books, 1973.

——. *The Spirit of the Laws.* Trans. and ed. A.M. Cohler, B.C. Miller, and A.S. Stone. Cambridge: Cambridge UP, 1997.

Munck, Thomas. *The Enlightenment: A Comparative Social History, 1721–1794.* London: Arnold Publishers, 2000.

Muthu, Sankar. *Enlightenment against Empire.* Princeton and Oxford: Princeton UP, 2003.

Nuix, D. Giovanni. *Riflessioni Imparziali Sopra l'Umanità degli Spagnuoli nell'Indie Contro i Pretesi Filosofi e Politici per Servire de Lume alle Storie de' Signori Raynal e Robertson.* Venice, 1780.

Outram, Dorinda. *The Enlightenment.* New Approaches to European History 7. Cambridge: Cambridge UP, 1995.

Pocock, J.G.A. *Barbarism and Religion. Vol. 2: Narratives of Civil Government.* Cambridge: Cambridge UP, 1999.

——. 'Enlightenment and Counter-Enlightenment, Revolution and Counter-revolution: A Eurosceptical Enquiry'. *History of Political Thought,* 20:1 (1999): 125–39.

Porter, Roy. *Enlightenment: Britain and the Creation of the Modern World.* London: Allen Lane, 2000.

Raynal, Guillaume-Thomas François. *A Philosophical and Political History of the Settlements and Trade of the Europeans in the East and West Indies.* Trans. J.O. Justamond. 3rd edn, 4 vols. Dublin, 1779.

Robertson, John. *The Case for the Enlightenment: Scotland and Naples, 1680–1760*. Cambridge: Cambridge UP, 2005.

Rothschild, Emma. 'Commerce and the State: Turgot, Condorcet and Smith'. *The Economic Journal*, 102 (1992): 1197–210.

——. 'Social Security and Laissez-Faire in Eighteenth-Century Political Economy'. *Population and Development Review*, 21:4 (1995): 711–44.

——. *Economic Sentiments: Smith, Condorcet and the Enlightenment*. Cambridge, MA: Harvard UP, 2001.

——. 'Global Commerce and the Question of Sovereignty in the Eighteenth-Century Provinces'. *Modern Intellectual History*, 1:1 (2004): 3–25.

Rudé, George. *Europe in the Eighteenth Century: Aristocracy and Bourgeois Challenge*. London: Weidenfeld and Nicolson, 1972.

Schui, Florian. 'Prussia's "Trans-Oceanic" Moment: The Creation of a Prussian Asiatic Trade Company in 1751'. *Historical Journal*, 49 (2006): 143–60.

Scott, H.M. *The Birth of a Great Power System, 1740–1815*. Harlow: Pearson Education, 2006.

Shovlin, John. 'Emulation in Eighteenth-Century French Economic Thought'. *Eighteenth-Century Studies*, 36:2 (2003): 224–30.

Small, Albion W. *The Cameralists: The Pioneers of German Social Policy*. Chicago: University of Chicago Press, 1909.

Spengler, Joseph J. *French Predecessors to Malthus: A Study in Eighteenth-Century Wage and Population Theory*. Durham: Duke UP, 1942.

Subirats, Eduardo. *La Ilustración Insuficiente*. Madrid: Taurus Ediciones, 1981.

Tomaselli, Sylvana. 'Moral Philosophy and Population Questions in Eighteenth-Century Europe'. In *Population and Resources in Western Intellectual Traditions*. Ed. Michael Teitelbaum and J.M. Winter. Cambridge: Cambridge UP, 1988.

Tribe, Keith. *Land, Labour and Economic Discourse*. London: Routledge and Kegan Paul, 1978.

——. 'Cameralism and the Science of Government'. *Journal of Modern History*, 56:2 (1984): 263–84.

——. *Governing Economy: The Reformation of German Economic Discourse, 1750–1840*. Cambridge: Cambridge UP, 1988.

Venturi, Franco. *The End of the Old Regime in Europe, 1776–1789. Vol. I: The Great States of the West*. Trans. R.B. Litchfield. Princeton: Princeton UP, 1991.

Westergaard, Waldemar. *The Danish West Indies Under Company Rule (1671–1754)*. New York: Macmillan, 1917.

Whelan, F.G. 'Population and Ideology in the Enlightenment'. *History of Political Thought*, 12:1 (1991): 35–72.

Winch, Donald. *Classical Political Economy and the Colonies*. London: London School of Economics & Political Science, 1965.

Womack, William R. 'Eighteenth-Century Themes in the *Histoire Philosophique et Politique des Deux Indes* of Guillaume Raynal'. *Studies in Voltaire and the Eighteenth Century*, 96 (1972): 129–263.

Miscellaneous

Reference:

Carande y Tovar, Ramón. 'Catálogo de la Colección de MSS e Impresos de Ciencias Económicas y Jurídicas de Don Juan Sempere y Guarinos'. *BRAH*, 136 (1955): 247–313.

Cejudo López, Jorge. *Catálogo del Archivo del Conde de Campomanes (Fondos Carmen Dorado y Rafael Gasset)*. Madrid: Fundación Universitaría Española, 1975.
Domíngue Bordona, Jesús. *Catálogo de la Biblioteca de Palacio. Tomo IX: Manuscritos de América*. Madrid: Palacio Real, 1935.
Fernández Duro, Cesareo. *Noticia Breve de las Cartas y Planos Existentes en la Biblioteca Particular de S.M. El Rey* (may be consulted at the BPR).
Gómez de Enterría, Josefa. *Voces de la Economía y el Comercio en el Español del Siglo XVIII*. Alcalá: Universidad de Alcalá, 1996.
Yolton, J.W. et al. *The Blackwell Companion to the Enlightenment*. Oxford: Blackwell, 1992.

General:

Appleby, Joyce Oldham. *Economic Thought and Ideology in Seventeenth-Century England*. Princeton: Princeton UP, 1978.
Armitage, David. 'The Fifty Years' Rift: Intellectual History and International Relations'. *Modern Intellectual History*, 1:1 (2004): 97–109.
Ball, Terence, James Farr and R.L. Hanson, eds. *Political Innovation and Conceptual Change*. Cambridge: Cambridge UP, 1989.
Ballantyne, Tony. 'Empire, Knowledge and Culture: From Proto-Globalization to Modern Globalization'. In A.G. Hopkins, ed. *Globalization in World History*. London: Pimlico, 2002.
Bayly, C.A. *The Birth of the Modern World, 1780–1914: Global Connections and Comparisons*. Oxford: Blackwell, 2004.
Bennett, Colin J. 'What is Policy Convergence and What Causes It?' *British Journal of Political Science*, 21:2 (1991): 215–33.
Benton, Lauren. *Law and Colonial Cultures: Legal Regimes in World History, 1400–1900*. Cambridge: Cambridge UP, 2002.
Black, Anthony. 'Concepts of Civil Society in Pre-Modern Europe'. In Sudipta Kaviraj and Sunil Khilnani, eds. *Civil Society: History and Possibilities*. Cambridge: Cambridge UP, 2002.
Coleman, D.C., ed. *Revisions in Mercantilism*. London: Methuen & Co. Ltd., 1969.
Cohen, Jean L. and Andrew Arato. *Civil Society and Political Theory*. Cambridge, MA, and London: M.I.T. Press, 1992.
Drayton, Richard. 'The Collaboration of Labour: Slaves, Empires and Globalizations in the Atlantic World, c. 1600–1850'. In A.G. Hopkins, ed. *Globalization in World History*. London: Pimlico, 2002.
Evans, Peter, ed. *State-Society Synergy: Government and Social Capital in Development*. Berkeley: University of California Press, 1991.
Evans, P.B., D. Rueschemayer and T. Skocpol, eds. *Bringing the State Back In*. Cambridge: Cambridge UP, 1985.
Eyestone, Robert. 'Confusion, Diffusion, and Innovation' *American Political Science Review*, 71:2 (1977): 441–7.
Gallagher, John and Ronald Robinson. 'Imperialism of Free Trade'. *Economic History Review*, 2nd series 4 (1953): 1–15.
——. *Africa and the Victorians: The Official Mind of Imperialism*. London: Doubleday, 1961.
Gaspar, David Barry and David Patrick Geggus. *A Turbulent Time: The French Revolution and the Greater Caribbean*. Bloomington: Indiana UP, 1997.
Gerschenkron, Alexander. *Continuity in History and other Essays*. Cambridge, MA: Belknap Press of Harvard UP, 1968.

Hecksher, Eli. *Mercantilism*. Revised edition. 2 vols. London: Macmillan, 1955.
Hirschman, Albert O. *The Passions and the Interests: Political Arguments for Capitalism Before its Triumph*. Princeton: Princeton UP, 1997.
Huizinga, Johan. 'The Task of Cultural History'. In *Men and Ideas: History, the Middle Ages, the Renaissance*. London: Eyre and Spottiswoode, 1960.
Keene, Edward. *Beyond the Anarchical Society: Grotius, Colonialism and Order in World Politics*. Cambridge: Cambridge UP, 2002.
Landes, David. *The Unbound Prometheus: Technological Change and Industrial Development in Western Europe from 1750 to the present*. 2nd edn. Cambridge: Cambridge UP, 2003.
Magnusson, Lars. *Mercantilism: The Shaping of an Economic Language*. New York: Routledge, 1994.
Nussbaum, Martha C. 'Patriotism and Cosmopolitanism'. In Nussbaum and Joshua Cohen, eds. *For Love of Country: Debating the Limits of Patriotism*. Boston: Beacon Press, 1996.
Paz, Octavio. *El Laberinto de Soledad*. Mexico City: Fondo de Cultura Económica, 2002.
Pigman, G.W. 'Version of Imitation in the Renaissance'. *Renaissance Quarterly*, 33:1 (1980): 1–32.
Sahlins, Marshall. *Islands of History*. Chicago and London: University of Chicago Press, 1985.
Symcox, Geoffrey, ed. *War, Diplomacy and Imperialism, 1618–1763*. New York: Harper & Row, 1972.
Wallace-Hadrill, J.M. *The Barbarian West, 400–1000*. Oxford: Basil Blackwell, 1997.
Weyland, Kurt, ed. *Learning from Foreign Models in Latin American Policy Reform*. Washington: The Woodrow Wilson Center for Scholars, 2004.
Wilentz, Sean, ed. *Rites of Power: Symbolism, Ritual and Politics Since the Middle Ages*. Philadelphia: University of Pennsylvania Press, 1985.
Williams, Eric. *Capitalism and Slavery*, [1944]. Chapel Hill: University of North Carolina, 1994.

Unpublished dissertations

Arregui Martínez-Moya, Salvador. 'El Real Consulado de La Habana, 1794–1834'. PhD Dissertation, University of Murcia, 1992.
Bonilla Bonilla, Adolfo. 'The Central American Enlightenment, 1770–1838: An Interpretation of Political Ideas and Political History'. PhD Dissertation, University of Manchester, 1996.
Callahan, William J. 'The Crown and the Promotion of Industry in Eighteenth-Century Spain'. PhD Dissertation, Harvard University, 1964.
Castillo Díaz, Adolfo. 'La Concepción de la Historia en Chile Durante la Epoca Colonial'. *Memoria de Licenciatura*, Pontificia Universidad Católica de Chile, 1988.
De Onis, Carlos William. 'Juan Bautista Muñoz: Ensayista de la Ilustración'. PhD Dissertation, University of Colorado at Boulder, 1980.
Edwards, David Hugh. 'Economic Effects of the Intendancy System in Chile: Captain-General Ambrosio O'Higgins as Reformer'. PhD Dissertation, University of Virginia, 1973.
Fernández-Sanz, Amable-Angel. 'Utopia y Realidad en la Ilustración Española. Pablo de Olavide y las "Nuevas Poblaciones"'. PhD Dissertation, Universidad Complutense de Madrid, 1990.
Garrido de Payan, Margarita. 'The Political Culture of New Granada, 1770–1815'. PhD Dissertation, University of Oxford, 1990.

Hart, Jonathan C. 'Representing the New World: English and French Uses of the Example of Spain, 1492–1713'. PhD Dissertation, University of Cambridge, 1997.

Lampros, Peter J. 'Merchant-Planter Cooperation and Conflict: The Havana *Consulado*, 1794–1832'. PhD Dissertation, Tulane University, 1980.

Nava Rodríguez, María Teresa. 'Reformismo Ilustrado y Americanismo: La Real Academia de la Historia, 1735–1792'. PhD Dissertation, Universidad Complutense de Madrid, 1989.

Noel, Charles Curtis. 'Campomanes and the Secular Clergy in Spain, 1760–1780: Enlightenment Versus Tradition'. PhD Dissertation, Princeton University, 1969.

Paquette, Gabriel. 'Governance and Reform in the Spanish Atlantic World, c. 1760–1810'. PhD Dissertation, University of Cambridge, 2006.

Wilhite, John F. 'The Enlightenment and Education in New Granada, 1760–1830'. PhD Dissertation, University of Tennessee, 1976.

Index